Rethinking Labour's Past

Rethinking Labour's Past

Edited by
Nathan Yeowell

I.B.TAURIS
LONDON · NEW YORK · OXFORD · NEW DELHI · SYDNEY

PROGRESSIVE
BRITAIN

I.B. TAURIS
Bloomsbury Publishing Plc
50 Bedford Square, London, WC1B 3DP, UK
1385 Broadway, New York, NY 10018, USA
29 Earlsfort Terrace, Dublin 2, Ireland

BLOOMSBURY, I.B. TAURIS and the I.B. Tauris logo are
trademarks of Bloomsbury Publishing Plc

First published in Great Britain 2022

A catalogue record for this book is available from the British Library.

Library of Congress Cataloging-in-Publication Data
Names: Yeowell, Nathan, editor.
Title: Rethinking Labour's Past / edited by Nathan Yeowell.
Description: New York : I.B. TAURIS, 2022. | Includes bibliographical references and index.
Identifiers: LCCN 2021037623 (print) | LCCN 2021037624 (ebook) | ISBN 9780755640171
(Hardback) | ISBN 9780755640164 (Paperback) | ISBN 9780755640188 (ePub) |
ISBN 9780755640195 (PDF) | ISBN 9780755640201 (eBook other)
Subjects: LCSH: Labour Party (Great Britain)–History. | Great Britain–Politics and government.
Classification: LCC JN1129.L32 R48 2022 (print) | LCC JN1129.L32 (ebook) |
DDC 324.24107–dc23/eng/20211001
LC record available at https://lccn.loc.gov/2021037623
LC ebook record available at https://lccn.loc.gov/2021037624

ISBN: HB: 978-0-7556-4017-1
          PB: 978-0-7556-4016-4
          ePDF: 978-0-7556-4019-5
          eBook: 978-0-7556-4018-8

Typeset by Integra Software Services Pvt. Ltd.
Printed and bound in Great Britain

To find out more about our authors and books visit www.bloomsbury.com
and sign up for our newsletters

Contents

Part 4

Part 5

Contributors

Robin Bunce is a historian based at Homerton College, Cambridge. He is co-author of *Diane Abbott: The Authorised Biography* (2020, with Samara Linton) and of *Renegade: The Life and Times of Darcus Howe* (2017, with Paul Field). With Field, he served as historical consultant on the Steve McQueen film *Mangrove* (2020), and the BBC documentary *Black Power: A British Story of Resistance* (2021).

Richard Carr is a Senior Lecturer at the Labour History Research Unit at Anglia Ruskin University. He is author of *March of the Moderates: Bill Clinton, Tony Blair, and the Rebirth of Progressive Politics* (2019) and a political biography of Charlie Chaplin (2017).

Krista Cowman is Professor and Head of the School of History, Politics and International Relations at the University of Leicester. She has published widely on women's suffrage and on women's political activism in a variety of sites throughout the twentieth century, including *Women of the Right Spirit: Paid Organisers of the Women's Social and Political Union (WSPU) 1904–18* (2011) and *Women in British Politics, c. 1968–1979* (2010).

Jonathan Davis is Associate Professor in Modern European History and Director of the Labour History Research Unit at Anglia Ruskin University. He is author of a number of books, including *The Global 1980s: People, Power and Profit* (2019) and *The Second Labour Government 1929–1931: A Reappraisal* (2011) and co-editor (with Rohan McWilliam) of *Labour and the Left in the 1980s* (2018).

Patrick Diamond is Director of the Mile End Institute and Senior Lecturer in Public Policy at Queen Mary University, London. He was previously Senior Policy Adviser to the Prime Minister (2001–05), and Head of Policy Planning in Ten Downing Street (2009–10). He is author of a number of books including *The British Labour Party in Opposition and Power* (2020), *The Crosland Legacy: The Future of British Social Democracy* (2016) and *Endgame for the Centre Left? The Retreat of Social Democracy Across Europe* (2016).

Steven Fielding is Professor of Political History at Nottingham University. He is the author and editor of a number of works including *The Churchill Myths* (with Bill Schwarz and Richard Toye, 2020), *Interpreting the Labour Party: Approaches to Labour Politics and History* (co-edited with John Callaghan and Steve Ludlam, 2004) and *England Arise! The Labour Party and Popular Politics in 1940s Britain* (with Peter Thompson and Nick Tiratsoo, 1995). He is currently writing *The Labour Party from Callaghan to Corbyn* for Polity Books.

Nick Garland is an adviser to a member of the Shadow Cabinet, DPhil candidate in Modern History at the University of Oxford and commissioning editor for *Renewal: A Journal of Social Democracy*.

Andrew Hindmoor is Professor of Politics and International Relations at the University of Sheffield, editor of *Political Studies* and associate editor of *New Political Economy*. He is author of several books including *12 Days that Made Modern Britain* (2019) and *What's Left Now? The History and Future of Social Democracy* (2018).

Ben Jackson is Associate Professor of Modern History at the University of Oxford and co-editor of *Political Quarterly*. He is the author of *The Case for Scottish Independence: A History of Nationalist Political Thought in Modern Scotland* (2020), *Equality and the British Left* (2007) and co-editor (with Robert Saunders) of *Making Thatcher's Britain* (2012).

Samara Linton is an award-winning freelance writer and content producer who previously worked as a junior doctor in London. She is author of the *Colour of Madness: Exploring BAME Mental Health in the UK* (2018) and co-author (with Robin Bunce) of *Diane Abbott: The Authorised Biography* (2020).

Rohan McWilliam is Professor of Modern British History and Director of the Labour History Research Unit at Anglia Ruskin University. He has published widely on a range of social, cultural and political topics covering Victorian and twentieth-century Britain. His most recent books include *London's West End: Creating the Pleasure District* (2020), *Labour and the Left in the 1980s* (co-edited with Jonathan Davis, 2018) and *New Directions in Social and Cultural History* (co-edited with Sasha Handley and Lucy Noakes, 2017).

George Morris is a PhD candidate in Modern British History at the University of Cambridge and is co-editor of *Renewal: A Journal of Social Democracy*.

Colm Murphy is a Deputy Director of the Mile End Institute at Queen Mary University, London, and Past and Present Fellow at the Institute for Historical Research.

Jeremy Nuttall is Senior Lecturer in Modern British History at Kingston University, London. He is co-editor (with Hans Schattle) of *Making Social Democrats, Essays for David Marquand* (2018), author of the book *Psychological Socialism: The Labour Party and Qualities of Mind and Character* (2006) and of articles on British social democracy in leading journals including *Historical Journal* and *English Historical Review*.

Glen O'Hara is Professor of Modern and Contemporary History at Oxford Brookes University. A former schoolteacher and journalist, he is the author of *The Politics of Water in Post-War Britain* (2017) and *Governing Post-War Britain: The Paradoxes of Progress* (2012). He is currently principal investigator on an Arts and Humanities Research-funded project on the history of rights of way in England and Wales and is writing a book on the domestic policies of the Blair government for Manchester University Press.

Daisy Payling is a Senior Post-Doctoral Research Fellow at the University of Essex working on the Wellcome-funded project 'Body, Self and Family: Women's Psychological, Emotional and Bodily Health in Britain, c. 1960–1990'. When she is not writing about the history of women's health, she can be found working on her book on local government and grassroots activism in 1980s Sheffield, soon to be published by Manchester University Press.

Karl Pike is a Deputy Director of the Mile End Institute and Lecturer in British Politics and Public Policy at Queen Mary University, London. He has published articles in a number of academic journals, including *Political Studies* and *The British Journal of Politics and International Relations*. He is currently working on a book about Labour's traditions after the 2010 general election. Prior to academia, he worked as an adviser to the Shadow Foreign Secretary and Shadow Home Secretary.

Rachel Reeves is the Labour MP for Leeds West and a member of the Shadow Cabinet. She is the author of *Women of Westminster: The MPs Who Changed Politics* (2019) and *Alice in Westminster: The Political Life of Alice Bacon* (2016).

Charlotte Lydia Riley is a Lecturer in Twentieth-Century British History at the University of Southampton, specializing in the intersections between foreign and domestic policy, politics and popular culture. Recent works include *The Free*

Speech Wars: How Did We Get Here and Why Does It Matter (editor, 2021) and 'The winds of change are blowing economically: The Labour Party and British Overseas Development, 1940s–1960s' in *Britain, France and the Decolonization of Africa: Future Imperfect* (co-edited by Andrew W. M. Smith and Chris Jeppesen, 2017).

Emily Robinson is Senior Lecturer in Politics at the University of Sussex and co-editor of *Renewal: A Journal of Social Democracy*. Emily is the author of *The Language of Progressive Politics in Modern Britain* (2017), *History, Heritage and Tradition in Contemporary British Politics* (2012) and is writing (with Jonathan Moss and Jake Watts) *An Emotional History of Brexit Britain* for Manchester University Press.

Florence Sutcliffe-Braithwaite is Associate Professor in Twentieth-Century British History at University College London and co-editor of *Renewal: A Journal of Social Democracy*. Florence is the author of *Class, Politics and the Decline of Deference in England, 1968–2000* (2018) and is currently working on a study of women's activism in the miner's strike of 1984–85 (with Natalie Tomlinson).

Nick Thomas-Symonds is the Labour MP for Torfaen and a member of the Shadow Cabinet. He is the author of *Attlee, A Life in Politics* (2010) and *Nye, The Political Life of Aneurin Bevan* (2015). His biography of Harold Wilson will be published in 2022.

Nathan Yeowell is the Executive Director of Progressive Britain and Co-Director of Labour to Win. He was previously Head of Policy and External Affairs at the social sector think tank New Philanthropy Capital and Head of the Labour Group Office at the Local Government Association.

Acknowledgements

Rethinking Labour's Past was my lockdown project. Conceived, canvassed and commissioned during the first lockdown; drafted during the second; edited, reviewed, corrected (mostly) during the third. The idea first came to me as I scrolled through Twitter on the morning of 4 April 2020 and read David Edgerton's blog, 'As Labour elects a new leader, some thoughts on Labour's misunderstood history', as I awaited the result of the 2020 Labour leadership contest. David very kindly acted as an early sounding board for the project and, although he was unable to take part himself, has remained supportive throughout – as have Tomasz Hoskins and Nayiri Kendir, my editors at I.B. Tauris/Bloomsbury, who have championed this collection wholeheartedly (and indulged my habit of dancing around deadlines).

My first – and most important – round of thanks must go to the twenty-two contributors who have made this collection a reality. Quite frankly, I am still in awe at the depth, quality and sheer star power of the list of historians, political scientists and front-rank Labour politicians who willingly, indeed enthusiastically, answered my calls to take part, despite the strains and upheavals of lockdown life. My second round of thanks go to Jeremy Breaks, Joanna Reynolds, Anne Showstack Sassoon and the directors of the Lionel Cooke Memorial Fund for their generosity, without which the book would not have seen the light of day. I hope it meets their expectations. My third round of thanks go to the very many experts, friends and colleagues who were generous with their time, thoughts and observations, including those who read and commented on the various drafts and chapters I pressed upon them. In alphabetical order, they include Andrew Adonis, Claire Ainsley, Dimitri Batrouni, Laura Beers, Lise Butler, Kay Carberry, Richard Carr, John-Paul Cherrington, Charles Clarke, Barry Colfer, Tom Collinge, Patrick Diamond, Steven Fielding, Sally Gimson, Clare Griffiths, Andrew Hindmoor, Joseph Holland, Roger Liddle, Peter Mandelson, Rohan McWilliam, Colm Murphy, Glen O'Hara, Karl Pike, Frederick Harry Pitts, Anne Reyersbach, Tanya Sassoon, Henna Shah and Peta Steel. In particular, I would like to single out Nick Garland for his steadfast assistance and inspiration. He made me think and improved my judgement through the editing and reviewing process immensely. My fourth round of thanks go to my colleagues, directors and parents for their encouragement and forbearance, especially as the development of the book coincided with the launch of Labour to Win, the merger of Progress with Policy Network and the resulting transition to Progressive Britain. Again, alphabetically: Luke Akehurst, Nathan Burns, Lloyd Duddridge, Matthew Faulding, Mary Goudie, Frankie Grant, Joseph Holland, Kira Lewis, Margaret Prosser, Pearleen Sangha, Emily Wallace, and to my Mum and Dad, Jeannette and David Yeowell. Finally, not a round of thanks so much as an opportunity to acknowledge past debts. I am ashamed to admit that I have two incomplete PhDs to my name, the first under the late, great E. H. H. Green at the University of Oxford, the second under Kathleen Burk at University College, London, both looking at aspects of Labour's political economy and emerging ideology in the 1960s and 1970s. Editing this collection has allowed me to reconnect with my earlier studies, and if I have a dedication to make, then it is to Kathleen and to Ewen's memory. In some small part I hope it repays their early faith in me.

Nathan Yeowell

Foreword

Rachel Reeves

Labour's history matters. As a party we have always had a powerful sense of our own history, of the importance of continuity with our past and staying connected with our roots.[1] I have always believed we can learn and draw inspiration from our history. Our party's historic achievements help define what it is to *be* Labour. And it defines our place within the UK's wider national story. Labour was founded to give voice to working people at a time before all men, and any women, had the vote. Labour spoke for the whole nation in opposition to the vested interests that dominated politics.

Labour's history is one of nation-building – from municipal socialists building libraries, public baths, housing, utilities, hospitals and local parks – through to the construction of a new settlement after 1945, creating modern industries, the infrastructure of a modern welfare state and raising the standard of living for all. Over the postwar years, the people of Britain benefitted from modern railways, electric power and gas. Things were built to last. Labour spoke in the name of the people against private interests and insular elites which held back investment, that inhibited the modernization of the country and clung on to undue privilege. It stood for fair rewards for workers, and for greater security for families, communities and the nation.[2] I am certain those values resonate today as strongly as ever.

For me, exploring Labour's history has had a personal dimension too. When I was first elected to Parliament in 2010, I set out to explore the life story of Alice Bacon, the only woman before me to represent the city of Leeds in Parliament.[3] Alice's story is one that was not so uncommon in her generation, but which is all too rare today. From a working-class home in Normanton in West Yorkshire, the

---

[1] Jon Lawrence, 'Labour – The Myths It Has Lived By', in Duncan Tanner, Pat Thane and Nick Tiratsoo (eds), *Labour's First Century* (Cambridge: CUP, 2000); and see Ben Jackson's or Steven Fielding's contributions in this volume.

[2] See David Edgerton, *Rise and Fall of the British Nation* (London: Routledge, 2018).

[3] Rachel Reeves, *Alice in Westminster: The Political Life of Alice Bacon* (London: I.B. Tauris, 2016).

daughter of a miner, Alice became a teacher before being elected to Parliament in Labour's great landslide of 1945. Under Harold Wilson after 1964, Alice served as a minister in the Home Office and the Department for Education and Science, playing a key role in some of Labour's greatest achievements: the decriminalization of abortion and homosexuality, the abolition of the death penalty and the introduction and extension of comprehensive education. That research prompted me to go back and study the lives, experiences and achievements of Labour women across the last hundred years – from those interwar trailblazers like Margaret Bondfield (Britain's first woman cabinet minister), Ellen Wilkinson and Susan Lawrence; through to women who have inspired me personally in more recent decades, from Tessa Jowell to Harriet Harman.[4] Each faced common obstacles and their own distinctive challenges. Women in Labour politics brought their own sets of concerns and their own understanding of the struggles of working people. They sought to expand politics beyond the boundaries of the unionized workplace and parliament, into the community, the chapel and the home. As minister of education after 1945, Ellen Wilkinson introduced free school milk and – in the face of resistance from male colleagues – the raising of the school leaving age. Margaret Bondfield – a former shop assistant and trade union organizer – fought for the provision of footwear for poor children. And Susan Lawrence, radicalized by the low pay and poor conditions of cleaners employed by the London County Council, drove the charge for pensions for widows.[5] From Barbara Castle and Child Benefit to Tessa Jowell and the introduction of SureStart, to Harriet Harman and the Equality Act, Labour women followed in a proud tradition.

Writing this foreword in July 2021, just days after speaking in opposition to a Chancellor determined to roll back Britain's commitments to the world's most disadvantaged, I was struck by Charlotte Lydia Riley's emphasis on the role of international development as a moral obligation for so many Labour politicians, from Castle to Judith Hart to Tony Blair and Gordon Brown. I hope that, in defending those commitments, we stood in that tradition. But returning to Labour's past can't all be about celebrating our achievements and luxuriating in our own mythology, without taking a hard look at our history; lazy assumptions and self-congratulatory narratives do us no good. Colm Murphy's re-examination of the 1983 manifesto is just one reminder of the dangers of

[4]   Rachel Reeves, *Women of Westminster: The MPs Who Changed Politics* (London: Bloomsbury, 2018).
[5]   See ibid, ch. 1.

lazy assumptions; whilst powerful accounts of the – often slow, always uneven – progress of women and Black, Asian and minority ethnic activists within the party shows we can never take our progressive credentials for granted. It wasn't until 1987 that Labour's first Black MPs were elected to Parliament.

I first entered Parliament in May 2010; the first of four successive General Election defeats. It has rarely been easy. But history tells us we have been here before. A consideration of Labour's slow, painful process of political renewal before 1997 illustrates the scale of political, intellectual and organizational work that took place through the 1980s and 1990s to bring us to that point.[6] Historians played their part in that process too – from Eric Hobsbawm urging Labour to face up to the scale of its challenge without illusion in the darkest moments of the 1980s, to David Marquand's grappling with the 'progressive dilemma'.[7] Contributions to this book return us to past debates and stories told about Labour's purpose and how to adapt to a changing society. They remind us that few of the questions we face today are wholly new; and that they are best understood with an eye on how they have been negotiated, successfully or otherwise, in the past. These themes run through Ben Jackson and Steven Fielding's stimulating discussions of Labour's relationship to its own history, to Patrick Diamond's consideration of how the great 1950s revisionist Anthony Crosland adapted to the new challenges of the 1970s, to Nick Garland's exploration of the changing place of 'community' in progressive politics, to George Morris, Emily Robinson and Florence Sutcliffe-Braithwaite's account of the history of the journal *Renewal* – a product of 1990s modernization that continues to play an important part in today's debates about the future of social-democratic politics.

The struggle to adapt social democracy, and its enduring values, to a continually changing economy and an evolving society is *the* central feature of Labour's history since its first, short-lived experience of government in the interwar years.[8] That task – of applying those values, of building that stronger, fairer country and extending security and opportunity to all – remains the same as ever. Attention to that history tells us, however, that without a deep

---

[6] James E. Cronin, *New Labour's Pasts: The Labour Party and Its Discontents* (London: Routledge, 2004); Patrick Diamond, *The Labour Party in Opposition and Power 1979-2019: Forward March Halted?* (London: Routledge, 2021); Florence Sutcliffe-Braithwaite, *Class, Politics and the Decline of Deference in England, 1968-2000* (Oxford: OUP, 2018).

[7] Eric Hobsbawm, 'Labour's Lost Millions', *Marxism Today*, October 1983, 7–13; David Marquand, *The Progressive Dilemma: From Lloyd-George to Kinnock* (London: Heinemann, 1991).

[8] See Patrick Diamond's chapter in this volume.

understanding of how society has changed, of the big economic challenges we face, and of what people want from their lives – and an ambitious, inclusive vision for the future of the United Kingdom – then we will go nowhere and change nothing. When we win it is because we look to the future, inspire and modernize. We cannot repeat the formula of 1945, 1964 and 1997 – but we can certainly learn from how Labour leaders then steered our party from the wilderness to power. We can seek to understand their successes and failures in turn in order to follow them in transforming lives.

It's been a pleasure reading the contributions to this book, bringing cutting-edge academic historical insight, in a real spirit of pluralism, to debates that still feel so live and pressing in the political arena. It is a valuable contribution to a debate that needs to draw on the widest possible range of insight and experience over the coming years, as we work to reconnect and win back support for our movement and our cause.

Part One

Introduction: Rethinking Labour's past

Nathan Yeowell

The year 2020 represented a decisive, if not seismic, break in the history of the United Kingdom. This did not necessarily come as a shock. The collapse of Theresa May's premiership and the election of Boris Johnson as Conservative leader in the summer of 2019 heralded six months of constitutional and civil turmoil, unprecedented in modern times, as Johnson broke and then recast the Conservative Party in his image and as his personal political vehicle to 'get Brexit done'. He won a decisive victory in the December 2019 general election, securing for the Conservatives their largest parliamentary majority since 1987 and sounding the death knell of 'Remainer' hopes to prevent a hard Brexit by any legal, constitutional or extra-parliamentary means. The UK left the EU on 31 January 2020 – and this alone marked the year out as a turning point, for good or ill or merely as a moment of apparent closure after more than four and a half years of existential debate and division over the country's relationship with the rest of Europe and its place in the wider world.

Within three months, Covid-19, the worst pandemic for over a century, spread rapidly across the UK, heralding the gravest political and economic crisis since the Second World War, and necessitating the greatest ever peacetime extension and mobilization of state power. From March 2020 to March 2021, the UK suffered one of the worst recessions of any developed economy as well as sustaining one of the highest Covid-related mortality rates: 126,284 deaths as of 23 March 2021 (the first anniversary of lockdown). The crisis shone a light on the widening inequalities that scarred the country and had been exacerbated by the Conservatives' ideological commitment to economic austerity after 2010: in Labour leader Keir Starmer's memorable phrase, Covid crept into 'the cracks and crevices of … society and forced them open with tragic consequences'.[1] As *Renewal*'s Florence Sutcliffe-Braithwaite and Emily Robinson observed: 'the experience of the pandemic … [was] primarily structured by class, and its intersections with race and gender: by our ability to work from home, to avoid public transport, to access technology and good food, to draw on savings, to share the responsibility of caring, and by the spaces and conditions in which we live'.[2] Perhaps most tellingly, it brought the interconnectedness of the UK's fragmented society into sharp focus, illustrating how the consequences of inequality – the polarization of the labour market, the proliferation of insecure work and poor working conditions, soaring household debt, inadequate and overcrowded housing, fraying public services – impacted on everyone.

Taken together, the 'twin traumas of managing two exits' from the EU and Covid-19, combined with the continuing crisis of climate change, present 'a dire moment in our national history' and one that 'demands an urgent plan for national recovery'.[3] This has been a common refrain for commentators, academics and politicians alike. In an interview with *The Observer* in February 2021, former civil servant and social reformer Louise Casey called for 'a new Beveridge Report … The nation has been torn apart, and there's no point being defensive about that. We've got to gift each other some proper space to think. We've got to work out how not to leave the badly wounded behind'.[4] Hot on her heels, the British Academy released *Shaping the COVID Decade: addressing the long-term societal impacts of COVID-19*, calling for reforms to tackle widening digital, geographical and social inequalities, for the resolution of long-simmering tensions between local and central government, and for the rejuvenation of community-led social infrastructure that had been cut away since 2010. The report found that 'in many places there is a need to start afresh, with a more systemic view, and where we should freely consider whether we might organise

---

[1] Sir Keir Starmer, 'A New Chapter for Britain', 18 February 2021, https://labour.org.uk/press/full-text-of-keir-starmer-speech-on-a-new-chapter-for-britain/ (accessed 13 September 2021).

[2] Florence Sutcliffe-Braithwaite and Emily Robinson, 'Defending, restoring, transforming', *Renewal* 28, no. 3 (2020), https://renewal.org.uk/archive/vol-28-2020/editorial-defending-restoring-transforming/ (accessed 13 September 2021).

[3] Jagjit S. Chada, 'Whither After Covid-19 and Brexit: A Social Science Perspective', *National Institute Economic Review* 255 (February 2021), https://www.cambridge.org/core/journals/national-institute-economic-review/article/commentary-whither-after-covid19-and-brexit-a-social-science-perspective/F5EB0B41861A3539F9FFDB9025CB8F38 (accessed 13 September 2021).

[4] Rachel Cooke, 'Louise Casey: "Are we ever going to create a Britain for everyone?"', *The Observer*, 21 February 2021, https://www.theguardian.com/society/2021/feb/21/louise-casey-homelessness-tsar-food-banks-covid-rough-sleeping-poverty (accessed 13 September 2021).

life differently in the future'.[5] As a rallying cry for British social democrats, Labour MP Stella Creasy and academic Karl Pike argued that the

> list of failures, and devastating problems emerging or being made visible during the pandemic, is long. Many of them speak to decades-long problems of inequality, market failure, and a lack of political commitment or proficiency. The challenge for the left is to ensure the need to act on these problems is not lost after the crisis abates – but is part of a post-crisis politics that says *this* is why we should act now. That *this* is what's important.[6]

As Starmer himself wrote on the first anniversary of his election as Labour leader, the UK 'is at a fork in the road. We can attempt to patch up our broken system and hope it works next time. Or we can choose a brighter future, built on security and prosperity for all, one that harnesses everyone's talents'.[7]

If, to quote US President Joe Biden, Covid-19 represents the beginning of a 'progressive paradigm shift' in UK politics, then much will depend on the Labour Party. In the last two great turning points in British political history, in the late 1970s and in the immediate wake of the 2008 financial crisis, Labour – and progressives more widely – were unable to prevent their political opponents from framing events in ways that contributed to major rightward shifts in British politics.[8] In the face of Johnson's pandemic populism, is the party capable of bucking this trend, galvanizing British society and successfully translating the extraordinary revival of community solidarity seen in 2020–1 into an attractive, national political project?[9] Starmer, like Biden, acknowledged the gravity of this moment in his speech to the virtual *Labour Connected* event in September 2020,

---

[5] The British Academy, *Shaping the COVID Decade: addressing the long-term societal impacts of COVID-19*, The British Academy (London, March 2021), 6, https://www.thebritishacademy.ac.uk/documents/3239/Shaping-COVID-decade-addressing-long-term-societal-impacts-COVID-19.pdf (accessed 13 September 2021).

[6] Stella Creasy MP and Karl Pike, 'Nothing is inevitable: narrating the Covid crisis', *Renewal* 29, no. 1 (2021), https://renewal.org.uk/archive/vol-29-2021/nothing-is-inevitable/ (accessed 13 September 2021).

[7] Keir Starmer, 'We must end the idea that inequality is inevitable. Let's get Britain working again', *The Observer*, 4 April 2021, https://www.theguardian.com/politics/2021/apr/03/we-have-a-once-in-a-generation-chance-to-rethink-our-future-lets-get-britain-working-again (accessed 13 September 2021).

[8] Creasy and Pike, 'Nothing is inevitable'; see also, Colin Hay, 'Chronicle of a Death Foretold: The Winter of Discontent and Construction of the Crisis of Keynesianism', *Parliamentary Affairs* 63, no. 3 (July 2010): 446–70.

[9] See, for instance, research by the /together coalition, which found that large pluralities believe that the pandemic had made their community more united and showed Britain's unity more than its divisions, whilst 12.4 million adults had volunteered in the early months of the pandemic; 4.6 million for the very first time. Haroon Sadique, 'Covid has connected UK communities and spurred volunteering, report finds', *Guardian*, 28 February 2021, https://www.theguardian.com/world/2021/feb/28/covid-has-connected-uk-communities-and-spurred-volunteering-report-finds (accessed 13 September 2021).

arguing that the ravages of Covid-19 meant 'that even the challenges of 2019 already [seemed] like ancient history'.[10] These challenges may well feel like ancient history when viewed through the prism of Covid-19 but that does not make them any less monumental. The year 2019 was truly terrible for the Labour Party, a landmark year for all the wrong reasons. Jeremy Corbyn led the party to its fourth, successive general election defeat in nine and a half years, losing sixty parliamentary seats in the process. The new parliament saw only 202 Labour MPs return to Westminster, the smallest cohort since 1935. Labour's share of the vote fell by 7.8 per cent, from 40 per cent in 2017 to 32.2 per cent – a loss of over 2.6 million votes on a smaller turnout in two and a half years – with an average 4.7 per cent swing towards the Conservatives across Great Britain.[11] The election accelerated change in historic demographic and geographical voting patterns. The Conservatives breached stretches of the so-called 'red wall' of Labour seats that snaked north-eastwards from north Wales, through the Midlands and on to Yorkshire, Teesside and County Durham, turning long-standing Labour strongholds into relatively safe Conservative seats. To quote directly, and in full, from polling expert David Cowling:

> Based on the current composition of the House of Commons, the party needs to gain 123 seats at the next election simply to secure a majority of one. In order to secure a 40 seat [*sic*] majority, that might see a reforming government through a full term, they will need to gain 142 seats. Since 1900, there have been only three elections where Labour has gained more than 123 seats – 1929 (+126); 1945 (+199); and 1997 (+146).

The scale of the challenge that Starmer inherited in April 2020 is clear, with the possibility 'that the disastrous finale of Mr Corbyn's leadership has exiled his successor to the political wilderness for at least the best part of a decade'.[12]

The rejection of Corbyn at the ballot box also meant the rejection of Corbynism as Labour's dominant political project (although at the time of writing his political legacy remains bitterly contested and he himself is suspended from the Parliamentary Labour Party).[13] To its supporters, Corbynism was a moment of almost euphoric political transformation, 'an attempt to convert a centrist

---

[10] Keir Starmer's speech at Labour Connected, 22 September 2020, https://labour.org.uk/press/full-text-of-keir-starmers-speech-at-labour-connected/ (accessed 13 September 2021).

[11] For these statistics, and more analysis on the 2019 general election, see Nathan Yeowell, *Progress election review*, February 2020, http://progressonline.org.uk/wp-content/uploads/2020/04/PROGRESS-LT-review-FEB2020-1.pdf (accessed 13 September 2021).

[12] David Cowling, 'December 2019 general election: No! Jeremy Corbyn', 18 December 2019, privately distributed, quoted in ibid.

[13] For a contemporary snapshot of the academic debate raging about Corbyn's legacy see the 'Corbynism and its Aftermath' issue of *The Political Quarterly* 92, no. 2 (2021).

Labour Party into a radical socialist movement', a rejection of 'the lies of the Iraq war, the MP expenses scandal, the corruption of cash for honours – and, most of all, the failure of either side of the political divide to articulate meaningful policies for the country post-crash'.[14] Even to many sceptics, the period saw a necessary break with the intellectual timidity that had marked the party in the run-up to the painful 2015 election defeat, whilst the relative gains of the 2017 election challenged many dominant assumptions about British politics and revealed a deep frustration with the status quo. But to its critics, Corbynism brought the party to the brink of electoral, political and moral collapse. In the judgement of Labour MP Wes Streeting, it 'saddled' Labour

> with a manifesto [in 2019] that people didn't believe in, with an endless wishlist of promises that led to real questions about whether they were achievable, let alone desirable. It offered a worldview that people reviled, from the response of the poisoning of the Skripals in Salisbury to a back catalogue of public statements about terrorists that led voters to question whether the Labour Party would side with our country's enemies over our friends. It presided over a culture that people feared, with the unchecked spread of a toxic, antisemitic, conspiracy theorist politics that saw Jewish MPs and members hounded out of the Labour Party.[15]

Starmer's election in April 2020 gave the party a much-needed reprieve, an opportunity to repair the damage done to its reputation as a credible party of government. The success of Starmer's leadership will depend much upon the readiness of Labour Party members to adapt to this task of reconstruction and get stuck into the hard work of rebuilding their relationship with the public. It will also depend upon their ability to accept that the 'great crashes' of 2019–21 – the rise of Johnson, the demise of Corbynism, Brexit, Covid-19 and its aftermath – represent as much of a natural breakpoint in the life and history of the Labour Party as they do in those of the country. Labour has an opportunity to move on from increasingly sterile arguments about the rights and wrongs of the Corbyn years (and before) and craft a new narrative capable of defining a new future for country and party alike – if it has the confidence to grasp it.

---

[14] Andrew Fisher, 'I was at the heart of Corbynism. Here's why we lost', *Open Democracy*, 10 September 2020, https://www.opendemocracy.net/en/opendemocracyuk/i-was-heart-corbynism-heres-why-we-lost/ (accessed 13 September 2021).

[15] Wes Streeting MP, *Let Us Face the Future Again*, Fabian Ideas 651, The Fabian Society (London, March 2020), https://fabians.org.uk/wp-content/uploads/2020/03/FABJ8066-Fabian-Tract-COVER-200312.pdf (accessed 13 September 2021).

Historian David Edgerton believes that the ability to capitalize on this potentially critical juncture would be much improved if the party undertook a more honest reassessment of its past. Writing in anticipation of Starmer's victory, he argued that:

> British politics has an intimate relationship to history, not least Labour politics. But it's often a version of history that never really happened. In order to generate fresh thinking about policy – something sadly lacking in the leadership debate – Labour has to free itself from the shackles of its own invented histories. An intelligent and respectful politics of the left needs a richer account of what Labour has proposed and what has actually taken place ... Labour's past is a resource, an important one, for the party. But too often the usually recalled history does not do justice to the variety of Labour's policies, politics and practices, which were never fixed in time, nor easily understood on the usually defined left-right axis. To reinvent itself, as either a radical or a conservative force, it needs not only a better grip on the present but a much richer, more practical understanding of its past.[16]

The increased commodification of political history from the 1980s onwards has played a role in this subversion of historical reality. Emily Robinson believes that history has become 'an ever-present point of reference in political discourse, providing a source of lessons, warnings and precedents', appropriated by the dominant 'present-focused view of the past as "heritage", which can be embraced or rejected as politically expedient'.[17] The exponential growth of social media has exacerbated this, with the explosion of highly partisan commentators, with narrow political perspectives but enormous Twitter followings in the tens or hundreds of thousands, increasingly dominating the discussion online and frequently in traditional media. We need to strip away some of the myths, distortions and stereotypes that have built up, and been perpetuated, around Labour's history, and provide fresh perspective on the long-term effects and significance of Labour's role as one of the two main parties of state. As Jon Cruddas writes, Labour has to 'move beyond the ever-present trap of political binaries ... excavate history [and] reclaim progressive traditions absent from the modern conversation. A return to history might also help the party own its

---

[16] David Edgerton, 'As Labour elects a new leader, some thoughts on Labour's misunderstood history', 4 April 2020, https://www.davidedgerton.org/blog/2020/4/4/as-labour-elects-a-new-leader-some-thoughts-on-labours-misunderstood-history (accessed 13 September 2021), republished as 'Labour has to free itself from the shackles of its own invented histories' in *Prospect*, 5 April 2020, https://www.prospectmagazine.co.uk/politics/labour-party-history-keir-starmer (accessed 22 September 2021).

[17] Emily Robinson, *History, Heritage and Tradition in Contemporary British Politics, Past Politics and Present Histories* (Manchester: MUP, 2021), 3.

recent victories and dissect successive defeats.'[18] This collection is an attempt to do just that: excavate Labour's history, whilst remaining conscious of the dangers of lapsing into nostalgia or treating historical exploration as a displacement activity from the urgent task of understanding the sociological and economic complexities of contemporary British society.

Crucial to this is a better understanding of the ideological continuum that has sustained the Labour Party since 1900. I think that there have been three distinct phases during this period, defined by specific ideological and organizational themes, and covering the years 1900–31, 1931–79 and 1979–2019. None of these three 'ages' are particularly novel in Labour historiography, but I think that they provide an important framework for looking at the evolution of the party as a national political project and the changing nature of its relationship with the British people. The 'first age' began with the foundation of the Labour Representation Committee (LRC) in 1900, with the aim of securing greater working-class representation in parliament, followed by the creation of a distinct Labour Party in 1906. Over the next twenty-five years, Labour went from being a (very) junior partner in the Edwardian progressive alliance to becoming the country's dominant, anti-Conservative party as the UK adapted and acclimatized to universal suffrage. The political genius of Ramsay MacDonald – Labour's chief organizer in the 1900s, keeper of the socialist flame in the 1910s and first prime minister in the 1920s – was his ability to fuse disparate radical, liberal and conservative groups together to form the bedrock of Labour's post-1918 electoral coalition. Labour's rise in the 1920s owed as much to the realignment of working-class Tory voters as it did to the collapse and fragmentation of the Liberals. As the former Labour MP and academic David Marquand acknowledged in his review of Martin Pugh's revisionist *Speak for Britain! A New History of the Labour Party*, Labour 'was not just the heir of liberalism and the Liberal Party. It also drew on a long line of working-class Toryism: a rollicking, rambunctious, fiercely patriotic and earthy tradition, at odds with both the preachy non conformist conscience that saturated the culture of provincial liberalism and with the patronising, "we-know-best" preconceptions of metropolitan intellectuals.'[19] MacDonald kept this coalition together by rejecting political militancy, instead framing Labour's historic mission as uniting the working and 'useful' classes in the quest for national fellowship. He saw the state in organic terms, as a

---

[18] Jon Cruddas MP, 'Politics beyond binaries', *Renewal* 29, no. 1 (2021).
[19] Martin Pugh, *Speak for Britain! A New History of the Labour Party* (London: Bodley Head, 2010); David Marquand, 'Review of Speak for Britain! A New History of the Labour Party by Martin Pugh', *New Statesman*, 2 April 2010.

'body in which the various organs find a place in a unified personality, and discover their liberty in that personality'.[20] Socialism was a project of social transformation, devoted to the interests of the community, however defined, and in opposition both to individualism and 'any sectional interests that jeopardised the whole ... In particular, he repudiated any idea of socialism as a politics of interest representation or emancipation based on class'.[21] This conception of politics, and of the Labour Party more as guarantor than agent of social progress, held a powerful sway over contemporaries, and determined the evolutionary, gradualist nature of Labour's appeal to the nation. The idea of community, cooperation or fellowship was fundamental here too: early socialists sought to construct a society based on an alternative ethical basis to the socially destructive, individualistic and competitive ethos of industrial capitalism.[22] Compelling as this ethical socialism might have been, chiming particularly with Britain's pre-existing nonconformist tradition, it had some hard practical limitations, particularly the absence of an alternative philosophy for economic policymaking – nor a suitably critical view of the limits of the British state as a vehicle for socialist reform.[23] As the 1920s wore on, MacDonald's rhetoric, in David Howell's damning phrase, 'grew increasingly obscure as he endured the present and contemplated the beauties of the distant socialist paradise'.[24] Fixation on the future led to inflexibility in the present and MacDonald proved incapable of accommodating domestic economic needs in the aftermath of the Wall Street Crash in October 1929. With the eventual collapse of the second Labour government two years later, and his continuation in office at the head of the incoming national government, the curtain came crashing down on the party that MacDonald had knitted together since the early 1900s. The primacy of 'fellowship' and 'community' evaporated, dispersed on the wind, much like MacDonald's 'romantic air and rhetorical ambiguity'.[25]

Although bracketed by the general election defeats of 1931 and 1979, the Labour Party enjoyed more years in power during the 'second age' than at any

---

[20] James Ramsay MacDonald, *Socialism and Government*, vol. 1 (London: Independent Labour Party, 1909), 178–9, quoted in Kevin Morgan, *MacDonald* (London: Haus Publishing), 107.

[21] Ibid., 108.

[22] See for instance Ben Jackson, *Equality and the British Left: A Study in Progressive Political Thought, 1900–64* (Manchester: MUP, 2007), 6–9.

[23] Ross McKibbin 'Why was there no Marxism in Great Britain?', *The English Historical Review* 99, no. 391 (April 1984): 297–331; and *Parties and People: Britain 1914–1951* (Oxford: OUP, 2010), 83–6; Stephanie Mudge, *Leftism Reinvented* (Cambridge, MA: HUP, 2018), ch. 4.

[24] David Howell, *British Social Democracy, A Study in Development and Decay* (London: Croom Helm, 1976), 38.

[25] David Marquand, *The Progressive Dilemma*, 2nd edn (London: Phoenix, 1991), 61.

time before or since, covering the Wartime Coalition of 1940–5, the 1945–51 Attlee administrations and the Wilson and Callaghan governments of 1964–70 and 1974–9. The period was characterized by three, complementary themes: a conversion to economic theory as the touchstone of political activity; the rise (and eventual fall) of Labourism as the dominant expression of this activity; and the legitimization of the party as part of the national fabric of the UK as a result of it. As the party sought to renew itself after the catastrophe of 1931, it found new arguments for equality in terms of economic theory – in particular those of John Maynard Keynes – and a commitment to planning and public ownership. This was in part a conscious rejection of the ethical socialism preached by the apostate MacDonald but also a reflection of the growing influence of middle-class intellectuals in the formulation of party policy – and that of trade union leader Ernest Bevin from the Transport and General Workers Union (TGWU), who had become a convert, of sorts, to Keynes' economic theories after 1930.[26] Under Bevin's watch, the unions took back control of Labour's organizational and policymaking platforms, reaffirming the party's role as the political expression of the organized working class. Labour's inclusion in Churchill's Wartime Coalition, and Bevin's appointment as Minister of Labour, took this a step further, symbolizing the historic acceptance and co-option of the labour movement into the national political system, where it stayed until it was systematically removed by Margaret Thatcher in the 1980s. The apotheosis of Labourism in postwar Britain helped lead the way to the foundation (or, at least, the evolution) of the modern welfare state, and the new, broadly consensual national frameworks and orthodoxies that governed socioeconomic policy after 1945. It also gave the Labour Party its first real opportunity to navigate the transition from class to nation-based politics. This was the period in which the 'British nation' was forged, as David Edgerton recounts; Labour played its part in building the economic and social infrastructure of that nation.[27] As Rachel Reeves reminds us: 'Labour's history is one of nation-building, of creating a thriving economy on strong, secure foundations.'[28] We should not lose sight of that today. Historian Jon Wilson argues that this essentially nationalist approach

[26] See Jackson, *Equality and the British Left* and Ross McKibbin, *Parties and People, England 1914–1951* (Oxford: OUP, 2010), 140–1. The year 1931 triggered the relegation of a generation of autodidact working-class journalists and agitators, to be replaced by the figure of the Keynesian economist – Durbin, Gaitskell, Crosland, Wilson – as the key source of expertise and authority within Labour politics, see Mudge, *Leftism Reinvented*, ch. 4.

[27] David Edgerton, *Rise and Fall of the British Nation: A Twentieth Century History* (London: Penguin, 2018). See also David Edgerton, 'How and why the idea of a national economy is radical', *Renewal* 29, no. 2 (2021): 17–22.

[28] Rachel Reeves, 'Our search for a national story', *New Statesman*, 8 March 2021.

to class was crucial to the party's electoral success in 1945, 1950 and again in the 1960s, when it confidently laid claim to speak and govern on behalf of the whole country, and not just one part of it. It might have divided 'people into specific interest groups, but [it] conceived of them all as members of one organised and planned national whole. In each case, Labour could push its strong class-based identity to one side when making its appeal to the broader public.'[29]

In the mid-1970s, Labour came perhaps as close as it ever has to being able to think of itself as a natural party of government: winning twice (albeit narrowly) in 1974 on the basis that it was the party best able to guarantee economic stability and social peace. But despite these victories, the structural integrity of postwar social democracy was creaking. The same social change that Labour's postwar reforms had done so much to promote was changing the electorate, chipping away at the reliability, even the very nature, of the party's working-class base. The global economic crises of the early 1970s fatally undermined the form of Keynesian demand management practised in the UK, coinciding with renewed interest in the free market, monetarist economic policies that came to be championed by Mrs Thatcher, who became the leader of the Conservative Party in 1975. In an increasingly antagonistic political environment, the trade unions objected to the income policies of successive Conservative and Labour administrations, and negotiation between nationally organized workers and businesses broke down. The ultimate failure of Labourism was foreshadowed by new prime minster James Callaghan's repudiation of Keynesianism in 1976 and later epitomized by the strikes of the so-called 'Winter of Discontent' in 1978–9. The latter shredded Labour's immediate claims to economic competence and heralded the popular exclusion of trade union involvement in national politics that was to characterize the decade to come. Fundamentally, the very obvious and public division between the two wings of the labour movement undermined Labour's claims to national legitimacy, raising questions from across the increasingly broad spectrum of Labour opinion and, crucially, in the minds of the public as to just what the Labour Party stood for.

The 'third age' lasted from 1979 until 2019, another span of years bookended by election defeat, but this time accompanied by two bouts of internal, political sectarianism for good measure. It also contained, of course, the Blair and Brown governments of 1997–2010 – by far the most electorally successful, continuously sustained period of government in Labour's history. The early 1980s were an

---

[29] Jon Wilson, 'Our People', *Renewal*, 10 April 2020, https://renewal.org.uk/our-people/ (accessed 13 September 2021).

existential battlefield for the Labour Party. Whilst Thatcherism administered shock therapy to the British economy and dismantled the various national institutions that Labour had helped create and then inhabit since 1945, the party came close to dismantling itself through two, separate but related bouts of factional warfare. The first was between the party leadership and 'mainstream' members on the one side, and the left-wing Bennite insurgency on the other. The left railed against the 'betrayal' of the 1974–9 governments, demanding the transfer of power away from party elites towards rank-and-file members. In the midst of this battle, a second front opened up in 1981 with the defection of twenty-eight sitting Labour MPs to form the new Social Democratic Party (SDP), 'a seismic event threatening to replace Labour as the dominant centre-left party'.[30] The impact of all of this was profound. It accelerated the degeneration of Labourism as a viable political system and exposed the tripartite threat of Labour's alienation from the hopes and aspirations of a sizeable minority of the working class, a growing, socially mobile 'new middle-class', and professional middle-class voters drawn to the SDP.[31] It gave the Conservatives carte blanche to reconfigure the British economy along Thatcherite lines, replacing 'a society of institutions and interests with a single homogenous people which shared her moral and economic "convictions", enforced by the state. Groups that challenged that position were cast from the nation into an anti-national residuum, whether they were striking miners, the unemployed who refused to "get on their bikes", academics, non-traditional families, public-sector workers, [or] ethnic minorities.'[32] By the time it clawed back some kind of competitive position at the 1987 general election, Labour had, by default, become the champion of these dispossessed groups, protecting 'our people' in the face of sustained Conservative attack, and shifting its political locus away from economic production towards social protection.

There is a symmetry to the Labour Party after 1987, delineated by the uphill climb towards, and long recessional from, the achievements of 1997–2010. The political genius of Tony Blair lay in his ability to connect with the British public and tell a story about his party as an agent of change and renewal, in tune with

---

[30] Patrick Diamond, *The British Labour Party in Opposition and Power, 1979–2019* (London: Routledge, 2021), 138.

[31] For Labour's difficulty in reconciling the competing impulses of the post-1945 settlement and the need to adapt to changing social demands and expectations, the decline of deference and a population clamouring for greater individual agency and autonomy, see James E. Cronin, *New Labour's Pasts: The Labour Party and its Discontents* (London: Routledge, 2004), 236; Emily Robinson et al., 'Telling stories about post-war Britain: popular individualism and the 'crisis' of the 1970s', *Twentieth Century British History* 28, no. 2 (2017), 268–304.

[32] Wilson, 'Our People'.

the needs of the British people, regardless of supposed class or background. This connection helped propel the party to two record-breaking parliamentary majorities in 1997 and 2001. Blair had the great fortune to serve as prime minster during the 'great moderation' of the world economy in the 1990s and 2000s.[33] He also benefitted from the intellectual renaissance and reappraisal of contemporary social democracy that blossomed in the late 1980s, driven by growing interest in a wealth of new political issues (especially the need for constitutional reform), by the urgent need to face up to the reality of successive election defeats and by the collapse of Communism in Eastern Europe. As Patrick Diamond contends, 'Invented *within* the Left's distinctive ecosystem, New Labour's governing project was the result of vigorous intellectual debate over Labourism's long-term decline … A multitude of ideas from diverse sources and intellectual traditions were crucial in revitalising the Labour Party.'[34] One tradition to make a reappearance was a contemporary take on the power of community. In their modernizing text, *The Blair Revolution*, Roger Liddle and Peter Mandelson characterized community as a 'robust and powerful idea … It means teamwork – working and acting together in companies, in local neighbourhoods, in the country as a whole to get things done. It means mutuality – rights and responsibilities going hand in hand.'[35] Blair's own promotion of communitarianism in the 1990s was potentially interesting, but it existed in tension with some of the government's other priorities – including its reticence to intervene in a flexible labour market – and ultimately petered out in government.[36] This speaks to one of the tragedies of New Labour: the inability to sustain and replicate the intellectual creativity of the 1990s into government, and the ultimate failure to renew sufficiently whilst in office, despite the existence of a lively infrastructure of sympathetic left-of-centre think tanks and other organizations keen to influence the direction of government policy. Labour failed in this task again in opposition. Instead of promoting 'a wide-ranging and candid debate about why Labour had been defeated in 2010, [new leader Ed] Miliband found a simplistic target in the accusation that New Labour was the inheritor of Thatcherism … His own leadership echoed the claim that the party under Blair and Brown was the ideological bedfellow of neo-liberalism.'[37] With

---

[33] See chapter 14 of this volume.

[34] Diamond, *The British Labour Party in Opposition and Power*, 8

[35] Roger Liddle and Peter Mandelson, *The Blair Revolution: Can New Labour Deliver?* (London: Faber & Faber, 1996), 19.

[36] Diamond, *The British Labour Party in Opposition and Power*, 376.

[37] Ibid., 331.

no compelling, alternative narrative to light the way ahead, the anti-Thatcherite politics of welfare and protection that sustained the party through the 1980s and 1990s returned with a vengeance after 2010:

> Labour's politically active supporters … [returned to the] emotional heartland of defending our institutions and 'our people' against Tory attacks and cuts, with higher public spending if necessary. Corbyn and Corbynism, with resistance to austerity as their key concepts … [were] the consequence … Corbyn's dominance was rooted in instincts mainstream to centre-left politics since Thatcher. It was only led by the party's far left because they were the only ones able to connect with the broader British left.[38]

Despite New Labour's success in creating a new, more inclusive political framework in the late 1990s, taken as a whole, Labour's 'third age' was an age of 'welfarism', dominated by the need and instinct to defend 'our people' from the worst excesses of Thatcherism and austerity in opposition, and to provide for them whilst in government. In Edgerton's terms, this 'welfarism' was shaped by the scarring experience of defeat (and the knowledge of its consequences), by the need to redress the alarming growth in inequality from the late 1970s onwards and by a pessimism about the ability of government to shape the productive side of the economy. As Florence Sutcliffe-Braithwaite describes, New Labour's success could in part be attributed to its development of a language of 'ordinary working people' which incorporated its working-class base and the poor into a broader social grouping that resonated with people's changing conceptions of themselves.[39] However, after 2010, members of the incoming Coalition government took every opportunity to excoriate Labour as the party of scroungers and benefit cheats, turning the welfare state, that 'tribute to solidarity', into a bitter dividing line between party and people.[40] Jon Wilson argues that the urgent need to defend the vulnerable and excluded

> has meant that Labour has been unable to forge an inclusive, progressive story about the nation as a whole, because people who identify with those terms are nowhere near a majority. The 2019 general election showed that its emotional affinity with its supposed constituency [was not] reciprocal. When the Labour Party talked about 'our people', most people thought it wasn't talking about them.[41]

[38] Ibid.
[39] Florence Sutcliffe-Braithwaite, *Class, Politics and the Decline of Deference in England, 1968–2000* (Oxford: OUP, 2018), ch. 8.
[40] David Miliband, Keir Hardie lecture, 9 July 2010, https://labourlist.org/2010/07/david-milibands-keir-hardie-lecture-full-speech/ (accessed 13 September 2021).
[41] Wilson, 'Our People'.

As it contemplates its post-Brexit, post-Covid 'fourth age', Labour must choose who it speaks for and how it speaks to them. It must decide what intellectual, ideological and organizational themes it wants to pursue and, equally importantly, those it wants to disavow. And it must refine and champion a new progressive, social democratic vision for life in twenty-first-century Britain. I fervently believe that by rethinking and re-engaging with its past, Labour is better equipped to reframe and command its present position, and in doing so improves its chances of shaping the future of the nation for the greater good.

This book is not a linear, narrative history of the Labour Party. Neither is it a comprehensive assessment of every period, trend or tradition over the past hundred years or so. There are a number of important areas that barely raise a mention. There is no serious consideration of the coming together and evolution of the Labour Party, of the crucial early role played by the trade unions, or of the highs and lows of the 1920s and 1930s. There is no in-depth analysis of the changing structures of the party, of the shifting demographics underpinning (or undermining) electoral success, or of the at times contradictory dynamics at play between the constituent parts of the wider labour movement. The struggles of the 1950s, the schism of the early 1980s, the reaction against New Labour following the global crash of 2008 – these events are glimpsed but not explored in detail. There is no study of continuity and change in Labour's positions regarding specific policies per se, meaning no contemporary account of Brexit, the full historical enormity of which will take years to understand. For similar reasons, there is no attempt to analyse Jeremy Corbyn's tenure as Labour leader after 2015. My own views, I think, are reasonably clear, and a number of contributors conjecture what long-term effects they think the Corbyn ascendancy might have on the party, but as this is a collection devoted principally to re-interpreting and re-engaging with Labour's past and its relationship with the present, and not in providing more *reportage* on the later 2010s, the comprehensive and critical, long-term consideration it demands will have to wait.[42]

The topics covered in the chapters in this volume emerged following discussions with the relevant authors, evolving over time as the narrative structure of the book itself evolved. In large part, this means that the essays in this collection are the essays that their authors themselves wanted to write (with some prodding and cajoling from me). Contributors were given no political or factional editorial line and come from a variety of points on the Labour spectrum (or no point on

---

[42] As an interim appraisal, I would recommend Matt Bolton and Frederick Harry Pitts, *Corbynism: A Critical Approach* (London: Emerald Publishing, 2018).

that spectrum). The collection does not seek to push a progressive interpretation of Labour history as such, although readers may well agree that the beginnings of such interpretations are revealed during the course of the book. Indeed, if insights from this book help build the foundations of a renewed progressive, social democratic project within the Labour Party, then all the better.

With one exception (and not including references made in this introduction), the chapters all take place in my 'second' and 'third ages' of the Labour Party, namely from the 1930s onwards, and the structure of the book, which is split into five parts, reflects this. **Part I** consists of this introduction and Ben Jackson's discussion of the 'disenchantment' of Labour's relationship with its own history (Chapter 2), with particular reference to the different ways that Attlee, Wilson and Blair wove themselves into (and out of) the tapestry of the labour movement's past struggles and triumphs. Emerging from the trauma of the 1980s, Blair pointed to a tattered legacy of myth and nostalgia that increasingly alienated British society and urged his party to rethink and reposition itself in the realities of 1990s Britain. As Jackson maintains, in what also serves as a challenge for the rest of the book, the 'task for the Labour Party today is to reconnect with the inspiring aspects of its past without sliding back into the self-congratulatory and uncritical historical ambience that was dispelled by the ruptures of the late twentieth century'.[43]

Part II contains four essays devoted to issues and individuals in Labour's 'second age', from the 1930s to the late 1970s. As Joe Biden seeks to inspire to a generation of progressives across the Atlantic, Richard Carr delves back into the history of Democratic and Labour Party co-operation from Franklin D. Roosevelt's New Deal in the 1930s to John F. Kennedy's New Frontier in the 1960s in Chapter 3. In particular, he shows how the practical, progressive advances of Democratic government in the 1930s helped change and moderate the views of left-wingers and isolationists in the UK – and how the bonds of friendship between revisionist political and literary elites here and in America helped shape a common, liberal agenda in the 1960s. In Chapter 4, Steven Fielding turns to 1945, that most iconic of years in the annals of the Labour Party, with an essay that looks at the historical and historiographical significance of Attlee's postwar government, and in particular debunks the historical and rhetorical repositioning of the hard left through the prism of Ken Loach's 2013 documentary film, *The Spirit of '45*. He goes on to ask whether Labour activists have identified with idealized notions of Attlee and his governments and to what extent Covid-19

---

[43] 46, below.

and the brazen *realpolitik* of Prime Minister Johnson mean that 'the kind of interventionist state associated with Attlee's administration is now taken more seriously'.[44] We move forward to the 1960s and 1970s with Chapters 5 and 6: Glen O'Hara's reassessment of Harold Wilson, and Patrick Diamond's analysis of Anthony Crosland's writings in the 1970s. Between 1963 and 1966, Wilson captivated the public, pioneered a brand of 'scientific socialism' that galvanized both wings of the Labour Party, and delivered two general election victories on the bounce in 1964 and 1966, the latter with a majority of almost one hundred seats. Crosland, having already authored the definitive statement of postwar revisionism in 1956, would in the 1960s and 1970s be one of the pre-eminent intellectual forces, and one of the more dynamic and effective ministers in a series of cabinets full of heavyweight political figures. To quote Jackson, the 'Labour governments of 1964–70 and 1974–9 introduced significant political initiatives designed to advance an egalitarian agenda, but the work of these governments was ultimately constrained by the formidable political and economic crises that engulfed them.'[45] Long consigned to the political-historical dustbin, O'Hara asks whether the vicissitudes of the 2010s have given Wilson new lustre. As the country grapples with the grave economic consequences of Brexit and Covid-19, Diamond looks at whether Crosland's writings from an earlier period of economic turmoil have anything to say to today's generation of policymakers.

We step out of our chronological framework for **Part III** and turn our attention to a number of important thematic issues revolving around identity, community and place. In Chapter 7, Krista Cowman surveys the evolution of women's activism in the Labour Party from the early 1900s until the 1980s, paying particular attention to the close connections between 'municipal socialism and municipal feminism'. She describes a long, rich history of Labour women organizing and campaigning locally to 'bring about solutions to the problems that had a disproportionate effect on women's lives', working together in an inclusive, supportive environment that helped foster a feminist 'sense of possibility' sadly lacking on the national stage. She predicts that the future of progressive feminism will be local. In Chapter 8, Nick Garland explores one of our recurring themes – the politics of 'community' and the idea that the actions of Labour governments can sometimes serve to undermine those values of community and solidarity that give life to the movement. Where critics of Labour governments have often described a binary between a top-down, redistributive egalitarianism and a

---

[44] 72, below.
[45] Jackson, *Equality and the British Left*, 224.

grassroots ethos of community, solidarity and mutual aid he reminds us that, in fact, social democracy and the welfare state have been, and remain, powerful agents for building community and fostering participation. In Chapter 9, Daisy Payling presents us with a case study of how place and community have shaped Labour's policies and local politics: the cheap bus fares policy implemented across South Yorkshire in the 1970s and 1980s. She shows that, even at the height of Thatcherism, Labour local authorities provided a space for political renewal, 'where policies could be designed and enacted' and local politicians 'develop distinctive and varied municipal or local socialisms'.[46] Should they need it, this is a lesson for contemporary Labour politicians. In Chapter 10, Robin Bunce and Samara Linton appraise the 1980s 'Black Sections debates' – the high-profile campaign by Black and Asian activists to secure formal representation within the Labour Party's constitution. In part, this push was an attempt to reshape Labour into a more multiracial party in terms of representation, and a more anti-racist party in terms of politics, but the debate became bogged down in the sectarian arguments that stalked much of the decade. The episode is a timely reminder that the Labour Party has often struggled to represent a multiracial society and be a welcoming space to incoming communities – and that there remains no settled view on the rights and wrongs of assimilation versus liberation within the UK. Part III comes to a close with Chapter 11, Charlotte Lydia Riley's essay on the important role played by overseas aid in the development of the Labour Party's ethical identity following the retreat of the British Empire. Riley believes that

> aid and development policies are an integral part of Labour ideology, as central to the party's identity as the welfare state at home … Labour's most successful leaders have been those who have advocated with clear voices for overseas aid spending, and should continue to make a case for aid, not only for short term political gain, but as part of the moral framework of the Labour Party itself.[47]

We turn to Labour's 'third age' in **Part IV**. In Chapter 12, Colm Murphy asks 'What did the 1983 manifesto ever do for us?' as he aims to return Labour's early 1980s policy platform to its true context, namely the political and social upheavals of the 1970s, and its true purpose, mainly as a reaction to the intellectual collapse of Labourism. Crucially, he argues that the 1983 manifesto owed a debt of gratitude to the electorally successful (if factionally contentious) manifestos of 1974 – and even provides a couple of intellectual threads to the landslide-inspiring New Labour manifesto of 1997. He also issues a warning to social democrats

---

[46] 162, below.
[47] 211, below.

against 'stereotyping the ideas of other traditions in the labour movement and broader left ... Otherwise, they can find themselves ... marginalized from the dynamic debates of their day', which certainly resonates with the experiences of 'moderates' during the period of the Corbyn ascendancy.[48] Jonathan Davis and Rohan McWilliam seek to reassess the leadership of Neil Kinnock in Chapter 13, with specific reference to the process of political and intellectual transformation that he oversaw from the mid-1980s onwards. They place his leadership in a global context, his actions as part of a wider realignment of socialist parties in the face of market liberalization and consumer individualism. Ultimately, Kinnock remains the key transitional figure in Labour's recent history, and potentially the only contemporary figure capable of inaugurating 'the process of reconciliation with the new global order emerging as deindustrialization and the turn towards the free market gathered pace'.[49] To put it another way, whether

> we think Kinnock was the saviour of the Labour Party or its gravedigger depends very much on what we think of New Labour, and how far we agree with [Roy] Hattersley that Kinnock was seeking not to abandon socialism but to introduce a new and improved form of it. Somebody had to disembarrass Labour of the infantile disorders of the early 1980s and Kinnock did that very well.[50]

The process of reconciling the Labour Party with the wider electorate fell to his protégé, successor-but-one as leader and the subject of Chapter 14, Tony Blair. Critics and supporters alike tend to write about Blair and 'Blairism' as a single, coherent phenomenon that arrived fully formed, and unalterable, in the mid-1990s. Andrew Hindmoor and Karl Pike argue that this does a disservice to Blair and his continuing legacy. They suggest that we need to think instead about 'five phases of Blair and New Labour' covering the breadth of his public career – a form of historical and political analysis that both contextualizes his contribution and reveals his interpretations of long-standing Labour traditions. As the title of the chapter suggests, a challenge of interpreting Blair is that he is both past and present. 'Blairism' – a term thrown around so much today, and often attached to Blair's contemporary observations on political strategy or judgements on recent Labour leaders – isn't particularly helpful for understanding Blair the opposition leader, nor Blair the early prime minister. As we have already established, one of the more iconoclastic hallmarks of New Labour in opposition in the early to

---

[48] 230, below.

[49] 232, below.

[50] Ross McKibbin, 'The Luck of the Tories', *London Review of Books* 24, no. 5 (7 March 2002), https://www.lrb.co.uk/the-paper/v24/n05/ross-mckibbin/the-luck-of-the-tories (accessed 13 September 2021).

mid-1990s was the intellectual ferment it both drew upon and encouraged. One of the key publications to emerge from this period was *Renewal: A Journal of Labour Politics*, first published in 1993 (known as *Renewal: A Journal of Social Democracy* since 2007). In Chapter 15, George Morris, Emily Robinson and Florence Sutcliffe-Braithwaite tell the story of *Renewal*: its origins in the factional fights of the 1980s; how it carved a niche for itself as a space for fresh thinking in the 1990s; its growing disenchantment with New Labour in the early 2000s; and its engagement with 'Corbynomics' between 2015–19. They argue that, because *Renewal* does not actively identify with any faction within the party, 'it has been able to deal with the … extremes of contemporary Labour history, whilst remaining committed to a core set of values: a guiding belief in the need for radical action to create a more egalitarian and democratic country'.[51]

Bringing the collection to a close with **Part V**, Jeremy Nuttall makes a stirring case in Chapter 16 for the enduring importance of aspiration to Labour's political and electoral success. Comfortable with subjects like equality and community, Labour's historians have felt uneasy in engaging with those of aspiration and opportunity. He explores how debates over how far the party needed to speak a language of aspiration created divisions, both between Labour's left and right, and within those factions. He then considers how the party at its governing best, specifically, in 1945, 1964 and 1997, forged an agenda of equity and aspiration – and how this remains absolutely crucial to any future revival of fortunes. In his conclusion, Nick Thomas-Symonds draws on Labour's history, and on the experience of the pandemic, to offer a rallying cry, calling on the party to meet the moral imperative of the moment and channel the spirit of a post-pandemic Britain, which has been given a vivid demonstration of the consequences of inequality and social injustice. In doing so, he underlines one of the central messages of the collection, namely the 'challenge for every generation of Labour politicians [to apply themselves] to the circumstances of the country they find them themselves in, to offer practical policies that can improve people's lives' and build towards a better future.

How do we shape that future? Three closing thoughts from me. First, it is imperative that the Labour Party ditches the 'them-and-us' rhetoric of the more recent past, moves away from binary, antagonistic political positions and sets out a new framework that allows it to develop as a genuinely national political project once again. It is right both on the grounds of electoral strategy and of principle that we emphasize what people hold in common and de-escalate our

---

[51] 285, below.

divisions. An obvious priority for this would be redefining the role, nature and scope of work in modern Britain, embracing a realistic assessment of ongoing sociological and demographic shifts in the process.[52] This would need to champion the diverse experiences and forms of contemporary work; most people like their jobs but quite rightly dislike the insecurity that comes with too many jobs and want to ensure that flexibility works for them and not just for their employer. The success of the Johnson government's furlough scheme, and the growth in support for a greater role for workers in the running of companies, illustrates the exciting possibility of a renewed role for labour within our national politics, in the making of key economic decisions by the state and within the private sector, for the first time in decades.[53] As both an activist and political practitioner, I have developed rather a tin ear for the 'romantic' class rhetoric of the past decade, a condition I share with a majority of the public. History shows us that when Labour reaches out beyond its self-defined sectional interests, and positions itself as an agent of progressive, consensual and *fundamentally national* change, it can connect with the electorate. To do this, it must craft a narrative and deliver a message that is ebullient, optimistic and aspirational. As Nuttall explains, if 'modern British history shows anything, it is that an aspirational agenda, generously and progressively defined, and articulated by convincing leadership, has an appeal which bridges many of the apparently immutable divides, between young and old, city and small town, and even nations'.[54]

Second, the advent of Labour's 'fourth age' gives it an opportunity to recast its ideological foundations, or at least synthesize the underpinnings I sketch out above, namely a belief in community, a revitalized economic (and, crucially, environmental) theory and an enduring commitment to social policy and welfare provision, in a manner that guarantees parity of esteem between the three. I make no bones of the fact that I am an avowed localist and champion of the 'progressive case for place'. As we level up, or build back better, we must ensure that our places – and the people within them that make them so unique – become the building blocks of political, economic and social renewal.[55] If

---

[52] See Claire Ainsley, *The New Working Class* (Bristol: Policy Press, 2018).

[53] For an interesting contemporary discussion about the future and possibility of work as the lodestone for Labour's political revival, see Jon Cruddas in conversation with Frederick Harry Pitts, 'The Labour Party and the future of work, parts I-III', *Renewal* (8–12 June 2021), https://renewal.org.uk/labour-and-the-future-of-work-1/ (accessed 13 September 2021).

[54] 305, below.

[55] See Dan Corry and Gerry Stoker (eds), *The New Localism* (London: New Local Government Network, 2003); Joe Simpson, *The Politics of Leadership* (London: Leading Edge Publications, 2008); Nathan Yeowell, 'Radical roots to practical action – the case for place', *New Philanthropy Capital*, 23 April 2019, https://www.thinknpc.org/resource-hub/radical-roots-to-practical-action-the-case-for-place/ (accessed 13 September 2021).

Labour is to turn back the Conservatives' advances beyond the 'red wall' and reconstruct the geographically diverse coalition necessary to win in the future, it needs to reconnect with local, regional and devolved political identities as a source of strength and inspiration. David Miliband's words are as apposite today as they were in 2010: 'Default statism turns citizens into consumers and makes government a giant problem solver, which only increases our technical managerialism ... We need a creed that could combine solidarity with responsibility, freedom and equality. Without community ethics, lived and upheld, it is difficult to generate the civility we value.'[56] The combination of Brexit and pandemic has prompted a wider shift across the political spectrum towards a more interventionist, post-austerity state. Labour must capitalize on this as it brings forward a new economic settlement fit for the future – and robust enough to maintain and improve the welfare state.

Third, and in terms of a new progressive, social democratic vision for the country, Labour must seek to construct a broad-based coalition committed to tackling deep-rooted structural inequalities, and advancing opportunity, economic efficiency, climate and social justice. Our long-term aim must be to create a new social contract and nurture the sustainable rehabilitation of compelling and electorally successful centre-left politics across the UK. As Rachel Reeves argues, we can draw inspiration from Labour's historic achievements, but we should also pay attention to where we have failed; we should be aware of both where today's challenges mirror those of the past and of where the context in which we find ourselves is wholly new. This book is only one part of a long and essential task of political renewal – learning from the best of Labour's achievements and from its failings, as well as from the realities of a changing country that deserves better leadership.

---

[56] Miliband, Keir Hardie lecture.

2

The disenchantment of the Labour Party: Socialism, liberalism and progressive history

Ben Jackson

History is both a source of inspiration and a burden for the Labour Party. Labour activists and politicians often see themselves as part of a dissenting egalitarian tradition that stretches back to the formation of the welfare state in the 1940s, and before that to nineteenth- and early-twentieth-century struggles for workplace rights and for votes for women and workers. Conceptualizing the political struggles of the moment as but the latest episode in this long-running crusade electrifies otherwise prosaic party matters. On this account, to be Labour is to be part of a righteous cause that has been vindicated by history. But such a historical perspective can also be problematic, insofar as it raises the bar of expectations for the Labour Party to a very high level. For the unlucky leaders who found themselves steering the party after the bold, heroic age of 1945 (and even to some extent for those who were in charge between 1945–51), a failure to initiate deep structural change was often understood by supporters as a betrayal of the glorious party lineage disclosed by history. Equally, a preoccupation with the history of industrialization and democratization in the nineteenth and twentieth centuries could appear out of step with the concerns of electorally decisive segments of the public, who were in the first instance looking for a government that could competently manage a modern economy and deliver public services. Across the twentieth century, Labour leaders have had to assuage the tension between a support base that believes the party to be the historic vehicle of social transformation, and the constraints that hem in the freedom of action of the Labour Party in opposition and in government. Yet it is fair to say that it was only under Tony Blair's leadership of the party that the management of this tension tipped decisively in one direction, as Blair promulgated a much less starry-eyed view of Labour history than any of his predecessors. Just as Max

Weber once wrote about the 'disenchantment of the world' as science dispelled religious and mystical beliefs in favour of rationally grounded knowledge, in a more minor key Blair – and associated advisers and thinkers – sought to bring about a disenchantment of the Labour Party that would root it more firmly in what they saw as the rational demands of the pursuit of office rather than a utopian vision of building the world anew.[1]

This chapter will investigate how Labour leaders have interpreted the party's past, comparing the rhetoric used by the three postwar, election-winning Labour prime ministers – Attlee, Wilson and Blair – in order to identify what was distinctive about Blair's understanding of Labour history. However, the aim of this comparison is not to castigate Blair as a regrettable anomaly but rather to understand why the more traditional historical self-understanding of the Labour Party lost its allure in the late twentieth century. The chapter will conclude by considering, as the party looks to the future, how we might delineate a new account of the Labour tradition which accepts that Blair made some trenchant points about the myths that have populated Labour discourse, whilst still seeking to reinject into Labour's account of the past the idealism that the architects of New Labour so scrupulously removed. Weber acknowledged that 'disenchantment' risked leaving the modern world adrift from meaning or purpose in the absence of agreed ethical and spiritual values. The task for the Labour Party today is to reconnect with the inspiring aspects of its past without sliding back into the self-congratulatory and uncritical historical ambience that was dispelled by the political ruptures of the late twentieth century.

Clement Attlee

Although his social background was upper middle class, and his qualities as a leader and prime minister were quintessentially technocratic, Clement Attlee nonetheless personally embodied the historic rise of the labour movement to its new status as a party of government. Attlee had spent his early adult life embedded within the Edwardian and interwar Labour Party. Living in the East End of London, he had been, amongst other things, an activist campaigning in the classic political battles over poverty and inequality of the early twentieth century. He helped organize the campaign for the 1909 *Minority Report on*

---

[1]   Max Weber, 'Science as a Vocation', in Hans Heinrich Gerth and Charles Wright Mills (eds), *From Max Weber* (London: Routledge, 2009), 155.

Poor Law Reform, largely authored by Beatrice Webb.[2] Attlee therefore spoke about Labour's history with the authority of one who had in fact lived through, and contributed to, the movement's formative years. He could stand before an audience and casually remark that 'when I was young I found my leader in Keir Hardie', praising from first-hand knowledge 'the strength, the tenderness and the crusading zeal' that Hardie embodied.[3] Speaking in parliament during the second reading of the National Insurance Act in 1946, Attlee eloquently characterized the implementation of the Beveridge Report as the culmination of the Edwardian debates about the Poor Law that he had participated in (and acknowledged the role of Liberal politicians such as Lloyd George in driving forward welfare provision).[4] As Attlee wrote in 1937, for Labour politicians of his generation 'the emergence of the Labour Party as a great political force is still something of a miracle'.[5]

Both Jon Lawrence and Steven Fielding have observed that the idea of an inexorable upward 'rise of Labour' was commonplace amongst Labour politicians and activists before 1945, but that this trope took on a much more triumphalist tone in the wake of Labour's general election victory of that year.[6] Attlee himself contributed to this by depicting his government as the crest of a great historical wave that had been building for decades – or perhaps even for centuries. Attlee recognized that a simple teleological story of social progress was unsatisfactory in the wake of the Second World War. He noted that the immense destruction of two total wars and the atrocities committed by the Nazis drove home that 'the progress of the human race is very unequal; that in one part of the field there is advance, in another retreat'. But he did argue that 'in the particular fields in which I have worked, I have seen great changes of conception', as older ideas that poverty and unemployment should be seen as the responsibility of the individual had been displaced by 'a far greater sense of social obligation than has ever existed in our country before'.[7] Attlee depicted Labour

[2] John Bew, *Citizen Clem* (London: riverrun, 2016), Part I; Ben Jackson, 'Citizen and Subject: Clement Attlee's Socialism', *History Workshop Journal* 86 (2018): 291–8.

[3] Clement Richard Attlee, 'An Address to the General Assembly of the Church of Scotland', 25 May 1946, in Clement Richard Attlee, *Purpose and Policy: Selected Speeches* (London: Hutchinson & Co., 1946), 112.

[4] Clement Richard Attlee, speech to the House of Commons on the Second Reading of the National Insurance Bill, 7 February 1946, in Attlee, *Purpose and Policy*, 92–3.

[5] Clement Richard Attlee, *The Labour Party in Perspective* (London: Gollancz/Left Book Club, 1937), 27.

[6] Jon Lawrence, 'Labour – the Myths it Has Lived by' and Steven Fielding, 'New Labour and the Past', both in Duncan Tanner, Pat Thane and Nick Tiratsoo (eds), *Labour's First Century* (Cambridge: CUP, 2000), 360–1, 367–8.

[7] Attlee, 'Address to the General Assembly of the Church of Scotland', 111–12.

in quasi-Christian terms, as a righteous sect that had come into its inheritance: 'Through many years of adversity we have kept our faith, we have striven for the opportunity to translate our socialist policy into action.'[8] Labour was, he said, 'a party of idealists inspired by a living faith in freedom, democracy and social justice', ultimately upholding 'the Christian principle that all men are brothers one of another'.[9] In historical terms, Attlee understood Labour as standing in a long line of popular – and ultimately successful – struggles that had formed Britain into a democracy. As he explained in 1945 in an address to a joint session of Congress in the United States, Labour stood in the tradition of those who had fought for freedom against monarchs, religious oppression, landowners and now 'the overwhelming strength of moneyed interests'. Labour was 'in line with those who fought for Magna Carta and *habeas corpus*, with the Pilgrim Fathers, and with the signatories of the Declaration of Independence'.[10]

Attlee therefore told a positive and redemptive historical story about the Labour Party, as the rightful inheritor of a long tradition of democratic dissent, which had superseded earlier radicals and Liberals because Labour was more broadly representative of Britain's modern industrialized society. He did not offer any substantial critique of Labour's historical trajectory but rather rejoiced in the heroic story of how a hardy few socialist pioneers and trade unionists had ultimately built a movement powerful enough to govern the British state and to equalize and democratize British society. As Attlee had argued at greater length in his pre-war book, *The Labour Party in Perspective* (1937), Labour's rise should be understood as the British version of a worldwide movement in which the issues of the nineteenth century – centred around political and civil liberty for the individual – had now given way to protest against the economic injustice of capitalism, and the need for collective action to secure 'economic freedom and social equality'.[11]

---

[8] Clement Richard Attlee, speech to Labour Party Conference, 11 June 1946, in Attlee, *Purpose and Policy*, 49.

[9] Attlee, speech to Labour Party Conference, 1946 and speech to Trades Union Congress, 12 September 1945, both in Attlee, *Purpose and Policy*, 49, 107.

[10] Attlee, speech to Congress, 13 November 1945, in Attlee, *Purpose and Policy*, 148.

[11] Attlee, *Labour Party*, 29–40, quote at 33–4.

Harold Wilson

Although Harold Wilson was born into a less privileged social background than Attlee, he did not in fact share Attlee's deep connection to the labour movement. Wilson was from a younger, more technocratic generation who joined the party once it had become established as the principal political party of the left and offered a clear career path for bright young people keen to push state policy in a more egalitarian direction.[12] As party leader, Wilson was also conscious of the need for Labour to present itself to voters as a modern, dynamic force that engaged with the pressing problems of the 1960s and 1970s, rather than dwelling on the accomplishments of the 1940s or the heroic struggles of Labour's early years. Reflecting the prevailing ideological atmosphere of that period, though, Wilson's account of what would represent a 'modern' Labour response consisted of a strong commitment to a more rationally planned economy, in order to keep Britain on pace with the economic achievements that stronger forms of planning appeared to be yielding in the Soviet Union and other Western European states.[13] He had of course been a cabinet minister during the 1945 Labour government – and even concluded the 1964 election campaign at a rally alongside Lord Attlee himself – so Wilson was also personally part of the lineage of Labour history.[14] Meanwhile, within the party, Wilson addressed a membership with firm socialist beliefs about the movement's purpose and identity. As he recollected in his memoirs, Wilson felt that his predecessor, Hugh Gaitskell, had failed to grasp this aspect of Labour's culture, since 'from the Party's earliest days, a great number of converts had joined Labour because they believed that socialism was a way of making a reality of Christian principles in everyday life'.[15]

Wilson was undoubtedly more cautious than Attlee about framing Labour historically in his public rhetoric, preferring to signal his radicalism in more personal terms, through his image as an anti-metropolitan, provincial figure

---

[12] Ben Pimlott, *Harold Wilson* (London: William Collins, 2016), 67–9.

[13] Ibid., 276; Glen O'Hara, *From Dreams to Disillusionment? Economic and Social Planning in 1960s Britain* (Basingstoke: Palgrave, 2007), 9–36.

[14] Pimlott, *Harold Wilson*, 317.

[15] Harold Wilson, *Memoirs: The Making of a Prime Minister* (London: Weidenfeld and Nicolson, 1986), 182, quoted in Pimlott, *Harold Wilson*, 235. For detailed studies of this aspect of Labour's internal life – and its clash with the social change of the period – see Lawrence Black, *The Political Culture of the Left in Affluent Britain, 1951–64: Old Labour, New Britain?* (Basingstoke: Palgrave, 2002), 12–64; Steven Fielding, *The Labour Governments 1964–70, Vol. 1: Labour and Cultural Change* (Manchester: MUP, 2003); Richard Jobson, *Nostalgia and the Post-War Labour Party* (Manchester: MUP, 2018), 60–84.

ranged against the privilege of the British political class. As Wilson put it before becoming party leader:

> The Yorkshire socialist revolts from poverty, not so much because it is a product of inefficiency and a badly-run social system, but because it is a crime against God and man. Our socialism does not come from the London School of Economics or any other seat of learning. It comes from revolt, revolt against the inequality that is endemic in Tory freedom.[16]

Nonetheless, when addressing Labour members, Wilson hewed to a similar position to Attlee, namely that Labour's programme represented 'a distillation of the thinking and the idealism of the democratic traditions of this country over a century past'.[17] Casting his mind back to the history of the movement, Wilson recapitulated the idea that Labour had developed, rather like Christianity, from a small persecuted sect of the faithful, to a broad-based movement to redeem the nation (and perhaps even the world):

> It is easy to be a Socialist today. It no longer means victimization, eviction from one's home, persecution or worse. But the founders of our Movement, men of courage, men of infinite faith, were prepared to face persecution and even death that a generation still to come might realize their ideals, might be permitted to create that new and just society which their vision could see gleaming above the squalor and exploitation and ugliness of Victorian industrialism.[18]

Labour entered government in 1964, said Wilson, as a fortunate generation chosen to bring this vision to fruition: 'The day for which we and those that went before us have waited is here. It is our task to be worthy of the torch they have handed on to us.'[19] Like Attlee, Wilson expressed an impregnable historical confidence in the rise of Labour and of its allotted role as the agent of social progress in modern Britain. It was an eloquent, powerful and romantic view, but not one that could survive the vicissitudes of the next three decades intact.

---

[16] Harold Wilson, 'The War on Poverty', *New Statesman*, 1959, reprinted in Harold Wilson, *Purpose in Politics: Selected Speeches* (London: Weidenfeld and Nicolson, 1964), 241–2.

[17] Wilson, speech to Labour Party conference, 1964, http://www.britishpoliticalspeech.org/speech-archive.htm?speech=162 (accessed 8 December 2020).

[18] Ibid.

[19] Ibid.

Tony Blair

Although Tony Blair is sometimes depicted as an unusual Labour leader because of his social background, in fact, he shared his middle-class family origins with Attlee (both, as it happens, had fathers who were lawyers). A more important difference between Blair's leadership and that of Attlee and Wilson was that Blair was much less reverential about Labour's past. Where Attlee and Wilson had told a story about Labour as the culmination of the broad movement towards democracy and social progress over several centuries, Blair sounded a more cautionary note about Labour's historical role, since in his view the party had failed to win as much popular support as it ought to have. Blair's reservations about Labour's historical track record were in part an anachronistic projection of his own contemporary worries about Labour's electoral travails after 1979 onto quite different eras of electoral competition. But Blair's argument also drew on a significant body of historical research and political commentary that had demythologized the Labour Party's self-congratulatory account of its rise. Such arguments had been commonplace on the New Left from the 1960s onwards. The searing critique of the limits of 'labourism' articulated by Ralph Miliband, Perry Anderson and Tom Nairn had diagnosed the historical weaknesses of Labour's socialism when compared to the continental Marxist tradition, notably its lack of ideological rigour and its excessive respect for British constitutional conventions.[20] Whilst the New Left offered a Marxist disenchantment of Labour aimed at radicalizing it or starting a new socialist party, an intriguingly similar analysis was also developed a few years later from the liberal centre, with the opposite political objective of moderating Labour's socialism or building a new, non-socialist political alliance that could replace it. The common ground between these two positions was the historical argument that Labour was indebted ideologically and culturally to British Liberalism. Peter Clarke and Michael Freeden, for example, wrote influential books in the 1970s and 1980s that downplayed the ideological differences between socialists and left liberals in the early twentieth century, suggesting that Labour's political thought was best seen as one wing of a wider 'progressivism' that encompassed both Liberals and Labour before the First World War. Clarke also argued that, had it not been for the 'accidental' impact of the First World War, the Liberal Party had been

---

[20] Ralph Miliband, *Parliamentary Socialism* (London: Allen & Unwin, 1961); Perry Anderson, 'Origins of the Present Crisis', *New Left Review*, no. 23 (1964): 26–53; Tom Nairn, 'The Nature of the Labour Party I', *New Left Review*, no. 27 (1964): 38–65; Tom Nairn, 'The Nature of the Labour Party II', *New Left Review*, no. 28 (1964): 33–62.

on course to emerge as a broad-based, centre-left party that promoted social welfare and economic redistribution, with Labour remaining a junior partner within a 'progressive alliance'.[21] These historical arguments were given a more immediate political heft by David Marquand, whose book, *The Progressive Dilemma* (1992), was a major source for Blair's speeches and writings on this subject (perhaps through intermediaries such as Roy Jenkins, Andrew Adonis and David Miliband). Marquand made a powerful case that Labour's reign as the main party of the left after 1918 had been less successful than the Liberal Party's efforts in the decades before when it came to the crucial metric of defeating the Conservative Party in general elections. Marquand, who had been a founding member of the SDP, attributed this to Labour's undue narrowness of appeal as a socialist and trade union-dominated party, when a less doctrinaire and class-conscious party (such as the Edwardian Liberals or the Democratic Party in the USA) would probably have fared better in staving off decades of Conservative government.[22]

Tony Blair drew on these claims to position Labour under his leadership as aligned with this broader 'progressive' tradition that earlier versions of the Labour Party had (he argued) cut itself off from.[23] As Blair put it in 1999:

> Born in separation from other progressive forces in British politics, out of the visceral need to represent the interests of an exploited workforce, our base, our appeal, our ideology was too narrow. People were made to feel we wanted to hold them back, limit their aspirations, when in truth the very opposite was our goal.[24]

Labour was, he stressed, now a non-doctrinaire party, less concerned with a specifically socialist agenda than arraying itself as 'part of the broad movement of human progress, the marriage of ambition with justice, the constant striving of the human spirit to do better, to be better'.[25] Daringly, Blair even acknowledged that Labour's ideas drew from liberal as well as socialist sources: 'Our economic and social policy today owes as much to the liberal social democratic tradition

---

[21] Peter Clarke, *Lancashire and the New Liberalism* (Cambridge: CUP, 1971); Peter Clarke, *Liberals and Social Democrats* (Cambridge: CUP, 1978); Michael Freeden, *The New Liberalism* (Oxford: OUP, 1978); Michael Freeden, *Liberalism Divided* (Oxford: OUP, 1978).

[22] David Marquand, *The Progressive Dilemma* (London: Heinemann, 1992; rev. edn, 1999).

[23] On Marquand's influence on Blair and other political figures in the 1990s, see Emily Robinson, *History, Heritage and Tradition in Contemporary British Politics* (Manchester: MUP, 2012), 122–52.

[24] Tony Blair, speech to Labour Party Conference, 28 September 1999, http://www.britishpoliticalspeech. org/speech-archive.htm?speech=205 (accessed 8 December 2020).

[25] Tony Blair, speech to Labour Party Conference, 3 October 1996, http://www.britishpoliticalspeech. org/speech-archive.htm?speech=202 (accessed 8 December 2020).

of Lloyd George, Keynes and Beveridge as to the socialist principles of the 1945 Government.'[26] Looking back at the 1945 government and its legacy, Blair observed that it was often forgotten that Attlee's achievements 'had cut decisively with, not against, the grain of political thinking', channelling a wider national mood and ideological turn.[27] Drawing on Marquand's work, Blair argued that the 1940s was in fact an exceptional episode in Labour's history because Labour's socialist ideology and trade union roots had usually prevented the party from becoming a majoritarian one.[28]

All of this marked a rather startling departure from the account of Labour's history that had been offered by Attlee and Wilson. Where previously Labour members had been told that they were the sole inheritors of the British radical tradition, Blair impressed upon his audiences that Labour had other progressive political partners that it had worked with – and had even neglected to its political cost. Rather than thinking of the Labour pioneers as a marginalized group that had escaped persecution to beat back the forces of reaction, Blair argued that Labour had failed to remain in touch with the broad direction of public opinion and had become preoccupied with socialist doctrine at the expense of the underlying ethical ideals that had historically animated socialism. This line of argument was itself one that ran with the grain of the politics of the late twentieth century, since it reflected growing anxiety on the left – and triumphalism on the right – about the trajectory of British and world history. In Britain, the pulverizing success of the Thatcher government in pushing back public ownership, the state's commitment to full employment, and union collective bargaining brought into question the easy teleological assumption that had infused Labour rhetoric since the early twentieth century: namely that an irreversible trend towards greater collective action sponsored by Labour was underway. From a global perspective, the end of the Cold War brought with it the conviction that socialism as an alternative model of economic organization was no longer credible or desirable. Labour had of course long distinguished its understanding of socialism from Soviet-style authoritarian central planning, but the fall of the communist regimes were nonetheless widely taken to mark the demise of attempts to devise a distinctly non-capitalist model of economic organization. In this context, the dreams of qualitative social transformation

---

[26] Tony Blair, speech to Labour Party Conference, 2 October 2001, http://www.britishpoliticalspeech. org/speech-archive.htm?speech=186 (accessed 8 December 2020).

[27] Tony Blair, *Let Us Face the Future: The 1945 Anniversary Lecture* (London: Fabian Society, August 1995), 3.

[28] Ibid., 10–13.

that had dominated Labour discourse for generations lost their appeal, leaving a party leader who was probably personally more religious than either Attlee or Wilson to foster a more secular and disenchanted historical rhetoric than either of them had ever contemplated.

As Richard Toye and Emily Robinson have argued, the version of history told by Tony Blair was in its own way as mythological as the heroic narrative that he sought to dispel.[29] Blair's analysis was fundamentally about Labour's electoral failures in the 1980s and early 1990s, which he garbed in a grander historical analysis by claiming that the same shortcomings could be discerned in the 1930s or the 1950s. Equally, Blair's interest in a 'progressive' tradition surely also reflected an electoral context in which third-party voting was now very significant – and an incoming Labour government might require a coalition with the Liberal Democrats (or so it seemed before the 1997 landslide). Blair had nonetheless made an important point that should still be taken seriously by ardent Labour supporters (even if Blair's own political practice did not live up to his rhetoric): it is inaccurate and off-putting for the Labour Party to claim that it is the monopoly-provider of social and political reform as the sole inheritor of the radical tradition in British politics. The Labour Party should instead seek to build alliances with other parties and social movements. Although it can be useful to place contemporary political battles in a longer-run account of social progress, Blair was also right to puncture the complacency of Labour supporters who saw the party's rise to power as in some sense guaranteed by underlying historical trends rather than as a hard struggle that required strategic political agency at every stage, including decisive revisions to Labour's approach to fit a changing social and economic context. Indeed, the 'progressive dilemma' view of British history could even help with the pessimistic twin of a narrative about Labour's inevitable forward march, namely the sociological claim that Labour was doomed to decline because of the decomposition of the industrial working class. The Marquand/Blair account instead suggested that the problem for Labour had *always* been how to build an electoral coalition that could knit the middle and working classes together. Finally, Blair was correct to say that an important lesson of 1945 is that the Labour Party cannot wish socialism into existence by itself. Rather, the party has to grapple with pre-existing expert opinion, state capacity, economic structures and public opinion and to conjure up what social democratic policies may be summoned from those materials.

[29] Richard Toye, "'The smallest party in history'? New Labour in historical perspective', *Labour History Review* 69 (2004): 83–103; Emily Robinson, *The Language of Progressive Politics in Modern Britain* (Basingstoke: Palgrave, 2017).

After disenchantment

Amid the lively and at times acrimonious debate that ensued after Labour's exit from office in 2010, New Labour's place in history emerged as an important point of contention. For Maurice Glasman, and other figures associated with the 'Blue Labour' movement, New Labour was in fact just the latest iteration of a Labour tradition that had become entangled with the state and liberalism from the mid-twentieth century onwards and had lost touch with the movement's roots as an insurgent democratic force that sought to tame the power of capital.[30] This counter-narrative objected to the Marquand-style history of the progressive dilemma championed by Blair and his colleagues on the grounds that the authentic Labour tradition was not at all a Liberal one – liberalism being, on this account, tied up with the pursuit of abstract concepts such as 'justice' and 'rights'. For Glasman, the true expression of Labour politics was to be found in the mutualist associational culture of the working classes in the late-nineteenth and early-twentieth centuries – the co-operatives and the trade unions – which had subsequently been diluted by an admixture of middle-class technocratic expertise focused on the hierarchical exercise of state power. One weakness of this view was that it was above all an attempt to return to an enchanted idea of the Labour Party, seeing it as an organization that could stand apart from an otherwise rationalized and bureaucratized society and which had only ever been betrayed by periods in government, even in 1945. Likewise, it is not necessary to agree with Tony Blair's assessment that the creation of a Labour Party outside of an alliance with the Liberal Party was a historical wrong turn to acknowledge that Labour has been heavily influenced by the British Liberal tradition.[31]

Part of the romance that attracts so many idealistic people to the Labour Party is the sense of continuity with a long tradition of radical protest and reform. But it is possible to retain that sense of continuity without lapsing into an uncritical hagiography that overlooks Labour's tensions and limitations. Attlee and Wilson offered an account of the rise of Labour that worked because it was tied into assumptions about the direction of history, and about the character of socialism, that are much harder to sustain today. Blair highlighted these problems in

---

[30] Maurice Glasman, 'Labour as a Radical Tradition', in Maurice Glasman, Jonathan Rutherford, Marc Stears and Stuart White (eds), *The Labour Tradition and the Politics of Paradox* (London: Soundings, 2011), 14–34.

[31] I expanded on these criticisms of Glasman in Ben Jackson, 'Labour History and Glasman's Labour Tradition', in Glasman et al., *Labour Tradition*, 38–41.

Labour's historical self-understanding, but in doing so failed to fill in a more positive account of what remains of persisting value in the Labour tradition. There is scope now for a Labour rhetoric that can do this, not merely by invoking 1945 or 1964 or 1997, but by envisaging Labour's contribution to modern British history as the result of a series of contingent political struggles for freedom and equality, which were never guaranteed to succeed and indeed sometimes did not. When Labour *did* successfully take the lead in these struggles, it was because of the alliances that the party forged with social movements, new ideas, state power, changing social attitudes and even other political parties. This more modest but pluralistic understanding of Labour's past would stand the party in good stead as it grapples with the diverse and fragmented electoral landscape of the 2020s. Labour faces a daunting prospect over the next few years, though the green shoots of a new progressive coalition may be starting to peep through. Perhaps the trickiest challenge for the Labour leadership will be finding a way to bring together the new demands for social and environmental justice that energizes the party's base, with the resurgent politics of place and nation that have curtailed Labour's electoral performance in recent years. The reassurance of studying history for Labour supporters is that we can learn that the party has in the past forged successful electoral coalitions in demanding circumstances. But the past cannot tell us whether Labour will do so again in the future. As always, that depends on what party leaders, activists and supporters do next.

Part Two

3

'A party not unlike the Democrats': Labour, the left and encounters with America from the New Deal to the New Frontier

Richard Carr

On 14 September 1959, Roy Jenkins began, in his famous timbre, to dictate a brief letter. With Britain set to go to the polls in a few weeks there was certainly much to report. '[Prime Minister Harold] Macmillan has at last cleared up our doubts about the date of the election', he told his correspondent. 'And I think we can therefore now make firmer plans.' Jenkins had had a busy decade, and his Penguin book *The Labour Case*, which outlined a detailed and moderate agenda for government, had made a real splash earlier that summer (the *Guardian* at least found it 'lucid and persuasive').[1] As his pen pal noted elsewhere, Jenkins was by now 'one of the most prominent coming figures [in the Parliamentary Labour Party and] would seem to be a certainty for a high cabinet post' should Labour win power. In September 1959, however, Jenkins' aforementioned plans were not those of high office. For the future reforming Home Secretary, the odds 'on this wretched Government winning again … still look pretty heavy'. As such, it was already time to discuss 'a nicely timed consolation prize': a speaking tour of the American East Coast. Jenkins' 'gloomy' views of the contemporary climate were, he noted, 'for private consumption only'. But he had no real fears they would be passed on. For the recipient was his friend, the noted Harvard economist John Kenneth (J. K.) Galbraith.

Jenkins wasn't wrong – Hugh Gaitskell's Labour would indeed be defeated in October 1959, with Harold Macmillan's Conservatives extending their parliamentary majority by twenty seats. But his letter was indicative of more than just good political antennae. This chapter outlines its wider relevance: the

---

[1] *Guardian*, 16 September 1959. See also footnotes 47 and 48 for this paragraph.

political connections between American Democrats and prominent figures in the UK Labour Party. There is, of course, a wider, well-trodden story here. In terms of transnational dialogue per se, the travels of Labour figures in Soviet Russia, or their relationship with the German SPD have been ably explored by historians such as Jonathan Davis and Stefan Berger.[2] The Commonwealth has also proven an inspiration of sorts, particularly the practical examples of Labour in government in New Zealand from Michael Savage to Jacinda Ardern.[3] Indeed, Hugh Dalton and Ernest Bevin were but two Labour politicians to make the trip to the Antipodean world in the 1930s – whilst Tony Blair and Gordon Brown sketched out much of the agenda for what became New Labour on the same arduous journey several decades later.[4]

But for reasons of language, economic might and wider twentieth-century diplomacy, America has held a particular place of importance for British progressives. In more modern times, whether it be Joe Biden's borrowing of a Neil Kinnock speech, Gordon Brown's affinity for the Kennedys or the Blair-Clinton 'March of the Moderates' (which I have discussed elsewhere), many elements of the Labour-Democrat relationship have been outlined by academics and political journalists alike.[5] This is probably a phenomenon nudged along of late by an enduring fascination with *The West Wing, Veep* and *House of Cards*. Ed Miliband's plea to his advisers that they should 'let Miliband be Miliband' formed something of an apogee here – even if his leadership never quite hit the heights of Jeb Bartlett.

Culture aside, some of this transatlantic intrigue has been generational. As the sociologist Karl Mannheim noted, political and social norms are not just innate, but often framed by some common early experience. This might include dramatic collective circumstances such as service in a war, but it can also be more mundane levels of shared exposure to particular stimuli in early adulthood. And for most would-be politicians, certainly in recent decades, this has meant university study. By way of example, Bill Clinton encountered two of his future senior colleagues (Robert Reich and Strobe Talbott) in the same year

---

[2] Jonathan Davis, 'An Outsider Looks In: Walter Citrine's First Visit to the Soviet Union, 1925,' *Revolutionary Russia* 26, no. 2 (2013): 147–63; Stefan Berger, 'Organising Talent and Disciplined Steadiness: The German SPD as a model for the British Labour Party in the 1920s', *Contemporary European History* 5, no. 2 (1996): 171–90.

[3] On the Commonwealth, see for example Glen O'Hara and John Stewart, '"The land with the Midas touch": British perceptions of New Zealand, 1935–1979', *New Zealand Journal of History* 52, no. 2 (2018): 42–65.

[4] See Gordon Brown, *My Life, Our Times* (London: Bodley Head, 2017), 81–2.

[5] Richard Carr, *March of the Moderates: Bill Clinton, Tony Blair, and the Rebirth of Progressive Politics* (London: I.B. Tauris, 2019).

of Rhodes Scholars at Oxford, whilst his personal lawyer (David Kendall) had taken the same path two years earlier. Two decades later, Ed Balls and David Miliband took in university life in Boston, whilst Douglas Alexander was a few hours south in Pennsylvania. As well as later parliamentary and congressionally funded research trips, modern transatlanticism certainly owes much to such early moments. These encounters helped foster direct personal connections, but they also elevated the ideological importance of the country in which the future politician was temporarily resident (Wilson's devaluation of the pound, for instance, really did put more pounds in the young Bill Clinton's pocket). To paraphrase Neville Chamberlain, Britain and America may well be 'far away countries', but they are not nations of whom their political class 'know nothing'.

That said, this chapter argues that there are two ways the transatlantic progressive story should be extended. Firstly, it has not only been moderate Blair or Jenkins types who have sought to learn from their American cousins. Whilst it is true that the generally smaller-state, decentralized and lower-tax nature of American democracy has made it easier for the centre or right of the Labour Party to think in a truly transatlantic sense; figures on the Labour left have not been shy about adopting best practice from US figures they approve of, either. We shouldn't let diplomatic *contretemps* – such as Wilson (correctly) not sending British troops into Vietnam in the 1960s, or Foot (incorrectly) kicking up a major fuss about giving a state visit to Ronald Reagan in the 1980s – cloud this long-term story. In short, whilst we deal with some moderates in what follows, they are not the only travellers we will encounter.

Secondly, the above caveats aside, we should consider that the tale goes back further than sometimes acknowledged. Advances in the speed and comfort of long-haul travel certainly made it easier to hop on an airplane in the 1990s than taking a boat (or boat-plane) had been in the 1930s, but the point was that there *were* such earlier progressive pioneers. If nothing else, arriving on a steamship to New York was certainly more glamorous than cramming into the economy aisles of a flight to Dulles. As such, those seeking the renewal of Labour from all sides of the party's spectrum have sought to learn from America, and for a far longer period than sometimes acknowledged within institutional folklore. We shouldn't go overboard – the wider goal for the British left was always to win power itself, and degrees of interest in America fluctuated to the extent it could help deliver that. But nor were Britain and America just 'two countries divided by a common language' – at least when it came to politics.

To frame its argument, this chapter considers three such cases: John Strachey's relationship to Roosevelt's New Deal, Mary Agnes Hamilton and her changing belief in the need for military interventionism and Roy Jenkins (and other moderates) from the 1950s to the Kennedy era. In the first two cases, their American travels have either been ignored by the standard accounts of Labour history and transatlanticism – including Henry Pelling – or significantly downplayed.[6] The latter postwar story has been given more airing, not least lately by Ilnyun Kim, but even here there is more to say. Certainly, such visits were impressionistic, and America was but one influence acting on some complex politicians. But, as we will see, it was clearly a significant one – providing rhetorical inspiration and practical ideas in equal measure.[7] If nothing else, the staggering success of the Democrats – winning seven of nine presidential elections from 1932 to 1964 – meant there was a broad range of experience from which to draw.

John Strachey and a renewed faith in democratic governance

In a crowded market, few politicians had a stranger 1930s than John Strachey. Having first been elected to parliament in 1929, Strachey left the Labour Party alongside Oswald Mosley to form the New Party in 1931 and lost his seat in the national government landslide that autumn. Though he and Mosley shared the idea that Keynesian economics could arrest the economic slump, the latter was falling in love with the totalitarian regime of Italian strong-man Benito Mussolini. This led Strachey to break with Mosley, later denouncing him as an example of *The Menace of Fascism*.[8] As Mosley went right, Strachey went further left – applying for Communist Party membership in 1932 (though rejected by the CPGB on the grounds that he was ideologically unreliable) and helping Victor Gollancz form the *Left Book Club* in 1936. He would eventually find his way back to Labour, winning Dundee in 1945, and later briefly served as Secretary of State for War.

---

[6]   Henry Pelling's classic *America and the British Left* (London: Adam & Charles Black, 1956) mentions Strachey's trips in passing, but neither of the other two.

[7]   See for example Martin Pugh, *Speak for Britain! A New History of the Labour Party* (London: Bodley Head, 2010) where we learn the (admittedly excellent) fact that Strachey had chocolate cake and creme de menthe for breakfast when at Oxford, but not that he regularly visited the United States in later life. Roosevelt and the New Deal do not figure at all. Likewise, Pugh, *Speak for Britain!*, and Ralph Miliband, *Parliamentary Socialism: A Study in the Politics of Labour* (London: Allen & Unwin, 1961) do not mention Mary Agnes Hamilton at all. Jenkins' American jaunts have fared better, not least in Ilnyun Kim, 'The Party of Reform in the Doldrums: The Convergence of Anglo-American Political Progressivism', *Modern Intellectual History* 18, no. 3 (2021): 782–805.

[8]   John Strachey, *The Menace of Fascism* (London: Victor Gollancz, 1933).

It is, however, Strachey's keen observation of American politics in the 1930s that interests us. His contemporary contacts give something of a flavour: Earl Browder, the general secretary of the American Communist Party, was one regular correspondent. Another was the English film star Charlie Chaplin, whose left-leaning sympathies eventually led to his exile from America in 1952, but who in the mid-1930s, shared such an affinity with Strachey that the pair worked on a script together for a movie about Napoleon. In the end, Chaplin made the capitalism critiquing *Modern Times* instead, which Strachey was 'quite sure … will be the biggest thing you've done'.[9] In short, Strachey, despite his failure to join the Communist Party itself, was clearly a figure of the far left – associating with radical leftists and Marxists alike.

To further such credentials, he visited the United States several times. As well as staying with Chaplin in Los Angeles, Strachey's 1934–5 US trip was marked by major political controversy. Having sailed to New York, he was subject to the usual questions by US immigration services. However, his answer of 'no' when asked if he was 'a person who believes in or advocates the overthrow … of the government' landed him in hot water – and temporary arrest – as his US speeches veered in an increasingly anti-capitalist direction. Immigration officials thus picked up on Strachey's rhetorical flourish that he was 'a Communist drummer selling Marxism instead of pills',[10] though many in the American press recognized that in reality he was no 'agitator', and mostly addressed 'middle and upper class audiences interested in the opinions of an Eton and Oxford educated "radical"'.[11] Strachey was something of a prototypical troll and criticized, as the *Springfield Leader and Press* noted, 'fascism and the capitalist economists and … the New Deal' in turn.[12] He would eventually pay a $500 bond, get out of his temporary arrest, and leave the country. 'Everyone treated me swell', he told reporters before boarding his Cunard liner bound for Southampton. 'And I will soon be back.'

Whilst this was true, his next visit, in October 1938, went more or less the same way. Detained at Ellis Island on the now very familiar accusation that he was a communist, Strachey set about correcting the proofs of his next book to pass the time. All this was good publicity, as Strachey riffed on the authorities' supposed evidence: 'If [having] an article in the *Daily Worker* makes me a communist,

9   See Richard Carr, *Charlie Chaplin: A Political Biography from Victorian Britain to Modern America* (London: Routledge, 2017) for more.
10   *The New York Times*, 17 March 1935.
11   *The Baltimore Sun*, 14 March 1935.
12   *Springfield Leader and Press*, 13 March 1935.

doesn't one in the *Spectator* make me a Tory?'[13] But the furore also ensured that his most recent text, *What Are We To Do?*, would be widely reviewed in the American media.[14] As such, for this supposed revolutionary (and indeed his publishers), controversy created cash.

The reality was arguably more interesting. In its review, Virginia's *The Times Dispatch* was amongst many to note that Strachey's views were shifting. Whereas Strachey argued that Roosevelt's first term had been 'devoted to saving capitalism and big business', his second offered far more hope for the American worker: 'We have had the Wagner Act applied, farm legislation in favor of tenants, and finally wages and hours regulation.'[15] Many agreed. The future cabinet minister Richard Crossman, then an Oxford don, wrote to Strachey to tell him that, 'Having finished *What Are We to Do?* this morning, I find it difficult to see where a right-winger and a communist differ, if they are both under 40 and realize the fact of declining capitalism. The general tone and policy of your book seems to be completely correct.' As his biographer Hugh Thomas thus observed, 'It seems obvious that in 1938 Strachey was beginning quietly but explicitly to move away from Communist ideology.' In this move, 'Keynes and his followers, Roosevelt, [and] patriotism ... were interconnected'.[16]

Though the ignominy of the 1939 Nazi-Soviet Pact would prove to be the death knell of his communism, Roosevelt and the New Deal were Strachey's lifeboat back to respectability. FDR's attempts to redistribute purchasing power, to Strachey, were worth 'supporting to the uttermost'.[17] Surveying the stranglehold that big business had for so long on the American worker, Strachey increasingly felt by 1938 and 1939 that there was no point in making perfect the enemy of the good. Roosevelt was a reformer, on the right side of the argument, and so one should support him wholeheartedly. Though Strachey wanted the president to go further, it had become increasingly clear that, 'What the reactionaries cannot stand about Mr Roosevelt is ... that for the first time for many years, they have encountered serious opposition to their own dictatorship!'[18] Economist and Labour leftwinger Harold Laski, whose own belief in Roosevelt had seen him encourage Strachey to temper any earlier barbs towards the president, watched on approvingly.[19]

[13] *The Gazette* (Montreal), 12 October 1938.
[14] John Strachey, *What Are We to Do?* (London: Victor Gollancz, 1938).
[15] *The Times Dispatch*, 9 October 1938.
[16] Hugh Thomas, *John Strachey* (New York: Harper & Row, 1973), 175–6.
[17] John Strachey, *Hope in America* (New York: Modern Age New, 1938), 206.
[18] Ibid., 96.
[19] On Laski, see Pelling, *America and the British Left*, 143–5.

In 1940, Strachey's *Programme for Progress* went a stage further. Selected as the Left Book Club choice for January that year, Strachey argued that the real goal for the masses should be out and out socialism, but, pending the electoral success of this, there needed to be a programme that ameliorated the excesses of capitalism. And here, again, he turned to FDR. 'The vital lesson to be derived from the rich experience gained by the progressive forces during the two Roosevelt administrations is, then, the familiar political precept that boldness always pays.' In short, 'The New Deal did the right things, but not enough.'[20] It was thus the job of the American left to 'supersede [the New Deal] with another progressive programme, cast in the same general mould, but built upon incomparably more secure political and financial foundations'.[21] *A Programme for Progress* urged 'the extension of public enterprise, low interest rates on loan capital, increased social services, including monetary allowances to individuals, and redistributory taxation; [and] there would also be a state controlled banking system and strict public control over foreign exchanges'.[22]

As Hugh Thomas noted, whilst Strachey's earlier bestseller *The Coming Struggle for Power* had made some people communists, *A Programme for Progress* made them Keynesians.[23] Anthony Crosland, writing years later, found it all 'incomparably more modest' than the short-term economic programme put forward by Labour in 1937. The New Deal was 'the rich store of experience' from which Strachey was drawing, and to some degree this put him on the centre or right of British progressive opinion at the time.[24] This was quite the shift. As Strachey later told Hugh Gaitskell, 'I became a communist supporter in 1931, because I saw no way through the dilemma that the moment a democratic socialist policy began to be implemented, the economy got into crisis … and so democratic socialist governments were bound to [be] impotent.' However, 'Keynes and your own group – Douglas [Jay], Evan Durbin and yourself, and the experience of the New Deal, had converted me by 1940 to the view … that a way through did exist.'[25] Here, then, the very atypical Strachey followed the path of others. As Theodore Rosenof later noted, 'Whilst radicals on both sides of the Atlantic tended initially to dismiss the New Deal as a mere holding operation for capitalism … by the later 1930s the tendency increasingly was to see the

[20] John Strachey, *A Programme for Progress* (London: Victor Gollancz, 1940), 254.
[21] Ibid., 242.
[22] Thomas, *John Strachey*, 187.
[23] Ibid.
[24] Ibid.
[25] Ibid., 273.

transition in long-range terms and to view New Deal reforms as useful both in themselves and as transitional devices.'[26] A progressive Democrat in the White House might not always lead to Valhalla, but it was a damn sight better than the available alternatives.

Mary Agnes Hamilton and the flight from pacifism

It was not just attitudes to the economy that could shift upon contact with America. Mary Agnes Hamilton had entered parliament at the same 1929 election as Strachey. Unlike the future minister however, she would only serve a single term – being one of many Labour MPs unseated in 1931 and never returning to Westminster. A former suffragist and arch pacifist, she had helped draft the constitution for the anti-war Union of Democratic Control (UDC) in 1914. During the Great War, she had felt that, 'War was for the entire world so frightful a disaster that nothing could justify it: a "just war" is a contradiction in terms.'[27] An accomplished novelist, much of this went on to shape her literary work. Though one American reviewer found her 1916 *Dead Yesterday* slightly plodding, they did note that, 'A feature of its chapters is the boldness with which England's policy and her substantial right to enter the war are questioned.'[28] Later, her 1930 *Three Against Fate* ably documented what another dubbed 'the suffering and loss and degradation that follow as a result of war'.[29]

Hamilton visited the United States every couple of years from the 1920s onwards. Some of this was to sell her novels, make decent fees on the lecture circuit and establish political connections. But it also served as a means to stress test her own opinions on future diplomacy. Through the 1930s she began to shed her pacifism – coming out in favour of sanctions backed by force against Italy, after Mussolini's invasion of Abyssinia in 1935. As Hitler's armies marched through Europe, she became, in the words of Hugh Dalton, 'quite anti-German as opposed to her attitude in World War One'.[30]

Indeed, during a boat trip across the Atlantic in early 1938, Hamilton began to further review her pacifist views. As she later noted, 'I sank with shame as I

---

[26] Theodore Rosenof, 'The American Democratic Left Looks at the British Labour Government, 1945–1951', *The Historian* 38, no. 1 (1975): 98–9.

[27] Mary Agnes Hamilton, *Remembering My Good Friends* (London: Jonathan Cape, 1944), 67–8.

[28] *Evening Capital News*, 2 December 1916.

[29] *Brooklyn Daily Eagle*, 29 January 1930.

[30] Janet Grenier, 'Hamilton [née Adamson], Mary Agnes', Oxford Dictionary of National Biography, https://doi.org/10.1093/ref:odnb/39455.

reviewed mentally the policy of British governments since 1931 and their refusal to see what we did not want to see – the meaning of Hitler and Hitlerism.'[31] The country she was about to enter, however, was scarcely more pro-war. 'In 1938, opinion in America was perplexing', she recorded.[32] Indeed, with pro-appeasement voices like ambassador to London Joseph Kennedy feeding back the idea that the British couldn't beat the Nazis, and various of *Hitler's American Friends* on Capitol Hill lapping up this message, nine in ten US citizens wanted nothing to do with any European war – even after the Nazi invasion of Poland.[33] The 'America First' Committee – a phrase Donald Trump would later come to repopularize – numbered 800,000 supporters at its height, including film stars like Lillian Gish. Isolationism was in – as other British speakers in the United States during this era, such as Conservative MP Alfred Duff Cooper, would see for themselves.[34] As such, FDR was largely hamstrung by a Congress where four Neutrality Acts ever decreased his room for diplomatic manoeuvre.

Despite her own long-held anti-war views, Hamilton knew she had to make a stand. In doing so, she mirrored the shift Labour had made in moving from the leadership of the pacifist George Lansbury to the more muscular form offered by (Major) Clement Attlee. In January 1938, at a debate in Pittsburgh, Hamilton therefore told her audience that, 'The Rome-Berlin Axis is a threat to the people of Europe and the world.' Admitting that the British Empire had also been spread through force in decades past, she told the three-hundred-strong crowd that it was now solely 'interested in the preservation of democracy'.[35] 'If you have a children's party and one little boy insists on making faces and succeeds', she noted, 'he can go on provoking the rest of the children until they have to hit him back. That is the way with Germany and Italy.'[36] If some of America's 'best minds' were 'temporarily blinded' to the threat, it was all the more necessary to make her case.[37]

This bristled not only with some of those in the audience but also with her personal contacts. Referencing her friend Mary Blankenhorn, an American with whom she shared a love of Independent Labour Party (ILP) pacifist James

---

[31] Hamilton, *Remembering My Good Friends*, 236.

[32] Ibid., 240.

[33] Bradley W. Hart, *Hitler's American Friends: The Third Reich's Supporters in the United States* (London: Thomas Dunne Books, 2018).

[34] See Bradley W. Hart and Richard Carr, 'Promoting Britain's Fight: Duff Cooper's 1939–40 Lecture Tour and American Public Opinion During the "Phoney War", *Historical Research* 94 (2021), 158–180.

[35] *Pittsburgh Post Gazette*, 27 January 1938.

[36] *Pittsburgh Sun Telegraph*, 26 January 1938.

[37] Hamilton, *Remembering My Good Friends*, 242.

Maxton, she noted, 'Mary and I have constantly disagreed, for instance her pacifism remaining absolute, pretty much until [the attack on] Pearl Harbor.'[38] Hamilton, however, knew the threat of figures like Senator Gerald Nye and the aviator Charles Lindbergh: seductive voices preying on a society where so many didn't want to risk future soldiers' lives, even against an enemy as repugnant as Adolf Hitler. During the war, Hamilton joined the British civil service, and subsequently became head of the US section of the Ministry of Information. Much of her work there, sometimes tacitly, sometimes more explicitly, was to try and convince the American public of the need to join the conflict.

As Stephen Wertheim points out, from its entry into the Second World War onwards, America would play a bigger role in global affairs than the Lindberghs and Nyes (or even George Washington) had intended.[39] In 1947, Hamilton would go on to give a speech that in many ways lauded this shift. Though she acknowledged that her old ideology of pacifism 'is strong [in America]: it has some queer bedfellows. But, unmistakably, [a] change has taken place ... the realization that America is a world power and carries world responsibilities has come to stay. The responsibilities are terrifying ... [but] they are inescapable.' For Hamilton, Pearl Harbor had 'ended an epoch ... and now the possession of the atomic bomb carried the demonstration a stage further.'[40] This meant engagement with global institutions like the new United Nations, a firm line with dictators and, for Foreign Secretary and 'Labour's Churchill' Ernest Bevin, leading the charge for the creation of NATO.[41] For the vast majority of Labour voices, including Hamilton, there was now no doubt: better Truman than Stalin. Exposure to the US political scene had only deepened such convictions.

Roy Jenkins and the moderates

The postwar era brought not only a new set of Anglo-American challenges but also, technologically, a much easier means of reaching the United States: commercial air travel. As such, Hugh Gaitskell recorded in his diary in October 1950, 'I think it must be an event in anybody's life when he first crosses the

---

[38] Ibid., 226.

[39] Stephen Wertheim, *Tomorrow the World: The Birth of US Global Supremacy* (Boston: Belknap Press, 2020), passim.

[40] Mary Agnes Hamilton, 'The Place of the United States in World Affairs', Fifth Montagu Burton Lecture on International Relations (Nottingham: University of Nottingham, 1947), 8. Many thanks to the Churchill Archives Centre for providing a copy.

[41] Andrew Adonis, *Ernest Bevin: Labour's Churchill* (London: Biteback, 2020).

Atlantic. I had been trying to do this for a good many years.' On arrival, he noted, 'First of all perhaps one notices more than anything else two things.' The first was the significant African American population – far exceeding the numbers of Black British residents only two years after the arrival of the *Empire Windrush*. But 'above all [there were] the cars – endless streams on the roads even on Sunday afternoons'. Though Gaitskell's bags ended up on the wrong plane and he couldn't get used to the time difference, this first trip to the United States was a success. It was there that the final confirmation came through that, as expected, he would take over from Stafford Cripps as Chancellor of the Exchequer. Gaitskell promptly tucked into a celebratory whiskey and went out dancing.[42]

Such levity had a serious side for Labour moderates. Many, including Crosland, liked the atmosphere in America, and in some ways wanted to replicate it. The United States was a country where, 'Social relations are more natural and egalitarian, and less marked by deference, submissiveness, or snobbery, as one quickly discovers from the cab driver, the barman, the air hostess, and the drug store assistant.'[43] Its largely comprehensive school system naturally appealed to Crosland's own leanings in that regard, whilst its recent history – 'twenty years of New Deal and Fair Deal, of anti-business bias and "creeping socialism"', followed by 'a Republican Administration still committed to social security' – broadly mirrored the now Conservative-led, postwar consensus in Britain.[44]

With all this in mind, Roy Jenkins visited America for the first time in 1953. The cost of his trip was covered by a federal government scheme intended to bring 'young leaders' to the United States. Then in his early thirties, and having been in parliament for five years, Jenkins certainly qualified – and it was a wonderful opportunity to network. He met Harry Truman (of whom he would later pen a 1986 biography) and Hubert Humphrey. But it was a trip to Harvard that would prove most useful, connecting him to Arthur Schlesinger Jr and, even more importantly, the economist J. K. Galbraith.[45] As noted by his biographer John Campbell, these 'friendship[s] enabled him henceforth to feel at home in liberal circles on both sides of the Atlantic'.[46] Like Strachey and Hamilton before him, a literary background had helped give him an entrée into the American intellectual establishment.

---

[42] See Phillip M. Williams, *The Diary of Hugh Gaitskell 1945–1956* (London: Jonathan Cape, 1983), 201–13.

[43] Anthony Crosland, *The Future of Socialism* (London: Jonathan Cape, 1956), 249.

[44] Ibid., 223–4.

[45] Throughout, for clarity, the Schlesinger in question is the future Kennedy aide son, and not his equally distinguished father.

[46] John Campbell, *Roy Jenkins* (London: Jonathan Cape, 2014), 154.

However, when teeing up the later 1959 tour, with which we began this chapter, Jenkins had some logistical concerns. The first was that a pair of return plane tickets to New York cost £330, and Jenkins planned to travel with his wife, Jennifer. Given the then MP's salary of £1,750, this was a significant outlay. The trip was also long and arduous, prompting Jenkins' waspish comment to Galbraith that the pair were 'planning to subject ourselves to the rigours of economic class travel across the Atlantic'.[47] A ten-hour flight, usually with a refuelling stop in Ireland or Newfoundland, meant a long stay was necessary to justify the trip. Galbraith therefore acted, in effect, as Jenkins' commercial agent, making preliminary soundings about television and radio appearances for his time on the East Coast. He also did the potentially unseemly work of asking American universities for more money 'for someone like Jenkins'. He probed potential hosts: 'Could you possibly raise your fee a bit?'[48]

Jenkins' planned talks were general, though indicated his leanings. 'British Socialism – Modern Style' formed his 11 November address at Amherst, whilst 'The Future of the Labour Party' greeted Havard audiences the following day. The nature of his audience, even in the well-informed surroundings of New England academia, precluded much policy deep dive. But his American listeners got much of the same material he had rehearsed in an address to the Fabian Society earlier that month. 'Don't depend on a slump saving us', he had told the Fabians. 'First, we don't want to be a party which can do well only out of misery. Secondly, it is not very likely to happen.' Equally, if the left was just about nationalization – the desire, as he noted, to 'pop more and more industries into the bag' – it would face repeated electoral ruin.[49] Certainly not everyone agreed with this. For the Bevanite Richard Crossman, revisionists like Jenkins were getting it wrong. Rather than Labour being 'the anti-establishment party', Jenkins and his allies had in mind becoming 'an alternative team of management inside the establishment – a party not unlike the Democrats in the United States'.[50] This of course was not a compliment and followed the broad *Tribune* view, summarized by the historian Peter Jones, that: 'The Labour government should reassert its independence and demand that the Atlantic alliance is put on an even keel.'[51]

---

[47] Jenkins to Galbraith, 14 September 1959, John K. Galbraith papers, JFK Presidential Library, Boston, Box 39.

[48] Galbraith to Neumann, 10 July 1959, Galbraith papers, Box 39.

[49] *Guardian*, 5 November 1959.

[50] Richard Crossman, *Labour in the Affluent Society* (London: The Fabian Society, 1960), 3.

[51] Peter Jones, *America and the British Labour Party: The 'Special Relationship' at Work* (London: I.B. Tauris, 1997), 96.

Internecine battles within Labour aside, one candidate who understood the broad message that there were limits to what the state could do was John Fitzgerald Kennedy. Indeed, he would famously go on to urge his fellow citizens, during his inaugural address: 'Ask not what your country can do for you – ask what you can do for your country.' Backed by figures such as Schlesinger, Kennedy was always likely to take something of a mixed approach to economic management. In his 1949 book *The Vital Center*, Schlesinger had approvingly noted that Britain had, through the 1945 Labour government, 'already submitted itself to social democracy; [and] the United States will very likely advance in that direction through a series of New Deals'.[52] In a *New York Times* column the previous year, Schlesinger had expanded his definition of 'the vital centre' to include 'all those-non-Communist Left, Center and moderate Right – who believe in political freedom and in the democratic control of economic life'.[53] It was this latter big tent approach that marked JFK's world view. After all, as Kennedy declared in 1962, the reality was that the most important government concerns were 'technical problems, administrative problems' that did 'not lend themselves to the great sort of passionate movements which have stirred this country so often in the past'.

Jenkins saw much of this first-hand. During the tightly contested election against Richard Nixon, Jenkins had stayed with the Galbraiths in Vermont, and spent a day following JFK when he campaigned in New York. He further gave his views on the American scene in an October talk to Dartmouth students entitled 'A Britisher Views the American Election.'[54] This was certainly a turbulent time in US affairs – but it was no calm period on the British left either. At the Labour Party conference in Scarborough, motions calling for unilateral nuclear disarmament were passed against the will of (the now leader) Hugh Gaitskell, who famously declared he would 'fight and fight and fight again to save the party we love'. A leadership challenge from Harold Wilson soon emerged, with two-thirds of the party (including Jenkins) staying loyal to the incumbent. On 5 November 1960, three days before their own polling day, Americans read that, 'The re-election of Mr Gaitskell is reassuring – that the men and women who would constitute a Labo[u]r government have a large majority inside the party for common sense policies.' In short, as the *Pittsburgh Press* had it, 'Wiser heads seem to have prevailed.'[55]

---

[52] Arthur Schlesinger Jr, *The Vital Center* (Boston: Houghton Mifflin, 1949), 153–4.
[53] *The New York Times*, 4 April 1948.
[54] *The Vermont Journal*, 6 October 1960.
[55] *The Pittsburgh Press*, 5 November 1960.

With JFK in the White House, there was the chance to make greater links with Labour's 'wiser heads' – including a visit to D.C. from Gaitskell in 1962. Early the next year Jenkins then made his own play – being sold to the president by Schlesinger as 'the leader of the pro-Common Market wing of the Labour Party' – as well as a 'historian of some ability' who was 'intelligent and agreeable'. Perhaps with an eye to Kennedy's penchant for gossip, as well as his own hardly perfect marriage, Jenkins was also described as a 'good friend of [Conservative politician] Ian and Caroline Gilmour (reputedly a particular friend of Caroline's)'. Whatever the reason, it got Roy in the room. On 30 January 1963, Jenkins had a forty-minute, off-the-record conversation with JFK. Jenkins noted that Kennedy asked 'a series of rapid-fire questions about all sorts of subjects – economic growth, Europe and de Gaulle, the Labour Party'. His host 'interrupted the answers, [Kennedy] gave his own views, he followed up a weak or unconvincing reply by forcing one hard against the ropes'.[56]

There was much to discuss. Hugh Gaitskell had died earlier that month (in tribute, Kennedy had the highest regard for his 'integrity, intelligence, and humanity') and the contest to replace him was well underway.[57] Wilson, Jim Callaghan and George Brown were all campaigning for the top job and, with a general election in sight, Washington was interested in the potential next prime minister. Here again Schlesinger's comments tell us much. On 8 February 1963, the day after Callaghan had been eliminated from the contest, and a few days before Wilson won the second round by forty-one MPs, Kennedy's advisor prepared some notes for the president. 'Our press', Schlesinger advised, 'will probably describe [Wilson's impending win] as a victory for the anti-American and extreme leftist wing of the party'. Given the *San Francisco Examiner* led its story with a picture of Wilson captioned, 'He'd withdraw from Polaris missile pact', this seems like a fair assessment.[58] But Schlesinger argued this was a 'premature conclusion'. Instead, he noted, 'Wilson has taken an anti-American line because he is the sort of man for whom politics is a game of musical chairs, and Gaitskell was already sitting in the pro-America chair'. It was just as likely therefore that Wilson would pivot back, and 'out-Gaitskell Gaitskell' in taking a conciliatory line towards the United States.[59]

[56] Campbell, *Roy Jenkins*, 233.

[57] Kennedy note on Gaitskell death, via www.jfklibrary.org, document ref: JFKNSF-171-002.

[58] *San Francisco Examiner*, 15 February 1963.

[59] Schlesinger note, via www.jfklibrary.org (accessed 13 September 2021), 8 February 1963, ref: JFKPOF-065a-012.

In any event, once Lee Harvey Oswald took aim from the Texas School Book Depository, there would be no Wilson–Kennedy Special Relationship. In the House of Commons, Labour's shadow foreign secretary, Patrick Gordon Walker, paid tribute to the fallen leader. Referring to a meeting he had had with the president in May, Gordon Walker remembered 'one of the most persuasive men that I have ever encountered'. His most important legacy was civil rights:

> Kennedy set himself to complete the task that had been begun by Abraham Lincoln, of reconciling the races in America. He showed the same clearsighted courage. He showed the same proud disregard for anxious political calculations. Cut off as he has been in mid-career, President Kennedy's assassination may shock into shamed silence the bitter men who sought to frustrate his race policies.

Such landmark actions aside, Gordon Walker recalled 'the man himself, his smile, his alert and probing mind, his electric energy, his assurance and, perhaps above all, his gaiety'.[60] The Labour Party, including Roy Jenkins who could barely sleep the night after the events in Dallas, was utterly distraught.[61] After 1964, they would seek to deliver on some of the same civil rights agenda themselves – with Jenkins at the forefront of this charge.

Conclusion

From the early 1930s to the early 1960s, then, the relationship between the US Democrats and the British Labour Party was fundamentally recalibrated. In early 1932 it was accurate enough for Mary Agnes Hamilton to declare that 'the Labo[u]r Party in England … is comparable to the American Socialist Party, and stands for many of the same principles'.[62] It was not, in other words, necessarily a mirror of the Democrats. But as the global economic crisis brought FDR into interventionism and, then, the gradual remaking of the Democratic coalition steered that party away from the 'solid south' and its racialized politics, it became more and more possible to see the connections between Labour and its potential American allies. The political cover for the 1945 government to go 'bold', the ability for Labour to move away from an electorally unpopular and often undesirable elevation of blanket pacifism, and the vision of what the left could

[60] House of Commons Debates, 25 November 1963, vol. 685, col. 38.
[61] See Jenkins' *Observer* obituary, 24 November 1963.
[62] *Democrat and Chronicle* (Rochester, NY), 6 March 1932.

be about when the big economic questions seemed to have been solved, all owed something to interactions with US Democrats.

And such mirroring would largely continue. Dealing with the maelstrom of the 1970s, both Labour and Democratic administrations tried to use the tools of the state, including raising taxes, but could not arrest the decline of two advanced Western democracies. They were then succeeded in office by tax-cutting leaders of the New Right, who allied economic populism to an emphasis on family values. Finally, progressives from Robert Reich to Gordon Brown worked out that the way to defeat Reaganomics and Thatcherism was to encourage private sector growth to create tax receipts for socially progressive ends, and to be seen to back an agenda of 'opportunity, responsibility, and community', rather than seem in hock to big government. In 1996 Bill Clinton (tactically) declared the era of the latter to be over. However, like Tony Blair, he also dramatically increased the role of the state in the tax credit system, delivered transformational new resources for education, and made huge strides in terms of the minimum wage. Progressives have much to learn from one another, and this chapter has attempted to sketch out some important previous ideological junctures.

Given this, what lessons are there for today's transatlanticists? Firstly, as electorates begin to tire of political amateurism – and certainly politicians claiming they have 'had enough of experts' – cultivating some intellectual seriousness seems a reasonable start. Strachey, Hamilton and Jenkins all gained access to the American political scene as authors on topics quite distinct from the machinations of Capitol Hill. Touring the United States for weeks is no longer an option in an age where the MP-constituency link has rightly assumed greater prominence, but our new world of daily videoconferencing opens up avenues for connections with like-minded forces in the United States that, even in the last decade, seemed improbable. And, although writing a serious book is of course easier said than done, several current Labour MPs have already done a better job than our prime minister's efforts.[63]

Secondly, for the left of the Labour Party, Bernie Sanders and Alexandria Ocasio-Cortez can no longer be the only idols in town. John Strachey said things in the 1930s that even Jeremy Corbyn may have baulked at, but he still had the good sense to consider the response to the depression by Franklin Delano Roosevelt as, on the whole, positive – and to learn accordingly. Good politicians cast their nets far and wide. In the 1980s, for instance, Neil Kinnock

---

[63] See for example Rachel Reeves, *Women of Westminster: The MPs Who Changed Politics* (London: I.B. Tauris, 2019); Nick Thomas-Symonds, *Nye: The Political Life of Aneurin Bevan* (London: I.B. Tauris, 2014); and Chris Bryant, *The Glamour Boys* (London: Bloomsbury, 2020).

was in touch with everyone from Jesse Jackson to Gary Hart. Later, Tony Blair discussed his 'stakeholder economy' with Dick Gephardt whilst imbibing Bill Clinton's positions on law and order.[64] This raised – rather than diminished – their international reputations.

For Keir Starmer, forging links with sensible leaders in the democratic world cannot therefore come soon enough. Close allies of Labour's leader have been keen to argue that 'we're not the Democrats' – by which they mean a loose coalition of social liberals, big-city progressives and some trade unions.[65] Certainly, Labour must remain true to its own history. But such a history includes the track record of transnational cooperation, and the crafting of better policy, that has arrived when progressive forces on both sides of the Atlantic get together. Roosevelt and Kennedy showed British progressives that no truck should be given to totalitarians. Clinton provided a blueprint for government that helped orient an agenda for three New Labour terms in office. And Joe Biden and Kamala Harris have shown that a plain spoken, direct message of hope can trump the incompetence of a populist. There are worse fates than becoming 'a party not unlike the Democrats'.

---

[64] Carr, *March of the Moderates*, 193.
[65] *New Statesman*, 9 September 2020.

4

The shifting significance of 'The Spirit of '45'

Steven Fielding

The general election of 1945 was one of the most critical turning points in modern British history. It saw the Labour Party win 47.7 per cent of votes cast and achieve its first ever Commons majority (of 145 seats) which it used, despite appalling economic difficulties, to introduce a 'cradle to grave' welfare state, at the centre of which stood the National Health Service; nationalize key industries; and guarantee full employment. By 1951, when Labour returned to opposition, Clement Attlee's government had moreover helped establish a political settlement that lasted for three decades, one which constrained the actions of even Conservative administrations. You would need a heart of stone – or be an implacable Thatcherite – not to feel there was something heroic about that moment. Reflecting on this unique achievement, when historians and other informed observers are asked who Britain's greatest prime minister was, Attlee is often placed first and never lower than third.[1]

As YouGov discovered in January 2020, two-thirds of Labour members, perhaps unsurprisingly, also looked favourably on Attlee. But nearly one-third admitted they did not know enough about him to express an opinion.[2] So, if '1945 and all that' is seen in overwhelmingly positive terms within the party, many in its ranks have an uncertain grasp of what happened and why. This means that those Labour figures who wish to use this good feeling to justify themselves and their own politics enjoy a relatively free hand to suggest an affinity – however spurious – between themselves and that glorious past.[3]

---

[1]   Historical rankings of prime ministers of the United Kindom, Wikipedia, https://en.wikipedia.org/wiki/Historical_rankings_of_prime_ministers_of_the_United_Kingdom (accessed 29 December 2020).

[2]   Matthew Smith, 'Five more things we discovered about Labour members', YouGov, 21 January 2020, https://yougov.co.uk/topics/politics/articles-reports/2020/01/21/five-more-things-we-discovered-about-labour-member?utm_source=twitter&utm_medium=website_article&utm_campaign=Labour_Members_Jan_2020_extra (accessed 5 January 2021).

[3]   For more on how politicians exploit the past for their own purposes, see Emily Robinson, *History, Heritage and Tradition in Contemporary British Politics* (Manchester: MUP, 2012).

For understandable reasons, therefore, party leaders have often made stirring references to Attlee's 1945 landslide and the legislative achievements that followed. But the alacrity with which supporters of Jeremy Corbyn's leadership used the 1945 moment as a point of justification and inspiration was unusual, especially in contrast to the more muted references made to the Attlee years during the New Labour period. For some on the Labour left, and others on the far left of British politics who joined the party after 2015, the recovery of what many increasingly referred to as the 'Spirit of '45' was vital to the success of Corbyn's socialist project, proof of its legitimacy within a mainstream Labour tradition, they wished to recast to look more like their own.

Certainly, as the December 2019 election approached, references to 1945 came thick and fast. When delegates gathered at Brighton for what would be Corbyn's last annual party conference as leader, Shadow Chancellor John McDonnell told them:

> It was the Attlee Labour Government that built a new society from the debris of the bomb sites, in the new era after the Second World War. Those men and women who had endured so much throughout the depression of the 1930s and who had sacrificed so much to defeat fascism, placed their trust in our party. My Dad was a sergeant in the army and my Mum a welder by day, in a munitions [*sic*] factory, and an ARP warden at night. They came out of the war with that spirit of 1945, inspired in them by the election of a Labour Government. And the Labour Party fulfilled its promise to them and all the other families by creating the welfare state, providing free education for their children, building them a decent home, investing in an economy based upon full employment. And, of course, creating that jewel in our crown, our NHS … We should never forget that we are part of that great Labour tradition and we should be so proud of it. So, as we now enter the next, new era, the era of the fourth industrial revolution, I tell you it is a Corbyn Labour Government that will rescue our country from the long years of austerity. And it will be up to us to lay the foundations of the new world that awaits us.[4]

The year before, McDonnell claimed that most members of Attlee's government had wanted to initiate a 'systemic change' that went beyond 'ameliorative reform' and had Labour remained in office beyond 1951, 'it may well have had the opportunity to demonstrate how radical transformation could be achieved'.[5]

---

[4] Shadow Chancellor John McDonnell speech to Labour Party Conference, https://labour.org.uk/press/shadow-chancellor-john-mcdonnell-speech-to-labour/ (accessed 4 January 2021).

[5] John McDonnell, *What is the Labour Party for?*, https://www.plutobooks.com/blog/what-is-the-labour-party-for-john-mcdonnell/ (accessed 4 January 2021).

McDonnell argued that the similarities between Attlee's Labour and the party led by Corbyn were striking. Indeed, as the election loomed, he even informed radio listeners: 'I think I'm in the tradition of the Attlee government.' Yet, whilst Labour under Corbyn, he went on, stood for 'the traditional Attlee commitment on public ownership', he wanted to go beyond that: 'We want a different type of democratic ownership', in which employees and consumers become involved in their management.[6] Indeed, Shadow Education Secretary Angela Rayner was cheered at a campaign rally when she declared that a Corbyn government 'would knock the socks off' Attlee's administration.[7]

The 2019 election did not, however, produce a Corbyn government; Attlee's socks remained unmoved. Instead of emulating the 1945 landslide, Corbyn's performance more closely evoked the sad haul of seats achieved by Labour in 1935. There was a surfeit of reasons for Labour's defeat, notably its complex Brexit policy, unfeasible number of radical commitments, widespread hostility to Corbyn and his failure to tackle anti-Semitism amongst members and supporters. But the belief that Corbynism represented a rearticulation of the 'Spirit of '45' and that Corbyn was Attlee reborn played its part in blinding many Labour members to flaws in the party's change of direction after 2015, and so helped lay the foundations for its disaster in December 2019.

This chapter looks at the far left's appropriation of Labour's 1945 victory and the government that followed by focusing on Ken Loach's widely praised 2013 documentary *The Spirit of '45*. But it first assesses how historians and others since the 1960s regarded that critical moment's relationship to the times in which they lived. Having focused on the status of 1945 within the Labour Party and across the left more generally, the chapter concludes with an analysis of how that election, and Attlee, are remembered by the wider public.

In 1963 the political journalist Anthony Howard claimed: 'Occasionally late at night at a Labour Party conference – or in the small hours of the morning at the more strenuous gathering of the T.U.C. – the cry can still be heard. "Where", a plaintive, maudlin voice will ask, "did it go wrong?"' Howard believed that whilst the government elected in 1945 achieved much, it was hobbled by a limited social ambition, one which allowed public schools to flourish and Oxbridge to accrue

---

[6]   Iain Dale, 'Iain Dale pushes John McDonnell on whether he is a Marxist', LBC News, 6 November 2019, https://www.lbc.co.uk/radio/presenters/iain-dale/iain-dale-pushes-john-mcdonnell-marxist/ (accessed 4 January 2021).

[7]   Henry Deedes, 'Angela Rayner is less knee jerk and more knee to the groin: Henry Deedes sees Jeremy Corbyn outshone', MailOnline, 12 November 2019, https://www.dailymail.co.uk/debate/article-7678497/Angela-Rayner-knee-jerk-knee-groin-HENRY-DEEDES-sees-Jeremy-Corbyn-outshone.html (accessed 30 December 2020).

even more prestige. This meant Labour's victory ironically 'brought about the greatest restoration of traditional social values since 1660', one which laid the foundations for what was, when his piece was published, the twelfth successive year of Conservative rule.[8]

Howard was a Labour partisan, although more of its right than its left. Even so, his critique was echoed in accounts written during subsequent decades by communist, New Left and Trotskyist authors. Whatever their doctrinal differences, writers such as Ralph Miliband, Jeremy Seabrook and John Saville shared the conviction that Labour in office, principally by not taking more of the economy into state hands, failed to express the widespread radical – even revolutionary – wartime mood which they believed had delivered the party its victory on a plate. They conceded that the government's reforms had ameliorated the worst aspects of interwar capitalism, but accused Attlee's ministers of turning their backs on the kind of state socialism demanded by their own members. By frustrating the wartime desire for real change, Labour's leaders are said to have fostered a popular political disenchantment which, such writers believed, was the main cause of the Conservatives return to power in 1951.[9] This visceral belief in Labour's betrayal went beyond the printed page and during the 1970s was dramatized by radical playwrights such as David Hare, Howard Brenton and Trevor Griffiths whose work found a place in the schedules of BBC television.[10]

In parallel with this perspective was another, expressed by more mainstream historians who saw the government in generally positive terms and believed its achievements broadly reflected the popular mood. The most significant example of this viewpoint was Paul Addison's *The Road to 1945* (1975).[11] Addison agreed with its left critics that the government had introduced a 'reformed style of capitalism', conceding that '[i]f capitalism is regarded as inherently productive of ruthless exploitation and inequality', then by definition it changed little. 'But', he continued, 'on the social democratic thesis that parliamentary democracy enables the labour movement to achieve worthwhile benefits within capitalism, … [it] might be regarded as radical in its effects'. And he inclined to the latter interpretation.[12]

---

[8] Anthony Howard, 'We are the Masters now', in Michael Sissons and Philip French (eds), *Age of Austerity, 1945–51* (Harmondsworth: Penguin, 1964).

[9] Ralph Miliband, *Parliamentary Socialism* (London: Merlin, 1964); Trevor Blackwell and Jeremy Seabrook, *The Politics of Hope* (London: Faber and Faber, 1988); John Saville, *The Labour Movement* (London: Faber and Faber, 1988).

[10] In plays such as *All Good Men* (broadcast on BBC One, 31 January 1974) and *Brassneck* (broadcast on BBC One, 22 May 1975).

[11] But see also Kenneth O. Morgan, *Labour in Power, 1945–51* (Oxford: OUP, 1984) and Henry Pelling, *The Labour Governments, 1945–51* (London: Macmillan, 1984).

[12] Paul Addison, *The Road to 1945* (London: Quartet, 1975), 276.

But Addison went further. He proposed that the settlement that emerged from the Second World War was the work of many hands, and not just those of Labour's leaders. He claimed that many of the reforms with which the 1945 government was associated were the product of members of 'the upper middle class of socially concerned professional people' who entered Whitehall during Winston Churchill's coalition government. This group included Liberals such as William Beveridge, whose 1942 Report into Social Insurance and Allied Services played a critical role in laying down what would be Labour's welfare policies. When the Report was published, James Callaghan, the future Labour prime minister, was serving in the Royal Navy. He kept a copy in his kit bag, 'like a missionary would carry the gospel', because despite its Liberal provenance, he saw it as 'a charter of human rights'.[13]

The influence of figures like Beveridge, who had been attempting to influence government policy since before 1914, was such that the historian Gareth Stedman Jones even called the Attlee government, 'the last and most glorious flowering of late Victorian liberal philanthropy'.[14] Beveridge and his ilk did not seek to destroy capitalism but to make its operation, as they saw it, more rational through state intervention. They consequently looked on the mass unemployment of the 1930s not as a class issue, but as a functional one (it was inefficient) and a moral problem (many were Anglicans). Attlee, himself a socially concerned professional person drawn from the upper middle class, welcomed their contribution even if their intentions were somewhat different to Labour's. According to Addison this combination even pulled a few leading Conservatives into its 'field of force'. This meant that even before the 1945 election there was cross-party agreement on postwar policy in home affairs, including education, social security, employment and health – although not, critically, public ownership.

Later historians have questioned the extent of this consensus; others suggested it took Labour's landslide to convince the Conservative Party to embrace it.[15] And whilst Addison was clear about the limits of the cross-party agreement that allowed Attlee to create what he called 'a more enlightened and humane society', others would subsequently highlight the extent to which it was underpinned by patriarchal and racist assumptions. The Attlee administration after all turned its back on equal pay and its immediate response to the arrival of eight hundred

---

[13] James Callaghan, *Time and Chance* (London: HarperCollins, 1987), 61.
[14] Gareth Stedman Jones, *Languages of Class* (Cambridge: CUP, 1983), 246.
[15] For example, Kevin Jefferys, *The Churchill Coalition and Wartime Politics, 1940–45* (Manchester: MUP, 1991).

West Indians on the *Empire Windrush* was to consider whether it should restrict Black immigration.[16] However, most historians accept the thrust of Addison's interpretation, and specifically his claim that Attlee fostered 'a politics of the Centre' in which the two front benches agreed to a historically remarkable degree on policy means, even whilst they continued to disagree about ideological ends.[17] Labour's leaders hoped the welfare state would promote social equality, whilst the most moderate Conservatives saw it as providing the necessary minimum to ensure a competitive economy. But in this consensus, Addison is clear, the left – both in and outside the Labour Party – played a minor part, remaining at loggerheads with Attlee notably over his reluctance to nationalize more industries. This is a view with which socialist historians have always concurred. As Simon Hannah puts it, during the 1940s the Labour left and their parliamentary leaders might have been in the same party but they pursued very different strategies.[18]

The Road to 1945 was published just as Attlee's consensus entered a crisis from which Thatcherism would emerge. However, many on the left initially hoped they would emerge victorious from this crisis: Britain in their view had always needed more public ownership than that established by Attlee, not less. In 1974 Harold Wilson became prime minister with a manifesto largely written by newly influential radicals led by Tony Benn promising, 'a fundamental and irreversible shift in the balance of power and wealth in favour of working people'. Benn believed the ultimate roots of this socialist insurgency lay in the Peasants Revolt of 1381. Most of his followers had shorter time horizons and considered they were living up to Labour's original socialist promise, embodied in Clause Four of its constitution, which since 1918 had formally committed the party to advance the common ownership of the economy.

From this perspective Attlee's government which nationalized one-fifth of the economy – was a socialist who, unlike many members of Wilson's Cabinet, according to Benn, 'didn't believe in running capitalism, he [Attlee] didn't believe in profits, he wanted the extension of public ownership'.[19] Indeed the Labour left maintained Wilson and his successor James Callaghan wanted to appease capitalism and so in no way could be considered Attlee's heirs. It was

---

[16] For example, Kenneth Lunn, 'The British state and immigration, 1945–51: new light on the Empire Windrush', *Immigrants and Minorities* 8, nos 1–2 (1989) and Denise Riley, 'The Free Mothers: Pronatalism and working women in industry at the end of the last war in Britain', *History Workshop Journal* 11 (1981).

[17] See Kevin Hickson, 'The Postwar Consensus Revisited', *The Political Quarterly* 75, no. 2 (2004).

[18] Simon Hannah, *A Party with Socialists in it* (London: Pluto, 2018), 95.

[19] Tony Benn, *Against the Tide: Diaries 1973–76* (London: Arrow, 1990), 436.

only natural that the party's 1983 manifesto, again largely written by Bennite hands, included inspirational references to the 1945 government. A radical Labour administration committed to returning all privatized industries to public hands, it asserted, could again abolish unemployment, which under Thatcher's Conservatives had reached 1930s levels. Even after that manifesto was decisively rejected at the polls, Benn saw the result as a vindication, given 8.5 million Britons had 'for the first time since 1945, [supported] a political party with an openly socialist policy'. Placing Attlee on his side of the argument, Benn argued Labour should remain true to its historic destiny by continuing in a leftward direction.[20]

Labour's 1983 defeat allowed the Conservatives to privatize even more industries nationalized by Attlee as part of Thatcher's attempt to push back the boundaries of the state. New leader Neil Kinnock reluctantly accepted many of these measures, if only because they seemed popular with voters. Labour's 1987 manifesto nonetheless still evoked the spirit of Attlee by describing the NHS – not public ownership – as Labour's 'proudest achievement', promising to save it from Thatcher's depredations. It helped that the NHS was the most popular of Attlee's creations, but references to the 1940s were increasingly the preserve of critics of Kinnock's move to the centre ground. Moreover, by the late 1980s the leadership had started to couch its strategy of moderation in the rhetoric of 'modernization': Labour, it was argued, needed to be relevant to the present by looking to the future, one seemingly defined by free markets and individualistic consumers. The place of the past in such a strategy seemed uncertain. Even so, during Kinnock's last campaign as leader in 1992 the party still deployed rousing if vague references to 1945, if only to give members hope that their efforts canvassing and posting leaflets would end with a Labour government.[21]

The 1992 election was Labour's fourth defeat in a row and by 1994 the party was led by Tony Blair – who four years earlier had boldly told conference delegates that they 'should leave the past to those who live in it'.[22] Once leader, in renaming his party 'New Labour', Blair dismissively called opponents 'Old Labour', a crude binary which appeared to confirm the charge of left critics that they were the true legatees of the Attlee government.[23] Blair did, nonetheless, challenge that belief by imposing his own meaning on 1945 when marking the

[20] *Guardian*, 20 June 1983.
[21] Richard Jobson, *Nostalgia and the post-war Labour Party* (Manchester: MUP, 2018), 119, 126.
[22] *Labour Party Conference Annual Report 1990* (London: Labour Party, 1990), 75.
[23] I owe this point to Robert Saunders, Twitter, 31 January 2021, https://twitter.com/redhistorian/status/1355883699301134336?s=20 (accessed 13 September 2021).

fiftieth anniversary of Attlee becoming prime minister.[24] Just a year into his leadership, Blair had recently won members' endorsement for his revised Clause Four, which no longer committed the party to common ownership. With that in mind, he distinguished between the 'enduring values' of 'fairness, freedom from want, social equality', which he claimed underpinned Attlee's government, and the time-bound means – by which he meant state intervention – it used to advance them. Therefore, Blair said, he remained committed to applying those values in government. Having relegated public ownership to an antediluvian means, he further challenged the left's interpretation of 1945 by claiming Labour won not because of its appeal to class consciousness but to a classless and patriotic message. Indeed, in formulating its policies the party was, he said, 'willing to draw on the resources of the whole progressive tradition'. Like Addison, Blair emphasized the contribution of Liberals going so far as to quote Attlee that, 'the aim of socialism is to give greater freedom to the individual'.

Blair's was an audacious attempt to paint Attlee as New Labour before New Labour. He failed to convince the left: they saw any attempt to move from the policies set down in 1945 – which they believed were umbilically linked to the achievement of the party's values – as treachery. So far as they were concerned, public ownership was more than a means. As the labour historian and left stalwart Royden Harrison wrote, the Labour tradition was defined by 'the settlement which followed victory in the Second World War: *it was and it will always be* the Party of full employment, comprehensive social services and extended common ownership with public accountability'.[25] Yet, this was a sentiment shared by a declining number of members, especially those who joined the party in the early years of the Blair leadership. Two years after Labour had won a landslide victory comparable with that of 1945, 44 per cent remained in favour of more nationalization. But if that represented a large minority it was significantly down from the 71 per cent who had expressed the same opinion in 1990.[26] Blair was – perhaps – winning the argument.

Under Blair, Labour won an unprecedented three general elections in a row whilst investment in public services reached new heights. But his record as prime minister was problematic for many in his party, who saw progress towards equality as too slow, capped as it was by the contentious invasion of Iraq. It was, however, the 2008 financial crash, which occurred whilst Gordon

---

[24] The following account is based on Tony Bair, 'Let Us Face the Future', Fabian Pamphlet 571 (1995).

[25] Royden J. Harrison, 'New Labour as Past History' (Nottingham: Socialist Renewal, 1996), 26–7; emphasis added.

[26] Patrick Seyd and Paul Whiteley, *New Labour's Grassroots* (London: Palgrave Macmillan, 2002), 50–3.

Brown occupied Number 10, which was the most electorally damaging. Many voters were persuaded by the Conservatives that Labour's spending on schools and hospitals made the impact of the crash worse than it would otherwise have been. But many in Labour's ranks believed the collapse of the banks was in contrast mostly due to Blair's embrace of the free market, which only a quarter ever looked on with favour.[27] His government's modest impact on inequality was also wiped away as the Conservative-led coalition cut back welfare spending under the guise of what it claimed was an economically necessary 'austerity'. Ed Miliband, elected leader in the wake of Labour's 2010 defeat, believed this proved the party needed to be more critical of the market.[28] Yet, this course failed to make an impression on the public; most disturbingly an increasing number of manual workers, once Labour's core constituency, were turning towards UKIP.

During this period of disorientation, the past became even more of an inspiration than usual, with some seeing members' attentiveness to history as part of a wider 'nostalgic resurgence' within its ranks.[29] In 2014 the elderly Harry Leslie Smith published *Harry's Last Stand*, widely quoted on the left, in which he contrasted the defeatism and timidity of the generation meekly living though austerity with the heroism and fortitude of his 1940s generation, one embodied by Attlee's government. Smith scolded the present for its failings, thereby hoping to revive those lost virtues in his readers' hearts. More generally, the Attlee government became a useful means to critique austerity. For, despite facing even more severe difficulties than the ones confronted by Cameron, Attlee had built the very welfare state and NHS the Tories were now undermining. The left, however, used Attlee not only to attack Cameron's programme of cuts but also to criticize what they took to be Miliband's tentative response to it. On the 2011 TUC March for an Alternative Against Austerity, a placard held by a member of the Tower Hamlets Labour Party contingent asked: 'What would Clem do?'[30] The question was posed in an ironic way – it knowingly echoed the Christian query 'What would Jesus do?' – but the answer was politically serious: keep on spending, just like Attlee. The question had first been printed on T-shirts and sold commercially in 2010, and they quickly became a bestseller for the company making them.[31] Soon, hundreds of these shirts appeared at left-wing

---

[27] In 1999 only 27 per cent of members believed the free market was the best means of delivering goods and services whilst 54 per cent disagreed; ibid.

[28] Eunice Goes, *The Labour Party under Miliband* (Manchester: MUP, 2016), 51.

[29] Jobson, *Nostalgia*, 175.

[30] 'TUC March for an Alternative: What would Clem do?', John's Labour blog, 9 April 2011, https://www.johnslabourblog.org/2011/04/tuc-march-for-alternative-what-would.html (accessed 11 January 2021).

[31] Based on email correspondence with a representative of RedMolotov.com.

demonstrations and Labour meetings. It was no accident therefore that during this period Labour members looked on Attlee as the model to follow: in 2015, 36 per cent voted him their greatest ever leader, over twice the proportion of those who chose Blair.[32]

It was during this moment that Ken Loach made *The Spirit of '45*. Released in 2013, the film prefigured arguments associated with Corbyn's leadership, and in *Harry's Last Stand,* that if it was to again win power, Labour needed to return to a lost socialist and proletarian authenticity as exemplified by the Attlee government's commitment to public ownership.

Loach was, however, at the time not a party member, being one of the Miliband leadership's fiercest left critics.[33] He had joined Labour in 1964, although flirted with various far-left groups critical of the party's moderation. His early work as a BBC television director similarly took aim at the limitations of Attlee's welfare state, as in *Cathy Come Home* (1966); or claimed Labour's pursuit of the parliamentary road helped capitalism by suppressing working-class militancy, historically (*Days of Hope* [1975]) and in the present (*Big Flame* [1969]). He endorsed Ralph Miliband's assertion that, 'one of the biggest obstacles to developing socialism in this country is the Labour party', a claim the author of *Parliamentary Socialism* partly based on his analysis of the Attlee government.

Loach remained a member even as Kinnock moved Labour towards the centre ground, 'because there was still a radical element that was critical of the leadership'. He was also an implacable anti-Zionist, seeing Israel as an imperialist state. In the late 1980s Loach even attempted to stage *Perdition*, a play which suggested the founders of Israel had been helped by the Nazis, provoking accusations of anti-Semitism. His movie *Hidden Agenda* (1989) promoted another kind of conspiracy, suggesting Margaret Thatcher became Conservative leader thanks to an MI5 plot and that the intelligence services had provoked the 'Winter of Discontent' to ensure she won the 1979 general election. These were hardly mainstream

[32] 'Clement Attlee chosen as Labour's greatest ever leader', LabourList, 2 September 2015, https://labourlist.org/2015/09/clement-attlee-chosen-as-labours-greatest-ever-leader/ (accessed 2 February 2021).

[33] This account of Loach's political background is based on: https://www.newstatesman.com/arts-and-culture/2007/09/ken-loach-labour-party-film (accessed 4 January 2021); Simon Hattenstone, interview, 'Ken Loach: "If you're nopt angry, what kind of person are you?"', *Guardian*, 15 October 2016, https://www.theguardian.com/film/2016/oct/15/ken-laoch-film-i-daniel-blake-kes-cathy-come-home-interview-simon-hattenstone (accessed 4 January 2021); Salman Shaheen, 'Ken Loach discusses his hopes for Left unity', *Huffpost*, 20 November 2013, https://www.huffingtonpost.co.uk/salman-shaheen/ken-loach-left-unity_b_4302871.html (accessed 4 January 2021); Kira Cochrane, interview, 'Ken Loach: "the ruling classes are cracking the whip"', *Guardian*, 28 August 2011, https://www.theguardian.com/film/2011/aug/28/ken-loach-class-riots-interview?INTCMP=SRCH (accessed 4 January 2021).

Labour views, although it was not till the mid-1990s that Loach finally quit the party. Considering Blair had definitively turned Labour into 'a party of business', his immediate reason for leaving was, somewhat idiosyncratically, the ending of door-to-door collections of membership subscriptions. Loach subsequently became a leading member of the far-left coalition Respect which in a 2012 by-election defeated Labour in its former stronghold of Bradford West.

In *The Spirit of '45* Loach played down his hard-line politics so the movie might appeal to as wide an audience on the left as possible. Superficially, *The Spirit of '45* was an emotionally charged celebration of Labour's landslide and the government which transformed the country. It juxtaposed what Loach cast as the hopes of the 1940s with the despair of austerity Britain, hoping this would inspire a new generation to realize a market-dominated society could be overturned: the past – or his version of that past – proved it. This was history with a strong dose of propaganda. Some of the archive footage uncovered by Loach's researchers, such as Churchill being booed during the 1945 campaign, is nonetheless remarkable. The elderly nurses, miners and steelworkers who recalled that time similarly imbue the film with vivid authenticity. But the seemingly authoritative experts who contextualize the events depicted were mostly drawn from the Communist Party, Militant, the Socialist Workers Party, the Trade Unionist and Socialist Coalition and the Stop the War campaign. Tony Benn was the only Labour politician of any standing to be interviewed. As an accomplished film maker, Loach also made his case through other kinds of manipulation, such as the mixing of beguiling images and emotive music. This was a view of 1945 seen through the prism of visceral far-left sentiment with the kind of impact no book could rival.

The film consequently left out those awkward questions historians of the period have made it their business to ask. In particular the complex and contingent character of 1940s popular politics was completely overlooked. To sum up working-class views, Loach left it to one grey-haired nurse who said it was: 'All for one and one for all, no greed and selfishness'. As with *Harry's Last Stand*, the film suggests that a whole generation was united by a shared uplifting goal. Yet, whilst a plurality of voters supported Labour in 1945, a majority did not. The war failed to magically transform them into idealists – in fact many observers commented on the peoples' continued political scepticism and disengagement.[34] That the policies implemented by Labour were anything other than socialist in origin is ignored: Beveridge is mentioned but his status as

---

[34] See Steven Fielding, Nick Tiratsoo and Peter Thompson (eds), *'England Arise!' The Labour Party and Popular Politics in 1940s Britain* (Manchester: MUP, 1995).

a Liberal is not. In contrast, Loach twice shows the same clip of Attlee describing his as a 'socialist policy' and leaves it at that. Appropriate excerpts from the 1945 Labour manifesto are also anachronistically spoken in a regional working-class accent although it was written by former barrister Michael Young. Loach, in other words, does his best to convey the impression that 1945 was the moment when socialism and the working class met their historical destiny, through the agency of a principled Labour Party.

The film made some modest criticisms of the Attlee government, specifically of the top-down management of the nationalized industries. This muted critique did not in fact reflect Loach's own more severe views: like others on the far left he saw the government as a failure thanks to its commitment to a mixed economy.[35] Even friendly reviewers admitted the movie 'undoubtedly glosses over a lot'.[36] Suppressing this critique enabled Loach to finish with the crowd-pleasing conclusion that, as one speaker asserted, Attlee's achievements 'rank along the greatest achievements of any other government there has ever been anywhere in the world'. How this exemplary regime lost power in 1951 with many of its accomplishments reversed by 1980s Conservatives is, however, never explained. The film simply jumps from the Festival of Britain to Mrs Thatcher entering Downing Street: Attlee's collectivism is unaccountably replaced by individualism and the country set on the path to austerity and a 1930s redux. The means by which contemporaries could recapture the 'Spirit of '45' is nonetheless outlined. With a brass band echoing over footage of young Occupy activists, various speakers argue that capitalism has to be resisted on the streets and through trade union militancy, by breaking laws if needs be, whilst Labour – having been 'hijacked' by the middle class – must return to its proletarian and socialist roots. Building on this time-worn, hard-line analysis, immediately after making the film, Loach established Left Unity in hopes of creating an electoral alliance across the far left. In the 2015 election it stood candidates against Labour. Indeed, in launching his new party, Loach used *The Spirit of '45* to attack Ed Miliband's 'neo-liberalism', declaring that now only Left Unity could continue Attlee's work.[37]

---

[35] Salman Shaheen, 'Ken Loach discusses his hopes for Left unity', *Huffpost*, 20 November 2013.

[36] Alex Nunns, 'Days of hope: The Spirit of '45 review', Red Pepper, 25 April 2013, https://www.redpepper.org.uk/days-of-hope-the-spirit-of-45/ (accessed 12 January 2021). For a more honest appraisal of what the authors frankly admit is the Attlee government's 'problematic legacy for the left', Christine Berry and Joe Guinan, *People Get Ready! Preparing for a Corbyn Government* (London: Orbooks, 2019), 35–9.

[37] Ken Loach, Kate Hudson and Gilbert Achcar, 'The Labour party has failed us. We need a new party of the left', *Guardian*, 25 March 2013, https://www.theguardian.com/commentisfree/2013/mar/25/labour-party-left (accessed 14 January 2021).

At most two thousand people joined Left Unity. But the impact of Loach's film was much more impressive, becoming popular with many in the Labour Party and beyond, especially those who supported Corbyn's two leadership campaigns. Its screenings provoked 'an emotional atmosphere and a real political discussion'.[38] Local Momentum groups also showed the film, and to support Corbyn's 2016 successful defence of his leadership, the organization sponsored a national tour which saw Loach discuss the film's themes with audiences. At the Derby screening, sometime-Labour MP Chris Williamson made direct comparisons with what the film depicted and the movement then mobilizing behind Corbyn: the working class was coming together again he said.[39] This was a view Loach endorsed, for by then Left Unity had effectively shut up shop with many of its members having joined – or re-joined – Labour. Loach even became an unofficial spokesperson for the Labour leader, defending him especially from accusations of condoning anti-Semitism.

Corbynites were right to believe it was advantageous to claim Labour's 1945 moment as their own. It legitimized their resetting of the party's direction amongst members most of whom regarded the period positively if hazily. Appropriating the 'Spirit of '45' also helped persuade members that, just like Attlee, Corbyn would lead another great Labour administration.

On this basis, some supporters even suggested Attlee and Corbyn were as one in a number of ways but most significantly because both demanded 'social progress at a time of economic disaster'.[40] If, to some, Corbyn was Attlee reborn, that was not necessarily the view of many historians. As already noted, professional students of the past habitually rank Attlee as one of Britain's best prime ministers. But, so far as his most recent biographers are concerned, whilst they agree about Attlee's stature, they by no means all see him as a Corbynite before Corbynism. For Francis Beckett, a long-time left Labour activist, who *hoped* Corbyn would turn out to be an Attlee-like figure, the man who won the 1945 election was a principled socialist, in fact, 'the greatest changemaker who ever occupied 10 Downing Street'. A reassuring revolutionary, given his modest personal manner, Attlee was a revolutionary just the same, one who moreover never expressed

---

[38] Tess Noonan, 'Ken Loach: The Spirit of '45 and Q&A at Warwick Arts Centre', *The Boar*, 26 November 2014, https://theboar.org/2014/11/ken-loach-spirit-45-warwick-arts-centre/ (accessed 30 December 2020).

[39] *The Spirit of '45* film screening Q&A session with director Ken Loach hosted by Chris Williamson at the QUAD cinema in Derby, 17 August 2016, https://www.youtube.com/watch?v=sNHTj3bpPiI (accessed 13 September 2021).

[40] Danny Dorling and Sally Tomlinson, 'Is Corbyn as lacking in drive and personality as Attlee? Let's hope so', *Guardian*, 9 May 2017, https://www.theguardian.com/commentisfree/2017/may/09/jeremy-corbyn-clement-attlee (accessed 4 February 2021).

'the hero-worshipping prattle about big business and rich people that was such a feature of the Blair years'.[41] If Beckett hoped for continuity between Corbyn and Attlee (and identified a huge chasm between the latter and Blair), John Bew – soon to become advisor to Prime Minister Boris Johnson on defence and foreign policy – stressed the extent with which they were at odds. In particular, Bew looked beyond public ownership and the NHS. He argued Attlee was able to implement his radical domestic programme because the public trusted him 'to keep Britain safe in a dangerous world'. Attlee helped create NATO, commissioned nuclear weapons and reinforced Britain's alliance with the United States.[42] Corbyn and his anti-imperialist followers disagreed with that. Bew's view was echoed by the Anglo-American author Michael Jago, describing Attlee as a 'Britain-first patriot' who in retirement recalled that his greatest problem as prime minister was not capitalism: it was Russia.[43] Standing astride these contrasting emphases was Nick Thomas-Symonds, Keir Starmer's future shadow home secretary. He highlighted Attlee's procedural competence, stressing his effectiveness as an administrator and manager of government business. But Thomas-Symonds also underlined the importance of Attlee's conventional patriotism, about which Corbynites were often deeply uncomfortable.[44]

Biographies are a popular way through which the past is consumed. Even so, sales are usually measured in the thousands rather than millions. How do those who rarely open a serious work of history regard Attlee, and by implication the achievements of the government he led? If one-third of Labour members don't know enough to have an opinion, what of the wider public? The evidence, such as it is, suggests they know very little. Most strikingly, in 2002 when BBC viewers voted Winston Churchill the Greatest Briton, Attlee did not even make it into the top 100.[45]

As he ensured Britain fought on against the Nazis, Churchill's position as a central character in British history is undoubtedly justified. But if Churchill made Britain safe from Hitler, Attlee surely made Britons safe from the dire economic consequences of ill-health. Attitudes to common ownership might

[41] Francis Beckett, *Clem Attlee: Labour's Great Reformer* (London: Haus, 2015), x–xi, xx, https://www.breadandrosestheatre.co.uk/news/a-modest-little-man-comes-to-the-bread-roses-theatre (accessed 25 January 2021).

[42] John Bew, *Citizen Clem* (London: riverrun, 2017), xxi–ii, xxiv.

[43] Michael Jago, *Clement Attlee: The Inevitable Prime Minister* (London: Biteback, 2017), 3, 368–70.

[44] Nicklaus Thomas-Symonds, *Attlee: A Life in Politics* (London: I.B. Taurus, 2010), 270.

[45] BBC Press Office, 'BBC TWO reveals the nation's top 100 Greatest Britons of all time', BBC, 21 August 2002, http://www.bbc.co.uk/pressoffice/pressreleases/stories/2002/08_august/21/100_britons.shtml (accessed 30 December 2020).

have changed since 1945 but it is remarkable that the man whose government established the National Health Service – today more highly regarded than the Royal Family – remains in the shadows.[46] The NHS shapes how many Britons think of their nation, most notably expressed in the opening ceremony to the 2012 London Olympics. The Covid-19 crisis has only strengthened the emotional bond between the British and their health service. Churchill and Attlee are, then, comparable in terms of their historical significance. To make this point, Leo McKinstry recently wrote a dual biography of the two figures.[47] But his was a rare attempt. In terms of television documentaries, biopics on the big and small screen and statues – Churchill beats Attlee hands down.[48]

Churchill's prominence owes something to his facility with words: 'History will be kind to me, for I intend to write it' he once said. And if Churchill is famous for his rhetoric, Attlee is best known for his lack of it. Politics experts believe Attlee was such an effective leader because he worked in a collegial way. But to their frustration the public remains in awe of more bombastic if less efficient 'strong leaders'.[49] Critically, after 1945 Churchill was adopted by Americans who saw him as a useful soldier in the Cold War, allowing them to draw parallels between his opposition to appeasement and warnings about Stalin's ambitions. In contrast many in Washington saw Attlee – despite his role in forming NATO – as the unwelcome progenitor of 'socialized medicine'. There has therefore never been a bust of Attlee in the White House Oval Office, nor Hollywood cash for an Attlee biopic.

It is, then, culture more than actual achievement that accounts for Attlee's popular obscurity. But it is also a result of Labour's own failure to take culture seriously. And, for that, Attlee is partly to blame. For whilst his government wrought huge changes – as Anthony Howard suggested fifty years ago and the historian Ross McKibbin more recently – it left the leading institutions of national life in the hands of the traditional elite.[50] Scion of Haileybury School and University College, Oxford, Attlee called himself a socialist but as all his biographers note he was deeply imbued with conventional upper-middle-class

---

46 Matthew Smith, 'The House of Parliament are the institutions Britons are least proud of', YouGov, 4 July 2018, https://yougov.co.uk/topics/politics/articles-reports/2018/07/04/nhs-british-institution-brits-are-second-most-prou (accessed 30 December 2020).

47 Leo McKinstry, *Attlee and Churchill: Allies in War, Adversaries in Peace* (London: Atlantic Books, 2019).

48 On Churchill's mythic dominance, see Steven Fielding, Bill Schwarz and Richard Toye, *The Churchill Myths* (Oxford: OUP, 2020).

49 For example, Archie Brown, *The Myth of the Strong Leader* (London: Vintage, 2015).

50 Ross McKibbin, *Classes and Cultures: England, 1918–1951* (Oxford: OUP, 1998), 534–6.

values. His Labour Party was economically radical but culturally conservative and unwilling to challenge those forces that ensured it was Churchill who would be regarded as Britain's leading historical figure. It was perhaps that mix of the radical and the traditional which helped Labour win power in 1945 and achieve so much; but it did not help Attlee leave a strong mark on the public memory.

The significance of the Attlee government within the Labour Party has undoubtedly grown in recent years. This is partly due to the passage of time promoting an idealization of that government, and of those who assumed a leading role within it. The 1940s remains a decade of unique achievement, one whose stature grows the longer Labour remains out of office. The combined effect of the 2008 financial crash, the impact of the ensuing austerity, Brexit and now the economic consequences of Covid-19 have also prompted even some Conservatives to embrace the idea of bigger government. Having been cast into the policymaking wilderness for four decades the kind of interventionist state associated with Attlee's administration is now taken more seriously.

Until the 2019 disaster, those Corbyn supporters who annexed Labour's 1945 moment to their cause also prospered – within the party at least. But the uses to which the left put the 'Spirit of '45' were glib and misleading. That Labour only needed the right leaders willing to revive that same (alleged) spirit and the party would be propelled into power as it was in 1945: for party members, this was an enthralling idea. But it reduced the politics of the 1940s to a matter of mere hope and exhortation, ignoring its complexity and contradictions, thereby suggesting that socialism in the second decade of the twenty-first century was ultimately just a question of will. No wonder the 2019 election result – which saw voters reject a Labour manifesto even more radical than the one presented in 1945 – came as such a shuddering shock.

Labour won in 1945 and achieved what it did in government due to more than the 'spirit' of a generation and the principles of its leaders. As historians almost without number have pointed out, Labour benefitted from the consequences of one of the twentieth century's great discontinuities: the Second World War.[51] The need to fight Hitler turned Britain almost upside down, requiring as it did the full mobilization of the country's resources. This meant the market simply had to give way to the state: even Churchill recognized that. Thereby the war legitimized government intervention in a way no political speech could. Previously impotent advocates of a greater peacetime role for the state, the Labour Party included, now found themselves in positions of influence. Many Britons also realized they

---

[51] It is, however, an idea most closely associated with the work of Arthur Marwick.

need no longer accept mass unemployment and poverty as inevitable. All this did not make a Labour victory inevitable. Nor did it mean the Attlee government would ineluctably be one of great achievement. Individuals and politics played their part in both and that required argument and compromise – the mixing of radical and conservative impulses – and the skilful manipulation of power.

The very complexity of '1945 and all that' is why historians still debate it – and why very different elements within the Labour Party have been able to claim it for themselves. There is something for its socialist, radical, liberal, moderate, progressive and traditional strands. That Labour managed to navigate that complexity should be celebrated by the party, although its leaders might ask why so few outside its ranks do so. To believe in *the* 'Spirit of '45' might also provide comfort in hard times and hope for the future. But it is a fake comfort and a bogus hope if it leads Labour members to pray for the revival of an imaginary pristine historical moment and so encourages them to denigrate the necessary compromises of their very messy present.

5

The fall and rise of Harold Wilson

Glen O'Hara

The afterlife of a political 'ghost'

Nearly sixty years on from his first election victory in 1964, Harold Wilson now seems like a more substantial figure than he once did, his period in office ripe for further revaluation. Although his years in power were marked by rising inflation and industrial strife, Wilson held the country together in an age of deepening economic and social policy dilemmas, managed the Labour Party as an instrument of government, and secured the UK's place in Europe. Above all, his governments passed legislation that still stands today as the foundation stones of a more civilized society: on crime and justice, race relations and equal pay. Yet, despite these achievements, Wilson has almost become the great unmentionable of Labour politics. Derided by left and right alike, depicted as a failure who never lived up to his early, era-defining promise, Wilson was written off as a prime minister unwilling or unable to make the hard choices required to shake Britain out of its collective apathy.[1] Most of all, he became most commonly understood as a tactical genius without a strategic endpoint in sight, a leader whose only and overriding goal was to hold the Labour Party together. As Andrew S. Crines and Kevin Hickson recently and rightly observed: 'this involved a fine balancing act, and would result in Wilson being regarded as a rather Machiavellian character'.[2] The idea of a lost opportunity, or raised hopes and dashed expectations, has sat alongside the idea of tactical successes that led nowhere. In some ways, it could hardly be otherwise: Wilson created an intoxicating vision, in his most famous 1963 Conference speech, of 'new industries, the revitalisation of declining

---

[1]   Lawrence Black, 'Revaluing Wilson', *Parliamentary History* 24, no. 3 (2005): 378–9.
[2]   Andrew Crines and Kevin Hickson, 'Introduction', in Crines and Hickson (eds), *Harold Wilson: The Unprincipled Prime Minister? Reappraising Harold Wilson* (London: Biteback, 2016), xxvi.

industries ... hope for the nation's youth' and 'the application of scientific planning to ... the war on world poverty'.[3]

A great deal of this impression arose from ideological hostility towards a leader without an absolutely secure camp in any part of the Labour coalition. Labour's left had once voted for him as their standard-bearer against the right's champion, Hugh Gaitskell, in 1960; they supported his election as party leader after Gaitskell's death in 1963. Wilson had, after all, resigned from Attlee's government alongside Aneurin Bevan in 1951 unable to accept even minimal charges within the National Health Service. But from the late 1960s onwards, the left fused their criticism of his compromises in power with their traditional suspicion of British state structures, especially the power of the Treasury. Michael Foot's belief was always that

> you had to have a more deliberate Keynesian plan for dealing with the blight of economic crisis, and we didn't have it. At the first signs of the economic threat Harold Wilson gave in ... The Treasury is the place we've got to get under control if a Labour government comes in. In that case the Treasury was allowed to get away with it.[4]

His nephew, the crusading journalist (and revolutionary socialist) Paul Foot, argued in his classic 1968 polemic *The Politics of Harold Wilson* that the prime minister's restrictive economic measures of July 1966 were a betrayal of his promises: 'now he was abandoning growth for stagnation, social justice for a strong pound and freely negotiated agreements for a wage freeze. Every aspect of his policy was now reversed – with hardly a word of intelligent analysis or justification.'[5]

For Labour's right, Wilsonian 'modernization' did not go anything like far enough, made too many compromises with underperforming industries and obstructive unions and failed to challenge many of the shibboleths of a Labour Party committed above all to defending the public sector. This analysis was taken up with gusto by future generations. As Tony Blair himself put it to the 2005 Labour Party conference:

> the seeds of 18 years of opposition were not sown in 1979, but in the 1960s when great challenges came upon us. And instead of understanding we were simply being tested by the forces of change, we lived out a sad episode ... we were not

---

[3] Labour Party, *Labour's Plan for Science* (London: Labour Party, 1963), 6.

[4] Austin Mitchell and David Wiener, *Last Time: Labour's Lessons from the Sixties* (London: Bellew, 1997), 195.

[5] Paul Foot, *The Politics of Harold Wilson* (Harmondsworth: Penguin, 1968), 181.

ready then to see change was coming, accept it and then shape it to progressive ends ... if we had been, how many fewer lives would have been destroyed?[6]

Blair's pollster and ally, Philip Gould, thought the Wilsonian moment 'a deceit, a compromise', which delayed hard decisions that had to be taken. For Gould, 'Wilson failed to modernize Labour, which put the genuine modernization of Britain beyond his reach. His failure to resolve the competing claims of left and right, and to move beyond both in a new modernizing solution, made civil war in the Labour Party inevitable'.[7]

Wilson's colleagues could be devastating about his personal qualities (or lack of them). When Hugh Gaitskell died in office as Labour's leader in 1963, his friends and political heirs accepted Wilson only with some despair: as Richard Crossman noted, they thought that 'if Harold Wilson was an odious and impossible man, George Brown was just impossible'.[8] The choice between George Brown from the right and Wilson from at least the nominal left was 'between a crook and a drunk', Anthony Crosland complained. Roy Jenkins, contacted by a journalist for a quote on his mentor's passing, was told that Wilson had given a statement 'without difficulty': 'you have to remember that he was very fond of Gaitskell', replied Jenkins bitterly.[9]

Denis Healey, Wilson's Defence Secretary in 1964–70 and later his Chancellor, was excoriating in his memoirs: 'his short-term opportunism, allied with a capacity for self-delusion which made Walter Mitty appear unimaginative, often plunged the government into chaos. Worse still, when things went wrong, he imagined everyone was conspiring against him'.[10] Healey never reconsidered this highly negative opinion: as he later told the journalist Andy Beckett, 'he was a terrible Prime Minister, actually'.[11] It was all the easier, then, for 'New' Labour to relegate him to the sidelines.

None of these prejudices were challenged by Wilson's final two years in power between 1974 and 1976, during which time he often gave the impression of being listless or bored. He was losing his edge, drinking too much, becoming

---

[6]   Glen O'Hara and Helen Parr, 'Conclusions: Harold Wilson's 1964–70 Governments and the Heritage of "New" Labour', in O'Hara and Parr (eds), *The Wilson Governments 1964-1970 Reconsidered* (Abingdon: Routledge, 2006), 171.

[7]   Philip Gould, *The Unfinished Revolution: How the Modernizers Saved the Labour Party* (London: Abacus, 1998), 35.

[8]   Peter Paterson, *Tired and Emotional: The Life of Lord George-Brown* (London: Chatto & Windus, 1993), 125.

[9]   Giles Radice, *Friends and Rivals: Crosland, Jenkins and Healey* (London: Abacus, 2003), 125, 122.

[10]   Denis Healey, *The Time of My Life* (Harmondsworth: Penguin, 1989), 331.

[11]   Andy Beckett, *When the Lights Went Out: What Really Happened to Britain in the Seventies* (London: Faber and Faber, 2010), 162.

forgetful – possibly a sign of the Alzheimer's that was eventually to reduce him to a peripheral figure.[12] In the end, with his memory mostly gone and his legacy not so much contested as erased, Wilson became what Steve Richards calls a 'ghostly figure': 'from being the most talked-about figure in British politics for more than a decade, Wilson was rarely referred to'.[13] Ben Pimlott's magisterial biography of Wilson, published in 1992, contained a final chapter simply entitled 'Ghost'.[14] When Wilson left Number 10 for the last time, his close adviser Bernard Donoughue regarded him with human sympathy: 'I felt sorry for him as I watched him go, in an affectionate and I hope in a completely unpatronising way, I don't know how he will cope in the real world … after a lifetime of political power and fantasy. He has too few genuine interests of his own, inside him, to keep him interested.'[15] The so-called 'Lavender List' of honours issued at Wilson's resignation – the name referred to the lavender notepaper Marcia Williams was supposed to have written it on – tarnished him with a faint whiff of self-interest, even corruption.[16]

In truth, it became harder and harder to govern during the 1960s and 1970s – as inflation rose under the shock of oil price rises, unemployment increased alongside it and industrial strife mounted in Britain's traditional manufacturing industries. Although there had never been a complete 'consensus' about how government should work after 1945, there had at least been some agreement about the broad aims of policy – especially in terms of keeping unemployment down. Now even that basic level of agreement frayed, as the conviction politics of Margaret Thatcher on the right, and Tony Benn on the left, strained some of the social contract Wilson aimed at – broadly technocratic in method, egalitarian in aim, but dependent on a level of co-operation across economy and society that was increasingly difficult to secure.[17]

But the passage of even more time allows us to see Wilson in a new light, shaping as he did a new and more progressive Britain – kinder, gentler, more

---

[12] Ibid., 164–5.

[13] Steve Richards, *The Prime Ministers: Reflections on Leadership from Wilson to May* (London: Atlantic Books, 2019), 31.

[14] Ben Pimlott, *Harold Wilson* (London: HarperCollins, 1993), 724.

[15] Donoughue diary, 5 April 1976: Bernard Donoughue, *Downing Street Diary: With Harold Wilson in No. 10* (London: Jonathan Cape, 2005), 721–2.

[16] Philip Ziegler, *Wilson: The Authorised Life* (London: HarperCollins, 1995), 494–8; Pimlott, *Wilson*, 685–90.

[17] The classic statement of how Britain was becoming harder to govern is Anthony King, 'Overload: Problems of Governing in the 1970s', *Political Studies* 23, nos 2–3 (1975): 284–96. On the 1970s overall, amongst recent works the reader can most usefully consult Lawrence Black, Hugh Pemberton and Pat Thane (eds), *Reassessing 1970s Britain* (Manchester: MUP, 2013).

outward-looking, more equal. In this the man matched the moment. As Donoughue has put it in the introduction to his diaries from the mid-1970s, Wilson himself was both 'an immensely professional politician' and 'a warm and remarkably tolerant human being'.[18] For Alan Johnson, Wilson was more broadly in fact a 'statesman and visionary', whose 'vision was of a society characterised by greater equality and moral decency where poverty had been eradicated and opportunity was available to all'.[19] As that vision has spluttered and faltered, so Wilson's own clarity has become increasingly evident.

Strange rejuvenation

From the early 1990s onwards, a strange recrudescence has lifted Wilson's reputation. Pimlott's sensitive and sympathetic treatment was one key development, emphasizing just how successful Wilson had been, both electorally and politically, and how barren the years since his resignation had been, but there were others.[20] The passage of time, and its lending of perspective, had begun to smooth over some of the bad impressions Wilson's many manoeuvres had created – because the point of his continual politicking came sharply into focus. The unemployment and social division of the Thatcher years had begun to burnish his reputation; divisions over Europe brought into focus his achievement of keeping the UK inside the European Community; the social reforms of his era came to look far-sighted; Labour's civil war and splits demonstrated that only a political virtuoso could hold the party together. Ross McKibbin's reassessment, in a famous article published in *The London Review of Books* in 1991, was particularly bracing, and bears repeating in full:

> The historical record suggests that, as against the post-1979 Conservative governments, Wilson and Callaghan glow with a particular lustre ... Both governments, particularly the 1964–70 government, deserve a much more positive evaluation than they have usually received. Indeed, apart from Attlee's, the 1964 government is probably the only post-war British government whose record we can read with some satisfaction. Whilst it would be too much to say that in 1970 the horizon was cloudless – amongst other things ... the relationship

[18] Donoghue, *Downing Street Diary*, 19.
[19] Alan Johnson, 'Harold Wilson: Statesman and Visionary', Speech at the University of Bradford, 3 November 2016, https://www.bradford.ac.uk/50/events/alan-johnson-transcript/ (accessed 17 December 2020).
[20] Pimlott, *Wilson*, 728.

of the trade unions to society and the Labour Party remained highly problematic – the sky was pretty blue. Unemployment and inflation were low, the balance of payments was in equilibrium, productivity growth was by British standards high.

'The Wilson and Callaghan governments', McKibbin continued, were more 'competent than their predecessors and successors … and … their policies, though … imperfect, were better suited to a sluggish, rather uncohesive society than the alternatives'.[21]

Wilson's political achievements, especially in the early 1960s, seem vastly impressive with the benefit of hindsight. Along with Blair, he is the only Labour leader to pull the party straight out of opposition and into government. He did this in an unpromising environment. The old nostrums of the left had not always worked as Labour had hoped: nationalized industries were unpopular, and full employment with stable prices were not always easy to maintain. On the other hand, the so-called social democratic revisionists who looked to Gaitskell for leadership had not always proved prescient either. The combination of endless growth and the concomitant decline of poverty they believed the managed economy heralded seemed far away by the early 1960s. Wilson's genius was to fuse together the two traditions, in a way that was appealing to the electorate. For Wilson, there had to be a directing and moral state; but it had to work in an up-to-date and efficient manner. Nationalization would focus on growing whole new sectors of the economy, and investing in new techniques, rather than simply taking over the decline of old staple industries: national planning would direct resources to the same sectors.[22]

By framing the whole arena of Britain's future as a combination of what was technically proficient as well as what was right, Wilson pulled away the Conservatives' mantle of economic competence. He also deprived the resurgent Liberals, already keen on planning and 'modernity', of one of their trump cards with younger, more educated but increasingly frustrated voters.[23] As *The Economist* noted in 1964, Labour's image of extremism and division had been replaced in the public mind by 'Mr Wilson's capture of the more positive image of the white laboratory coat'.[24] But there was more to Wilson than the obviously successful political leader, as this chapter will demonstrate.

[21] Ross McKibbin, 'Homage to Wilson and Callaghan', *London Review of Books* 13, no. 20 (1991): 3–5.

[22] Illaria Favretto, *The Long Search for a Third Way: The British Labour Party and the Italian Left since 1945* (Basingstoke: Palgrave Macmillan, 2003), 38–44, 61–71.

[23] Peter Sloman, *The Liberal Party and the Economy, 1929–1964* (Oxford: OUP, 2015), 224–6.

[24] Kevin Jefferys, *Retreat from New Jerusalem: British Politics, 1951–64* (Basingstoke: Palgrave Macmillan, 1997), 193.

Economic policy

The new Labour government's 'failure' to devalue the pound in October 1964 is usually cited as one of Wilson's main failures.[25] The struggle to maintain sterling's value involved continual fights with the financial markets speculating against sterling, at a time when currencies were pegged to the value of gold and the dollar in the so-called 'Bretton Woods system' created at the end of the Second World War. Even given those supposedly fixed exchange rates, regular rounds of bad news about the balance of Britain's trade exerted downwards pressure on sterling. Financial markets came to believe that Britain's currency might be devalued in the near future in order to boost exports, a perception only reinforced by Britain's much-discussed 'balance of payments' problem – a chronic deficit that plagued successive governments in the way that budget deficits moved to the centre of expert and public attention after the Global Financial Crisis of 2007–8. Every release of unfavourable data could therefore lead to runs on the pound.[26]

Trade deficits bringing sterling's gold peg into doubt forced the government into successive economic packages designed to restrain domestic demand (and thus discourage imports and raise exports) in July 1965 and July 1966.[27] In a system where the value of sterling could not float downwards to take the strain of Britain's apparently faltering productivity (and therefore sales abroad), domestic demand and public spending had to absorb the pressure instead. Wilson's vow to end 'stop-go' economic policies, in which every economic expansion led to financial crisis and then to another phase of restraint, sometimes came to seem like a hollow promise, however hard he pushed it.[28]

The original decision not to devalue sterling immediately, once Labour returned to office, was made for a series of reasons. Wilson and James Callaghan, as his Chancellor, feared for the forced savings of sterling holders with their money in London, since they were often developing countries inside the Commonwealth. Likely American dismay also weighed with them.

---

[25] See for example Peter Sinclair, 'The Economy – A Study in Failure', in David McKie and Chris Cook (eds), *The Decade of Disillusion: British Politics in the Sixties* (London: Macmillan, 1972), esp. 112–14.

[26] Jim Tomlinson discusses the debates and language surrounding the 'balance of payments problem' in Jim Tomlinson, *Managing the Economy, Managing the People: Narratives of Economic Life in Britain from Beveridge to Brexit* (Oxford: OUP, 2017), 215–23.

[27] Frank Blackaby, 'Narrative, 1960–74', in Frank Blackaby (ed.), *British Economic Policy 1960–74: Demand Management* (Cambridge: CUP, 1979), 33–9.

[28] Labour's (and Wilson's) opinion poll ratings were very low from the last quarter of 1967 to the late summer of 1969: see Pimlott, *Wilson*, 547.

But the overriding reason for their scepticism was that they did not think that devaluation would work without an industrial shake-out that they wanted to conduct in a 'planned' manner, and that insofar as it did would only change the situation through exactly that austerity they were seeking to avoid.[29] As Wilson had already told those economic advisers he was bringing into Downing Street, devaluation 'would water the weeds as well as the flowers'.[30]

Instead, 'socialist' measures were to perform the role that devaluation could not. This led Labour in power to bring in a temporary import surcharge, allow more export credits, to set up an Industrial Reorganisation Commission and provide for quick-acting capital grants rather than slower tax allowances for investment.[31] Such measures were designed to boost productivity, increase investment and therefore increase exports under a brief set of protective tariffs.[32] These direct interventions certainly might have made some difference in calmer times, and in 1966 they were allied to a new Selective Employment Tax (SET) that sought to subsidize manufacturers (and therefore exporters) at the expense of service industries. But as Edmund Dell, at the time a junior trade minister in Wilson's government, later put it: 'their effect was insufficient both in time and quality to rectify the fundamental disequilibrium'. These types of measure were not only bureaucratic and hard to operate, but they simply could not take effect on the time horizon sterling needed.[33] The attempt to avoid devaluation via 'direct measures' was perhaps unlikely to succeed from the start.

The aim of the November 1967 devaluation itself, when it was for the most part forced on Wilson, was also to avoid binding restrictions – not to embrace yet another period of 'stop-go' with nothing to show for it. Wilson evaded the concept of a strong tie between a pro-American foreign policy and currency support during the summer of 1966.[34] When the Americans floated the idea of a massive multilateral loan during a period of relative market calm in March 1967, Wilson again rejected this: it could come with the condition that Britain's armed forces stayed east of Suez, a risk too far for the country's room for manoeuvre and even sovereignty.[35] Meeting as part of their work in the Organisation for

---

[29] Kenneth Morgan, *Callaghan: A Life* (Oxford: OUP, 1997), 212–13.

[30] Ziegler, *Wilson*, 190.

[31] Glen O'Hara, '"Dynamic, Exciting, Thrilling Change": The Wilson Government's Economic Policies, 1964–70', in O'Hara and Parr (eds), *Wilson Governments*, 87.

[32] Richard Roberts, '"Unwept, Unhonoured and Unsung": Britain's Import Surcharge, 1964–1966, and Currency Crisis Management', *Financial History Review* 20, no. 2 (2013): 209–29.

[33] Edmund Dell, *The Chancellors: A History of the Chancellors of the Exchequer, 1945–90* (London: HarperCollins, 1996), 332.

[34] Jonathan Colman, *A 'Special Relationship'? Harold Wilson, Lyndon B. Johnson and Anglo-American Relations 'At the Summit', 1964–68* (Manchester: MUP, 2004), 84.

[35] John W. Young, *The Labour Governments 1964–1970, Vol. 2: International Policy* (Manchester: MUP, 2003), 48; Pimlott, *Wilson*, 475.

Economic Co-Operation and Development (OECD), the main capitalist economies made clear early in the week of devaluation itself that any large-scale international bailout would come only on very restrictive terms – including binding rules on credit control and growth.[36]

This Labour government's refusal to accept help with foreign policy conditions also had direct economic effects. When devaluation did require an international loan to fend off further speculation, Wilson and his ministers were able to avoid any obligatory terms being inserted into the Letter of Intent issued by the International Monetary Fund laying down the conditions for short-term help – something they might not have been able to achieve had they struggled on into 1968.[37] It was a sense of relief that detailed limits had not been imposed from outside, as much as the inevitable sense of release once a decision is finally made, that caused Wilson to speak optimistically in the Commons about the opportunity 'to break clear from the dilemma of more than a decade'.[38]

That feeling of release actually did further damage to Wilson's reputation. A deeply unwise prime ministerial broadcast, in which Wilson assured voters that 'the pound in their pocket' had not lost its value, did do a great deal of political damage – though the prime minister quickly adjusted his tone in later interviews. Lord Cromer, who as Governor of the Bank of England Wilson had fought over deflation or expansion on coming to power and who in November 1967 had recently ended his five-year Governorship, was given the chance to crow on television that the prime minister's statement was nonsense.[39] Cromer continued to get his revenge, both in the media and the House of Lords, over the following days: he portrayed devaluation as a 'default' that would harm Britain's overseas investment business for years to come. For Cromer, this was a moral as well as an economic reverse: 'how can those responsible for this default and those who condone a default command respect as worthy leaders of this nation?'[40]

Despite the diplomatic defeat, the incessant emphasis on a British economy 'in crisis' seems very overheated. It was government spending, not the private sector, that caused the so-called 'balance of payments' deficit throughout this entire period: the very reason why Wilson rejected 'American' diplomatic terms

[36] William Davis, *Three Years Hard Labour: The Road to Devaluation* (London: Andre Deutsch, 1968), 152; Wilson, *Labour Government*, 453.

[37] Glen O'Hara, *Governing Post-War Britain: The Paradoxes of Progress, 1951–1973* (Basingstoke: Palgrave Macmillan, 2012), 81.

[38] Davis, *Hard Labour*, 163.

[39] Ibid., 161–2.

[40] David Blaazer, '"Devalued and Dejected Britons": The Pound in Public Discourse in the Mid-1960s', *History Workshop Journal* 47 (1999): 136.

on loans to defend sterling. Defence spending, in particular, so unbalanced the external picture that it was this, not a rather nebulous crisis inside the British economy, that was the real weight Labour and the country were bearing. It would have had to rise, not fall, if the British fought in Vietnam alongside the Americans, or kept all their bases east of Suez.[41] The record here was again positive, but mixed. On returning to power in 1964, Labour decided to cap defence expenditure at current levels (in cash terms) by 1969–70. That implied savings of £360 million on planned programmes, and the government did indeed manage to stick to this target.[42] British military spending in the Persian Gulf and the Far East fell quickly, though it could not be cut back in Western Europe. In total, defence spending abroad and net of receipts did stay flat in nominal terms between 1964 and 1970.[43]

It is also important to see these problems as ministers did, given the statistics they had to work with at the time – all of which indicated they might avoid further crises. In the early summer of 1967 not just the Treasury, but also the National Institute of Economic and Social Research, thought that there would be a small basic surplus for the year as a whole.[44] The payments situation improved more than expected in 1966, in part because of the government's own restrictive measures in July. By the time of the 1967 Budget, a surplus was expected in both 1967 and 1968.[45] As Roger Middleton has shown, the economy was expanding much more rapidly than anyone understood at the time, and in both 1965 and 1966 balance of payments forecasts got much worse suddenly, frustrating the efforts of both ministers and officials to understand what was happening.[46] There was a systemic undercounting of exports that made the deficit look much worse than it really was.[47]

It was against this background of poor forecasting that Wilson's government made a series of errors that, looking back, made devaluation much more likely. SET could not take effect quickly during 1966 and was therefore ineffective as any restraint on demand.[48] Callaghan cut interest rates three times in the first

---

[41] J. H. B. Tew, 'Policies Aimed at Improving the Balance of Payments', in Blackaby, *Economic Policy*, table 7.1, 305.

[42] Young, *Labour Governments, Vol. 2*, 35.

[43] J. H. B. Tew, 'Balance of Payments', in Blackaby, *Economic Policy*, table 7.3, 321 and table 7.4, 323; C. D. Cohen, *British Economic Policy 1960–1969* (London: Butterworths, 1971), table 8.5, 197.

[44] Davis, *Hard Labour*, 141.

[45] Cohen, *Economic Policy*, table 2.3, 17, and 26–7.

[46] Roger Middleton, *Inside the Department of Economic Affairs: Samuel Brittan, the Diary of an 'Irregular', 1964–6* (Oxford: OUP, 2012), table 4, 203. table 2, 194–5.

[47] Glen O'Hara, 'Towards a New Bradshaw? Economic Statistics and the British State in the 1950s and 1960s', *The Economic History Review* 60, no. 1 (2007): 16–17.

[48] Dell, *Chancellors*, 334.

half of 1967; Hire Purchase restrictions were relaxed.[49] Ministers were also simply unlucky, though depending on never being unlucky may be thought unwise at the best of times. As Wilson later noted, the Six Day War of 1967 between Israel and her Arab neighbours, and the consequent closing of the Suez Canal, made a huge difference to Britain: before its outbreak, the overall balance of payments deficit had closed to 'only' £87 million. The crisis in the Middle East cost Britain about £200 million in lost trade over the whole year: it made a difficult situation much worse.[50] The most one can say about this is that Wilson's attempt at strategic reorientation had not been able to rectify Britain's financial position before a run of international crises – inevitable in any era – derailed the whole effort to hold sterling's value at the same time.

In Place of Strife

The other area in which the Wilson government has been found wanting is industrial relations, with a major White Paper on workplace reform – *In Place of Strife* – going down to ignominious defeat. The concept of establishing a new legal framework for employers and unions, in a country where the whole field had grown up piecemeal and on an ad hoc basis, was a powerful one. Here, too, the traditional narrative – of over-mighty unions resisting 'reform' – needs severe qualification. *Strife* would have made unions more powerful, not less. Collective bargaining was to be underpinned in law; compulsory recognition of trade unions was to be legally enforceable; workers would be reserved places in the boardroom.[51] The whole point of these measures was to re-centralize and rationalize power in the industrial relations system. For some years an increasingly powerful shop steward movement had been undermining the power of national unions, helping to make effective management more and more difficult.[52] *Strife* was an attempt to bring the trade unions within the law without the harsh, head-on attacks of the Thatcher years.

---

[49] Davis, *Hard Labour*, 143–4.

[50] Harold Wilson, *The Labour Government, 1964–1970: A Personal Record* (London: Weidenfeld and Nicolson, 1971), 400, 440.

[51] Steven Fielding, *The Labour Governments 1964–1970, Vol. 1: Labour and Cultural Change* (Manchester: MUP, 2003), 105.

[52] Andrew Thorpe, 'The Labour Party and the Trade Unions', in John McIlory, Nina Fishman and Alan Campbell (eds), *British Trade Unions and Industrial Politics, Vol. 2: The High Tide of Trade Unionism, 1964–79* (Aldershot: Ashgate, 1999), 136–7.

The emphasis on strikes was unfortunate, for although poor industrial relations surely did not help the British economy, its problems went deeper. The focus on relations between labour and management was overdone. Strike-prone factories such as Longbridge in Birmingham, owned by what became in this era British Leyland, in fact turned out successful models that dominated the home private purchase market until well into the 1970s. There is little evidence that Britain was particularly strike-prone in this period when compared to other developed nations, and most companies did not experience walkouts.[53] That focus was bound up with Wilson's view of what 'productivity' was in the first place, which he had imbibed during his time as a minister in Attlee's government: the question for him was one of *labour* productivity and the correct use of the workforce given full employment. That was the thrust of the 1965 National Plan's declared intention to root out 'under-employment' in the 'wrong' sectors and using the 'wrong' techniques; behind the Wilson government's Productivity Conferences of 1966–7, virtuous though many of their recommendations were; and the creation of a new Department of Employment and Productivity in 1968.[54]

The ideas in *Strife*, however, tested beyond limits what the Cabinet and the Parliamentary Labour Party would bear. Middle opinion, including within the Cabinet, was very sceptical that the relevant Secretary of State, of all people, should have the power to mandate ballots for strike action or impose a 'cooling-off period' of up to twenty-eight days. Many reasoned that it would be far better to let an independent body decide on such matters. The government's ideas also went far beyond what the Donovan Royal Commission on Trade Unions and Employers' Associations (1964–8) had recommended, partly designed as it was to outflank the Conservatives' attempts to reform industrial relations. Long-term policy formulation and short-term electoral calculation were both at fault here.[55] The whole plan had to be dropped, with only the consolation prize of reformed TUC processes in return – and a great deal of ill-will having been stirred up.[56] It was a rare Wilsonian misstep, though an entirely explicable one in the circumstances.

---

[53] Alan Booth, *The British Economy in the Twentieth Century* (Basingstoke: Palgrave Macmillan, 2001), 117, 148–9.

[54] Jim Tomlinson, *The Labour Governments 1964–1970, Vol. 3: Economic Policy* (Manchester: MUP, 2004), 179, 183.

[55] Peter Dorey, *Comrades in Conflict: Labour, the Trade Unions and 1969's 'In Place of Strife'* (Manchester: MUP, 2019), 76–7, 44, 46–7; Crossman diary, 18 June 1969: Anthony Howard, *The Crossman Diaries* (London: Mandarin, 1991), 628–30.

[56] Dorey, *Comrades in Conflict*, 178–3.

Progress to limits – but progress nonetheless

If hostility to Wilson himself often originated with prior ideological commitment on left and right, it was also an entirely unrealistic outlook, failing to grasp at the forces arrayed against 'Wilsonism'. His governments had to find a way between the international markets, the Parliamentary Labour Party and Labour's membership; between employers and trade unions; between declining Commonwealth trade, General de Gaulle and popular scepticism about the European Economic Community (EEC). At home, it wanted to build more New Towns, but found its way blocked by local authorities; to reorganize the NHS, but became enmeshed in fiendish difficulties of jurisdiction and authority; and to foster better race relations, faced by an increasingly poisonous debate about immigration.[57] As with the proposals contained in *Strife*, it is all very well setting out to settle these issues from above: but they needed careful fostering from below, and much more time, if they were to come to fruition.

Even so, Wilson's time in office involved a long list of enormous achievements, some of which were forgotten in the long years when his reputation was in the doldrums. Britain became a much more liberal, equal and tolerant place to live under his leadership, for instance. Although technically dependent on a series of free votes, capital punishment was brought to an end after direct assistance from Wilson as prime minister. Ministers were ordered to abstain if they objected; an initial attempt to filibuster the bill was headed off with the help of the Labour Whips.[58] The 1967 Sexual Offences Act meant that a 'homosexual act in private shall not be an offence', so long as only two men over twenty-one were involved.[59] Jenkins as Wilson's second Home Secretary secured crucial parliamentary time for the key backbench bill involved – despite, in this case, some ambivalence in both Wilson's and much of the PLP's minds.[60]

Labour passed the Equal Pay Act in 1970 – a measure which owed much to Castle's perseverance though the law would come into effect only in 1975, and still did not really grapple with the reasons for women's lack of access to training and promotion.[61] Wilson's 'University of the Air', the ambition of which was to

---

[57] Brian Lapping, *The Labour Government 1964–70* (Harmondsworth: Penguin, 1970), 12.

[58] Neville Twitchell, 'Abolition of the Death Penalty', in Peter Dorey (ed.), *The Labour Governments 1964–1970* (Abingdon: Routledge, 2006), 332–3.

[59] 'Sexual Offences Act 1967', https://www.legislation.gov.uk/ukpga/1967/60/pdfs/ukpga_19670060_en.pdf (accessed 11 August 2020).

[60] Peter Dorey, 'Homosexual Law Reform', in Dorey, *Labour Governments*, 347–54.

[61] Fielding, *Labour Governments, Vol. 1*, 131–2; 'Equal Pay Act, 1970', https://www.legislation.gov.uk/ukpga/1970/41/enacted (accessed 10 August 2020).

teach remotely and to widen access to top-quality courses, achieved more than its founder could have hoped for. The Open University has, to date, welcomed more than two million students: it is one of Europe's largest universities, with over 168,000 learners, a quarter of whom live in the UK's 25 per cent most deprived areas.[62] Questions connected to the quality of life, as well as its equality, were also attended to. The appointment of a minister for sport and the setting up of the Sports Council gave sport a huge boost, backed up by the contemporary burst of investment in public sector leisure infrastructure such as swimming pools and youth clubs. Central government funding for sports grew rapidly, though not to the extent Labour had promised it would.[63]

The welfare state also continued to develop and progress. Supplementary Benefits were introduced to replace the invasive and discretionary payment of the old National Assistance benefits, with an additional earnings-related element (though with a means test for sickness, unemployment and widows' benefits).[64] These new benefits rose by some way faster than post-tax wages during the later 1960s. Since these benefits were paid as of right, and integrated more surely into the welfare system as a whole (replacing for instance the unpopular 'two book' system, under which other claimants could see who was on National Assistance), these benefits' stigma declined and take-up increased.[65] As wages moved upwards, benefits increased even more quickly, and public services improved, many of Labour's ambitions for a fairer society were gradually achieved. For these reasons amongst others, the Gini coefficient that simply if crudely measures income inequality hovered around the same level through the later 1960s, and then fell towards all-time lows just as Wilson left office.[66]

The National Health Service was not only better funded: like the machinery of the central state and the welfare system, the aim here was to make the NHS more responsive, more accessible, more human. General Practice was in a state of crisis when Wilson brought Labour back to power in 1964. Family doctor numbers were declining; GPs were threatening to set up their own insurance

---

[62] Open University, 'Facts and Figures', http://www.open.ac.uk/about/main/strategy-and-policies/facts-and-figures (accessed 12 August 2020).

[63] Glen O'Hara, *The Politics of Water in Post-War Britain* (Basingstoke: Palgrave Macmillan, 2017), 155; Kevin Jefferys, 'Sport Policy: An Unheralded Success Story', in Crines and Hickson, *Reappraising*, 187–92.

[64] Derek Fraser, *The Evolution of the British Welfare State* (Basingstoke: Palgrave Macmillan, 3rd edn, 2003), 276.

[65] Michael Stewart, 'The Distribution of Income', in W. Beckerman (ed.), *The Labour Government's Economic Record 1964–1970* (London: Duckworth, 1972), tables 2.16–2.17, 100, and 98–101.

[66] IFS Briefing Note, 'No Growth in Household Incomes Last Year – For Only the Fourth Time in the Last 30 Years', 28 March 2019, https://www.ifs.org.uk/publications/14015 (accessed 11 August 2020).

system; a majority sent in undated resignations in a fevered bout of negotiations with the new health minister, Kenneth Robinson, and a handful actually did resign from the NHS. Eventually a large-scale package of support for group practices and help with staff and training averted the most serious threat to the NHS since its founding.[67] The building of Health Centres, which brought different practitioners together, and allowed for teamwork between different parts of the NHS, had fallen into abeyance during the 1950s: by 1958, only twenty-eight new centres had been approved in England and Wales. Labour under Wilson gave them another start, with 131 opened by 1970, and 153 more either approved or being built.[68] Indeed, the Wilson government's understanding of the key role GPs played in the Service amounted to a type of NHS refoundation: without this new package for local doctors, the NHS might have locked up completely.

Final stretch, 1974–6

Even Wilson's much-criticized premiership of the mid-1970s contained great successes. The government could hardly be blamed for the major part of the huge spike in inflation that occurred worldwide in the mid-1970s. The doubling of oil prices during the first OPEC shock of 1973, and its knock-on effect in commodity markets, was the main reason for that.[69] Agreement of a £6 pay norm with the unions, reached in late 1975, heralded a period of recovery and greater economic 'normality' than Britain had known for some years. That 'Stage One' of a new effort on income policy, to be followed by a relatively successful 4.5 per cent norm during the 'Stage Two' of 1976–8, did help to bring the situation under control.[70] Although public expenditure rose very quickly in 1974 and 1975, not only could this be explained yet again by poor data (in this case, a £5 billion Treasury underestimate of public borrowing) but by IMF and OECD advice to hold back from immediate deflationary measures.[71] From the publication of the

[67] Nicholas Timmins, *The Five Giants: A Biography of the Welfare State* (London: Fontana, 1996), 222–3.

[68] Glen O'Hara, *From Dreams to Disillusionment: Economic and Social Planning in 1960s Britain* (Basingstoke: Palgrave, 2007), 192.

[69] Richard Coopey and Nicholas Woodward, 'The British Economy in the 1970s: An Overview', in Coopey and Woodward (eds), *Britain in the 1970s: The Troubled Economy* (London: UCL Press, 1996), tables 1.4–1.5, 6–7.

[70] Kenneth Morgan, *Labour People: Leaders and Lieutenants, Hardie to Kinnock* (Oxford: OUP, 1987), 258; David Coates, *Labour in Power? A Study of the Labour Government, 1974–1979* (London: Longman, 1980), 64–7.

[71] Dilwyn Porter, 'Government and the Economy', in Coopey and Woodward, *Troubled Economy*, 44.

February 1976 White Paper on public expenditure, the huge and unsustainable boom inherited from the Conservatives was deliberately slowed.[72]

Above all, Wilson's final term saw him fight and win a referendum that cemented Britain's place in Europe. The prime minister himself did not particularly care for 'Europe', or its culture. He had little interest in what he regarded as the unrealistic aims or theology of Europe as a political project. But, in general, he thought first that Britain was better off in the Community than outside, and that secondly the British left was more likely to hold together if the country was a member. Roy Jenkins and the pro-Europeans, committed as they were, could never have achieved what Wilson did, and the prime minister resented having to make up for what he regarded as their self-indulgence: 'wading in shit … to allow others to indulge their conscience', as he called it.[73]

Wilson promised the left a referendum on the question to hold the party together, and then – when it came to renegotiating Britain's membership – showed a keen eye for what could realistically be won, and for what might be popular. Quite modest though not inconsequential concessions, some way from Britain's original objectives, were thus made to seem more important than they were.[74] The question of trade relations with Australia and New Zealand, he told officials, should be highlighted instead of the esoteric matter of the European budget. Wilson was also shrewd enough not to make the campaign about himself at all, staying above the fray for most of it, thus preventing the issue becoming a matter of his own leadership. His interventions in the referendum campaign itself came late and were sober, reasoned contributions, all the better to pose as the voice of reason in a heated, ideological contest. It would be possible to secure free trade via EFTA, he conceded, but Britain would then have to accept all the rules of a free market without any say in setting them at all – an argument that David Cameron failed to land in 2016.[75] The Yes vote he achieved – 67 per cent – was a personal triumph that few others could have achieved.[76]

---

[72] Coates, *Labour in Power?*, 37–8.

[73] Hugo Young, *This Blessed Plot: Britain and Europe from Churchill to Blair* (London: Macmillan, 1999), 274.

[74] Mathias Haeussler, *Helmut Schmidt and British-German Relations* (Cambridge: CUP, 2019), 80–5.

[75] Robert Saunders, *Yes to Europe! The 1975 Referendum and Seventies Britain* (Cambridge: CUP, 2019), 82, 91, 114–17; Richards, *Prime Ministers*, 39–40.

[76] David Butler and Uwe Kitzinger, *The 1975 Referendum* (London: Macmillan, 1976), 263.

A leader with many faces

As Labour struggled in the 1970s and the early 1980s, all those achievements seemed to wither. Wilson bore some responsibility for this, not just in trying to keep Labour together whatever happened, but in the speed, range and scope of the changes he had invoked. In many ways he had overpromised, with grand talk of one hundred days of action in the mould of President Kennedy – only to preside over a culture of backroom deals, manoeuvring, unattributable leaking and personal retribution.[77] Most leaders of the opposition do this, and so do incoming prime ministers. As Dell once put it, 'British governments have learned few lessons from the history of economic management … Political Parties continue to promise what they cannot deliver'.[78] But the intoxicating atmosphere of a rapidly changing Britain, in its fashionable mid-1960s mood, made the subsequent dawn of reality feel much harsher than it might have.

Wilson's blizzard of images and poses did not help. He was, in Kenneth Morgan's words, 'an enigma … there was Dunkirk Harold in Churchillian garb, white-coated Harold caught in the white heat of technological revolution, Walter Mitty Harold about to amaze the world with deeds that would be the terror of the earth, even World Cup Harold, appealing to the populist instinct for razzmatazz'.[79] One could add to this: statesman Harold flying to Washington to negotiate about Vietnam; joker Harold, taking on the hecklers; economist Harold happily picking through statistics with his advisers; ordinary Harold, walking on holiday in the Scilly Isles with Paddy, his Labrador dog.[80] In some ways, he was so successful in image-making that he made too many, deepening the sense that there was nothing real behind the façade.

Just as there were many Mr Wilsons, so there were two Harolds in private. Wilson was usually a good judge of personality, spotting for instance that the veteran left-winger Michael Foot was keen to play a constructive role in his government during the mid-1970s.[81] He was also notable for his sympathy and compassion, as his humanistic reforms and concern for ordinary voters demonstrated again and again. Benn, a bitter enemy in the 1970s, was later to praise him personally: 'he was a kind man and a man of imagination and … and although he's been very badly hammered and I criticised him and he criticised

---

[77] Morgan, *Labour People*, 256.
[78] Dell, *Chancellors*, 553.
[79] Morgan, *Labour People*, 259.
[80] Pimlott, *Wilson*, 468, 605.
[81] Richards, *Prime Ministers*, 43.

me ... I think I look back on my association with him with a great deal of – tenderness'.[82]

Britain, in the Wilsonian era, came to seem a lot like its leader: perhaps it had seen better days, and maybe its reputation had become a little shabby and dogeared around the edges. But it had also become a more human and more equal place to live and work, in which your birth and wealth had less and less effect on your later life. Most of all, despite devaluation and *Strife*, Britain's strategic reorientation from world power to European state had been achieved and safeguarded. Sterling's reserve role was dissolved. Britain's bases east of Suez were closed. Human capital was to replace military might. Defence spending fell in real terms by nearly 1 per cent a year between 1963 and 1964 and 1969 and 1970: education and health spending, in contrast, rose by 5.5 per cent and 5.1 per cent respectively: the share of Gross National Product taken up by those two latter services sprang upwards.[83] Education spending overtook that on defence for the first time in 1969.[84]

For these reasons, Wilson's transformation from 'crook' and 'ghost' to human leader, replete with narratives of defeat and victory, seems more than secure. Alan Johnson has summed up Wilson's novel understanding of what Labour could do with those much-derided shifts of image and tone. Whilst Wilson

> recognised Labour's enduring dilemma of how to speak persuasively for the poor, the secure worker and the socially mobile, he felt that if the Party could align itself with the public thirst for change and modernity it had a unique opportunity to become the natural party of government in the way that the Tories had been throughout most of their existence. Only then could it reshape public morality, rights at work, access to education and public services.[85]

Wilson, above all, had a real and intuitive feel for the future. That included his concept of the 'scientific revolution': new telecommunications, networking and computer technologies were indeed to change the world. But Wilson's surprising grasp of likely future trends also incorporated the need for Britain to find a strategic home inside 'Europe', cut her defence cloth to her means, link public

---

[82] Peter Hennessy, *Muddling Through: Power, Politics and the Quality of Government in Post-War Britain* (London: Indigo, 1997), 266.

[83] Tomlinson, *Labour Governments, Vol. 3*, table 9.1, 202; Stewart, 'Distribution of Income', in Beckerman, *Economic Record*, table 2.19, 105.

[84] O'Hara, 'Economic Policies', table 3, 90.

[85] Johnson, 'Harold Wilson: Statesman and Visionary'.

and government closer together, expand education and health care and refashion Labour's appeal to the emerging electorate of skilled workers and graduates: all fronts on which he made a great deal of progress.[86] These were formidable strategic achievements. It is long past time for Labour to take another long look at that list of the impossible turned into the possible.

---

[86] O'Hara and Parr, 'Introduction', in O'Hara and Parr, *Wilson Governments*, xii.

6

Crosland in the seventies: Revisionist social democracy in a cold climate

Patrick Diamond

Anthony Crosland is widely regarded as one of Labour's leading postwar intellectuals. His most celebrated work, *The Future of Socialism*, is interpreted as articulating socialism for a modern affluent society. This chapter will focus on Crosland's published work in the 1970s, particularly his treatise, *Socialism Now*. The chapter contends that Crosland's writings during that period are of particular importance, even if they have received less attention within the scholarly literature. They illuminate Crosland's attempt to comprehend the political and economic failures of the Wilson years. Moreover, these writings highlight the obstacles to achieving radical social reform in a Western industrialized society. *Socialism Now* points towards the economic and institutional crises of the 1970s, alongside the challenge of pursuing social democracy in a cold climate.

The chapter argues that by the mid-1970s, Crosland's influence was perceptibly waning. Polarization meant the ideological momentum increasingly lay with the Bennite left. The Labour right appeared exhausted, devoid of ideas and defeated politically. The landscape of UK politics was being redefined by the New Right and the upsurge of Scottish nationalism. The historical particularities of the period make it difficult to read-off lessons for the future. Nonetheless, what is of unquestionable relevance is Crosland's determination to maintain a radical cast of mind, undertake rigorous analysis drawing on social science and uphold the ethical tradition of conscience and reform.

The Future of Socialism and *Socialism Now*

Socialism Now (1974) was a consequential work, even if it never had the political impact of *The Future of Socialism*. *Socialism Now* was certainly not as intellectually audacious. *The Future of Socialism* was written in the aftermath of the Attlee government's defeat, launching a major attack on the shibboleths of state socialism. Although presented as a critique of Marxist theory and its application in the British context, Crosland's target was the knee-jerk desire to bring swathes of industry into public ownership. He insisted nationalization was not only unpopular with traditional working-class voters. It would not provide Labour with the distinctive ideological purpose it required, given the structural alterations underway in postwar Britain. The tactic of making commitments to nationalize 'the top 500' industries, a feature of Labour's 1955 election manifesto, bred alarm. Crosland stated that, 'the definition of capitalism in terms of ownership has wholly lost its significance and interest now that ownership is no longer the clue to the total picture of social relationships ... it would be more significant to define societies in terms of equality or class relationships'.[1]

More significantly, Crosland provided a trenchant critique of Fabianism. He famously wrote that, 'total abstinence and a good filing system are not now the right signposts to the socialist utopia: or at least, if they are, some of us will fall by the wayside'.[2] He was sceptical of the 'statist' instincts of the Webbs. He recorded in his diary:

> [The Webbs'] considerable indifference to all forms of art or culture, their lack of temptation towards any of the emotional or physical pleasures of life, the consequent priggish puritanism – all of this is v. unattractive & would, if universally influential, make the Socialist State into the dull functional nightmare which many fear.[3]

The sociologist Michael Young developed an authoritative critique of planning and state bureaucracy. Crosland similarly believed the material austerity of Fabian socialism risked placing Labour on the wrong side of the affluent society. *The Future of Socialism* went beyond economic strategy, urging cultural reforms to make Britain a more tolerant, cultured and civilized society, celebrating the emergence of mass consumption.[4] Whereas the early ethical socialism of William Morris and John Ruskin was instinctively romantic and backward-looking, Crosland sought to align social democracy with the forces of the future.[5]

---

[1] Anthony Crosland, *The Future of Socialism* (London: Jonathan Cape, 1956), 75.
[2] Ibid., 524.
[3] Cited in Susan Crosland, *Tony Crosland* (London: Jonathan Cape, 1982), 47.
[4] Giles Radice, *Friends and Rivals: Crosland, Jenkins and Healey* (London: Little Brown, 2002).
[5] On this point, I am grateful to Professor Michael Savage at the London School of Economics.

The Future of Socialism was an ebullient and intellectually fearless expression of confidence in that future society. Despite painful defeats in 1951 and 1955, Crosland believed history was moving in an irrefutably 'progressive' direction. He insisted the affluent society could be reshaped to realize social democratic aspirations. America and Sweden demonstrated that modern capitalism was no longer 'red in tooth and claw'. The separation of ownership from management weakened the influence of profit. Like Eduard Bernstein, Crosland insisted capitalism could be modified by the liberal democratic state. Managerial capitalism was compatible with Labour's belief in equality. Moreover, if the dividend from growth was split between personal consumption and public expenditure, Labour could continue the welfare state's postwar expansion. Crosland was writing against the backdrop of the Cold War and the imperative of defending liberal democracy, accommodating the working class within the established political order.

Crosland envisaged that Labour governments would entrench the vision of citizenship enunciated by the LSE sociologist T. H. Marshall. Civil and political rights would be augmented by inalienable social rights. Citizens would have access to collective goods irrespective of their market position, eroding class inequalities and decommodifying social relationships.[6] As liberties were entrenched by social reform, Labour promised both greater freedom from restraint, alongside greater freedom to realize the unique talents, creativity, capacities and potential of each citizen. The left would wholeheartedly embrace personal freedom.

By the 1970s, Crosland's faith in that vision was waning, given the travails of governing accompanied by the painful experience of election defeat. Yet whilst their tone may be pessimistic, Crosland's later writings are significant. In the 1950s, Crosland was writing as an academic economist and intellectual who served one full term as an MP, linked politically to the leader of the party, Hugh Gaitskell. By 1974, he was writing as a former cabinet minister with practical experience of British government. The dominant themes of *Socialism Now*, published eighteen years after *The Future*, are very different. They capture Crosland's response to the traumas and tribulations of the Wilson era. Many of the essays reflect Crosland's involvement in major government departments: education, local government, the environment and housing. In the light of that bruising experience, he was more sanguine about the constraints of initiating

6 See Ben Jackson, *Social Democracy* (Oxford: OUP, 2013).

social reform. After the crises of the 1960s, Crosland was compelled to confront what it meant to pursue social democracy in hard times.

From 1964 to 1970, Crosland served as a cabinet minister in three departments of state. His time in office was inevitably shaped by the distrustful relationship he 'enjoyed' with Harold Wilson, alongside growing rivalry with Roy Jenkins. Although he was, 'an extremely outspoken critic of Wilson', questioning the government's strategy of ruling out devaluation as 'the unmentionable', Crosland was quickly promoted.[7] Yet it was Jenkins who held the great offices of state as home secretary and chancellor of the exchequer. Both Crosland and Jenkins were Gaitskellites who had refused to support Wilson for the leadership in 1963, dismissing him as shallow and unprincipled. Yet Jenkins enjoyed a far closer relationship. They were compatible personalities, inspired by a shared fascination with railway timetables. Wilson thought Jenkins was an able minister, his natural successor. With Crosland, relations remained uneasy. Crosland confided after a lunch in 10 Downing Street: 'No one could say that Harold is the most elevated conversationalist. We don't all agree with Roy [Jenkins] that prime ministers should be elegant and erudite. But one did have to drag him back to serious conversation: he was constantly breaking off with a fresh anecdote. Really all he wants to do is chitter-chatter.'[8] Wilson found Crosland indecisive, recoiling at his intellectually superior Oxford common room manner. The most able economist in the government, Crosland was distraught at being passed over as chancellor. Inevitably, the experience soured his experience of the Wilson years, leaving him embittered and disillusioned.

The 1970 defeat then left an indelible stain. It was hardly Crosland's first experience of defeat. The squandering of Labour's majority was not unexpected. Whilst the polls narrowed in the preceding months pointing to a Wilson victory, Labour's position was precarious for much of the parliament. Real wages and living standards fell precipitously, whilst unemployment grew. Yet amongst ministers, there were hopes that Labour had established itself as the natural party of government. Wilson insisted he offered a technically competent administration augmented by the phalanx of economists and scientists brought into Whitehall as expert advisers. Moreover, it appeared that industrial peace rested on sustaining the tripartite relationship between the state, employers and the trade unions. It was claimed only Labour was capable of preserving industrial harmony. Edward Heath was not regarded as an electorally appealing leader of the Conservative

---

[7] Crosland, *Tony Crosland*, 126.
[8] Ibid., 184.

Party. The so-called 'Selsdon manifesto' (named after the hotel in Croydon where the discussions over it took place), was attacked by Wilson as a recipe for radical small state conservatism, a major assault on the living standards of workers. Labour still lost the election, suffering a heavy swing amongst the skilled and semi-skilled working class, leaving many members shellshocked. The considerable advantage gained by the party in 1966 evaporated. Crosland's writings constitute a sustained effort to understand the root causes of Labour's failure.

Naturally enough, Crosland stoutly defended the achievements of the post-1964 administrations. He noted that public spending grew significantly. The distribution of income was fairer. Education reforms were enacted including circular 10/65 promoting comprehensive schools, Education Priority Areas and the expansion of higher education following the Robbins report. There was progress in improving the quality of public housing. Regional policy advanced through development areas and investment grants. The libertarian reforms pioneered by Jenkins as home secretary led to an extension of personal liberty. Britain's national strategy became more credible following the decision to reduce military commitments east of Suez, alongside the proposal to join the European Economic Community (EEC). Crosland even grew to respect Wilson's prime ministerial skills: 'Harold is a bastard, but he's a genius. He's like Odysseus. Odysseus also was a bastard, but he managed to steer the ship between Scylla and Charybdis.'[9] Yet Crosland was the first to acknowledge that a pall of failure hung over the Wilson era. In 1966, it secured a majority of almost a hundred seats. Within four years, Labour was disastrously swept from office. The great hopes of a 'New Britain' were dashed.

Economic failure

Without question, Crosland believed the key difficulty of the Wilson governments lay in their mismanagement of the economy. Growth was 'sluggish' by international standards. Germany and France swept past Britain after the Second World War. The UK was in danger of being overtaken by Japan and Italy. Economic growth from 1964 to 1970 averaged 2.3 per cent per annum, compared to 3.8 per cent from 1958 to 1964. Like many social democrats who supported devaluation in 1964, Crosland believed growth had been sacrificed to the imperative of maintaining a strong pound. Wilson's experience as a Minister

---

[9] Ibid., 172.

during the 1949 crisis made him uncomfortable with devaluation. The danger, he believed, was that Labour would be labelled permanently as the party of devaluation, never acquiring a reputation for economic competence.

Between 1964 and 1967, Wilson sought to avoid devaluation, introducing import controls alongside the import surcharge. Yet the measures proved ineffective. The balance of payments crisis continued. As Crosland noted, the administration was excessively optimistic that planning and industrial intervention through the National Plan and the Department of Economic Affairs (DEA) would deliver results. Crosland accepted he had been wrong to take growth for granted. Since the late 1950s, governments had used stop/go policies and deflation to regulate the economic cycle, deliberately suppressing the growth rate.

The lower rate of growth consequently created acute political problems. Macroeconomic management was fraught. The Treasury simultaneously sought to pursue growth, full employment and public expenditure controls, whilst avoiding a balance of payments crisis. Not surprisingly, the strategy failed. Low growth was attributed by Crosland to two major factors. The first was low productivity. Labour's policies for science and technology proved 'no short-term panacea'. They lacked the instruments to modernize the British economy. The second weakness was the decision to pursue deflation. Labour governments needed to allow greater flexibility in the exchange rate, as part of a more effective solution to inflation, reducing the imperative for stop/go policies. That inevitably meant incomes policies. Yet the 'In Place of Strife' White Paper (1969) was defeated in Cabinet. Despite opposing the White Paper, Crosland believed Labour had to assert its credentials as 'a national party', rather than being constrained by historic ties to the trade unions.

As a result of declining growth, public expenditure was lower. It was difficult to meet social priorities, notably reducing poverty. There was greater antagonism with the trade unions over wage settlements. Taxes on the average worker rose. There was a squeeze on living standards. Personal consumption was declining rapidly. Crosland reflected: 'The popular mood is one of intense resentment of high taxation and of certain forms of public spending.'[10] After six years of Labour, Britain still exhibited 'persistent and glaring inequalities', alongside deeply entrenched class divisions amplified by the education system.[11] The difficulty was that after two decades of full employment and rising personal prosperity,

---

[10] Anthony Crosland, *Socialism Now and Other Essays* (London: Jonathan Cape, 1974), 74.

[11] Ibid., 23.

an increase in real wages (even if it could be achieved) was not sufficient to win the election.

The 1964–70 administrations failed to appreciate the obstacles to growth and social reform in British society. Crosland identified pervasive national traits. Britain was, 'a protestant country ... the first to embrace capitalism' and retained its tradition 'of free enterprise and Manchester Liberalism'. As a consequence, priority was accorded to 'private commercial enterprise' over long-term competitiveness. Society was insular, hierarchical and divided with a strong bias against welfare spending. Britain was pervaded by 'exceptionally low cultural expectations and an extraordinary passivity in the face of squalor'.[12] By 1970, Crosland was compelled to acknowledge that, 'to carry through a radical, egalitarian programme, involving a major redistribution of resources, is a formidable task'.[13]

Loss of working-class support

Another major cause of defeat was conflict between 'liberal progressivism' and 'Labourist-populism'. Crosland believed Labour lost office due to the discernible erosion of working-class support. Critics of Wilson's strategy, notably John Gyford and Stephen Haseler, the authors of the seminal Fabian pamphlet *Social Democracy: Beyond Revisionism*, claimed the major achievements of the 1964–70 administrations related to individual freedom – divorce, penal reform, abortion, outlawing racial discrimination.[14] They averred that economic and social equality was neglected. Gyford and Haseler highlighted:

> The sense of estrangement felt by many working-class voters towards a government whose policies sometimes seemed to bear little relation to the realities of the everyday life of ordinary people, and whose concern for permissive legislation, the arts, higher education, and technological efficiency could not mask its failure to deal adequately with housing, unemployment and the cost of living.[15]

Crosland accepted Labour's increasingly middle-class leadership meant the party risked losing focus on its traditional supporters. The danger was that, 'the

[12] Anthony Crosland, *The Conservative Enemy* (London: Jonathan Cape, 1960), 127.
[13] Crosland, *Socialism Now and Other Essays*, 87.
[14] John Gyford and Stephen Haseler, *Social Democracy: Beyond Revisionism* (London: Fabian Society, 1971).
[15] Ibid., 9.

temptation becomes even stronger to seek the esteem of the liberal audience of columnists and TV commentators, college graduates also, with essentially middle-class values, who since childhood, have seldom ventured out of the introverted world of central London into the rougher provincial world where most Labour voters live.'[16] Immigration was a particular fault-line, as Crosland (who prided himself on his understanding of his Grimsby constituents) noted:

> Large sections of our working-people have real grievances which they believe to be intensified by continued immigration. Where there is a desperate shortage of housing for young people, and jobs are scarce, and schools already under strain, the priority given to new immigrants inevitably causes dismay. And people of an older generation, who have spent their lives in a close-knit working-class community, inevitably feel bitter when they find the local pub or cinema or corner-shop taken over by a different community with an unfamiliar culture.[17]

Crosland was adamant that disquiet about immigration reflected pervasive insecurity and economic anxiety. If the leadership were perceived as indifferent to the adversities of life in working-class communities, an opening would be created for Powellite extremism. There was a swing against Labour amongst the semi-skilled and unskilled working class who felt 'a sense of estrangement' from the government. The defeat of Democratic candidate George McGovern in the 1972 US presidential election demonstrated, 'the appalling danger to a left-wing party of neglecting its traditional working-class supporters in the interests of a largely middle-class "new Politics" appeal'.[18] Crosland believed the Swedish social democrats were more effective in combining the focus on living standards and welfare with an appeal to personal liberty, underlining the importance of culture and quality of life.

False trails

Crosland was conscious that following Labour's defeat, new themes were emerging on the left following the growth of post-materialism. Elaborated by the American sociologist Seymour Martin Lipset, post-materialism inferred that affluence meant Western electorates were turning their attention to environmentalism, democracy, liberty and cultural self-fulfilment. Yet Crosland

---

[16] Crosland, *Socialism Now and Other Essays*, 100–101.
[17] Ibid., 106.
[18] Ibid., 104.

believed post-materialism was a political dead end. He was doubtful the majority were interested in influencing the democratic process. Most voters:

> Prefer to lead a full family life and cultivate their gardens. And a good thing too. For if we believe in socialism as a means of increasing personal freedom and the range of choice, we do not necessarily want a busy bustling society in which everyone is politically active, and fussing around in an interfering and responsible manner, and herding us all into participating groups. The threat to privacy and freedom would be intolerable.[19]

What voters wanted was not participation, but the right to be consulted on key decisions affecting their lives, accompanied by machinery to 'redress grievances' perpetrated by institutions – schools, the National Health Service (NHS), social housing, the planning system.[20] The problem was 'large local government units' failed to consult individuals and communities. Crosland was aware of the danger of imposing central government's will on localities, insisting, for example, that the existing structure of schooling must not be 'forcibly dismantled'.[21] As Secretary of State for Education, despite his wish to abolish grammar schools, Crosland was cautious about interfering in Local Education Authorities (LEAs). He believed reforms were more likely to 'stick' if they were achieved voluntarily rather than imposed through legislation.[22] 'Persuasion' was preferred to 'coercion'. The 1965 circular insisted educational provision should be determined by local areas. In his 1970 Local Government White Paper, Crosland advocated neighbourhood 'urban parish councils', weakening the bureaucratic centralism of town halls.

As a politician, Crosland was conscious of declining faith in government. Fault-lines were emerging, notably a surge in support for Celtic separatism, alongside the structural crisis of the British state, provoking a major realignment of the party system. Crosland reflected:

> It may be true that, as Robert Nisbet has recently written, 'we live in a kind of twilight age of government, one in which the loss of confidence in political institutions is matched by the erosion of traditional authority in kinship, locality, culture, language, school, and other elements of the social fabric'.[23]

[19] Ibid., 68.
[20] Ibid., 69.
[21] Crosland, *The Future of Socialism*, 198.
[22] Crosland, *Tony Crosland*.
[23] Crosland, *Social Democracy in Europe*, Fabian Tract 438 (London: The Fabian Society, 1975), 13.

It has been claimed Crosland failed to take civic participation seriously. Crosland was criticized by John Mackintosh and David Marquand for his apparent self-satisfaction about the status quo. He allegedly scorned political reform:

> [Crosland] does say in *Socialism Now* that he would be against constitutional and political reform that led to an artificially contrived idea of equality of participation because 'we don't want more and more people engaged and fussing about'. He had great scepticism about big claims for increased participation that many constitutional reformers wanted to lay claim to.[24]

Mackintosh claimed Crosland was not radical enough in rejecting bureaucratic statism and public ownership. The new generation believed personal liberty was as important as social and economic equality. Yet in a lecture given in the mid-1970s, Crosland warned:

> We must take seriously the fears about the growth of state power, especially given the *penchant* of some socialists for the continual spawning of giant new institutions under centralized control ... We should not be in the business of creating endless giant Leviathans managed by armies of bureaucrats; and we must therefore heed this warning ... The fact is that we want democratic control over all concentrations of power.[25]

In contradistinction to the Webbs, he insisted socialism meant equality, not 'spawning new pieces of state bureaucracy'.[26] Like his friend Michael Young, Crosland was aware of the postwar Keynesian welfare state's limitations. Moreover, he was sceptical of institutional reforms mandated by the central state in improving equality of opportunity. He told an interviewer in 1974: 'There has been a lot of American research which suggests that we were inclined 20 years ago to exaggerate the effect of education taken alone on people's life-chances'.[27] Of course, Crosland never lost faith in the capacities of the British state. He implored there was, 'no substitute for institutions, with their bureaucracy, rules, clerks and computers ... they are the only instruments of social reform'.[28] He deplored the idea the private sector should take over the public sector, or that public officials were self-interested bureaucrats who ought to be subject to political control. The threats facing the world – pollution, over-population and

---

[24] Interview with Lord Raymond Plant, House of Lords, 23 February 2015.

[25] Crosland, *Social Democracy in Europe*, 6.

[26] Crosland, *Socialism Now and Other Essays*, 44.

[27] Interview between Anthony Crosland and George Gale, London, BBC, 25 April 1974, Crosland archive 13/20 (326), LSE.

[28] Crosland, *Socialism Now and Other Essays*, 69.

nuclear proliferation – required 'an increasing degree of social and institutional control' through the democratic state.

Where next?

By 1975, Crosland concluded that British social democracy had lost its way. The imperative was to rediscover the left's egalitarian purpose. He argued revisionists should restate their fundamental commitment to equality – a position distinct from Roy Jenkins who insisted on a trade-off between liberty and equality. There was no need 'for revisionists to revise our definition of socialism', still, 'basically about equality'.[29] Whilst Wilson emphasized class conflict which centred on the division between meritocratic scientific professions and the exploitative capitalist elite, Crosland focused on the ideal of a classless society. He believed that a classless society would be achieved through the redistribution of income, overhauling the structure of industrial power, access to education and the dispersal of property rights. Crosland insisted 'greater clarity about egalitarian objectives' was necessary. It was plausible to increase public spending by raising the growth rate and reforming the tax system.

He grew exasperated with long-winded theoretical debates. The central question was how to address 'harsh, specific and unmerited inequalities' in the present day.[30] Crosland understood that social mobility was necessary, but not sufficient to achieve a more equal and just society.[31] He wrote:

> By equality we mean more than a meritocratic society of equal opportunities, in which the greatest rewards would go to those with the most fortunate genetic endowment and family background – what Rawls has subsequently called the 'democratic' as opposed to the 'liberal' conception.[32]

Crosland came to believe that the 'Keynes plus Beveridge' formula that had shaped the social democratic 'golden age' was plainly inadequate. Despite stagflation in the early 1970s, Crosland continued to endorse the main postulates of Keynesian political economy: budgetary policy was an important instrument of macroeconomic management; public debt was not inherently inflationary;

---

[29] Ibid., 15.
[30] Ibid., 17.
[31] David Lipsey, 'The meritocracy myth – whatever happened to the old dream of a classless society?', *The New Statesman*, 26 February 2015.
[32] Crosland, *Socialism Now and Other Essays*, 15.

wages and prices were sticky and did not find a self-correcting equilibrium; finally, state intervention could raise productivity and improve long-term economic performance. Nonetheless, Crosland admitted the Keynes/Beveridge framework had no obvious solution to relative decline since 1945, managing the shift in the UK's comparative advantage away from heavy industry towards manufacturing and services.

Moreover, the Keynes/Beveridge synthesis was oblivious to environmental concerns. A major debate emerged in the 1960s concerning the ecological threat, focusing on the trade-off between economic growth and environmental sustainability. Crosland maintained it was vital to restrict the rights of private individuals. There were costs to economic growth: higher production led to more pollution; the demand for space meant encroachment on the countryside; urban clearance imperilled historical buildings and heritage.[33] He was concerned about improved planning of urban centres, acknowledging that many housing estates failed to provide privacy, amenity or a sense of community. Yet he opposed the environmentalist 'anti-growth lobby ... indifferent to the needs of ordinary people', reiterating that:

> My working-class constituents have their own version of the environment, which is equally valid and which calls for economic growth. They want lower housing densities and better schools and hospitals; they want washing machines and refrigerators to relieve domestic drudgery; they want cars, and the freedom they give on weekends and holidays; and they want package tour holidays to Majorca ... why should they too not enjoy the sun?[34]

Instead, advances in technology and social planning would permit solutions to environmental degradation, lead to cleaner rivers and better waste disposal. Crosland insisted static national income would hinder environmental progress. Growth was necessary to enhance human welfare and increase public expenditure: 'an allocation of resources which is not determined by market forces but our social priorities'.[35] Crosland maintained that 'the case for growth is unshaken'.

Socialism Now rejected the abandonment 'of the revisionist analysis of socialism in favour of a refurbished Marxism'. Still, 'a move to the Left was needed [Crosland believed] ... in the sense of a sharper delineation of fundamental objectives, a greater clarity about egalitarian priorities and a stronger determination to achieve them'.[36] Crosland was unquestionably a

---

[33] Ibid., 76.
[34] Ibid., 44.
[35] Ibid., 77.
[36] Ibid.

subtle and advanced thinker. He recognized Britain had not swung ineluctably between collectivism and individualism after the Second World War. Society was shaped by cross-currents of popular individualism combined with demands for collective institutions.[37] Moreover, he understood individualism was not only concerned with material greed or self-interest. It entailed self-actualization, freedom and personal autonomy, liberating individuals from moral norms and strictures that predominated in mid-twentieth-century Britain. Crosland recognized: 'The 1970s was a key moment in the spread of a popular, aspirational form of individualism in post-war Britain', building on the libertarian reforms of the Wilson era.[38]

The fundamental difficulty, as Crosland acknowledged, was that whilst it proved relatively straightforward for the governments of the 1960s to advance 'negative' liberty, freedom from restraint, advancing positive liberty, the freedom through which the capacities of each citizen would be realized, proved far harder. That weakness related to factors acknowledged in Crosland's writings, particularly the reduced rate of growth and the consequent squeeze on public expenditure.

Yet there were bigger questions Crosland was only beginning to confront when Labour returned to government, somewhat unexpectedly, in 1974. Fabian social democracy invested enormous faith in the power of institutions to bring about egalitarian objectives. Amongst the most important was the commitment to comprehensive education, and its ability 'to extend the rights of citizenship' creating a 'platonic meritocracy' in Britain.[39] More could be achieved, Crosland thought, if Labour governments, '(1) choose & announce [a] limited number of priorities and (2) create [a] sense that [we] still have [a] vision despite constraints – [we] haven't given up long-term goals'.[40] Yet intervening decades had proved that tackling Britain's deep-seated social and educational inequalities was a far more difficult task.

The limitations of Crosland's analysis

Whilst this chapter avers Crosland's writings of the early 1970s ought to be revisited, their limitations must clearly be acknowledged.

---

[37] See Jon Lawrence, *Me, Me, Me: The Search for Community in Post-War England* (Oxford: OUP, 2019).

[38] Emily Robinson et al., 'Telling stories about post-war Britain: popular individualism and the "crisis" of the 1970s', *Twentieth Century British History* 28, no. 2 (2017): 268–304.

[39] Crosland, *Socialism Now and Other Essays*, 202.

[40] Crosland, *Tony Crosland*, 306.

The challenge of the New Right

In the circumstances, Crosland was complacent about the New Right's challenge, which he saw as intellectual 'froth'. He underestimated market liberalism's capacity to delegitimize the pursuit of equality, rolling back the postwar settlement. In an interview with the *Financial Times* commentator, Samuel Brittan, Crosland dismissed the views of New Right thinkers as insignificant. Their growing prominence, he believed, 'didn't presage some fundamental shift in how British intellectuals thought about economic policy and the role of the state'.[41] Yet Crosland was proved wrong. Raymond Plant attests Crosland was too dismissive of his adversaries. He refused to take Friedrich Hayek seriously. Crosland wrote: 'No one of any standing now believes the once popular Hayek thesis that any interference with the market mechanism must start us down the slippery slope to totalitarianism.'[42] That insouciance was not shared by other revisionists, notably Evan Durbin and Hugh Gaitskell. They took Hayek's critique of state control more seriously.

As the counter-revolution against collectivism gained momentum, Croslandite revisionism offered a weak defence. The revisionist case had little coherent philosophical or moral underpinning.[43] Crosland believed the Attlee government advanced Britain irreversibly towards equality, eroding class-based disadvantage. The system of managed capitalism blurred the distinction between the public and private sectors.[44] The advance was not merely a consequence of social reform. Structural change and 'post-capitalist' society redefined the ideological consensus. In the post-1945 era, Crosland wrote: 'Ostentation is becoming vulgar; rich men tend to disclaim their wealth; and a general modesty in consumption becomes the fashion. This naturally reinforces the trend towards equality in outward style of life.'[45] The scale of inequality in the rich market democracies since the 1970s indicates Crosland was unduly optimistic.

The problem was that market liberal ideology appeared better equipped to explain alterations underway since the early 1960s. In the economy, industrial production as a share of employment was in rapid decline. The service sector was expanding dramatically, alongside burgeoning affluence and mass education.

---

[41] Interview with Lord Raymond Plant, House of Lords, 23 February 2015.

[42] Crosland, *The Future of Socialism*, 343.

[43] Raymond Plant, 'Democratic Socialism and Equality', in Anthony Crosland, David Lipsey and R. L. Leonard (eds), *The Socialist Agenda: Crosland's Legacy* (London: Jonathan Cape, 1981).

[44] Steven Fielding, *The Labour Governments 1964–70: Labour and Cultural Change* (Manchester: MUP, 2003).

[45] Crosland, *The Future of Socialism*, 214.

Society was reshaped by the emphasis on freedom and liberalization, reinforcing both the rise of consumerism and reaction against established moral norms.[46] There was the growing mood of rebelliousness and self-reliance enshrined in new social movements, particularly feminism and gay liberation. Crosland did not foresee the challenge to social democracy these developments posed.

Moreover, Crosland remained contemptuous of the left's intellectual critique. He thought Tony Benn (to whom he had been tutor in economics at Oxford) was a crank. He regarded the premise of the Alternative Economic Strategy (AES), of a fundamental shift in capitalist power to global corporations, as fundamentally misleading.[47] The capitalist class was becoming weaker, whilst the rate of profitability was falling. He remained sceptical about global capital's constraining power. Stuart Holland's analysis was the forerunner of contemporary debates about globalization. In one sense, Crosland's views were prescient, foreseeing the tendency to exaggerate globalization's impact on state capacity. Yet he was too dismissive of Holland's arguments. Social democracy was compelled to confront the spectre of worldwide 'turbo-capitalism', orientated to finance and increasingly internationalized – evidenced by the growth of offshore financial centres, tax competition and downward pressure on tax in the global market for 'talent'. These forces created a markedly less propitious climate for egalitarian policies after 1980.

Means and ends

In *Socialism Now*, Crosland made the case for an egalitarian strategy. Yet he struggled to identify reform instruments to remedy the deficiencies of the Wilson governments in 1960s, and to spell out how equality should be achieved given low growth. Whilst his argument rested on expansion of the economy, Crosland had relatively little to say about indicative planning or measures to boost productivity. He shifted his position on public ownership, admitting the nationalized industries had improved performance. Crosland endorsed 'competitive public enterprises' alongside a state investment trust – points of agreement with Holland.[48] However, traditional Labour voters were becoming suspicious of state control.

Crosland admitted British society was more 'slow-moving, rigid and class-ridden' than he originally envisaged and, 'much harder to change than was supposed'.[49] He accepted that revisionists in the 1950s proposed ambitious

---

[46] Jackson, *Social Democracy*.
[47] Crosland, *Socialism Now*, 33.
[48] Ibid., 58.
[49] Ibid., 44.

programmes, but gravely underestimated the difficulty of achieving them in the British context. Crosland was forced to confront Max Weber's exhortation that, 'Politics is a strong and slow boring of hard boards … Even those who are neither leaders nor heroes must arm themselves with that resolve of heart which can brave even the failing of all hopes.'[50]

Intellectual paralysis

By the mid-1970s, Crosland had less time to think. He told the Labour MP Giles Radice that he was 'too bloody busy' to reappraise revisionism. By the late 1970s, the revisionist project was faltering under sustained assault from the Bennite left. The right was fracturing following the split in the PLP over Europe, affirmed by the Social Democratic Party's (SDP) subsequent breakaway in 1981. Social democracy had little sense of direction. It had lost its radical edge. Crosland by the time of his death was a 'party man', cultivating leadership ambitions. He was close to the prime minister, Jim Callaghan, consequently more reluctant to rock the boat within the labour movement. There was less of Bernstein's revisionist iconoclasm. Nor was there any successor generation of 'Croslandites'. Figures who once extolled revisionist ideas, including David Marquand, Shirley Williams and Bill Rodgers, eventually defected to the SDP. Many found Crosland arrogant and aloof, unwilling to cultivate the next generation. He 'gave them little encouragement in their own efforts to think out new strategies.'[51] Rodgers recounts that social democrats shifted their allegiance to Roy Jenkins: 'Tony was our hero, but stage by stage we transferred our loyalty, support and affections [to Roy Jenkins], because Tony had no loyalty to his own friends.'[52]

Another controversy was council house sales. The former head of the Downing Street Policy Unit, Bernard Donoughue, complained that Crosland 'didn't have a sense of what ordinary Labour voters wanted' and was influenced by party views in local government, recalling that 'Crosland and his advisers

[50] Max Weber, 'Politik als Beruf', lecture delivered before the Freistudentischen Bund of the University of Munich (S. H. trans.), in *Gesammelte politische Schriften* (Bonn: Utb Gmbh, 1988), 560.

[51] Kevin Jeffreys, 'The Old Right', in Raymond Plant, Matt Beech and Kevin Hickson (eds), *The Struggle for Labour's Soul: Understanding Labour's Political Thought Since 1945* (London: Routledge, 2004), 78; Interview with Giles Radice, House of Lords, 16 December 2014.

[52] Interview with William Rodgers, 2 March 2015.

(although not most of the regular officials) were disappointing in their reactions' to Number 10's proposals.[53] Contrary to received wisdom, Crosland was not opposed to selling local authority properties. His stipulation was that housing stock must be replenished, using revenue from sales. The Thatcher governments prevented councils from reinvesting, the root cause of the contemporary crisis in housing provision.[54] Crosland accepted home ownership 'need not offend socialist principles'.[55] He went further in *The Conservative Enemy*, insisting, 'If property is well distributed, a property-owning democracy is a socialist rather than a conservative ideal.'[56] Crosland was influenced by the economist James Meade, who insisted social democracy's aim was 'to equalise the distribution of private property'.[57]

Radice believes Crosland's formula for ideological revitalization in *Socialism Now* was inadequate. Crosland struggled to explain why the middle classes should support egalitarian policies given absolute poverty was apparently falling. Crosland declared that to advance egalitarianism, 'we shall require higher taxation of the whole of the better-off section of the community'.[58] Yet he never actually specified who the better-off were. Crosland failed to anticipate the 'tax revolt' contributing to Labour's defeat in 1979 and the Thatcherite insurgency.

To give credence to his ideas, Crosland turned to the writings of the political theorist John Rawls. In *A Theory of Justice* (1971), Rawls emphasized the importance of 'the difference principle': that inequalities were only legitimate where they aided the least advantaged. This position chimed with Crosland's egalitarian outlook. Yet Rawls' influence on public policy in the advanced democracies proved less enduring. He failed to anticipate the rise of market individualism that rendered legitimate many inequalities scarcely to the benefit of the less advantaged. Liberal democracies came to resemble 'pure meritocracies' where talent was rewarded according to market incentives. The expansion of the global market for talent in financial services, for example, justified the explosive growth of rewards. As Raymond Plant noted, once the counter-reaction against collectivism gained momentum, it was apparent Croslandite egalitarianism offered weak resistance.

---

[53] Interview with Bernard Donoughue, 26 February 2015; Bernard Donoughue, *Prime Minister: The Conduct of Policy under Harold Wilson & James Callaghan* (London: Jonathan Cape, 1987), 108.

[54] Interview with David Lipsey, House of Lords, March 2015.

[55] Cited in David Reisman, *Anthony Crosland and the Mixed Economy* (London: Palgrave Macmillan, 1997), 96.

[56] Crosland, *The Conservative Enemy*, 39.

[57] James Meade, *Efficiency, Equality, and the Ownership of Property* (London: Routledge, 1964).

[58] Crosland, *Socialism Now and Other Essays*, 55.

Crosland's relevance today

The historian Ben Pimlott remarked that Crosland was one of few figures from the postwar era that contemporary Labour politicians were not embarrassed to be associated with. What Crosland bequeathed was a distinctive and persuasive conception of social justice that excited the liberal progressive intelligentsia without alienating ordinary voters. Mark Wickham-Jones speculated that Crosland's work was taken seriously since he reconnected 'New' Labour with its forgotten past, allowing the modernized party to feel less insecure. He also believed that Crosland's analysis betrayed the insular character of British social democracy, offering merely a vision of 'revisionism in one country'. Despite that, Crosland is still celebrated because he insisted that Labour had to do more than act as a responsible governing party. It must offer an uplifting vision of the just society. Moreover, his egalitarian ideas resonated with activists and the intelligentsia, concerned, as they were, to work through the practical implications for public policy.

Crosland's contribution as Labour's intellectual par excellence has almost inevitably been romanticized. His work cannot possibly serve as an oracle or guiding-post to the future. Nevertheless, his radical thrust is too easily dismissed. In his memoir, *A Journey*, Tony Blair states that *The Future of Socialism* was helpful in the 1980s, given the need to embrace the mixed economy and private sector, but had become largely irrelevant in the twenty-first century. Blair's view is surely mistaken. Crosland still offers important insights, understanding the dilemmas of achieving social democracy in a liberal society. He was adamant that social democrats must maintain a radical cast of mind, upholding the tradition of conscience and reform. Crosland believed they must employ rigorous analysis drawing on the eclectic disciplines of the social sciences.

Rigorous analysis

The building blocks of Crosland's writing were analytical precision and intellectual meticulousness. He used all the available tools of social science, notably sociology, a discipline still unfashionable in the late 1950s, alongside economics, political theory, history and organizational psychology. As secretary of state for education, Crosland appointed Michael Young as chair of the newly established Social Science Research Council.[59] Young expanded the discipline in the UK, challenging the dominance of economics in postwar public policy. Crosland agreed with the Polish philosopher Leszek Kolakowski that, 'the social democratic idea … requires, in addition to a number of basic values, hard knowledge and rational calculation'.[60] Crosland was part of the generation of Oxbridge educated social scientists who placed their expertise at the service of the state in the decades after the Second World War.

The record of these intellectuals was by no means faultless. For all their scholarly brilliance, the postwar socialist economists did not prevent the British economy from prematurely derailing successive Labour governments. What is more, they were invariably attached to a mechanical, reductionist and fundamentally elitist conception of society that exaggerated what could be achieved by formal legislative action (as Crosland subsequently acknowledged).

All that said, whilst Crosland remained a committed social scientist and economist, he believed firmly in ethical values. He did not accept all that mattered in political life was 'what works', an arid empiricism. The values of egalitarianism and social justice, Crosland believed, were timeless. The task for each generation was to determine the most effective means to achieve social democratic reform through public policy.

A radical cast of mind

Throughout his career, Crosland maintained an egalitarian impulse, the fundamental belief in a classless society. What mattered was the quality of social relationships in a dynamic and open community. Vast economic inequalities, he wrote, erected barriers between communities and classes that inhibited the full development of the individual. Crosland's concerns nearly fifty years ago still resonate amongst social democrats today. The Covid-19 pandemic accelerated the growth of economic and health inequalities around the world. The public health crisis merely exacerbated the pre-existing drivers of inequality. Even

---

[59] Lise Butler, *Michael Young, Social Science and the British Left 1945–70* (Oxford: OUP, 2020).

[60] Leszek Kolakowski, *Main Currents of Marxism: Its Rise, Growth and Dissolution* (New York: OUP, 1979).

before the pandemic, anger and despair were growing within advanced industrialized democracies. Relative decline, the loss of industrial jobs and the manifest unfairness of the established economic system were eroding faith in liberal democracy.[61] The work of Anne Case and Angus Deaton revealed how stark inequalities lead to ill-health and premature 'deaths of despair' in post-industrial communities. There was little effort to advance the 'economics of belonging'. The driving force of discontent was not only globalization but also technologies that eroded industrial employment, damaging 'left behind places'.[62] For the last thirty years, growth was increasingly focused on cities, leading to deep and entrenched spatial inequalities.[63]

Unquestionably, the pandemic deepened those long-term forces. Firstly, the pandemic led to prolonged shutdown of the economy, which disproportionately damaged younger generations. It then hit working-age women who, as a group, were more likely to be employed in the low-waged service sector, facing rising childcare demands. Thirdly, Covid-19 deepened inequalities, as those with capital had buffers to withstand economic insecurity. Fourthly, in the advanced economies, states were compelled to spend vastly more. Yet support focused on sectors such as finance, providing freely available loans for incumbent businesses by ramping up quantitative easing. The question remained: who pays for the pandemic and who benefits most from government action?

Crosland was an advocate of wealth taxes and capital levies, acknowledging inequality of wealth was as important as income inequality. Wealth taxation should now be back on the political agenda. Crosland argued forcefully for education reform, paying attention to the future of independent (public) schools. He recognized the divide between independent and state schools was a primary cause of Britain's entrenched divisions. Despite dramatic improvements in state education, those concerns remain. More reforms are necessary. Public schools should be fully integrated into the state sector whilst their operational independence is protected. Those remaining in the private sector should no longer be treated as charities. Tax relief should be withdrawn, whilst Value-Added Tax (VAT) is levied on private school fees. The state system must be further improved through a decisive advance in early years' provision, integral to a genuine 'cradle to grave' system. The provision of higher education should be revolutionized through innovation, opening up access to non-traditional groups.

[61] Mark Blyth and Eric Lonergan, *Angrynomics* (New York: Agenda Books, 2020).
[62] Martin Sandbu, *The Economics of Belonging* (Princeton: PUP, 2020).
[63] Paul Collier, *The Future of Capitalism: Facing the New Anxieties* (London: Penguin, 2018).

Meanwhile, as Crosland acknowledged, social democracy must address culture and quality of life, not only wages and living standards. Fabianism retains deep roots on the left. The danger is social democracy is perceived as bureaucratic and joyless. The Conservative Party captured the mantle of 'freedom for the individual'. Voters often felt 'the Labour party would put you in a group'.[64] The conscience and reform tradition recognizes that the means to freely pursue the good life should be available to all citizens.

Conclusion: social democracy in the new hard times

The Future of Socialism was Crosland's most celebrated treatise. Yet his later works capture Labour's pre-eminent postwar intellectual wrestling with questions of timeless importance: how can social democracy be fulfilled in a cold climate for the left? Crosland was writing as a former minister, reflecting on the practical impediments facing Labour governments. His admirers were unquestionably frustrated. Radice wrote after the publication of *Socialism Now*: 'There was a strong case for a Future of Socialism Mark II but as he admits himself, Mr Crosland has not written it.'[65] Nonetheless, Crosland's later works remain of continuing value, less for their theoretical lucidity than their subtle consideration of how social democratic priorities should be achieved in a mature liberal democracy.

[64] Cited in Robinson et al., 'Telling stories about post-war Britain', 281.
[65] Giles Radice, *Friends and Rivals: Crosland, Jenkins and Healey* (London: Little Brown, 2002), 224.

Part Three

7

Municipal socialism and municipal feminism: Women and local Labour politics from the 1900s to the 1980s

Krista Cowman

Introduction

Since its earliest days, the role of women in the Labour Party has been a matter of discussion. In August 1895, when the *Liverpool Labour Chronicle* welcomed the popular socialist propagandist Caroline Martyn to Liverpool, John Edwards, president of the local Fabians, posed an interesting question: 'When the story of the progress of Socialism in England comes to be written, I wonder what the historian will say about the little band of women who have done so much to inspire the movement ... '[1]

Edwards named Martyn, Enid Stacy, Margaret McMillan and Katharine St John Conway as key socialist pioneers. Historians have expanded the list, arguing that concentrating on the 'Famous Four' underplayed women's wider work.[2] The ILP (Independent Labour Party), Fabian and socialist women were visibly active in their communities, laying the ground for the formation of the LRC (Labour Representation Committee) in 1900. This, Enid Stacy explained, was because the 'objects of the ILP are calculated to especially enlist the sympathy and support of women. The party makes no distinction between men and women, all are equally eligible for membership and office.'[3]

---

[1] John Edwards, 'Caroline E. D. Martyn', *Liverpool Labour Chronicle*, August 1895, 1.

[2] June Hannam, '"In the Comradeship of the Sexes Lies the Hope of Progress and Social Regeneration"': Women in the West Riding ILP', in Jane Rendall (ed.), *Equal or Different? Women's Politics, 1800–1914* (Oxford: Blackwell, 1895), 214–38, 215. For expansion, see for example Krista Cowman, '"Giving them something to do": How the early ILP appealed to women', in M. Walsh (ed.), *Working Out Gender* (Aldershot: Ashgate, 1999), 118–34. June Hannam and Karen Hunt, *Socialist Women* (London: Routledge, 2012).

[3] Enid Stacy, 'Women's Work and the ILP', *The Labour Annual*, 1895, 118.

Such political equality was unusual; both the Liberal and Conservative parties only recognized auxiliary women members before the First World War. When the LRC became the Labour Party in 1906, its affiliated membership system retained the principle of sexual equality. Many women affiliated via the ILP and, whilst the preponderance of trades unions amongst Labour's affiliates mitigated against women's affiliation given the weak state of their unionization, the foundation of the Women's Labour League in 1906 and of local Women's Sections in 1918 offered alternative ways to participate.[4] Women made up at least half of party membership in the interwar years – as many as 300,000 – and between 41–43 per cent up to the 1970s.[5]

These numbers mask a complicated picture of women's experience of Labour politics. Studies of party women, particularly in Labour's first fifty years, identify numerous obstacles to their activism.[6] Few women achieved positions in the party hierarchy and although Labour consistently returned more women MPs than other parties, their proportion was way below the percentage of women members until direct measures were introduced to address this in the 1990s.[7] Several accounts point to the structural barriers within the party's systems that claimed to facilitate women's participation, whilst simultaneously marginalizing it.[8] The postwar reforms that ushered in individual membership of the Labour Party and established Women's Sections in 2018 also reserved a number of NEC seats for women, but these were not solely elected by women members. Resolutions passed at the women's conference were not binding (unlike those passed at the main conference) and the NEC's Women's Advisory Committee could not set party

---

[4] John Callaghan, 'Ross McKibben: Class Cultures, the Trade Unions and the Labour Party', in John Callaghan, Steve Fielding and Steve Ludlam (eds), *Interpreting the Labour Party: Approaches to Labour Politics and History* (Manchester: MUP, 2003), 116–33 (118, 126). On the Women's Labour League, see Christine Collette, *For Labour and for Women: The Women's Labour League, 1906–18* (Manchester: MUP, 1989).

[5] Pat Thane, 'The Women of the British Labour Party and Feminism', in Harold L. Smith (ed.), *British Feminism in the Twentieth Century* (Aldershot: Edward Elgar, 1990), 123–43, 125; Steven Fielding, *The Labour Governments 1964–1970*, vol. 1 (Manchester: MUP, 2003), ch. 5 'Appealing to Women', 113–38, 115.

[6] For overviews of this literature, see Martin Francis, 'Labour and Gender', in Duncan Tanner, Pat Thane and Nick Tiratsoo (eds), *Labour's First Century* (Cambridge: CUP, 2000), 191–220; June Hannam, 'Women as Paid Organizers and Propagandists for the British Labour Party Between the Wars', *International Labour and Working-Class History* 77 (2010): 69–88.

[7] Sarah Childs, 'The New Labour Women MPs in the 1997 British Parliament: Issues of Recruitment and Representation', *Women's History Review* 9, no. 1 (2000): 55–73.

[8] For discussion of structural impediments, see Harold Smith, 'Sex vs. Class: British Feminists and the Labour Movement, 1919–1929', *The Historian* 47, no. 1 (1984): 19–37; Pamela Graves, *Labour Women: Women in British Working-Class Politics, 1918–1939* (Cambridge: CUP, 1994), ch. 3; Martin Francis, *Ideals and Policies Under Labour, 1945–51* (Manchester: MUP, 1997), ch. 5; Amy Black and Stephen Brooke, 'The Labour Party, Women and the Problem of Gender', *Journal of British Studies* 36, no. 4 (1997): 419–52; Christine Collette, *The Newer Eve: Women, Feminists and the Labour Party* (Basingstoke: Palgrave Macmillan, 2009).

policy.[9] The precarity of women's employment, much of which was under or un-unionized in the pre- and interwar period, mitigated against fuller influence as the larger male unions wielded considerable power at party conferences.[10] Other research highlights the role of party ideology and culture in sidelining female members. Many Labour men feared that external, sex-based feminist movements would dilute class-based politics. Party iconography privileged masculinity; male workers appeared as heroic, whilst their female counterparts were exploited, sweated and in need of rescue.[11] And, if party language did shift from the lexicon of pre-war socialism, where the seemingly gender-neutral status of 'comrade' was too frequently undermined by the qualification 'woman comrade', other aspects of its political culture were more intransient.[12] Men and women even had different coloured party cards until the 1970s.[13]

Early historiography positioned party women in a series of binary oppositions. Structural approaches emphasized their lower success rates at ascending party hierarchies, whilst cultural approaches pointed to the marginalization of feminism in debates over the primacy of sex or class.[14] Later studies adopted a more complex view, suggesting that the numerous divergencies of age, class, gender and race complicate – if not nullify – the idea of a single category of 'Labour Woman'.[15] Much of this later research looks to the local level, capturing the work of branch members and grass roots activists rather than MPs or national leaders.[16] The local level offers a different view of Labour women's activism.

---

[9] Graves, *Labour Women*, 23–7, 109–14; Francis, 'Labour and Gender', 196.

[10] June Hannam, 'The Labour Party and Women', in Matthew Worley (ed.), *The Foundations of the British Labour Party: Identities, Cultures and Perspectives, 1900–1939* (Aldershot: Ashgate, 2009), 171–92, 174

[11] Francis, 'Labour and Gender', 212–14.

[12] For the gendered language of socialism, particularly up to 1920, see Krista Cowman, *Mrs Brown is a Man and a Brother! Women in Merseyside's Political Organisations, 1890-1920* (Liverpool: LUP, 2004), 58; Karen Hunt, 'Fractured Universality: The Language of British Socialism Before the First World War', in John Belchem and Neville Kirk (eds), *Languages of Labour* (Aldershot: Ashgate, 1997), 67–8.

[13] Steven Fielding, *The Labour Governments, 1964–1970, Vol. 1, Labour and Cultural Change* (Manchester: MUP, 2018), 123.

[14] Francis, 'Labour and Gender', 199, 201.

[15] Hannam, 'The Labour Party and Women', 175; Black and Brooke, 'Labour Party, Women and the Problem of Gender', 430.

[16] Key work taking this approach includes: Hannam, 'Women as Paid Organizers'; Karen Hunt, 'Making Politics in Local Communities: Labour Women in Interwar Manchester', in Matthew Worley (ed.), *Labour's Grass Roots: Essays on the Activities of Local Labour Parties and Members, 1918–45* (Aldershot: Ashgate, 2005), 170–93; Neil Evans and Dot Jones, '"Help Forward the Great Work of Humanity": Women in the Labour Party in Wales', in Duncan Tanner, Chris Williams and Deian Hopkin (eds), *The Labour Party in Wales, 1900-2000* (Cardiff: University of Wales Press, 2000); Cathy Hunt, '"Success with the Ladies": An Examination of Women's Experiences as Labour Councillors in Interwar Coventry', *Midland History* 22 (2007): 141–59; Lowri Newman, 'Count up to twenty-one: Scottish women in formal politics, 1918–1990', in Esther Breitenbach and Pat Thane (eds), *Women and Citizenship in Britain and Ireland in the 20th Century* (London: Bloomsbury, 2011), 29–44.

In contrast to the national leadership, women were very much a presence at this level. Pat Thane remarked on women's 'significant part in building and sustaining local Labour parties' before the First World War, whilst in the interwar years Stuart Ball, Andrew Thorpe and Matthew Worley found that 'many local and divisional women's sections [were] amongst the most active sites for party members, with female membership sometimes outnumbering men'.[17] Women were more likely to take on official positions or to stand for election when they could fit their activism around the daily demands of work, housekeeping and maternal duties.[18]

Convenience was not the only attraction of local activism.[19] Before winning the parliamentary vote, women could stand for election to boards of guardians and school boards from the late nineteenth century and for borough and county councils from 1907.[20] In the interwar period, socialist women regarded local legislatures as an 'important level' for them to be 'active in formulating and promoting policies' and to 'participate in their implementation'.[21] Later, the municipal socialism of the 'new urban left' in the 1970s and 1980s saw Labour women pursuing radical agendas with real impact.[22] By charting these periods through the lens of local activism, this chapter describes Labour women's activism across a century. Focusing on particular aspects of ideology and activity, it will demonstrate the continued importance of local politics as a site for feminized – and sometimes feminist – socialist politics, even when these appeared marginalized in the party's national policies and structures.

[17] Pat Thane, 'Labour and Local Politics: Radicalism, Democracy and Social Reform 1880–1914', in Eugenio F. Biagini and Alastair J. Reid (eds), *Currents of Radicalism: Popular Radicalism, Organised Labour and Party Politics in Britain, 1850–1914* (Cambridge: CUP, 1991), 259. Stuart Ball, Andrew Thorpe and Matthew Worley, 'Election Leaflets and Whist Drives: Constituency Party Members in Britain between the Wars', in Worley, *Labour's Grass Roots*, 7–32, 12.

[18] Ruth Davidson, 'Working-class Women Activists: Citizenship at the Local Level', in Peter Akers and Alistair Reid (eds), *Alternatives to State Socialism in Britain: Other Worlds of Labour in the Twentieth Century* (Basingstoke: Palgrave, 2016), 93–120.

[19] Pat Thane, 'Labour and Local Politics: Radicalism, Democracy and Social Reform 1880–1914', in Biagini and Reid, *Currents of Radicalism, 1850–1914*, 244–70, 244.

[20] For a full analysis, see Patricia Hollis, *Ladies Elect: Women in English Local Government, 1865–1914* (Oxford: Clarendon Press, 1987).

[21] Pat Thane, 'Visions of Gender in the Making of the British Welfare State: The Case of Women in the British Labour Party and Social Policy, 1906–1945', in Pat Thane and Gisela Bock (eds), *Maternity and Gender Politics: Women and the Rise of European Welfare States, 1880s–1950s* (London: Routledge, 1991), 93–114, 93.

[22] John Gyford, 'The New Urban Left: Origins, Style and Strategy', London: UCL Town Planning Discussion Papers, 1983. See also Patrick Seyd, *The Rise and Fall of the Labour Left* (Basingstoke: Macmillan, 1987), 140–1.

Pre-war politics and the Women's Labour League

Labour women could first organize separately in the Women's Labour League, inaugurated at Leicester in June 1906 to 'work for Independent Labour Representation in connection with the Labour party' and 'to obtain direct Labour representation of women in Parliament and on all local bodies'.[23] Despite initial suspicion from some Labour men, the League became an affiliate body in 1908. It had five thousand members, a 500 per cent increase on its founding conference, by 1913, and one hundred branches by 1918.[24] Its membership was socially mixed; League President Margaret MacDonald explained how 'many professional women, teachers, nurses, doctors … etc' had joined along with 'the wives and daughters of Trade Unionists and Socialists'.[25] League members fought elections, organized educational programmes and devised 'a politics of home' through campaigns that widened the boundaries of politics, connecting with women's daily concerns to draw them into activism.[26] One early initiative focused on state provision of meals for schoolchildren. Parliament had passed an Education (Provision of Meals) Act in 1906 (introduced by Labour MPs) which gave local authorities discretionary power to arrange school meals. League branches petitioned their local authorities to demand enforcement of the Act.[27] One particularly high-profile campaign was in Leicester, the constituency home of Margaret MacDonald and her husband (and local MP) Ramsay MacDonald, who had introduced similar legislation for Scotland. Leicester City Council attempted to postpone any discussion of the Act until September. Local branches of charities opposed municipal school meals. The Charity Organization believed it 'unnecessary for ratepayers' to have to bear the extra expense of 'a farthing in the pound', and the NSPCC feared it would 'lessen parental responsibility'.[28] The Women's Labour League held a protest meeting and delivered a petition of over a thousand signatures to the Council which then moved to meet its obligations. Other League campaigns demanded better maternity services, mother and baby clinics and nursery schools and pithead baths in mining communities.[29]

---

[23] Middleton, 'Women in Labour Politics', 26.

[24] Collette, *The Newer Eve*, 35; Caroline Rowan, 'Women in the Labour Party, 1906–20', *Feminist Review* 12 (1982): 74–91, 75.

[25] Middleton, 'Women in Labour Politics', 28.

[26] Karen Hunt, 'Gendering the Politics of the Working Woman's Home', in Elizabeth Darling and Lesley Whitworth (eds), *Women and the Making of Built Space in England, 1870–1950* (Aldershot: Ashgate, 2007), 107–22, 108, 121.

[27] 'Iona', 'Our Women's Outlook', *Labour Leader*, 1 November 1907, 13.

[28] Anonymous, 'Provision of Meals for School Children', *Leicester Daily Post*, 31 July 1907, 4. Anonymous, 'Summary of News', *Leicester Daily Post*, 22 July 1907, 1.

[29] Ferguson, 'Labour Women and the Social Services', in Middleton, *Women in the Labour Movement*, 38–56.

Labour women were also active inside elected authorities. By 1913, Labour had five female borough councillors, one rural district councillor plus thirty-one members of boards of guardians across Britain.[30] Thane's study of the radicalism of pre-war Labour local politics reminds us that its real 'powers to transform essential features of everyday life – and death' held 'more immediate prospects of democratic control of policy making and administration' than central government.[31] Several authorities delivered progressive agendas before the First World War; radical Progressives dominated London County Council until 1906, whilst in Liverpool a radical Liberal administration (1892–5) declared itself 'for the people, for the poor'.[32] Local boards of guardians were considered a particularly suitable field for Labour women. Katharine Bruce Glasier (writing as 'Iona') reminded readers of the *Labour Leader* that there was 'no public office today where a Socialist woman with quick sympathies and creative imagination can do better work'.[33] Just how creative Labour women could be was demonstrated by Leicester guardian Miss M. J. Bell, who told of how, when her attempts to pass a motion banning 'the degrading work of oakum picking for women' in the local workhouse failed, she waited until a fresh order for oakum appeared on the requisition book and quietly crossed it off, whereupon the work had to stop.[34]

Sex, class and votes for women

Women's contribution to Labour's first phase of electoral politics, and the principles of sexual equality underpinning their membership, belied a more complex attitude towards women's parliamentary suffrage, the key political question of the day. Unlike other contemporary parties, Labour and the ILP supported women's suffrage, but the party was conflicted over how to approach the growing women's movement. Some saw suffrage as an equality issue but others, fearing that giving women votes on the same terms as men would tip the balance of voters even further away from the working class, argued for

---

[30] Lucy Middleton, 'Women in Labour Politics', in Middleton (ed.), *Women in the Labour Movement* (London: Croon Helm, 1977), 22–38, 31.

[31] Pat Thane, 'Labour and Local Politics: Radicalism, Democracy and Social Reform 1880–1914', in Biagini and Reid, *Currents of Radicalism, 1850–1914*, 244–70, 244.

[32] Sam Davies, *Liverpool Labour: Social and Political Influences on the Development of the Labour Party in Liverpool, 1900–39* (Keele: KUP, 1996), 119. Krista Cowman, *Mrs Brown is a Man and a Brother: Women in Merseyside's Political Organisations, 1890–1920* (Liverpool: LUP, 2004), 48.

[33] 'Iona', 'Our Women's Outlook', 13.

[34] Ibid.

full adult suffrage. Socialist women were equally divided. Some felt that they were 'women first and socialists afterwards', but others agreed with Margaret McMillan that their party 'was not formed to champion women. It was born to make war on capitalism and competition'.[35] By 1903, some were convinced that whilst the Labour Party 'welcomed [women] in the work of elections', when male leaders were asked to press for votes for women, 'they express, at the best, vague sympathy'.[36]

The WSPU (Women's Social and Political Union) grew out of this concern and was originally formed as a 'ginger group' to pressure the ILP and LRC to move the matter forward. Nationally the union had distanced itself from Labour (and other political parties) by 1906. Whilst some Labour members felt betrayed by the WSPU's shift to political independence, there was accommodation with the National Union of Women's Suffrage Societies, a less militant body which set up an Election Fighting Fund to support Labour candidates from 1912, and with the Women's Freedom League, a militant group that drew the line at the WSPU's arson. At local level these distinctions were less apparent, and many Labour women remained active in both the WSPU and the party at the grass roots.[37] The question of whether to prioritize socialism or feminism continued to be a vexing issue for the party at national level throughout the twentieth century.

The interwar years: accommodating women voters

The Representation of the People Act in 1918 changed how political parties engaged with women. As voters, they were a new constituency to be addressed; each party was determined to capture the 'women's vote'.[38] In the wake of the 1918 reforms, the Labour Party appointed a chief woman's officer for the first time (Dr Marion Phillips, 1918–32, succeeded by Mary Sutherland, 1932–60) along with regional organizers (three in 1918, rising to nine by 1919). Phillips explained the logic of perpetuating spaces for separate organization in Women's Sections to new women voters:

[35] Lily Bell, 'Matrons and Maidens', *Labour Leader*, 13 April 1895, 4; Margaret McMillan, *The Life of Rachel McMillan* (London: J. M. Dent, 1937), 131.
[36] 'The Women's Social and Political Union', *Clarion*, 30 October 1903, 8; *Labour Leader*, 31 October 1903.
[37] Krista Cowman, '"Incipient toryism?" The Women's Social and Political Union and the Independent Labour Party, 1903–14', *History Workshop Journal* 53 (2002): 128–48.
[38] For a comparative discussion, see Krista Cowman, *Women in British Politics c. 1689–1970* (Basingstoke: Palgrave Macmillan, 2010), 131–50.

It is felt that women are so newly come into political life that their development will be hindered ... thus losing the value of women's rich experience, if the whole of their work is conducted in organizations including both sexes. The present scheme of separation is partial ... but it is sufficient to give full opportunity for the special qualities of women to make themselves felt in every constituency.[39]

Women's experience remained an important dimension of political activity. Wartime government had recognized women's 'special qualities' when the need to conserve resources such as fats (now needed for explosives rather than soap) transformed everyday domestic knowledge into a matter of national importance.[40] Women were engaged in official consultancy roles in the Ministry of Food, and then in the radical Ministry of Reconstruction where the Liberal (soon to be Labour) MP Christopher Addison appointed a Women's Advisory Committee to address 'questions more particularly affecting women' in postwar planning.[41] Improving housing was high on the ministry's agenda. As the Women's Labour League (WLL) had recently campaigned on this area, Labour women were enrolled onto the ministry's Women's Housing Sub-Committee, to look at the question 'from a housewife's point of view'.[42] Averil Sanderson Furniss (who had headed the WLL campaign) joined, with Eleanor Barton, Sybilla Branford and Councillor Rosalind Moore from the WCG (Women's Co-Operative Guild). '[T]wo more Labour women', Alice Jarrett and Annie Foulkes Smith, were added in July 1918.[43] Drawing on the results of the WLL campaign, supplemented with information gathered at countless local meetings, they provided the ministry with around ten thousand responses and a detailed report that showed women's 'unanimous' wishes for indoor sanitation, hot and cold running water and a separate parlour.[44]

This work, described by housing historian Alison Ravetz as women's 'most significant input ... into house design', demonstrates how Labour women viewed political action.[45] Women's domestic experience was considered vital, but not

---

[39] Marion Phillips, 'Introduction', in Phillips (ed.), *Women in the Labour Party* (London: Headley, 1918), 9–17, 13.

[40] Krista Cowman, '"From the Housewife's Point of View": Female Citizenship and the Gendered Interior in Post-First World War Britain, 1918–1928', *English Historical Review* 130, no. 543 (2015): 352–83, 358.

[41] Ministry of Reconstruction, *Report on the Work of the Ministry for the Period ending 31st December 1918* (London: HMSO, 1919).

[42] Women's Labour League Leaflet, 'The Working Woman's House', 1918; TNA, RECO 1/631, A. Sanderson Furniss, 'Report of Enquiry Conducted by Women in the Labour Party', 19 June 1918. For more on the campaign, see B. McFarlane, 'Homes Fit For Heroines: Housing in the Twenties', in Matrix (ed.), *Making Space: Women and the Built Environment* (London: Pluto, 1985).

[43] TNA, RECO 1/627, Gertrude Emmott to Dr Addison, July 1918.

[44] Averil Sanderson Furniss, 'The Working Woman's House', in Phillips, *Women and the Labour Party*, 74–85. For more details, see Cowman, 'From the Housewife's Point of View'.

[45] Alison Ravetz, 'A View from the Interior', in Judy Attfield and Pat Kirkham (eds), *A View from the Interior: Feminism, Women and House Design* (London: Women's Press, 1987), 187–206, 194.

constraining. The League's housing campaign was outward looking, positioning home improvement as a working woman's 'first effort of citizenship' rather than her sole contribution.[46] Through their continued politicization of working-class domesticity, Labour women challenged the gender imbalance in the party's trade union affiliates, arguing 'that work in the home should be seen in the same way as paid work in the labour market', as 'the woman's workshop is the home'.[47] June Hannam's study of Labour's women organizers found them actively recruiting housewives as employed women were likely to already be organized through unions.[48] This approach paid dividends in growing women's membership. Through Women's Sections, members could push their demands onto a broader Labour Party agenda in various ways, continuing to expand definitions of the political.[49] In Newport, for example, the Women's Section secured party support for linoleum to be fitted on two newly built housing estates, something male councillors had not considered important.[50] At the same time, Women's Sections broadened their members' political knowledge through a series of educational initiatives including reading programmes and summer schools on a wide range of subjects.[51]

Women could now raise issues in parliament themselves. Labour – just – provided the highest number of women MPs between 1918 and 1938; sixteen in total against fifteen Conservative and six others. The small number of women MPs punched above their weight, driving reforms on divorce, guardianship of children, widows' pensions and women's entry into professions, which addressed the needs of new women voters.[52] Some of the more radical measures were discretionary. The Maternity and Child Welfare Act 1918 allowed councils to appoint district nurses and health visitors, set up ante-natal clinics, supply milk and food in pregnancy and provide home help during the lying-in period, but the only requirement was a committee with at least two women members. *Labour Women*, the party's women's newspaper, urged its readers to press local authorities to use their new powers.[53] Local government remained 'the front line'

---

[46] Labour Party, 'The Working Woman's House'. This connection is discussed in more detail in Cowman, 'From the Housewife's Point of View'.

[47] Hannam, 'Women as Paid Organizers', 79; Sanderson Furniss, 'The Working Woman's House', 74.

[48] Hannam, 'The Victory of Ideals', 335.

[49] Ibid., 332.

[50] Stuart Ball, Andrew Thorpe and Matthew Worley, 'Election Leaflets', 12.

[51] Mary Agnes Hamilton, *The Labour Party Today* (London: Labour Book Service, 1937), 83.

[52] Pat Thane, 'Women and political participation in England, 1918–1970', in Esther Brietenbach and Pat Thane, *Women and Citizenship in Britain and Ireland in the 20th Century* (London: Bloomsbury, 2011), 19; MGF, *The Women's Victory & Afterwards*, 1920, 165.

[53] Pat Thane, 'Visions of Gender in the Making of the British Welfare State: The Case of Women in the British Labour Party and Social Policy, 1906–1945', in Thane and Bock, *Maternity and Gender Politics*, 106.

for women's activism, with elected women forming 'a significant part' of Labour's municipal growth.[54] Twenty per cent of London's Labour borough councillors (150) were women, whilst authorities such as Liverpool had around 10 per cent (or ten individuals).[55] Across the country, Labour women worked in town halls to enact improvements that made a material difference to their lives. This sometimes involved resisting national agendas. Susan Lawrence (later a Labour MP) was one of five women councillors sent to prison following the Poplar Rates Rebellion in 1920, under the slogan 'Better to break the Law than to break the Poor.' Elected Labour women helped organize local protests against the Means Test in the 1930s, but also did their best to ameliorate its impact through PACs (Public Assistance Committees). Hannah Mitchell challenged her male PAC colleagues as she 'knew just how much food could be bought out of the allowance', and made sure applicants were given tea and biscuits when being interviewed.[56]

Postwar politics: the personal becomes political

The 1945 election saw the Labour Party sweep to power with a slim majority of women's votes (just over 44 per cent) and a record number of women MPs (twenty-one out of a total of twenty-four). Many party activists attributed Labour's subsequent poll defeat in 1951 to its failure to retain the support of women, who found the Conservatives' affirmation of consumerism a more attractive proposition.[57] How accurate this was is debatable – at least one analysis suggests that men abandoned Labour in greater numbers.[58] Yet despite acknowledging that it needed 'to know more about voting by ... sex', Labour's leadership remained convinced that it had lost the women's vote in the 1950s and that, having regained it by the 1960s, 'it would be very satisfactory' to hold onto it.[59]

---

[54] Pamela Graves, *Labour Women* (Cambridge: CUP, 1994), 176.

[55] Pat Thane, 'Women of the British Labour Party', in Smith, *British Feminism in the Twentieth Century*, 124–43, 140; June Hannam, 'Women and Labour Politics', in Worley, *Labour's Grass Roots*, 171–92, 173; Davies, *Liverpool Labour*, 182–3.

[56] Hannah Mitchell, *The Hard Way Up* (London: Virago, 1977), 215, 214.

[57] See for example Ina Zweiniger-Bargielowska, 'Rationing, Austerity and the Conservative Party Recovery after 1945', *Historical Journal* 37 (1994): 173–98.

[58] James Hinton, 'Women and the Labour Vote, 1945–50', *Labour History Review* 57, no. 3 (1992): 59–68.

[59] Labour Party Report of General Election Sub-Committee, 22 October 1959; Home Policy Committee 'The General Election of 1966' both cited in Amy Black and Stephen Brooke, 'The Labour Party Women and the Problem of Gender, 1951–1966', *Journal of British Studies* 36, no. 4 (1997): 419–52, 419, 434.

Women's structural position in the party remained unchanged with Women's Sections, regional organizers, a chief woman's officer, the National Labour Women's Advisory Committee, an annual Women's Conference and reserved NEC places. Numbers remained between 41–43 per cent (approximately 286,000–351,000 women).[60] Yet by the 1960s it was clear that women *activists* were falling away. In 1918, as Labour struggled to work out how to accommodate individual women as members and voters, it seemed logical to meet them halfway and use familiar, domestic topics to develop their political citizenship. Forty years later, claims that Women's Sections helped develop this 'nervous' and 'less politically-minded' constituency of members were wearing thin for a new generation of political women.[61] Rather than functioning as a bridge to introduce women to wider political concepts, many sections concentrated on fundraising, canvassing and social matters. A tongue-in-cheek sketch of an anonymous party branch published in 1954 described how it had a young, right-wing leader, a small group of disruptive Trotskyists and

> … of course a women's section, engaged chiefly with knitting and not terribly interested in politics … They work very hard and without them the bazaars, socials and outings would flop miserably. Apart from detailed business they take little part in the debate, and tend to vote with 'the Member'.[62]

The numerical health of Women's Sections belied a different situation on the ground where many were stagnating – if they existed. Over four-fifths of Manchester's party branches had no active Women's Section in the 1950s.[63]

Centrally, the party had different priorities. Catherine Ellis has argued that by the 1960s, '[t]he "Youth Question" had assumed the place held by the "Woman Question" in earlier decades'.[64] Youth, rather than women, were now the main target for recruitment; developing the Young Socialists (YS), which replaced the Labour League of Youth, took precedent over rejuvenating Women's Sections.[65] Yet women continued to join the party. Those who found the gossipy ambience and 'cosy social life' of Women's Sections anachronistic in an age of espresso bars

[60] For precise figures, see Fielding, 'Appealing to Women', 115.

[61] Views from 1960s women members cited in Fielding, 'Appealing to Women', 116.

[62] A Correspondent, 'A Local Labour Party: All Colours of the Political Spectrum', *Manchester Guardian*, 9 November 1954, 5.

[63] Steven Fielding and Duncan Tanner, 'The "Rise of the Left" Revisited: Labour Party Culture in Post-War Manchester and Salford', *Labour History Review* 71, no. 3 (2006): 211–33, 215.

[64] Catherine Ellis, 'The Younger Generation: The Labour Party and the 1959 Youth Commission', *Journal of British Studies* 41, no. 2 (2002): 199–231, 202.

[65] Black and Brooke, 'Labour Party Women', 435. See Ellis, 'The Younger Generation' for fuller discussion of the YS.

and rock and roll looked to different activities.[66] Patrick Seyd, who identified women as one of three key groups responsible for the 1970s growth in CLP membership, suggested that they followed two routes into party life, union activism and an external WLM (Women's Liberation Movement).[67] Labour, finally succumbing to repeated calls from its women's conference, had included equal pay in the 1964 manifesto. Progress remained slow until the late 1960s when a number of strikes by women – most famously that of Ford workers portrayed in the 2010 film *Made in Dagenham* – pushed the issue higher up the political agenda culminating in the 1970 Equal Pay Act. Its author, Barbara Castle, hoped this would encourage greater unionization. Certainly, in the five years before its full implementation, a new generation of women trade unionists was politicized through a wave of strikes demanding equal pay for women workers in the Leeds textile industry (1970), at Wingrove & Rogers electronics, Liverpool (1974), at Salford Electrical Instruments (1975) and elsewhere.[68] One outcome of this new female militancy was the TUC's Working Women's Charter, adopted in 1974. This prompted local campaigns across the country in support of its demands for increased social and economic rights for women.

Other female union recruits came from expanding public sector unions reflecting another key social change.[69] The number of undergraduates in Britain leapt from 108,000 to 228,000 between 1960 and 1970, as beneficiaries of the 1944 Education Act came of age.[70] The new Robins Universities, opened to meet this demand, taught subjects such as sociology, psychology and politics. Campuses were hubs for innovative social movements campaigning around peace, race and sexuality. Most relevant of these here is the WLM, Britain's form of second-wave feminism. Decades earlier, first-wave feminists had worked in the Labour Party to achieve social, political and economic equality. WLM politics went way beyond the Women's Labour League's politicization of the domestic in its attention to areas previously considered private. Its slogan, 'the personal is political', demanded

---

[66] Kate Allen, Mildred Gordon, Sarah Roelofs and Clara Mulhern, 'The Women's Movement and the Labour Party: An Interview with Labour Party Feminists', *Feminist Review* 16 (1984): 75–87, 75; Fielding, 'Appealing to Women', 120; Fielding and Tanner, 'Rise of the Left', 215; Black and Brooke, 'Labour Party Women', 430.

[67] Patrick Seyd, *The Rise and Fall of the Labour Left* (Basingstoke: Macmillan, 1987), 44, 47–50.

[68] Fielding, 'Appealing to Women', 132. For Leeds, see L. Leicester, 'You're not a worker, you're a pair of hands', 2018, https://peopleandnature.wordpress.com/site-contents/youre-not-a-worker-youre-a-pair-of-hands-how-leeds-women-workers-struck-back-1970/ (accessed 13 September 2021); for Salford, see Marsha Rowe, 'What Happened at Heywood?' *Spare Rib* 31 (1975): 12–15; for Liverpool, see Anonymous, 'Wingrove and Rogers Strike', *Spare Rib* 28 (1974): 22–4.

[69] Sarah Perrigo, 'Women and Change in the Labour Party', *Parliamentary Affairs* 49 (1996): 116–29, 119.

[70] Harold Perkin, 'University Planning in Britain in the 1960s', *Higher Education* 1, no. 1 (1972): 111–20, 111.

political legitimacy for topics such as contraception, child-rearing, housework and sexuality. Initially WLM activists organized independently, but by the mid- to late 1970s significant numbers joined – or re-joined – the Labour Party.[71] Some did so because they felt that the WLM was 'in an impasse'.[72] On the left, but disillusioned with the 'hierarchical' and 'vanguardist' culture of revolutionary groups such as the International Socialists and International Marxist Group, they believed the Labour Party more open to the 'collective and collaborative' politics that had drawn them into the WLM.[73] This was particularly evident in a number of cities where a new generation of political activists were making their mark, sharing a determination to pursue a 'local road to socialism' against the growing centralization and disconnection of the state.[74] Although John Gyford, who identified this as a broad 'new urban left', classed its priorities (including nuclear-free zones, discussions of Northern Ireland and funding radical arts and community activism) as 'not hitherto seen ... as local government business', they represented familiar territory for activists who had moved into socialism from local branches of the new social movements. For women's groups in particular, '[l]eft wing municipal socialism ... held out the promise of concrete gains being won for women' on matters such as employment, childcare and personal safety.[75]

Socialism and feminism converged in the policies of a number of Labour-controlled local authorities in the 1970s and 1980s when councillors and CLP members from the new urban left pursued alternative strategies to those favoured by national government.[76] This included the seven Metropolitan County Councils (set up in 1973 and abolished in 1987 – in what many contemporaries interpreted as a political attack on their socialist agendas). Women's committees, subcommittees or units (collectively referred to as 'women's initiatives') appeared in various authorities.[77] The first, and largest, was the Greater London Council's Women's Unit. In 1981, the GLC had returned to Labour control after a four-year Conservative hiatus. The new council, according to its leader Ken Livingstone,

---

[71] Kathryn Harriss, 'New Alliances: Socialist-Feminism in the Eighties', *Feminist Review* 31 (1989): 34–54, 40

[72] Sarah Perrigo, 'Socialist Feminism and the Labour Party: Some Experiences from Leeds', *Feminist Review* 23 (1986): 101–8, 101.

[73] Harriss, 'New Alliances', 35.

[74] John Gyford, 'The New Urban Left: A Local Road to Socialism', *New Society* 21 (1983): 91–3, 91.

[75] Harriss, 'New Alliances', 42.

[76] For a useful summary of the literature on this point, see Tom Blackburn, 'The Capacity to Imagine: Labour in Local Government', *New Socialist*, 4 January 2001, https://newsocialist.org.uk/the-capacity-to-imagine/ (accessed 2 October 2021).

[77] Susan Halford, 'Spatial Divisions and Women's Initiatives in British Local Government', *Geoforum* 20, no. 2 (1989): 161–74. Cinnamon Bennett, 'Mainstreaming in Organisational Strategies for Delivering Women's Equality in UK Local Government', Unpublished PhD thesis, Sheffield Hallam University, 2000, 10.

reflected 'the post-1968 generation' emmeshed in the politics of that era's new social movements.[78] Its members and staff – including prominent WLM activists such as Sheila Rowbotham and Hilary Wainwright, who directed its Popular Planning Unit – actively sought to engage community groups and the extra-parliamentary left.[79] The GLC Women's Unit opened in 1981 with a budget of £300,000 and three staff, expanding to seventy staff and a budget of £10 million by 1987.[80] Others followed, and by 1987 forty-two Labour authorities had women's initiatives including Bristol, York, Wolverhampton and Aberdeen. Jan Parker from the GLC Women's Unit explained how none of these had 'come out of the blue ... feminists ... ha[d] been working very hard in the Labour Party' to achieve them.[81] Women's initiatives focused on three main areas. They pushed for gender equality around employment (and set up training schemes to achieve this). They carried out enquiries into local women's wants and needs then pursued policies to meet these. Simultaneously, they made real efforts to connect with a wider constituency beyond the town hall. Meetings were held at different times of day (echoing the earliest practices of the Women's Labour League) and childcare was provided or funded for attenders. Some authorities who were suspicious of separating women's issues, came round to the idea. Sheffield's David Blunkett was clear that local socialism should aim to alleviate the 'struggle of working people ... not a separate struggle for women'. Sheffield started a Women's Section in its Employment Department but socialist feminists soon broadened its remit, starting with offering women training in non-traditional areas such as plastering then moving to campaign against workplace harassment.[82]

Women's initiatives committed to broadening links with local communities, a key priority for new urban left activists who had often started in politics via this route. Grant aid was an important strategy to give women's groups autonomy to arrange their own activities rather than have authorities acting for them. Many women's initiatives experimented with co-opting women from community groups onto their formal committees, drawing a new layer of activists closer to Labour Party structures.[83] One recalled: 'A lot of my friends

---

[78] Owen Hatherley, *Red Metropolis: Socialism and the Government of London* (London: Repeater Books, 2020), 109.

[79] Alexandre Campsie, '"Socialism Will Never be the Same Again"'. Re-imagining British Left-Wing Ideas for the "New Times"', *Contemporary British History* 31, no. 2 (2017): 166–88, 168–9.

[80] Goss, 'Making Space', 141–2.

[81] Parker, 'Town Hall Take Over', 19.

[82] Daisy Payling, 'Socialist Republic of South Yorkshire: Grassroots Activism and Left Wing Solidarity in 1980s Sheffield', *Twentieth Century British History* 25, no. 4 (2014): 602–27, 620.

[83] Julia Edwards, 'Women's Committees: A Model for Good Local Government', *Policy & Politics* 17, no. 3 (1989): 221–5, 221; Parker, 'Town Hall Take Over', 19.

moved pretty seamlessly from being on the dole, volunteering for women's aid work or something similar, to getting a paid job in that area.'[84] This encouraged a further transference of feminist ideas into the Labour Party, precipitating shifts in practice and policy. For socialist feminists, activism in the WLM brought 'important insights … as to how we organize as socialists'.[85] As Sue Goss noted, many of the women who joined the party in the 1970s and 1980s took the lessons they had learned in campaigns for equal pay, abortion and employment rights into the 'previously moribund women's sections' where they 'abandon[ed] jumble sales and refreshments and began to campaign around sexism within the Labour Party'.[86] One woman who joined in the early 1980s described how this worked:

> [M]any of us within the party felt that we must do something to use the structures that were already there, that is to turn the women's sections outwards … Many young women then joined existing sections, and many more new sections were formed. I think the whole atmosphere within the women's sections changed.[87]

The sense of possibility feminists felt in municipal socialism had less impact on the wider party where the 'male, unionized industrial worker' remained the prominent version of an ideal activist.[88] Women associated with the Campaign for Labour Party Democracy started the Labour WAC (Women's Action Committee) in 1980, believing that reform was pointless unless 'extended to the large body of women … largely excluded from the party's powerful … bodies'.[89] The WAC's five key demands looked to strengthen the role of Women's Sections and the Women's Conference within the party (issues first raised by women in the 1920s) and increase the number of women in parliament by demanding that all short lists should include at least one woman. The final point was particularly pressing after 1979 when the party's women MPs fell to just 4.1 per cent.[90] The

[84] Adam Lent, 'The Labour Left, Local Authorities and New Social Movements in Britain in the 80s', *Contemporary Politics* 7, no. 1 (2001): 7–25, 17.

[85] Hilary Wainwright, 'Introduction', in Sheila Rowbotham, Lynn Segal and Hilary Wainwright, *Beyond the Fragments: Feminism & the Making of Socialism* (London: Virago, 1979), 13.

[86] Sue Goss, 'Women's Initiatives in Local Government', in Martin Boddy and Colin Fudge (eds), *Local Socialism? Labour Councils and Left Alternatives* (Basingstoke: Macmillan, 1984), 109–31, 110; Sue Goss, 'Making Space – Bringing Feminism into the Town Hall', in Stuart Lansley, Sue Goss and Christian Wolman (eds), *Councils in Conflict: The Rise and Fall of the Municipal Left* (Basingstoke: Macmillan, 1989), 142–59, 144.

[87] Allen et al., 'The Women's Movement and the Labour Party', 76.

[88] Sarah Perrigo, 'Gender Struggles in the British Labour Party from 1979–1995', *Party Politics* 1, no. 3 (1995): 407–17, 408.

[89] Meg Russell, *Building New Labour* (Basingstoke: Palgrave, 2005), 96–124, 97. See also Patrick Seyd, 'The Labour Left', PhD thesis, University of Sheffield, 1986, 358–60.

[90] Russell, *Building*, 99.

WAC put repeated motions to the party's Annual Conference. At first these were not well received. Mildred Gordon recalled how in 1982 men in the trade union section threw 'bags of sweets to each other' as she attempted to open a debate on women's issues.[91] Several WAC members felt that the overt hostility they sometimes encountered strengthened their resolve, bringing a 'real feeling of sisterhood' as one put it, and providing valuable lessons in how to operate inside party structures.[92]

In the 1980s and 1990s, the WAC's approach slowly began to show results. The NEC appointed its first spokesperson on women's issues (Jo Richardson) in 1984 and published a charter for equality for women in the party. There was also a shift towards women's demands from the trades union wing. Part of this reflected the growing changes in waged labour with traditional male industries giving way to the female-dominated service sector. Additional impetus came from Labour women's work in wider industrial struggles. During the miners' strike, for example, whilst popular representations such as that of the 2014 film *Pride* suggest that women's support groups politicized a generation of women, recent analysis of their composition has revealed its leaders as women already well embedded in Labour, feminist and sometimes communist politics.[93] Women's issues began to permeate party policy documents, helped by a rise in the number of women MPs in 1992 (from ten to twenty-one), many of whom identified as feminists. Finally, as polling data suggested that had women supported Labour as strongly as men, the 1992 election would have been won, the party began experiments in positive action that slowly turned around the percentage of women MPs.[94] An experiment in compulsory shortlisting of women candidates in 1987 failed to make much impact. Although quotas proved more successful in opening up the party hierarchy to women, they were resisted by some CLPs for candidate shortlists. Finally, in 1993, Labour introduced all-women shortlists for 50 per cent of its safe vacant and marginal seats. (The policy was deemed unlawful in 1996, and selection processes were re-run but by this point many women had been given a head start in the process.)[95] More broadly, initiatives

[91] Allen et al., 'The Women's Movement', 79.

[92] Ibid.; S. Perrigo, 'Women and Change in the Labour Party, 1979–1995', *Parliamentary Affairs* 49, no. 1 (1996): 115–29, 123.

[93] Florence Sutcliffe-Braithwaite and Natalie Thomlinson, 'National Women Against Pit Closures: Gender, Trade Unionism and Community Activism in the Miners' Strike, 1984–5', *Contemporary British History* 32, no. 1 (2008): 78–100.

[94] Perrigo, 'Gender Structures', 413.

[95] Clare Short, 'Women and the Labour Party', *Parliamentary Affairs* 49, no. 1 (1996): 17–25; Sarah Childs, 'The new labour women MPs in the 1997 British parliament: issues of recruitment and representation', *Women's History Review* 9, no. 1 (2000): 55–73, 59.

such as Emily's List and internal training courses focused on identifying women candidates and preparing them for working in national leadership roles. In 1997, Labour famously returned 101 women MPs.

Conclusion

Some may see irony in the fact that Labour women made significant progress in shaping a socialist feminist agenda for local authorities, just as Margaret Thatcher's national government waged ideological warfare against the British left. Recent historical analyses of the politics of the 1980s have attempted to shift away from viewing the decade purely in terms of defining 'Thatcherism' to provide a key point of reference.[96] In attempting to shift the focus away from Thatcher, it has been suggested that deeper attention to the local may provide a more optimistic picture of a politics not 'overdetermined by Thatcherism'.[97] This was certainly the case for Labour women who succeeded in 'rais[ing] gender as a legitimate political issue and ... making significant, practical improvements in many women's lives' when national politics was pushing in an opposite direction.[98]

In this, they were building on a longer tradition. For much of the Labour Party's first century, local government had offered one of the most exciting spaces for its women activists. Since before the First World War, socialist women had channelled their community activism through their Labour Party branches. In the 1920s new women voters continued this work, lobbying authorities to ensure that municipal housing schemes kept housewives' needs to the fore. Recognizing that the power to bring about solutions to the problems that had a disproportionate effect on women's lives – poor housing, bad education, unequal access to the labour market – lay largely with local authorities, they focused much of their energy on this arena.

By the 1960s, Labour women's politicization of the domestic had expanded to encompass issues such as childcare, contraception, sexuality and domestic violence. Working with local authorities they were instrumental in paving the way for a number of initiatives aimed at promoting gender equality. The

---

[96] Matthew Hilton, Chris Mores and Florence Sutcliffe-Braithwaite, '*New Times* Revisited: Britain in the 1980s', *Contemporary British History* 31, no. 2 (2017): 145–65.

[97] Stephen Brooke, 'Living in "New Times": Historicizing 1980s Britain', *History Compass* 12 (2014): 20–32, 20.

[98] Halford, 'Women's Initiatives', 258.

municipal socialist experiments of the 1980s were shot through with municipal feminism. Safer (and sometimes women-only) public transport, support for women fleeing abusive relationships and childcare schemes were accompanied by support for artistic and cultural events that were explicitly anti-sexist and anti-racist.[99] Much of this was achieved through a wider engagement with other local community groups, pursued by socialist feminists who had experience of the more collectivist politics of the WLM. The municipal feminism of the urban new left of the 1980s thus provided interesting examples of experiments with widening democracy.

These examples are more than historic curiosities. The short lived – but successful – socialist feminist initiatives have something to say to today's politics, where a national agenda of austerity is again being challenged by radical municipal initiatives, and internationally progressive women are finding that 'municipalism is well suited to pursuing the feminist aim of changing how politics is done'.[100] As the world emerges from the aftershock of a global pandemic, which has had a disproportionate effect on women, and the poor, the field of local politics may again prove to be a key site where socialist women can make a difference.

[99] See Bea Campbell and Martin Jaques, 'Goodbye to the GLC', *Marxism Today*, April 1986, 6–10.
[100] Laura Roth, Irene Zugasti Hervas and Alejandra De Diego Backer, *Feminise Politics Now* (Brussels: Rosa Luxemburg Stiftung, 2020), 127.

8

Social democracy, the decline of community and community politics in postwar Britain

Nick Garland*

A recurring theme in debate about the Labour Party and social democracy since 1945 has been the repeated idea that Labour took a historic wrong-turn in government, which led to the subordination of a more libertarian and fraternal socialist politics to a bureaucratic Fabianism.[1] A critique of social democracy centred on the alienating scale of state institutions, the disruptive effects of state planning upon 'traditional' working-class communities and the failure of social democracy to achieve a substantive change in human relationships and social values (to combine the social-democratic economy with a social-democratic society) was a feature of British political and cultural life throughout the postwar decades. That this has been a recurring trope suggests it merits serious engagement, but also that we should approach such claims with some caution.

We can crudely identify four stages in Labour's twentieth-century history in which a community-oriented critique of social democracy came to the fore. Firstly, the immediate period following the high watermark of 1945, through to the late 1950s: as the party struggled to come to terms with 'affluence' and the apparent disappearance of a wartime spirit of community and social solidarity, the decay of working-class community became a prominent concern

* The author wishes to thank Megan Corton Scott, Jeremy Nuttall, Colm Murphy, Sam Pallis, David Klemperer and Nathan Yeowell for generous feedback on earlier iterations of this chapter.

[1] There is at least an element of truth in this; Ben Jackson has charted the relative marginalization by revisionist social democrats of concerns with 'fraternity' or 'community', in favour of an emphasis on economic equality, in the 1930s. See Ben Jackson, *Equality and the British Left* (Manchester: MUP, 2007). The tension between Labour's commitment to delivering its social objectives via the state, and a concern for community closely parallels the tensions between its role as a movement, rooted in a historic dissenting tradition, and as a party of government. This is discussed in Ben Jackson's chapter in this volume.

for writers and thinkers, such as Richard Hoggart and Michael Young. The apparent erosion of localized working-class cultures by the 'massification' of culture, rise of new towns and suburbs, and physical decline or dismantling of 'traditional working-class neighbourhoods' featured prominently in such accounts. Secondly, by the late 1960s, 'community' was increasingly invoked by activists practising grassroots politics within Britain's 'crisis'-hit inner cities. Labour politicians saw the rise of community action in this period both as a challenge to the party's political primacy and to the central priorities of social democracy, yet also as an opportunity to align the party to new concerns and new constituencies. Thirdly, in the late 1970s and early 1980s, revisionist social democrats (including key founding figures of the SDP) and 'new urban left' councils would both try to channel these energies, drawing on related critiques of Labourism and its reliance on centralized state power. Finally, the 1990s would see the communitarian critique of social democracy take centre stage within the party, as New Labour sought to centre the concept of 'community' within its politics, and to distance itself from many of the perceived shortcomings of past Labour governments and the cultural politics of the left. However, this engagement would wane in government. By the 2010s, Blue Labour was levelling a similar critique at the Blair–Brown governments.

Exploring this history and drawing on some of the recent historical literature on class and community in postwar Britain, I suggest three conclusions. First, these varied examples illustrate the many contrasting uses to which so amorphous a concept can be put, and indeed the different geographies underlying it. Secondly, however, the enduring appeal of community might also indicate its worth. It is a concept that can resonate with Labour's own political traditions as well as with broad popular desires. That the term is vague whilst suggesting a high degree of specificity is a limitation, but it is also an asset in a time when there is an increasing expectation for politicians and policymakers to engage with place, but equally a need to speak in a language able to cross deep cultural fault-lines. The task is to construct a story about community and about lived communities, which resonates with popular attitudes, whilst being compatible with social-democratic values. Indeed, thirdly, we should push back against the idea that social democracy was inimical to community. Whilst acknowledging the flaws of the postwar welfare state, it is important to acknowledge its role in creating the conditions for numerous manifestations of community in postwar Britain. Social democracy was frequently a facilitator and not a disruptor of community. The 1970s were as much a moment of collective action and the assertion of community interests, as they were of 'crisis'.

And the state remains the most powerful weapon available to social democrats for creating the conditions whereby community, in myriad forms, can flourish.

Postwar: reaction against the state

It did not take long for Labour's high watermark to give way to a sense of crisis, both regarding the party's electoral prospects and its policy agenda. In 1948 the Attlee–Beveridge welfare state truly came into being. However, before the last bricks had been laid on the New Jerusalem, some of its architects were already disenchanted. Credited with the central part in shaping Britain's postwar welfare settlement, William Beveridge 're-emerged in the post-war years as a passionate defender of voluntarism, individual liberty, and small-scale private enterprise', culminating in his 1948 report *Voluntary Action*.[2] The same year, Michael Young, author of Labour's 1945 manifesto, published *Small Man, Big World*. The short pamphlet spelled out many of the preoccupations that would define Young's storied career as a sociologist and an extraordinary political innovator: an emphasis on smallness; upon democracy at the neighbourhood level; and on the central role of the social sciences in good government. The family, for Young, was the model on which a more democratic society should be based.[3] Throughout the postwar decades, he would argue that the overriding emphasis upon equality within Croslandite social democracy, whilst important, placed insufficient value on fraternity.[4] Young's communitarian, ethical brand of social-democratic revisionism was relatively marginal in the 1950s and 1960s, compared to the Croslandite emphasis upon economic equality-through-redistribution.[5] However, as Stephen Meredith has noted, his ideas foreshadowed a decentralist turn amongst post-Croslandite revisionists in the 1970s.[6]

---

[2]   Jose Harris, *William Beveridge: A Biography* (Oxford: Clarendon Press, 1997), ch. 18.

[3]   Michael Young, *Small Man Big World: A Discussion of Socialist Democracy* (London: Labour Party Publications Department, 1948). See also Lise Butler, 'Michael Young, the Institute of Community Studies, and the Politics of Kinship', *Twentieth Century British History* 26, no. 2 (2015): 203–24; Butler, *Michael Young, Social Science and the British Left* (Oxford: OUP, 2020); Stephen Meredith, 'Michael Young: An Innovative Social Entrepreneur', in Peter Ackers and Alastair J. Reid (eds), *Alternatives to State Socialism: Other Worlds of Labour in the Twentieth Century* (London: Palgrave Macmillan, 2016).

[4]   Meredith, 'Michael Young', 280.

[5]   Jackson, *Equality*, ch. 7.

[6]   Meredith, 'Michael Young', 271–3.

The 1950s were a period of painful retrenchment for Labour, with three successive electoral defeats. Although the party's base held up relatively strongly, these setbacks had a profound psychological impact. As Lawrence Black observes: 'More than votes, socialism lost confidence that history pointed towards its vision and, in part, its faith in the people.'[7] In response, intellectuals across the left played out a debate about Britain's changing class structure, the effects of affluence and the purpose of socialism in the welfare state and the mixed economy.[8] In this context, 'Many on the Left were beginning to question whether Labour could successfully reconnect with people's everyday lives.'[9] Sociologists – like Young himself – and cultural critics such as Hoggart and Raymond Williams showed an increasing interest in popular culture and in the everyday lives of working-class people. The emergence of the First New Left after 1956 saw a deeper engagement with culture and an emphasis on non-state forms of socialism from the Marxist left.[10] Meanwhile, a debate played out amongst social democrats about the apparent 'embourgeoisement' of parts of Labour's electoral base.[11]

The apparent decline of the inner-city community – the locus of everyday working-class life – served a particularly important role in these debates. A critical moment in the development of this thinking came in 1957, with the publication of Young and Peter Wilmott's *Family and Kinship in East London*, and Richard Hoggart's *The Uses of Literacy*.[12] Between them, these books 'came to define the concept of "working-class community" in British public debate.'[13] They enshrined an image of 'traditional working-class community' that would continue to exercise a powerful hold over the popular and political imagination for the rest of the twentieth century. This image implied communities rooted in

---

[7]   Lawrence Black, *The Political Culture of the Left in Affluent Britain 1951–64: Old Labour, New Britain?* (London: Palgrave, 2003), 10.

[8]   On the 'affluence' debate, see ibid.; Madeleine Davis, 'Arguing Affluence: New Left Contributions to the Socialist Debate 1957–63', *Twentieth Century British History* 23, no. 4 (2012): 496–528; Freddy Foks, 'The Sociological Imagination of the British New Left: "Culture" and the "Managerial Society"', c.1956–1962', *Modern Intellectual History* 15, no. 3 (2018): 801–20; 'Stuart Middleton, ""Affluence" and the Left in Britain, c.1958–1974', *The English Historical Review* 129, no. 536 (February 2014): 107–38.

[9]   Jon Lawrence, 'Inventing the "Traditional Working Class": A Re-Analysis of Interview Notes from Young and Wilmott's Family and Kinship in East London', *Historical Journal* 59, no. 2 (2016): 571.

[10] Dennis Dworkin, *Cultural Marxism in Post-War Britain* (Durham, NC: Duke University Press, 1997); Michael Kenny, *The First New Left: British Intellectuals After Stalin* (London: Lawrence & Wishart, 1995).

[11] See in particular Mark Abrams and Richard Rose, *Must Labour Lose?* (London: Penguin, 1960).

[12] Richard Hoggart, *The Uses of Literacy: Aspects of Working-Class Life* (London: Penguin Classics, 2009); Michael Young and Peter Willmott, *Family and Kinship in East London* (London: Penguin Classics, 2007).

[13] Lawrence, 'Inventing', 568–71.

the built environment of the 'urban village', strongly localized cultures, physical proximity, extended kinship networks, the central role of the matriarch, and the mutualistic values which this way of living apparently fostered. For Hoggart, it was the encroachment of a consumerist mass culture that was eroding the distinctive cultures and values of working-class communities. Young and Wilmott meanwhile focused their critique on planners, dismantling such communities through redevelopment, and relocating their inhabitants to new towns and suburbs, in which they would live a more privatized, home-oriented and indeed isolated existence.[14]

These accounts of community in decline would continue to play an important role in both the political imagination of the British left and centre-left, and in culture more widely, over the ensuing decades. Historians have noted the extent to which the growing attachment to the idea of the 'traditional working-class community' – and the redefinition of what were once called slums as 'neighbourhoods' – coincided with its gradual disappearance.[15] As slum clearances, redevelopment, and the relocation of working-class families to suburbs and new towns served to dismantle those neighbourhoods, the proletarian neighbourhood became sentimentalized and celebrated within academia and within popular culture, manifest in popular television programmes like *Coronation Street* and *Eastenders*. Into the 1970s, images of working-class life popularized by academics and social realist writers in the 1950s would exert a strong hold over British popular culture.[16] In a similar vein, Jörg Arnold has noted the extent to which the image of close-knit mining communities invoked during the 1984–5 miners' strike 'owed as much' to romanticized sociological studies of the 1950s and 1960s, such as the famous study *Coal is our Life*, 'as to careful observation of the social realities of miners' lives in the 1970s and 1980s'.[17]

The 1970s and 1980s would see a huge volume of journalism focused on the apparent decline of working-class neighbourhoods against the backdrop of

[14] On the 'long-standing mistrust' of the suburb in the twentieth-century socialist imagination, see also Jeremy Nuttall's chapter in this volume.

[15] Chris Waters, 'Autobiography, Nostalgia and Working-Class Selfhood', in George K. Behlmer and Fred M. Leventhal (eds), *Singular Continuities: Tradition, Nostalgia, and Identity in Modern Britain* (Stanford, CA: SUP, 2000), 178–95; Christian Topolov, '"Traditional Working-Class Neighbourhoods": An Inquiry into the Emergence of a Sociological Model in the 1950s and 1960s', *Osiris* 18, 2nd Series (2003): 212–33.

[16] Waters, 'Autobiography', 181–2; Jon Lawrence and Florence Sutcliffe-Braithwaite, 'Thatcher and the decline of class politics', in Ben Jackson and Robert Saunders (eds), *Making Thatcher's Britain* (Cambridge: CUP, 2012), 136.

[17] Jörg Arnold, '"That rather sinful city of London": the coal miner, the city and the country in the British cultural imagination, c.1969–2014', *Urban History* 47 (2020): 299.

unemployment and urban decline. Most vividly, in the pages of *New Society*, *Guardian* and *The New Statesman*, as well as numerous books, the journalist Jeremy Seabrook would chart what he saw as the effects of the welfare state, consumer capitalism and unemployment on once-solidaristic working-class communities:

> The malaise … in what remains of what we still call, sentimentally, our communities; [consisted in] loneliness, dissatisfaction; the powerlessness of parents over their children, the indifference of the young towards the old, the sense of reluctant acquiescence in values that seem to be beyond our control, the cynicism towards others.[18]

However, from the early 1970s, such accounts of community came under sustained criticism.[19] Coming particularly from feminist writers, such criticisms would frequently serve as a proxy for a wider critique of the shortcomings of social democracy and the culture of Labourism. These arguments stressed the gendered view of family and community life present in nostalgia for lost working-class communities; the need to look to political constituencies beyond the (shrinking) manual industrial working class; and the wrongheaded and politically disabling effect of the left's moralistic view of working-class consumption.[20] More recently, historians have uncovered the much more varied experiences and subjectivities of working-class people in mid-twentieth-century Britain. These have pointed both to the existence of individualism *within* 'traditional working-class communities', and the endurance of community outside of them. They have also stressed, contrary to the more pessimistic tone of some of social democracy's critics, to the empowering effect that the postwar welfare state – from education, to free orange juice, to the redevelopment of town centres – had on many working-class people and communities. Whilst these arguments by no means invalidate some of those earlier criticisms of the postwar welfare state, they suggest a need for a more pluralistic account of what community and belonging might entail, and a more optimistic view of the relationship between egalitarian social democracy and community.[21]

---

[18] Seabrook, *What Went Wrong?* (London: Gollancz, 1978), 72.

[19] See for instance Jennifer Platt, *Social Research in Bethnal Green: An evaluation of the work of the Institute of Community Studies* (London: Macmillan, 1971).

[20] See for example Beatrix Campbell, *Wigan Pier Revisited* (London: Virago, 1984); Anne Phillips, 'Fraternity', in Ben Pimlott (ed.), *Fabian Essays in Socialist Thought* (London: Heinemann, 1984), 130–41; Carolyn Steedman, *Landscape for a Good Woman* (London: Virago, 1987).

[21] Jon Lawrence, *Me, Me, Me?: The Search for Community in Post-War England* (Oxford: OUP, 2018); Selina Todd, 'Phoenix Rising: Working-Class Life and Urban Reconstruction, c. 1945–1967', *Journal of British Studies* 54, no. 3 (2015): 679–702; Butler, 'Politics of Kinship'.

The moment of 'community action'

Following race riots in Notting Hill in 1958, the idea that Britain's inner cities were in 'crisis' – characterized by deindustrialization, a backlash against Commonwealth immigration, population decline driven by the ongoing outward flow of people, and the physical decay of the built environment – would be a recurring theme of public discourse for several decades.

From the mid-1960s, this apparent 'crisis' was met by an explosion of grassroots activity in Britain's inner cities, frequently labelled 'community action'. Community groups campaigned against redevelopment of working-class areas or the building of motorways; for the preservation of historic landmarks, and for new or improved local amenities; and organized to provide legal, welfare and housing advice. Responding to that prevalent sense of crisis and widespread disillusionment with the bureaucratic state, community activists sought to meet need and mobilize working-class people at the grassroots.[22]

For radicals who had come to political maturity in the late 1960s, protesting against the Vietnam War or apartheid, community action represented a new strategic approach. Anti-apartheid activist, leading Young Liberal and future Labour minister Peter Hain saw community politics as a means of bridging the cultural divide between largely middle-class radicals involved in anti-Vietnam War and anti-apartheid protests in the late 1960s, and ordinary working-class people.[23] In a vein similar to Young, Hain argued that the 'facelessness of the new industrialism', alongside the remoteness of the social-democratic state, had served to fragment 'the old working-class communities' and in so doing 'destroyed the communal identity of interest which could have formed the basis of a unified political struggle springing from industrial action'. In a context in which increasingly few workers lived side by side in single-industry communities, Hain believed that community action within the residential community was the means to forge a new class solidarity. By fostering participation within residential communities, around issues of redevelopment or public service provision, it would be possible to 'forge a new community

---

[22] John Davis, 'Community and the Labour Left in 1970s London', in Chris Williams and Andrew Edwards, *The art of the possible: Politics and governance in modern British history, 1885–1997: Essays in memory of Duncan Tanner* (Manchester: MUP, 2015); David Ellis, 'On taking (back) control: lessons from Community Action in 1970s Britain', *Renewal* 25, no. 1 (2017): 53–61. For a contemporary account, see Peter Hain (ed.), *Community Politics* (London: John Calder, 1976).

[23] Peter Hain, *Radical Regeneration: Protest, Direct Action and Community Politics* (London: Quartet, 1975), ch. 1.

consciousness that can bring back some cohesion and a spirit of solidarity to social life'.[24] For Hain, this was a means of creating the capacity and confidence for a new sort of grassroots libertarian socialism: by mobilizing working people around a wide range of issues, 'a participatory spirit [would] be injected into the community and people will realise it is *they* who possess the real power: the power to confront, to challenge, to agitate, the power to create a participatory democracy'.[25]

However, it was not just the New Left which responded to a growing sense that the British state was too paternalistic, insufficiently undemocratic and remote from ordinary people's lives. Under Michael Young's stewardship, Labour, Conservative and Liberal MPs came together with local government bureaucrats and New Left activists in the Association for Neighbourhood Councils (ANC), campaigning for 'urban parish councils' in response to the mooted expansion of the area covered by local government. Such councils, they believed, would provide a greater voice to the individual citizen and local neighbourhood, create a stronger identification between people's sense of place and the area in which they were represented, and allow for a degree of local participation and autonomy around the provision of services and amenities.[26]

These actors by no means shared an understanding of what community meant. Whilst Young and the ANC placed great importance on people's identification with a specific geographical area and the relationships within it, community activists and community workers coming from a more orthodox Marxist perspective saw the concept of community as an obstacle to the development of class consciousness, serving to obfuscate real social divisions. Hence, the authors of *Community or Class Struggle* argued that, 'to speak of a "community" when working on issues such as housing, health, play or welfare can cause great confusion, since, however one looks at it, no community exists; on the contrary, one is confronted with a cluster of class positions, conflicts and interests, some of which are irreconcilable'.[27] They understood *community politics* as useful only in the sense that it distinguished new areas of class struggle from those that took place in the workplace: it signified struggle within the sphere of *social*

[24] Ibid., 154; Hain, *Community Politics*, 'Introduction'.

[25] Hain, *Regeneration*, 160.

[26] John Baker and Michael Young, *The Hornsey Plan: A Role for Neighbourhood Councils in the New Local Government* (Halstead, UK: Association for Neighbourhood Councils, 4th edn, 1973).

[27] John Cowley, Adah Kaye, Marjorie Mayo and Mike Thompson, *Community or Class Struggle?* (London: Stage 1, 1977), 5–6.

reproduction. These activists saw their role as connecting traditional workplace struggles with the community struggles outside it.[28]

Despite these differences, however, actors on the left in the period shared a number of concerns – not only with the shortcomings of the social-democratic state, but also with the need to expand the political concerns of the left beyond workplace struggle and the redistribution of wealth. The welfare state provided for a huge range of social needs, but equally it created new expectations from citizens and new sites of struggle. Community action was a powerful strategy for grassroots mobilization and an outlet to expose the shortcomings of conventional social-democratic politics. With increasing pressure on public finances from the late 1960s onwards, and both parties increasingly keen to rein in local government spending, community action would serve as an outlet for opposition to cuts and a means of channelling a new spirit of 'popular individualism' in a radical direction.[29]

Revisionism and 'community socialism'

It was the Liberal Party that was best placed to profit from a new spirit of grassroots participation and new forms of ultra-local campaigning. Propelled in particular by the radicalism of the Young Liberals, by 1970 the party had adopted an idea of 'community politics' which combined a commitment to grassroots democracy and participation, with a new ultra-local form of campaigning. This created tensions between a leadership which saw community politics as a useful campaigning strategy whilst remaining largely committed to conventional parliamentary politics, and the Young Liberals who saw this as an expression of libertarian socialism, which would eventually lead Peter Hain and others into the Labour Party. Nonetheless, the approach was seen to play a major part in the Liberals' electoral revival in the early 1970s.[30]

The fading promise of the Wilson government prompted internal critics on Labour's left and right to question the implicit means and ends of Wilsonism, and the very explicit means and ends of Croslandite revisionism. If 1968 was a year of advance for the radical left, for Harold Wilson's Labour government it was

---

[28] Ibid.

[29] Emily Robinson et al., 'Telling stories about post-war Britain: "popular individualism" and the "crisis" of the 1970s', *Twentieth Century British History* 28, no. 2 (2017): 268–304.

[30] Tudor Jones, *The Revival of British Liberalism: From Grimond to Clegg* (Basingstoke: Palgrave Macmillan, 2011), ch. 4. See also Ruth Fox, 'Young Liberal Influence and its Effects 1970–74', *Liberal Democrat History Group* Newsletter, no. 14, March 1997, 16–18.

anything but. For the then Labour MP David Marquand, the year provided proof not of the latent socialist radicalism within the British electorate, but of the reverse: with Labour's disastrous showing in that year's local elections, surging support for Scottish and Welsh nationalists, and open displays of support amongst trade unionists for Enoch Powell.[31] Marquand and a number of younger revisionists like David Owen and John Mackintosh had been advancing the case for greater attention to the need for political reform – and particularly decentralization – since 1967's *Change Gear!* pamphlet.[32] The year's events reinforced an existing sense of crisis within Britain's inner cities and an awareness of popular frustration with the remoteness of government. Increasingly, the government pursued more participatory policies, particularly in response to the 'rediscovery of poverty'.[33] In 1967 and 1968, establishment of the Community Development Projects, and the Plowden, Skeffington and Seebohm reports – setting out plans for citizen participation and greater responsiveness in education, planning and social services respectively – indicated a significant degree of engagement with these ideas. Meanwhile a number of ministers from across the party, like Judith Hart, Richard Crossman and – to an extent – Anthony Crosland, showed interest in decentralist constitutional reform.[34]

In opposition, the party's leading lights would debate the potential of community politics as a path to socialist renewal. For Tony Benn, the 'new politics' was an exciting development: the emergence of 'a new expression of grassroots socialism' driven by the 'new citizen'. This 'new citizen' was said to be more resistant to centralized authority, able to make more demands of government, and making their presence felt in community groups and a wide range of other grassroots organizations. For Benn, this offered Labour the opportunity 'to renew itself and move nearer to the time when it was seen as the natural Government of a more fully self-governing society'.[35] The left should, he argued, reorient itself around a whole range of new issues: the preservation of cultural diversity, greater participation in decision-making across society, an assault upon bureaucracy and the democratization of the media.[36]

By contrast, Crosland would argue vociferously that social democracy was not in need of reinvention, that participation was an overwhelmingly middle-

---

[31] David Marquand, 'May Day Illusions', *Encounter*, 1968, 54–6.
[32] David Marquand, John Mackintosh and David Owen, *Change Gear!: Towards a Socialist Strategy* (London: Socialist Commentary, 1967).
[33] Steven Fielding, *Labour and Cultural Change* (Manchester: MUP, 2003), ch. 3.
[34] Ibid.
[35] Tony Benn, *The New Politics* (London: Fabian Society, 1970), 2.
[36] Ibid., 12–28.

class preoccupation, and that Labour risked being blown off course by the preoccupations of middle-class radicals. In a much-cited intervention, he cautioned against:

> ... the siren voices of some Left-wing publicists, both in this country and the United States, urging us to gallop off in a totally different direction. They concede that the basic issues are still of some importance. But, having made that quick obeisance, they go on to say that the real issues of the 1970s will be quite different ones – alienation, communication, participation, atomisation, dehumanisation, the information network, student revolt, the generation gap or even Women's Lib. Now, no doubt these polysyllables all conceal an important truth, even though I cannot myself discern it in every case, and occasionally dislike what I can discern.[37]

What was needed was 'not a great shift of direction but a clear reaffirmation of those agreed ideals'. Increased public expenditure and regulation remained the key methods for achieving these objectives. Indeed, the changing nature of the capitalist economy and new challenges – including increased concerns around the environment and the growth of multinational corporations – necessitated more regulation and redistribution through the central state, not less.[38]

On one level, this was a debate about the extent to which community politics offered a new model for British socialism. But on another, this was a more fundamental debate about the nature and interests of working-class communities. If Benn sought to align Labour with activists working at the grassroots to bring the party closer to working-class communities, then Crosland believed that working-class people, in his Grimsby constituency and elsewhere, were largely uninterested in participation:

> ... only a small minority of the population wish to participate in this way. I repeat what I have often said – the majority prefer to lead a full family life and cultivate their gardens. And a good thing too. For if we believe in socialism as a means of increasing personal freedom and the range of choice, we do not necessarily want a busy bustling society in which everyone is politically active, and fussing around in an interfering and responsible manner, and herding us all into participating groups.[39]

Crosland's abandonment of the iconoclasm which had once inspired the revisionists, and apparent failure to provide the intellectual leadership that social democrats needed after 1970, would increasingly isolate him from former allies.

---

[37] Anthony Crosland, *A Social Democratic Britain* (London: Fabian Society, 1970), 12.
[38] Ibid., 1–10.
[39] Ibid., 13.

By the early 1970s, many of the younger revisionists who had clustered around Crosland during the 1966–70 parliament had moved on. With Crosland seemingly failing to challenge the party over a whole string of issues – from industrial relations to (most famously) Europe – his former acolytes grouped around the figure of Roy Jenkins and found themselves increasingly detached from the party.[40] Although younger revisionists from the 1966 intake, like Mackintosh, Marquand and Owen, had been arguing that Labour needed a shift in emphasis from economic equality to (decentralist) political reform since the mid-1960s, these calls would become increasingly prominent in the late 1970s. The liberal revisionists understood the failings of the Wilson governments as failings of Croslandism. Where Croslandite social democracy largely hinged upon the role of the nation-state, the liberal revisionists argued that social democracy required a twofold move away from the nation-state. This meant looking upwards, towards the level of supranational institutions, and in particular an embrace of the urgent need for entry into the European Community. But it also involved shifting power downwards. By the late 1970s, revisionists were taking a turn towards 'community socialism', and an embrace of decentralist ideas formed an integral part of this.

Revisionist politicians like Marquand, Evan Luard and Giles Radice became increasingly critical of the disempowering, bureaucratic state, advocating a social-democratic politics which replaced an emphasis on 'mechanical reform' with 'moral reform', or 'downwards-moving' movements with 'upwards-moving' movements.[41] Influencing the thinking of Roy Jenkins, Shirley Williams and David Owen in the months and years prior to the SDP split, these thinkers' 'community socialism' encompassed an emphasis on political and constitutional reform, especially decentralization and greater participation within public services and industry. In the most utopian expression of this vision, Luard envisaged a 'community socialism', or 'socialism at the grassroots', based on diffusing power away from large organizations and elites within large organizations. He envisaged a future characterized not by the monolithic socialist state, but by 'the socialist city or small town, where a number of local undertakings, commercial

[40] For more on the revisionists' move away from Crosland towards Jenkins, and on Crosland's apparent antipathy towards some of their new ideas, see Patrick Diamond's chapter in this volume.

[41] See for example David Marquand, 'Taming Leviathan: Social Democracy and Decentralisation', Eighth Rita Hinden Memorial Lecture, February 1980; Giles Radice, *Community Socialism* (London: Fabian Society, 1979) and *The Industrial Democrats: Trade Unions in an Uncertain World* (London: Allen & Unwin, 1979); Evan Luard, *Socialism at the Grassroots* (London: Fabian Society, 1980). Unlike the others in this group, Radice would remain in the Labour Party after 1981 and would go on to be an important figure within debates about the party's modernization going into the 1990s.

and industrial, are run jointly' and 'the jointly-run neighbourhood laundry, the neighbourhood bakery, the neighbourhood hairdresser, run not for profit but for the equal benefit of all who live within the neighbourhood'.[42] Whilst Luard's vision was more utopian and on a grander scale, the same themes recurred in the work of many of his colleagues – a number, but not all, of whom would join the SDP in 1981.

For the liberal revisionists, the language of 'community socialism' allowed them to lay claim to radical currents found within modern Britain *and* to an authentic socialist tradition, whilst distancing themselves from what they saw as the failings of social democracy. To some, this was not only a critique of the means – the state – but also the ends: the primacy of equality was called into question, and a far greater emphasis placed on individual freedom.[43] Unlike others who had made the case for a more decentralist social democracy centred around community, the liberal revisionists did not see this in terms of working-class community. Indeed, Marquand's criticism of Labour related directly to its ostensibly 'proletarian', anti-intellectual culture: the villain of the piece, for Marquand, was not Tony Benn but James Callaghan.[44] Perceptively, the historian Raphael Samuel noted that the SDP's primary constituency was the 'new middle class': its concept of participation represented 'a democracy of the well-placed, a natural extension of the new middle class capacity for sociability'.[45] On this question, the Marxist historian Samuel and the revisionist politician Crosland would likely have spoken as one.

Despite this, there was a striking consonance between critiques of centralism and bureaucracy emanating from the social-democratic (or was it liberal?) centre, and from the Bennite left. Indeed, many of those involved in community action had, by the early 1980s, come to prominence on the Labour left in local government.[46] For one revisionist who would remain within the party, Philip Whitehead, Luard's work in fact had much in common with that of Tony Benn, who also advocated a more decentralist socialist politics:

---

[42] Evan Luard, *Socialism Without the State* (London: Palgrave Macmillan, 1991), 152.

[43] See especially David Marquand, 'Taming Leviathan: Social Democracy and Decentralisation', Eighth Rita Hinden Memorial Lecture, February 1980; David Marquand, 'Introduction', in Marquand (ed.), *John P. Mackintosh on Parliament and Social Democracy* (Harlow: Longman, 1982).

[44] David Marquand, 'Inquest on a Movement', *Encounter*, July 1979, 8–17.

[45] Raphael Samuel, 'The SDP and the new political class', *New Society*, 22 April 1982, 124–7.

[46] See for instance Tony Benn, *Arguments for Democracy* (London: Jonathan Cape, 1981); Hilary Wainwright, *A Tale of Two Parties* (London: Hogarth, 1984). On the 'new urban left' in local government, see John Gyford, *The Politics of Local Socialism* (London: Allen & Unwin, 1985).

In their different ways, from what would be thought (not always appropriately) the left and right of the Labour Party, Tony Benn and Evan Luard have written books dedicated to restoring the human scale of socialism. Away from the cheap applause and backstairs intrigues of the Conference, the Party may find the common ground where these two meet.

Whitehead went on: 'Taken together, [their] books point to the way Labour could regain mass support, as the party of community socialism – the only reasonable alternative to the way we live now.'[47]

As Colm Murphy notes elsewhere in this volume, the failure of social democrats to engage seriously with the ideas underpinning the left's strategy may have represented a missed opportunity to find common ground and contributed to their political marginalization.[48] The possibility of finding such common ground was, perhaps, unrealistic, given the strength of feeling involved – and by 1981 Luard and Marquand were both in the SDP.

In the immediate run-up to the split, both David Owen and Shirley Williams would author books that attempted to set out a new political vision, with both placing a heavy emphasis upon community and decentralization. Once again, this allowed them to lay claim to a more authentic radicalism than that of the Labour Party which, they suggested, was implacably statist and paternalistic. Owen in particular sought to locate himself within an alternative, non-statist socialist tradition.[49] Unsurprisingly, the effort to claim libertarian socialism for the SDP did not go unchallenged by those within Labour who believed they had a far more genuine claim to that tradition. Indeed, it was not without justification that there was some pushback against the idea that the revisionists who had most enthusiastically embraced Croslandism before 1970, could lay claim to Labour's more state-sceptical traditions. Anthony (Tony) Wright, the academic and future Labour MP, noted a certain irony in the fact that 'those social democrats who became Social Democrats belonged precisely to that wing of the Labour Party that had been the most uncritical carrier of the centralist version of collectivism. Yet in abandoning Labour they claimed (at least initially) to be abandoning not socialism but the state.'[50] Likewise, the authors of a 1982 Labour Co-Ordinating Committee pamphlet – Peter Hain amongst them – charged the SDP with having 'hijacked' a set of preoccupations which had emanated from

[47]   Philip Whitehead, 'Labour Pains', *London Review of Books* 1, no. 2 (8 November 1979): 7–9.

[48]   See Colm Murphy's chapter in this volume.

[49]   David Owen, *Face the Future* (London: Jonathan Cape, 1981); Shirley Williams, *Politics is for People* (Cambridge, MA: HUP, 1981).

[50]   Anthony Wright, 'Decentralisation and the Socialist Tradition', in Anthony Wright, John Stewart and Nicholas Deakin, *Socialism and Decentralisation* (London: Fabian Society, 1984), 1–2.

the New Left.[51] The charge of opportunism was not without merit. Following the 1983 election, Owen swiftly exchanged the language of 'values, love, charity and altruism' (as well as community and fraternity), for an alternative set of values which he believed explained Thatcherism's appeal to working- and middle-class voters, such as 'personal ambition and enterprise'.[52]

New Labour: community to the fore

By the mid-1990s, a critique of postwar social democracy centred around community had migrated from the margins to become a core part of Labour's message. In *The Blair Revolution*, Roger Liddle and Peter Mandelson claimed that the 'distinctive emphasis' in the politics of New Labour was 'its concept of community'.[53] A lively debate would unfold in the media and in academia about the influence of 'new communitarian' thought – advanced by American social scientists like Amitai Etzioni and Robert Putnam – on the party leadership.[54] Meanwhile, some of the SDP's leading exponents of community – notably Michael Young and David Marquand – had returned to the Labour fold.

For New Labour, an appeal to 'community' enabled the party to distance itself from class-based collectivism and an alleged overreliance upon the state, whilst drawing a sharp distinction between itself and Thatcherism's apparent disregard for community and society.[55] Likewise, it allowed Blair to lay claim to an older socialist tradition, which he could define in stark contrast to both statism and Marxism. Hence, it was possible to claim that 'modernisation' was in fact 'about trying to get the Party back' to its 'traditional values'. Blair advanced an account of Labour's recent history in which scientific Marxist tradition hijacked the party and detached it from its ethical socialist traditions. He wrote: '[I]n the late 1970s and early 1980s … its intellectual temple was stormed and captured by a generation of

---

[51] Labour Co-Ordinating Committee, 'Realignment of the Right: The Real Face of the SDP' (London: LCC, 1982).

[52] Dean Blackburn, '"Facing the Future?": David Owen and Social Democracy in the 1980s and Beyond', *Parliamentary Affairs* 64, no. 4 (2011): 634–51.

[53] Roger Liddle and Peter Mandelson, *The Blair Revolution: Can New Labour Deliver?* (London: Faber & Faber, 1996), 19–21.

[54] See variously Mark Bevir, *New Labour: A Critique* (London: Routledge, 2005), ch. 3; Stephen Driver, 'New Labour's Communitarians', *Critical Social Policy* 17, no. 52 (1997); Sarah Hale, *Blair's Community* (Manchester: MUP, 2006); Sarah Hale, Will Leggett and Luke Martell, *The Third Way and Beyond: Criticisms, Futures and Alternatives* (Manchester: MUP, 2004), esp. chs. 5–7; Ruth Levitas, 'Community, Utopia and New Labour', *Local Economy* 15, no. 3 (2000): 188–97.

[55] See for example Liddle and Mandelson, *Revolution*, 19; on the place of community in Labour modernizers' view of class and social change, see Florence Sutcliffe-Braithwaite, *Class, Politics and the Decline of Deference in England, 1968–2000* (Oxford: OUP, 2018), 191–6.

politicians and academics who thought that values and concepts like community and social justice were too weak to guide the party.[56] As we have seen, this view of history was highly selective but rhetorically appealing.

The New Labour understanding of community, argued Liddle and Mandelson, was 'not a soft, romantic concept – conjuring up images of old dears attending bingo nights in draughty halls, or the world of the tightly knit mining community that now is dying away'. In fact, neither they nor Blair would give much clear indication as to the geographical or spatial dimension of community.[57] In this sense, New Labour shared with the liberal revisionists of the late 1970s and early 1980s a commitment to 'community' which was geographically and sociologically ambiguous, free of the distinctive class- or place-based character of the communities described by Young and Hoggart. Like the liberal revisionists, they deployed the rhetoric of community to distance themselves from social democracy's alleged overreliance on the state. For New Labour, 'community' frequently described a relationship between individuals and society as a whole. This emphasized the state's obligations to provide people with opportunity – through education – and a stake in society, understood almost exclusively in terms of employment.[58] Indeed, if 'community' had been evoked in the 1950s and 1960s as a means of broadening the domain of socialist politics beyond the workplace, in the 1990s New Labour worked on the assumption that community would be realized primarily through paid employment.

However, where the liberal revisionists of the late 1970s and early 1980s had seen 'community' as a means of moving social democracy away from collectivism and towards liberal individualism, by the end of the Thatcher period, there was a clear sense that the balance had shifted too far in the other direction. As David Marquand would argue from the vantage point of 1996, in a volume edited by Radice and carrying a foreword by Blair: 'In the 1960s and 1970s, British governments sacrificed community to equality; in the 1980s and 1990s they have sacrificed it, far more brutally, to liberty.'[59] Already by the late 1980s, Marquand had markedly changed his tone, concluding that individualism was the root cause

---

[56] Tony Blair, 'Introduction', in Giles Radice (ed.), *What Needs to Change* (London: HarperCollins, 1996).

[57] Roger Liddle and Peter Mandelson, *The Blair Revolution: Can New Labour Deliver?* (London: Faber & Faber, 1996), 19–21.

[58] As Mark Bevir has suggested, this perhaps reflects the 'new communitarian' tendency to 'fuse civil society with community in opposition to both the state and the market. Civil society appears, in their view, as the site of families and voluntary associations that embody a spirit of community that is at odds with the individualistic rationalism of the market as well as the impersonal bureaucracy of the state. The dubious fusion of community and civil society enables communitarians such as Etzioni to operate with three sharply distinguished categories – the state, the market, and communities in civil society – whilst also facilitating a neglect of the particularity and exclusion that historically have been associated with community.' See Mark Bevir, *New Labour: A Critique* (London: Routledge, 2005), 74.

[59] David Marquand, 'Community and the Left', in Radice, *What Needs to Change*.

of British decline.[60] The task was for social democrats to reinstate a collectivist *ethos* of some kind, even whilst they disavowed the form collectivism had taken in the postwar decades. 'Community' was a vehicle for articulating a belief in the essentially social nature of human beings, but also for a more conservative aspect of socialist politics. For New Labour, the key dimension of 'community' was the contention that the notion of individual rights had gone too far and needed to be counteracted with an emphasis upon responsibility or duty. There was a distinctively tough edge to this. Liddle and Mandelson identified 'New Labour's enemies' as those 'who ignore the feelings of community … the vested interests who want decisions to be taken to benefit them, not the community as a whole … the inefficient who let the community down and impede its success … [and] the irresponsible who fall down on their obligations to their families and therefore their community'.[61] With New Labour reluctant to impose further obligations on corporations and the better off, and with widespread concern about welfare dependency and long-term unemployment, the weight of policies aimed at community tended to fall on the worst off, through policies around welfare and antisocial behaviour. As Jeremy Nuttall has observed, this meant in practice that New Labour at times 'focused more on … the parental failings of ordinary people than the financial or environmental abuses of wealthy businesses' and demonstrated an 'overzealousness … in its willingness to curb liberties in the interest of supposed moral ends'.[62]

Whilst an ethical or communitarian critique of 'old-fashioned' social democracy had a powerful political appeal to Labour in opposition, putting such a politics into practice in government would prove more difficult.[63] As Peter Sloman recounts, Labour's critique of 'old Labour's' reliance on redistribution soon ran into the reality of an insufficiently generous welfare state and evidence indicating that financial transfers were the best means of combatting 'social exclusion'.[64] Nonetheless,

---

[60] David Marquand, *The Unprincipled Society* (London: Fontana Press, 1988).

[61] Liddle and Mandelson, *Revolution*, 20.

[62] Jeremy Nuttall, *Psychological Socialism: The Labour Party and Qualities of Mind and Character, 1931 to the Present* (Manchester: MUP, 2006), ch. 6.

[63] The argument that there is a structural tendency for ethical-socialist critique to be subordinated, upon contact with power, to Fabianism is an old one. Indeed, in his seminal critique of 'Labourism', published within weeks of Harold Wilson's first election victory, Tom Nairn would argue that the inability of ethical socialists to translate their ideas into a viable governing philosophy had ensured hegemony for Fabianism from the party's earliest days. As Nairn put it: 'Lacking ideas (that is, lacking intellectual cadres) capable of formulating what they felt, tied in the archaic web of neo-Protestant moralism', the ethical socialists of the ILP tradition 'never had a clear conception of what should be done practically in order to realise their socialist dream. The Fabians, on the other hand, invariably knew what to do … This meant, in effect, that within the limits of Labourism the actual modalities of action were dominated by the Fabians. The ILP tradition was destined to become – so to speak – the subjectivity of the political wing of Labourism, the emotions of the movement in contrast to its Fabian "mind" or "intellect".' Tom Nairn, 'The Nature of the Labour Party – Part I', *New Left Review* 1, no. 27 (1964): 47–8.

[64] Peter Sloman, *Transfer State: The Idea of a Guaranteed Income and the Politics of Redistribution in Modern Britain* (Oxford: OUP, 2019), ch. 7.

the language of 'community' served its intended purpose in offering a powerful rhetorical underpinning for social-democratic politics in an inhospitable climate. It housed a varied set of political priorities within a distinctive and powerful synthesis: localism, investment in public services and the prevention of crime amongst them.[65] That the balance within this synthesis was not necessarily the right one or that some elements of it were more suited to the politics of the 1990s than that of the 2020s, does not preclude us from learning important lessons from it.

The speed with which New Labour abandoned its original ethical-communitarian orientation has been lamented by some of those who were involved.[66] And after 2010, Blue Labour would in turn take aim at New Labour as another manifestation of a Croslandite inheritance of social liberalism and Fabian technocracy.[67] This tendency – more a group of intellectuals, than an organized faction – argued that the party needed to restore its relationship with a lost working-class base through reconnecting with suppressed aspects of its traditions, which could fuse radicalism and conservatism.[68] Given the iconoclasm of Blue Labour's pitch, it is in fact striking how much of this critique of New Labour echoed New Labour's own pre-1997 communitarian critique of social democracy.[69] Key figures associated with the movement, and with Labour's Policy Review in the run-up to the 2015 general election, looked back to Hoggart and Young as sources of inspiration for Labour's intellectual renewal (and a critique of the left's wrong-turns after 1956).[70] With reference to these figures, and a wide array of others, Blue Labour sought to (re)construct a lost genealogy

---

[65] For a more obviously 'progressive' argument framing New Labour policies in terms of 'community', see Tony Blair, 'New Labour and Community', *Renewal* 10, no. 2 (2002): 9–14.

[66] For instance David Blunkett and David Richards, 'Labour In and Out of Government: Political Ideas, Political Practice and the British Political Tradition', *Political Studies Review* 9 (2011): 178–92. In a similar vein, Jon Cruddas has often spoken admiringly of the 'early Blair'. See for instance David Goodhart, 'Interview: Jon Cruddas', *Prospect*, no. 170, May 2010; Jon Cruddas, 'The Good Society', lecture at the University of East Anglia, May 2012, https://joncruddas.org.uk/jon-cruddas-mps-recent-uea-lecture-good-society (accessed 10 January 2020).

[67] See Maurice Glasman, Jonathan Rutherford, Marc Stears and Stuart White, *The Labour Tradition and the Politics of Paradox* (The Oxford–London Seminars, 2011).

[68] See for example 'Maurice Glasman: My Blue Labour vision can defeat the coalition', *The Observer*, 24 April 2011.

[69] However those involved in Blue Labour's development would deny the characterization of the movement as either 'communitarian' or even necessarily concerned with 'community'. As one participant in early discussions noted, Blue Labour's key figures tended to 'use the word "relationship" far more often than "community"'. For a movement which self-consciously defined itself against abstraction, '"community" has a nebulous abstraction that contradicts Blue Labour's concrete sensibility'. Jon Wilson, 'Blue Labour Realism', on Open Democracy, https://www.opendemocracy.net/en/opendemocracyuk/blue-labour-realism/ (accessed 16 February 2021).

[70] Jonathan Rutherford, 'The First New Left, Blue Labour and English Modernity', *Renewal* 21, no. 1 (Spring 2013): 9–14; Jon Cruddas, 'Power and One Nation', speech to the New Local Government Network Annual Conference, 12 February 2014, https://labourlist.org/2014/02/power-and-one-nation-jon-cruddas-speech-to-the-new-local-government-network/ (accessed 17 February 2021).

that stood in opposition to Labour's liberal-Fabian tradition.[71] Alongside this intellectual effort, the 2010–15 period also saw a more practical manifestation of interest in community, as the party began its intermittent engagement with community organizing.

Conclusion: social democracy and community

The language of community has frequently served as a powerful device for criticizing the remoteness of social-democratic parties – in and out of government – from ordinary people, and of the dislocating effects of both state and market. It has signified the need to expand the domain of socialist politics – beyond the workplace *and* the state – and embrace a politics sensitive to people's everyday lives and, often, 'common sense'.

It has also served as a powerful critique of the uneven geographic impact of socioeconomic change. From the 1950s to the 1980s, the imagined locus of community-in-decline was the 'urban village' in the depopulating city, contrasted to the apparently rootless, materialistic way of life in new towns and suburbs. This picture has now changed significantly. With the benefits of growth in a globalized economy and a massively expanded army of graduates concentrated in Britain's cities, city-dwellers have become a shorthand for the rootless and materialistic; the 'Anywheres' of London and Manchester have been contrasted with 'Somewheres' outside the city limits – particularly in ex-industrial towns.[72] These arguments may support a necessary critique of Britain's geographical inequalities and political centralization, but they also serve to efface the far more nuanced reality of inequality, deprivation and housing crisis within Britain's biggest cities.

---

[71] For a more recent attempt to reconstruct such a tradition by one of the figures previously associated with Blue Labour, see Marc Stears, *Out of the Ordinary: How Everyday Life Transformed a Nation and How it Can Again* (Cambridge, MA: HUP, 2021).

[72] David Goodhart, *The Road to Somewhere* (London: Hurst, 2018). The shifting imagined geographies of community – whereby urban and suburban or rural have taken on shifting connotations, and places and professions have shifted in the popular imagination between being 'rural' and 'urban' – has been discussed elsewhere; however, it remains a fruitful avenue for further historical exploration. In the early 1970s, Raymond Williams would note the extent to which community activists campaigning against the redevelopment of Covent Garden echoed the language of commoners resisting enclosure two hundred years before, whilst Jörg Arnold has more recently traced the 'ruralization' of the mining community in the popular imagination since the 1970s. See Raymond Williams, *The Country and City* (London: Vintage, 2016); Jörg Arnold, '"That rather sinful city of London": the coal miner, the city and the country in the British cultural imagination, c. 1969–2014', *Urban History* 2, Special Issue 2 (May 2020).

Frequently, an arid social democracy has been decried as overreliant upon the state and for placing too little emphasis upon relationships, community and solidarity. And yet there is another story that can be told about community and social democracy in postwar Britain. The period from the mid-1960s had seen the proliferation of voluntary and community groups in all sorts of forms, from tenants associations, to neighbourhood councils, to welfare advice centres. Nor should we overlook trade unionism as an expression of participation and solidarity: British trade union membership peaked in 1979. In that period, social democracy was not an exhausted monolith; rather, as Guy Ortolano contends, it was 'dynamic', adaptable to new contexts and to changing demands, and indeed sensitive to the need to support 'community' and to enable a greater degree of participation within the workings of the welfare state.[73] From the Community Development Projects of the late 1960s, to the efforts that Ortolano recounts to foster community amongst the first generations of residents in Milton Keynes, Labour politicians and local officials tried to encourage and channel grassroots initiatives during this period to tackle social problems and revitalize social democracy. Of course – as both the CDP story and Ortolano's example show – often activists and community groups would then direct their energies in opposition to heavy-handed planning decisions, poorly maintained public amenities or the intense alienation many people felt when coming into contact with the welfare arm of the state.

But it would be reckless to ignore the evidence that the social democracy of the 1940s through to the 1970s brought with it a flowering of the sort of voluntarist initiatives that its communitarian critics desired. After a decade of austerity, which has seen the withering of much of the social infrastructure essential to a rich associational life, reinvestment in that infrastructure will be an essential component of any politics that seriously values community.[74] The critics of social democracy that have been discussed in this chapter frequently identified real shortcomings. However, recent decades have illustrated the extent to which other factors pose a far greater threat to the ideal of 'community' – whether of a stable, residential kind or of a wider sense of common purpose. In particular, inequality, a fraying public realm and Britain's uneven economic geography – whereby a deficit of opportunity outside Britain's cities is matched

---

[73] Guy Ortolano, *Thatcher's Progress: From Social Democracy to Market Liberalism Through an English New Town* (Cambridge: CUP, 2019).

[74] A point that has been made well by Jon Lawrence. See Lawrence, *Me, Me, Me?*, postscript.

by a housing crisis within them – have had a corrosive effect on social solidarity and local and national scales. Unless a 'communitarian' sensibility is synthesized successfully with more traditional social-democratic concerns and with an effective governing ethos, then it is unlikely to achieve widespread support within the party – or to avoid a cycle whereby such ideas are embraced in opposition, only to be abandoned upon contact with political power.

9

Linking up Labour: Place, community and buses in 1980s Sheffield

Daisy Payling

In November 2018, Museums Sheffield launched 'Who We Are: Photographs by Martin Jenkinson': the first retrospective of the photographer's work. Jenkinson, who became a photographer in 1979 when he was made redundant from one of the city's steel works, photographed Sheffield and its people, documenting thirty years of political and social change. Most famous for his photographs of protests, including the 1984–5 miners' strike, Jenkinson's work also captures the everyday details of the city's landscape in stark black and white.[1] Much of his work is explicitly political. The exhibition was described as a 'tribute to Jenkinson's commitment to justice and equality'.[2] But even in photographs that are not documenting protests, it is hard to avoid evidence of the city's political culture. The image chosen to promote 'Who We Are' is a prime example. It is a black-and-white portrait of Maxine Duffas, South Yorkshire Passenger Transport's first Black woman bus driver, sitting in her cab in 1983. She turns towards the camera, smiling in her uniform, as she holds the steering wheel; ready to pull out of the bus garage and start her shift.

Duffas attended the launch of 'Who We Are' with her family. Museums Sheffield posted a photograph of the Duffas family posed in front of the exhibition banner bearing Maxine's image on their social media pages, explaining that Jenkinson's photographs 'created a candid insight into Sheffield and the communities we're part of, offering a sometimes moving, sometimes humorous

---

[1] Mark Metcalf, Martin Jenkinson and Mark Harvey, *Images of the Past: The Miners' Strike* (Barnsley: Pen & Sword History, 2014).

[2] Hannah Clugston, 'Politics, passion, pride: Who We Are: Photographs by Martin Jenkinson review', *Guardian*, 27 November 2018, https://www.theguardian.com/artanddesign/2018/nov/27/who-we-are-photographs-by-martin-jenkinson-review-weston-park-museum-sheffield (accessed 14 October 2020).

window onto the city's character'.[3] Celebrated as representative of Sheffield, Maxine Duffas was welcomed as a guest of honour. But in choosing this particular photograph as one of the exhibition banners, Museums Sheffield also celebrated Sheffield's buses, and the role they played in shaping the city's political identity, nurturing and sustaining a local community in the 1970s and 1980s.

Cheap bus fares feature heavily in people's memories of Sheffield in the 1980s. As one of the best-known policies of the so-called 'Socialist Republic of South Yorkshire' – the nickname of the Labour-led South Yorkshire County Council – cheap buses shaped Sheffield residents' everyday lives in the 1970s and 1980s. They enabled people to explore the city and surrounding countryside, take part in community life, travel to work and maintain relationships with friends and family. Former councillor and current Labour MP Clive Betts argues that the cheap-fares transport policy was the reason Sheffield was known as a 'radical' local authority.[4] It was a keystone of Sheffield's municipal socialism; itself an important strand of Labour thinking around renewal in the 1980s. Even critics agreed to a certain extent, with activist John Lawson telling me that the 'Socialist Republic' was 'complete and utter bollocks apart from your two pence bus fares'.[5] A flagship policy with a large amount of local support, cheap bus fares represented the local Labour group's vision of community in Sheffield, whilst providing the means to link up the city.

This chapter details the rise and fall of cheap bus fares in Sheffield to explore how the Labour-controlled local authority made policy to suit the needs of the local community, and how that policy became part of the city's identity, in turn shaping the community it served. Situated in the politics of municipal socialism, cheap bus fares provide an example of how place and community have shaped Labour policy. The longevity of buses in Sheffield's cultural memory demonstrates the significance the policy had on people's lives and shows what a Labour-controlled local authority could do when it was permitted to raise and allocate its own budget.

First stop: municipal socialism

It is an understatement to say that the 1980s was a difficult decade for the Labour Party. It weathered the continued erosion of its industrial base, its allies in trade

---

[3] Museums Sheffield, Facebook Page, 29 November 2018, https://www.facebook.com/Museums. Sheffield/photos/a.451998330491/10161346601330492/?type=3 (accessed 21 October 2020).

[4] Interview with Clive Betts, 19 July 2013.

[5] Interview with John and Sue Lawson, 17 May 2013.

unions were vilified by politicians and the press and it suffered successive general election defeats in 1979, 1983, 1987 and 1992. Despite the unexpected rise in influence of 'socialism' within the party in the early 1980s, Labour's defeat in 1983 – after running on a manifesto since dubbed the 'longest suicide note in history' – put it on a path to 'modernisation', much to the disillusionment of sections of the left.[6] At the same time, two 1970s developments altered the shape of the left considerably: one within and one without. The first was the growth of separate but overlapping campaigns for greater, recognized equality for women and ethnic minorities. The second was the emergence of deregulation and free market economics leading to greater inequalities in terms of wealth and class.[7] The 1979 government's commitment to emerging 'Thatcherite' economic policies were seen to exacerbate wealth inequalities. In the 1980s unemployment rose above three million, and de-industrialization ground down Labour constituencies.[8] Many have argued that this break in the postwar consensus led to a widening of the gap between rich and poor and irrevocably changed the social and cultural fabric of Britain.[9]

Some on the left saw this as a period of 'crisis', but with the Labour Party in opposition there were opportunities to strategize and suggest paths back to power; to design a 'renewal' of the left. One area where policies could be designed and enacted was in Labour local government. Particularly in the metropolitan county councils created in 1974 as an upper tier of local government intended to provide strategic coordination in transport and planning, and the metropolitan district councils, a corresponding lower tier, which delivered the bulk of services.[10] These local authorities 'captured a sense of opportunity' otherwise missed by or unavailable to the national Labour Party, leading to the claim that

---

[6] Florence Sutcliffe-Braithwaite, '"Class" in the Development of British Labour Party Ideology, 1983–1997', *Archiv Für Sozialgeschichte* 53 (2013): 329; Mark Garnett, *From Anger to Apathy: The Story of Politics, Society and Popular Culture in Britain since 1975* (London: Vintage, 2008), 7; '1983 v 2017: how Labour's manifestos compare', *Guardian*, 11 May 2017, https://www.theguardian.com/politics/2017/may/11/how-labours-2017-manifesto-compares-with-1983 (accessed 11 June 2019).

[7] Thomas Borstelmann, 'Epilogue: The Shock of the Global', in Niall Ferguson, Charles S. Maier, Erez Manela and Daniel J. Sargent (eds), *The Shock of the Global: The 1970s in Perspective* (Cambridge, MA: HUP, 2010), 354.

[8] Arthur Marwick, *British Society Since 1945* (London: Penguin, 1996), 272.

[9] Paul Addison, *No Turning Back: The Peacetime Revolutions of Post-War Britain* (New York: OUP, 2010), 260; Jeremy Black, *Britain Since the Seventies: Politics and Society in a Consumer Age* (London: Reaktion Books, 2004), 176.

[10] The six metropolitan county councils were Greater Manchester, Merseyside, South Yorkshire, Tyne and Wear, the West Midlands and West Yorkshire. They were all were controlled by Labour. Each metropolitan county council provided strategic oversight for the smaller metropolitan district councils within it. In South Yorkshire these were Sheffield, Doncaster, Rotherham and Barnsley, which were also controlled by Labour.

left-wing politics was most vibrant in local strongholds.[11] Local authorities made attempts to combine class politics with elements of other new social movements to develop distinctive and varied municipal or local socialisms. These aimed to make local politics more democratic and develop 'new ideas about the future of socialism'.[12] Political scientists at the time identified common themes including the restructuring of local capital, decentralization of local services and increased participation in provision by users, and positive action towards women, the poor and ethnic and sexual minorities.[13]

Municipal socialism was practised by councils dominated by the new urban left, which included newer, younger councillors, Labour Party members, community workers and grassroots activists.[14] Labour's local election defeats in the late 1960s and local government reorganization in the 1970s had brought in a new generation of Labour councillors across Britain. A change of personnel brought a change in attitudes. New urban left councillors were trained in the activism of the 1960s and counter-culture – rather than Marxism and Methodism of older Labour traditions.[15] Municipal socialism was an attempt by some Labour-led local authorities to build mass movements; protecting old alliances and creating new ones. It was also explicitly *local* and rooted in the places where it was formed. Its varied characteristics depended on the political priorities of each area and aimed to answer the specific needs of its constituencies and communities.

From the mid-1980s, modernizing figures within the Labour Party acknowledged the importance of 'the local' when polling data and market research found that place and region were central to the composition of social identity.[16] Yet there is a lack of historical literature dealing with municipal or local socialism – a politics that recognized local differences – outside of London. Liverpool is the exception as the city has received some attention given the role of Militant and the disruption that entryism caused on the left.[17] Different cities

---

[11] Geoff Eley, *Forging Democracy: The History of the Left in Europe, 1850–2000* (Oxford: OUP, 2002), 460–2.

[12] John Gyford, *The Politics of Local Socialism* (London: Allen & Unwin, 1985), 1.

[13] Patrick Syed, *The Rise and Fall of the Labour Left* (Basingstoke: Macmillan, 1987), 141. Gyford, *Politics*, 18.

[14] Martin Boddy and Colin Fudge (eds), *Local Socialism? Labour Councils and New Left Alternatives* (Basingstoke: Palgrave, 1984), 5; Gyford, *Politics*,17.

[15] James Curran et al., *Culture Wars: The Media and the British Left* (Edinburgh: EUP, 2005), 31, 42.

[16] Sutcliffe-Braithwaite, '"Class" in the Development of British Labour Party Ideology', 339.

[17] David E. Lowes, *Cuts, Privatization, and Resistance: Neoliberalism and the Local State, 1974 to 1987* (London: Merlin Press, 2012), 96–111. Brian Marren, *We Shall Not Be Moved: How Liverpool's Working Class Fought Redundancies, Closures and Cuts in the Age of Thatcher* (Manchester: MUP, 2016). Diane Frost and Peter North, *Militant Liverpool: A City on the Edge* (Liverpool: LUP, 2013).

embraced municipal socialism in different ways. As Julia Unwin, who worked for Liverpool and Southwark councils as well as the Greater London Council in the 1980s, made clear, 'we have to bear in mind how very different things looked in different parts of the country': a statement that rings true today.[18]

In 1980, David Blunkett became leader of Sheffield City Council, having served on both the Labour-led South Yorkshire County Council and Sheffield City Council throughout the 1970s. Blunkett based his brand of municipal socialism on the needs of the local community, and made it clear that his idea of community meant the traditional institutions of the working class: 'We are going to have to rely on people in the community – the trade unions, the district Labour Party, tenants' groups – to help identify the worst effects of Government policy and to suggest ways of overcoming them.'[19] His aim was to bring local authority departments and these 'active groups in the community' together in a coordinated approach to Sheffield's problems. He reiterated this in the pamphlet *Building from the Bottom* published in 1983. Here, Blunkett and Geoff Green explained that Sheffield's community involved 'a sense of shared experience and interdependence ... built around principles long embodied in the trade union movement'.[20] By drawing on the opinions, skills and 'everyday experience of working people', and by winning 'hearts and minds', Blunkett and Green aimed to build a 'mass movement'.[21]

Blunkett was building on his experience as chair of the Sheffield City Council's Family and Community Services Committee in the 1970s where he had wanted people to 'feel that the services belonged to them, not to the council'.[22] Between 1980 and 1987, Blunkett prioritized bringing Sheffield's communities into the processes of local government. For him, and others within Sheffield City Council, collective action had a 'rightful place alongside electoral representation'.[23] For some, this emphasis went too far. Deputy leader Alan Billings recalls his frustration with 'talk about bottom up politics, bottom up industry, bottom up this, bottom up that', which was 'extraordinarily idealistic, optimistic' and 'naive, unrealistic'.[24] As the decade progressed, influence and necessity encouraged

---

[18] Nick Crowson et al., 'Witness seminar: the voluntary sector in 1980s Britain,' *Contemporary British History* 25, no. 4 (2011): 503.

[19] *The Sheffield Star,* 15 May 1980, 14.

[20] David Blunkett and Geoff Green, *Building from the Bottom: The Sheffield Experience* (London: Fabian Society, 1983), 2.

[21] Ibid., 2, 28.

[22] David Blunkett, *On a Clear Day* (London: Michael O'Mara Books, 1995), 147.

[23] David Blunkett and Keith Jackson, *Democracy in Crisis: The Town Halls Respond* (London: Hogarth, 1987), 7–8.

[24] Interview with Alan Billings and Veronica Hardstaff, 14 June 2013.

Blunkett to expand his sense of community, although he and Sheffield's other councillors originally built their municipal socialism on the values of the local labour movement and the kinship networks that held it together.[25]

Cheap fares

The best-known policy of South Yorkshire's municipal socialism was its cheap bus fares. Initiated by the South Yorkshire County Council, they were defended vociferously by Sheffield City Council. Cheap fares were first put forward by the South Yorkshire Labour Party's manifesto working group in December 1972 and developed into policy after the reorganization of local government came into effect in 1974. The Labour group saw cheap fares and free public transport for elderly and disabled people as an 'immediate objective', but originally planned to develop a programme of 'free transport for all' over the following years.[26] Whilst unable to make public transport free for everyone, South Yorkshire Transport Committee fought to keep fares low until the abolition of metropolitan county councils in 1986. In 1975 they froze bus fares; maintaining them at a constant level in cash terms.[27] Inflation reduced the real price of fares over the decade and the shortfall was subsidized by rates. Interviewed in the *Sheffield Star*, County Councillor Roy Thwaites, Chairman of South Yorkshire Transport Committee and Labour Group Chief Whip, couched the policy in socialist terms. Thwaites reportedly said: 'It's not simply a question of "Can we afford it?", we think it is right as Socialists. We think public transport should be a public service available to all.'[28] Answering the critique that some rate-payers never used public transport, Thwaites argued that, 'as a citizen, one must accept the responsibility that goes with it.'[29] For Thwaites, affordable transport linked everyone in the county. Defending the policy in the 1980s, Blunkett argued similarly that the policy was a 'practical contribution to the social and economic life of the [whole] community'.[30]

---

[25] Daisy Payling, 'Socialist Republic of South Yorkshire': Grassroots Activism and Left-Wing Solidarity in 1980s Sheffield', *Twentieth Century British History* 25, no. 4 (2014): 610–11.

[26] Blunkett and Jackson, *Democracy in Crisis*, 71.

[27] Jonathan P. Nicholl, Michael R. Freeman and Brian T. Williams, 'Effects of subsidising bus travel on the occurrence of road traffic casualties', *Journal of Epidemiology and Community Health* 41 (1987): 51.

[28] 'Prices, politics and our bus services', *The Sheffield Star*, 6 February 1975, 12.

[29] Ibid.

[30] Blunkett and Jackson, *Democracy in Crisis*, 71.

Spending on transport aimed to save rate-payers money in other areas, reducing the need for investment in larger roads and car parks, and encouraged other economic benefits such as increasing the amount of disposable income available to families across the county.[31] The policy directly benefitted a large number of Sheffield's residents. In 1981, 49.6 per cent of Sheffield's population did not own a car.[32] In wards such as Castle and Manor, car ownership was as low as 26.6 per cent and 30 per cent respectively.[33] In 1985 adults could ride buses for six miles for 10p, children for 2p, disabled people for free and pensioners for free outside of peak hours. Adults could travel from the city out to the surrounding Peak District for only 20p. The standard 10p adult fare compared with 58p in Manchester, 55p in London and 50p in Leeds. The benefit for residents can be seen in the numbers using services. During 1982–3 more passengers boarded per mile in South Yorkshire than anywhere else in England, and bus travel increased by 7 per cent between 1974 and 1984, compared to a 30 per cent decline in urban areas nationally.[34] This did not mean that buses were beyond criticism. Tony Fawthrop, Chairman of Sheffield's Passenger Association, complained that cheap fares dominated discussions to the extent that, 'nobody ever asks whether the transport executive is efficient and well run'.[35] The Passenger's Association had been calling for more buses to Bridge Street in Sheffield for years.

Cheap bus fares across the country were threatened in 1982 when the courts ruled the Greater London Council's 'Fares Fair' policy illegal. Alex Waugh, who had succeeded Roy Thwaites as Chairman of the South Yorkshire Transport Committee in 1979, argued that South Yorkshire's policy was legal as they had never had to levy a supplementary rate to support their subsidy. The Court of Appeal ruled that the GLC had broken the law under the Transport (London) Act of 1969, but South Yorkshire was governed by legislation under the Transport Act of 1968, which set out different rules.[36] In response, Sheffield's councillors came out in support of cheap fares. Clive Betts argued that constituents in South Yorkshire had consistently voted for them. Peter Price said that the fares were

---

[31] 'Sheffield's Most Powerful Man ... and he's only 32', *The Sheffield Star*, 15 May 1980, 14; Blunkett and Jackson, *Democracy in Crisis*, 75.

[32] Blunkett and Jackson, *Democracy in Crisis*, 73.

[33] Publicity Department, City of Sheffield, 'The Bus Booklet: The effects of rate capping and the Transport Act in Sheffield April-October 1986' (Sheffield, 1987), 8.

[34] Blunkett and Jackson, *Democracy in Crisis*, 73–4.

[35] Alan Clarke, *The Rise and Fall of the Socialist Republic: A History of South Yorkshire County Council* (Sheffield: Sheaf Publishing, 1987), 74.

[36] Ibid.

'one of the most progressive pieces of socialist planning ever seen' in Britain and that they were 'working'.[37] Blunkett and Jackson reiterated this sentiment, writing that cheap fares were a 'practical as well as ideological threat' to their political opponents.[38] Sheffield City Council and Labour supporters in Sheffield campaigned to keep cheap bus fares for economic reasons, but also for what they represented for left-wing local government. Blunkett wrote in the *Sheffield Star* in 1982 that bus fares could quadruple and that the effects would be 'horrific'; altering the social life of the community 'overnight'. Furthermore, he suggested that if courts were allowed to decide policies then councillors 'might as well pack up and go home'.[39] This was an issue of local democracy and control over resources as well as social and economic fairness. Michael Foot, then-Labour Party leader, agreed. He pledged to protect local government autonomy should Labour win the 1983 General Election.[40]

The threat to cheap bus fares galvanized support across South Yorkshire. In January 1982, a demonstration 'stoppage' of public transport in Sheffield was supported by engineering and steel workers.[41] Councillor Roger Barton made badges that read, 'The air is cleaner because of cheap bus fares'.[42] A petition to save South Yorkshire's cheap fares collected 100,000 signatures in its first week and more than 250,000 in total.[43] One tenants' action group in Sheffield collected more than 1,000 signatures.[44] Even the *Sheffield Star*, a newspaper usually sceptical of the 'Socialist Republic', published a favourable editorial. Explaining that 'neighbouring West Yorkshire has bus fares five times higher than South Yorkshire's and still pays a subsidy of £48.3 million (compared with £48.9 million)', it offered a 'reminder that the abolition of cheap fares is not a magic formula for low rates'.[45]

Whilst the legality of South Yorkshire's cheap fares policy hung in the balance, South Yorkshire Transport Committee continued with low fares and the campaign grew. Activists organized a Cheap Fares Festival in Sheffield to whip up support in 1983. Parking a South Yorkshire Transport double-decker bus on Fargate in the city centre, they displayed a rolling tally of signatures in the

---

[37] 'Prospect of no more cheap bus fares "horrific"', *The Sheffield Star*, 4 February 1982, 8.

[38] Blunkett and Jackson, *Democracy in Crisis*, 73.

[39] 'Prospect of no more cheap bus fares "horrific"', *The Sheffield Star*, 8.

[40] 'Foot backs buses', *The Sheffield Star*, 12 February 1982, 1.

[41] Blunkett and Jackson, *Democracy in Crisis*, 72.

[42] Interview with Alan Billings and Veronica Hardstaff, 14 June 2013.

[43] 'Foot backs buses', *The Sheffield Star*, 1; Blunkett and Jackson, *Democracy in Crisis*, 72.

[44] 'Marching to defend cheap bus fares', *The Sheffield Star*, 3 February 1982, 9.

[45] 'Editorial', *The Sheffield Star*, 21 January 1982.

upper deck windows, and used the sides of the bus to communicate the County Council's cheap fares policy. Collecting signatures for the new petition, County Councillor Doris Askham claimed, 'All sorts of people have signed. Quite a few say they usually vote Tory but will vote Labour to save the cheap fares policy.'[46] By March, a reported half a million people had signed the petition, which was roughly the population of Sheffield.

The Celebrated Sheffield Street Band kept onlookers at the festival entertained with 'La Cucaracha' re-imagined with the words: 'Save our cheap buses, save our cheap buses, let's fight to keep them on the road.'[47] Plastered to the bus were lyrics to another song, extoling the freedom offered by the 'people's bus':

From the pit and the forges roar
Twenty pence will buy you a ride
To the peace of the open moor.[48]

The words evoked the city's long labour history of coal mining and steel work, as well as the Mass Trespass campaigns of 1932 in which ramblers in Manchester and Sheffield challenged landowners to open moorland to the public. The 50th anniversary of Mass Trespass saw a revival, with three hundred people participating in a trespass on Bamford Moor and the formation of the Sheffield Campaign for Access to Moorland, who continued to campaign for people's right to roam.[49] Access to the countryside from the city was a hot topic, whether by bus or by foot.

A second verse highlighted that this was also an issue of local democracy:

A South Yorkshire bus is a people's bus
It's been that way for years
We decided long ago that cheaper fares were what we needed
If you've a mind to try to make us change our point of view
You're out of luck, our mind's made up
And it's nowt to do with you.

Brennan Bates, one of the organizers of the Save Our Cheap Fares Campaign, was 'astonished' by the support, suggesting that, 'people are obviously beginning

---

[46] Alan Clarke, *The Rise and Fall of the Socialist Republic*, 90.

[47] Celebrated Sheffield Street Band Facebook Group, https://www.facebook.com/media/set/?set=o.298 649060158251&type=3 (accessed 24 April 2015).

[48] Martin Jenkinson Image Library, Sheffield Celebrated Street Band, Cheap Bus Fares Festival, Sheffield, 1983: 83030515.jpg, shorturl.at/gqwxU (accessed 13 November 2020).

[49] David Price, *Sheffield Troublemakers: Rebels and Radicals in Sheffield History* (Andover, UK: Phillimore & Co, 2008), 135–6.

to regard cheap fares as a right'.[50] Over the course of the campaign the slogan changed slightly from 'Save Our Cheap Fares' to 'Save Your Cheap Fares', as Doris Askham explained: 'We thought it ought to be "your" because the bus fares are yours, the people's.'[51] People across South Yorkshire and Sheffield had voted for cheap fares. The fare policy became intrinsically linked to local democracy and the ability of Labour-led local and metropolitan authorities to set policies that suited the needs of their communities.

The 1985 Transport Act introduced privatized and deregulated bus services throughout Britain, putting an end to cheap fares subsidized by rates. South Yorkshire Transport Board's spending limit was cut by 27 per cent and resulted in a 250 per cent fare increase. Bus fares in Sheffield rose from between 5p and 25p to between 10p and 80p. Free travel for pensioners and people with disabilities was abolished, and child fares increased from 2p to 5p. March 1987 saw a further fare increase of 6.2 per cent.[52] The final bus to operate under cheap fares in Sheffield set off on 31 March 1986 – the last day of the South Yorkshire County Council.[53] Over the summer of 1986, bus use decreased by 23 per cent.[54]

Shortly after the fare increases were implemented, Sheffield City Council surveyed nearly a thousand people. Half of those interviewed were using buses less frequently, with unemployed people and those on low incomes reporting the most change. Almost two out of three unemployed people said they could no longer afford to travel as much, making it more difficult to 'look for work, shop, visit friends, use the markets and city centre or go to social events'.[55] As predicted by Frankie Rickford, writing in *Marxism Today* in 1982, fare increases hit women particularly hard.[56] One 'partner of an unemployed man' in Manor, an area of Sheffield, was quoted saying 'We have difficulty going to hospital with my baby. It's either paying £3 in bus fares or walking it.' Another mother of two young children in Storrs, a hamlet on the edge of the city, said 'I can't usually afford to make more than one social visit a week now.'[57]

---

[50] 'Cheap fares campaign gets show on the road', *The Sheffield Star*, 12 February 1982.

[51] Alan Clarke, *The Rise and Fall of the Socialist Republic*, 90.

[52] Publicity, City of Sheffield, 'The Bus Booklet', 3–4.

[53] Martin Jenkinson Image Library, Last Bus: 86031823.jpg, 31 March 1986, http://martinjenkinson. photoshelter.com/gallery-image/1980s-Protest/G0000ADCbo9sFqdI/I0000L6z4O.Tcau4/ C0000PXenaeUbs6c (accessed 4 August 2015).

[54] Publicity, City of Sheffield, 'The Bus Booklet', 6.

[55] Ibid.

[56] Frankie Rickford, 'The Hidden Victims', *Marxism Today*, May 1982, 32.

[57] Publicity, City of Sheffield, 'The Bus Booklet', 6–10.

The changes also affected employment in the region. The South Yorkshire Passenger Transport Executive cut 31 per cent of its workforce resulting in 1,500 job losses. Nearly a thousand of these were in Sheffield.[58] Every Leyland bus contained twenty-five tons of Sheffield special steel, and so declining demand for buses affected heavy industry – a sector already hard hit.[59] For some, the fare increases made travelling to work prohibitively expensive. A part-time worker in Beighton, to the east of Sheffield, was recorded saying, 'I have to journey into the city for two hours work at £1.60 an hour five times a week. It's not worth working, so I'm leaving at the end of the month.'[60] The end of cheap fares also affected other areas of local service provision. Sheffield's Family and Community Services department faced travel costs of £30,000 per year to fund home helps as families struggled with the added cost of travelling to look after elderly relatives. The cheap fares policy served the community in Sheffield – and in bringing people together, it had also helped to sustain it.

Terminus: rate-capping and the abolition of metropolitan county councils

The Save Our/Your Cheap Fares campaign was fought alongside campaigns against both rate-capping and the abolition of metropolitan county councils. Viewed together, the privatization and deregulation of buses, rate-capping and abolition look like a comprehensive attack on local government and were certainly perceived as such by Sheffield City Council and other new urban left local authorities. Yet this was not necessarily the original intention of the Thatcher government in 1979. In Margaret Thatcher's first term, the Conservatives aimed to reduce the proportion of public expenditure given to local authorities. Although controversial, attempting to reduce local government spending was not a radical break with previous governments. The 1980 Local Government, Planning and Land Act introduced financial penalties for councils that spent 'in excess of defined levels'.[61] Local authorities responded, not by reducing expenditure, but by raising their local rates to make up the shortfall. The 1982 Local Government Finance Act attempted to curtail this practice by

---

[58] Publicity, City of Sheffield, 'The Bus Booklet', 20–1.
[59] Blunkett and Jackson, *Democracy in Crisis*, 78.
[60] Publicity, City of Sheffield, 'The Bus Booklet', 6–10.
[61] Hugh Atkinson and Stuart Wilks-Heeg, *Local Government from Thatcher to Blair: The Politcs of Creative Autonomy* (Cambridge: Polity, 2000), 63–5.

outlawing supplementary levies: the practice of introducing rate increases more than once in a financial year. In response, local authorities increased their rates by more initially to make sure they were covered. Non-compliance by councils – especially those led by the Labour left who were formulating dynamic new ways of government in opposition to Conservative policies – provoked the Conservative government to introduce as many as six new measures to try to close loopholes. Across the development of new legislation, the government's emphasis shifted from reducing expenditure to controlling income streams. A subcommittee led by William Whitelaw was created to look into replacing the rates system. Unable to find a suitable alternative it instead recommended the abolition of the GLC and the metropolitan county councils. As tensions between the GLC and the government grew, the Conservatives made a 'last minute' promise to abolish the GLC in their 1983 manifesto, sealing the fate of top-tier local government, which would eventually be dismantled by the 1985 Local Government Act.[62]

Bolstered by their landslide win in the 1983 general election, the Conservatives brought in more stringent controls on local government in the form of the 1984 Rates Act. The Act gave the Secretary of State for the Environment power to impose an upper limit on the rates set by a local authority: to impose a general limit on all local authorities in England, Wales and Scotland, and to cap rates in individually specified local authorities. The Act was largely used against Labour-led local authorities and 'provoked a bitter ideological battle' as more than forty Labour-controlled local authorities refused to set a rate as an act of non-compliance.[63] Sheffield City Council was one of these local authorities. From the start they agreed to the principle of non-compliance in order to protect jobs and services. David Blunkett, as chair of the National Executive Committee Local Government Committee, had his own ideas about how to present this campaign. Rather than martyr Labour-led local authorities to a cause, Blunkett was determined to persuade central government and the electorate that high-spending councils were not necessarily inefficient and wasteful, and instead put forward the argument that high rates went towards necessary services. He put in place a 'continual review' of Sheffield's budget to reduce inefficient spending and identify priority areas, and in 1985 the Audit Commission deemed Sheffield a 'shining example' of local authority efficiency despite their high spending.[64]

---

[62] Ibid., 66–7.
[63] Ibid., 94.
[64] Stephen Pollard, *David Blunkett* (London: Hodder & Stoughton, 2004), 144.

As the campaign continued, Sheffield City Council carried public support with them. On 7 March 1985, fifteen thousand people marched against rate-capping in the city's biggest demonstration of the decade.[65] Yet nationally the campaign began to falter. The legal positions of local authorities differed. The GLC and the metropolitan county councils were legally required to set a rate by 10 March 1985, whereas other local authorities were under no such obligation. Divisions began to appear within and between local authorities, and the strategy of non-compliance crumbled.[66] One week before an arranged budget vote on 7 May 1985, Blunkett asked the district Labour Party to agree to set a maximum legal rate and combine it with a deficit budget in the hope that central government could be persuaded to make up the shortfall. The motion was rejected, and the official Sheffield Labour policy remained a refusal to set a rate.[67] However, on the night of the budget decision, moderate Labour rebels joined with Conservative and SDP-Liberal Alliance councillors to agree to set a rate, and left-wing rebels dismissed Blunkett's further calls for a deficit budget. On what Blunkett described as 'the worst night of [his] political life', Sheffield City Council set a legal rate and ended their campaign against rate-capping.[68]

Sheffield City Council was now tasked with trying to implement the new budget. The council claimed they could partially bridge the gap between income and planned expenditure with £17 million from council balances, and had identified £3 million in potential savings – but there was still a shortfall of £12 million.[69] To avoid having to make large and immediate cuts, the council found ways of postponing some of their spending, hoping the election of a Labour government in 1987 would bail them out. By 1988, local authorities nationally had a deficit of around £2 billion.[70] The new urban left in Sheffield went into retrenchment, 'both materially and ideologically'.[71] The council entered pragmatic partnerships with central government and the private sector, turning away from the 'bottom up' approaches of the early 1980s.

---

[65] Sheffield Local Studies Library, 396 SQ, *Double Shift*, Issue 18, March 1985.

[66] Atkinson and Wilks-Heeg, *Local Government from Thatcher to Blair*, 95.

[67] Pollard, *David Blunkett*, 147.

[68] 'City's rate defiance finally crumbles', *The Sheffield Star*, 8 May 1985, 9; 'Rate is set after split by Labour', *The Sheffield Star*, 8 May 1985, 1.

[69] 'Rate is set after split by Labour', *The Sheffield Star*, 1.

[70] Allan Cochrane, 'Book Review Essay', *International Journal of Urban and Regional Research* 12, no. 2 (1988): 319; John Gyford, Steve Leach and Chris Game, *The Changing Politics of Local Government* (London: Unwin Hyman, 1989), 309–10.

[71] Green, 'The new municipal socialism', 290; Gyford, Leach and Game, *Changing Politics*, 316.

Conclusion

Cheap fares live on in Sheffield's cultural memory. In 1992, Pulp recorded 'Sheffield Sex City', a song whose protagonist is thwarted from meeting his increasingly irritated lover by the distractions of the city – a character in her own right – and then, ultimately, by transport difficulties. In his explanation of the lyrics, published in 2011, Jarvis Cocker notes that the song refers to how 'in 1986 a two-tier system was introduced, making travel more expensive after 7pm on weekdays'.[72] Beyond Cocker's oeuvre, memories of South Yorkshire's cheap bus fares reverberate across digital community-interest spaces like the Sheffield Forum.[73]

In this chapter, I have used South Yorkshire's cheap bus fares and their popularity in Sheffield to highlight a Labour policy that was rooted in the place and the community it served. It not only served the community but also helped sustain it by allowing people to move around the city more freely: to work, socialize, volunteer and care for one another. In turn, Sheffield's communities came out in support of the policy, and a proportion of them remember it as something special about their region and still lament its loss. Cheap bus fares were just one innovation of the metropolitan county councils and new urban left local authorities. Leo Panitch and Colin Leys argue that the 'radical broadening of the public arena, tapping the talent and energy of ordinary people, and bringing them into new positions of power and responsibility' was the 'greatest achievement' of the new urban left.[74] These local authorities have also been celebrated for bringing a 'radically different and positive style' to local government and for imagining 'creative ways to promote social change'.[75] Yet with rate-capping and the abolition of metropolitan councils, the 'local socialism' practiced by the new urban left became unsustainable.

This did not mean the end of innovative local government. Atkinson and Wilks-Heeg suggest that perhaps the 'very existence of a hostile climate has led local authorities ... to attempt to make greater use of those resources and opportunities that they have open to them'.[76] In late-1980s Sheffield, new pragmatic partnerships emerged. Sheffield Development Corporation was set

---

[72] Jarvis Cocker, *Mother, Brother, Lover: Selected Lyrics* (London: Faber and Faber, 2011), 131.

[73] Sheffield Forum: https://www.sheffieldforum.co.uk (accessed 3 October 2021).

[74] Leo Panitch and Colin Leys, *The End of Parliamentary Socialism: From New Left to New Labour* (London: Verso, 2001), 266.

[75] Atkinson and Wilks-Heeg, *Local Government from Thatcher to Blair*, 109.

[76] Ibid., 78.

up in 1988 to bring economic regeneration to the Lower Don Valley area of Sheffield, facilitating the Meadowhall shopping centre and creating eighteen thousand jobs.[77] In the intervening three decades, local authorities have been making do and building expertise within the constraints of limited resources and autonomy. In recent years, discussions of devolution and the introduction of directly elected mayors suggest that Westminster might be taking note of local authorities, yet the austerity measures levelled at councils undermine much of what could be achieved. During the Covid-19 pandemic and consequent debates about local lockdowns we once again heard calls for Westminster to listen to local government, and for local government to have 'decent tax-raising and borrowing powers' and autonomy over resource allocation.[78] As the 'Socialist Republic' shows, with these in hand, Labour-led local authorities could enact measures tailored to the needs of their communities and put them centre stage in their policies.

---

[77] Hansard, 'Sheffield Development Corporation (Area and Constitution) Order 1997', HL Deb 6 February 1997, vol. 577, cc1801–4.

[78] John Harris, 'The rest of the country will suffer so long as Westminster holds the purse strings', *Guardian*, 26 October 2020, https://www.theguardian.com/commentisfree/2020/oct/26/rest-country-suffer-westminster-purse-strings-covid (accessed 13 November 2020).

10

Race and the left: From protest to power?
The story of Black Sections

Robin Bunce and Samara Linton[*]

Black representation is a cause whose time has come. We are moving from protest to politics. We are moving from protest to power.

Bill Morris, *The Guardian*, 5 October 1990

On 12 June 1987, Diane Abbott, Paul Boateng, Bernie Grant and Keith Vaz won election to the House of Commons, changing the face of parliament for good. Addressing a jubilant crowd, Boateng proclaimed, 'there are some of us who have been waiting four hundred years for this result, four hundred years!'[1] Yet despite the moment of triumph there was no triumphalism. Adelaide Tambo was one of Boateng's guests at the count, and together with her husband Oliver Tambo, the Deputy President of the African National Congress (ANC), she was living in exile in London. With Tambo next to him, Boateng recalls that he was 'well aware that the struggle against racism was an ongoing struggle, and a global struggle'.[2] His famous statement 'today Brent South, tomorrow Soweto!'[3] reflected the global aspirations of the Labour Party's Black Sections – and the global nature of white domination. Whilst the 1987 election was a bad night for Labour, it was a good night for democracy. The victories of this first cohort of Black MPs were the result of what became known as the Black Sections' campaign, won in the teeth of fierce opposition from the press, from rival parties – and from the Labour leadership. This chapter examines the origins of Black Sections and the

[*] The authors thank the Principal and Fellows of Homerton College for their ongoing support, as well as Rohan McWilliams and Brandon High for discussing many of the ideas which informed this chapter. We also thank Diane Abbott, Linda Bellos, Paul Boateng, Russell Profitt, Bell Ribeiro-Addy and Keith Vaz for their help and support during the composition of this piece. Thank you to Nathan Yeowell for including us in this project.
[1] Off-air recording of *VOTE '87*, ITV, 11 June 1987, British Film Institute Archive.
[2] Interview with Paul Boateng, 10 February 2020.
[3] Off-air recording of *VOTE '87*, ITV, 11 June 1987, British Film Institute Archive.

arguments surrounding the Black Sections campaign. It will also consider the radically different approaches taken to questions of racial equality within the labour movement during the 1970s and 1980s.

Trade unions and the problem of Black rights

Black Sections emerged in a specific context in the early 1980s. In many ways, the movement was a response to the victories achieved by Black radicals in previous decades, and ongoing racism within the labour movement.[4] The relationship between Black workers and white trade unions, the bedrock of the Labour Party, has always been contentious. During the nineteenth and twentieth centuries, maritime trade led many Black seamen and their families to settle in Britain's port cities. Ship-owners would frequently pay these seamen lower rates than their white counterparts, fuelling hostility. In 1911, for example, during the Seamen's Union strike in Cardiff, white workers turned their hostility on Chinese workers, destroying their properties.[5] During the interwar period, violent attacks on Black workers were commonplace, with attacks taking place in Cardiff, Glasgow, Hull, Liverpool, London, Salford, Newport and South Shields. The most notable of these were the South Wales race riots of 1919, which left three dead and hundreds injured.[6] In addition to violent attacks, Black workers struggled to find work due to colour bars.[7] By the 1930s, Black workers had begun to form their own organizations, such as the Indian Seamen's Union, the Coloured Seamen's Union and the Indian Workers' Association.

Following the Second World War, employers actively recruited workers from the Caribbean and the Indian subcontinent to meet the demand for labour. In accordance with the 1948 Nationality Act, these migrants were UK citizens. Yet, trade unions met Black workers with hostility. The National Union of Seamen (NUS) was in the vanguard of this discriminatory behaviour. Addressing the union's 1948 annual general meeting, North East Coast district secretary J. Ockleton asserted: 'we are not going to sit down and see white men pushed

---

[4] The meaning of the term 'black' was disputed in the period discussed in this essay. Radicals associated with Black Sections tended to embrace 'political blackness'. In that sense, they used the term black to encompass all people who had been oppressed by colonialism, or who had experienced racism in the metropolis. As this is a historical piece, the authors adopt the language used during the period but would challenge the appropriateness of this definition in contemporary contexts.

[5] Neil Evans, 'The South Wales race riots of 1919', *Llafur: The Journal of the Society for the Study of Welsh Labour History* 3, no. 1 (1980): 5–29.

[6] Ibid.

[7] Ibid.

out of employment by coloured men' and boasted of instances the union had been 'successful in changing ships from coloured to white'.[8] Other trade unionists insisted on the introduction of quotas for Black workers and banned their promotion over white workers.[9]

The 1955 TUC conference condemned racial prejudice and colour discrimination, but this had little influence on practice.[10] Also in 1955, bus workers in Wolverhampton banned overtime to protest against the rising number of Black and Asian workers, whilst bus workers in West Bromwich staged strikes in response to the employment of a solitary Indian conductor.[11] There were motions from transport workers to the Transport and General Workers Union (TGWU) annual conference calling on the union to ban Black workers from being employed on the buses. Famously, in 1963, Black communities boycotted the Bristol Omnibus Company which, supported by the local TGWU branch, refused to employ Black bus crews.[12]

The 1950s and 1960s saw anti-Black riots erupt across the UK, the root of which was deemed to be the presence of Black people in the country, rather than white racism. The 1962 Commonwealth Immigrants Act was the first legislation to restrict the rights of Commonwealth citizens to reside in the UK. Successive governments, both Labour and Conservative, continued to introduce further restrictions on immigration. Meanwhile, a number of far right 'empire loyalists' and neo-Nazis had begun to join forces, culminating in the formation of the National Front (NF) in 1967. The NF garnered considerable working-class support. They handed out leaflets to workers striking outside factories or on the docks, taking advantage of the widespread discontent being felt at the end of the postwar economic boom. In 1968, Enoch Powell's 'Rivers of Blood' speech brought the racist, anti-immigrant discourse associated with the NF into the political mainstream. When Powell was dismissed from the Shadow Cabinet, NF membership soared with a further bump in recruits in 1972 following the arrival of Asian refugees from Uganda.[13] As a former NF official put it, 'before Powell spoke, we were getting only cranks and perverts. After his speeches we started to attract, in a secret sort of way, the right-wing members of Tory organizations.'[14]

8   *The Liverpool Echo*, 10 August 1948, 4.
9   Peter Fryer, *Staying Power: The History of Black People in Britain* (London: Pluto Press, 2018), 373.
10 'Will there ever be black trade union leaders?', *The Times*, 1978.
11 Fryer, *Staying Power*.
12 Steven Ian Martin, *Unity in Diversity: A Celebration of Black and Ethnic Minority Union Members* (London: RMT, 2017).
13 Daniel Trilling, *Bloody Nasty People: The Rise of Britain's Far Right* (London: Verso, 2012).
14 Paul Foot, *The Rise of Enoch Powell: An Examination of Enoch Powell's Attitude to Immigration and Race* (London: Penguin Books, 1969), 126.

It was against this backdrop that the Labour Party passed its first Race Relations Act in 1965, making certain forms of racial discrimination a civil – but not criminal – offence. The Race Relations Acts of 1968 and 1976 outlawed direct and indirect racial discrimination in employment, housing and education, and created the Community Relations Commission. The TGWU's general secretary, Frank Cousins, was the commission's first chairman, but this did little to encourage trade unions to recruit and support Black workers.[15]

The early 1970s were marked by trade union strikes against the Conservative government's Industrial Relations Act, rising unemployment and limits to wage increases. However, the unions were notably reluctant to support Black workers' strikes. When Asian workers staged strikes at Mansfield Hosiery Mills in Loughborough and Crepe Sizes Ltd in Nottingham, it was the solidarity committees formed from the Black community that forced the unions to act.[16] Similarly, in 1974, when Asian workers at Imperial Typewriters went on strike over racial discrimination and exploitation, the TGWU negotiator said the group had 'no legitimate grievances' and the union refused to make the strike official, saying 'some people must learn how things are done'.[17]

The supposed turning point for race relations within the trade union movement occurred in 1976, when Asian workers at the Grunwick Photo Processing Laboratories in London staged strikes against unfair dismissals. Following the advice of their Citizen's Advice Bureau, they joined the local Association of Professional, Executive, Clerical and Computer Staff (APEX) branch.[18] When Grunwick's management rejected APEX's claim for recognition, sacking 137 workers in the process, the strike's focus shifted from discrimination to recognition. It encouraged white trade unionists and workers, for whom the strike was symbolic of workers' fundamental right to be a part of a trade union, to rally behind the Grunwick workers. By the end of the year, the strike had garnered support from the TUC and the local trades council – as well as from post office workers, car workers, miners and several MPs.[19]

Although the Grunwick dispute helped to bring the issue of equality and race relations onto the national trade union agenda, it only attracted significant

[15] Alastair J. Reid, *United We Stand: A History of Britain's Trade Unions* (London: Allen Lane, 2004).

[16] Wilf Sullivan, 'Race and trade unions', Britain at Work, http://www.unionhistory.info/britainatwork/narrativedisplay.php?type=raceandtradeunions (accessed 13 September 2021).

[17] Reid, *United We Stand*; BBC, 'Imperial Typewriters strike project recalls "shameful" union', BBC New, 15 June 2019, https://www.bbc.co.uk/news/uk-england-leicestershire-48586737 (accessed 13 September 2021).

[18] Reid, *United We Stand*.

[19] Rod Ramdin, *The Making of the Black Working Class in Britain* (London: Verso, 1987).

support once the focus of the dispute shifted away from race. Indeed, trade union leaders struggled to tackle racism within their own organizations. Along with concerns over the rise of the NF, the TUC were pushed to set up an Equal Rights and Race Relations Advisory Committee. Abbott explains the challenge of addressing institutional racism on the left in the late 1970s: they 'were fine to march against the National Front, but if you tried to say that there was institutional racism in the institutions where they worked, you got a certain amount of push-back'.[20] Once again, many Black workers turned to self-organization, for example, by establishing the Black Workers' Coordinating Committee, the Black Unity and Freedom Party, the Croydon Collective, the Black Workers' Movement and the Black Trade Unionist Solidarity Movement.

The origins of Black Sections

The push for Black Sections first emerged in the summer of 1983,[21] building on an ongoing postwar campaign for Black representation in and around the Labour Party.[22] The Standing Conference of Afro-Caribbean and Asian Councillors (SCACAC), founded in the late 1970s by Labour councillors Russell Profitt and Phil Sealey, was one of the tributaries from which Black Sections flowed. Born in Georgetown, British Guiana in the 1950s, Profitt moved to London in 1961, where he became involved in student politics and later with the Labour Party. Having been co-opted onto Lewisham Council as an alderman in 1973, and following his election as a councillor in 1978, Profitt recalls being 'frustrated with the lack of action on equality issues generally in local government and elsewhere', and therefore reached out to Black councillors for solidarity. In time, Profitt and Sealey's network developed into SCACAC.[23]

Whilst Profitt was organizing in south London, Ben Bousquet was working along similar lines north of the river Thames. Born in St Lucia, Bousquet had arrived in Britain in 1957 at the age of eighteen. By the late 1970s, he was a National and Local Government Officers' Association (NALGO) shop steward in Charing Cross Hospital, and a Labour councillor for North Kensington

[20] Diane Abbott, 'Race Relations Conference', in Robin Bunce and Samara Linton, *Diane Abbott: The Authorised Biography* (London: Biteback, 2020), 69–70.

[21] Ibid., 148.

[22] See Sydney Jeffers, 'Black Sections in the Labour Party: the end of ethnicity and "godfather" politics?', in Pnina Werbner and Muhammad Anwar (eds), *Black and Ethnic Leaderships in Britain* (London: Routledge, 1991), 43–6.

[23] Private correspondence with Russell Profitt, 23 January 2019.

in the Royal Borough of Kensington and Chelsea. Together with Labour councillors Ray Philbert and Billy Poh, Bousquet established a caucus which, he argued, would 'create the proper atmosphere' to support Black people in the Labour Party, to encourage them to join and to advance a Black agenda. In the winter of 1982, Bousquet, Philbert and Poh expanded what they were doing, writing to every Black councillor in the country inviting them to participate in the initiative.[24] Although the three were working within the Labour Party, their letter went to all members of the SCACAC, including the small number of Conservatives, Liberal and Independent councillors who were part of the organization.

The 1983 general election gave further impetus to the campaign. Labour went down to its worst defeat since 1935. But, significantly, the equalities' charity the Runnymede Trust's analysis of the election indicated that 'the black vote' had been crucial in preventing a complete Labour wipe-out.[25] Interviewed in 1986, Narendra Makenji (a left-wing activist from Zimbabwe who moved to Britain in 1974, joined the Labour Party the following year, and went on to serve as a councillor in Haringey, to work with Ken Livingstone's GLC and to take on the role of chair of Islington's Race Equality Unit) explained that:

> The black vote was fairly solid for Labour. If the black vote had collapsed to the SDP and the Tories as the white working-class vote collapsed, Labour would have definitely been the third party, we would have lost possibly another thirty parliamentary seats, at least. And if Labour was the third party, defections [to the SDP] would grow, because very often black people were voting anti-Tory.[26]

Makenji argued that the Runnymede Trust's analysis persuaded a number of black activists that the time was right to mount a campaign to force the Labour Party to stop taking the support of Black voters for granted, and to accept that Black members should exercise power within the party.

The Runnymede Trust's analysis was not the only impetus behind Black Sections. Makenji argued that changes in the Labour Party in the early 1980s persuaded many black voters to join the Party.[27] During the 1960s and 1970s, he argued, Labour governments had treated immigration as a matter of electoral expedience, rather than moral principle, which alienated black voters. The end

---

[24] Ben Bousquet interview, British Library, 1986.
[25] Marion Fitzgerald, 'Ethnic Minorities and the 1983 General Election', *Runnymede Trust Briefing Paper*, December 1983.
[26] Narendra Makenji interview, British Library, 1986.
[27] Interview with Narendra Makenji, 24 August 2018.

of the Wilson/Callaghan era led many black voters to re-evaluate the party. Moreover, efforts to democratize the party, which was spearheaded by Tony Benn and the Campaign for Labour Party Democracy (CLPD), persuaded Black people to join up in the hope that they might exercise real power.[28]

Diane Abbott, the child of Jamaican immigrants, Cambridge University history graduate and, by 1982, a Labour councillor in Westminster, situates the emergence of Black Sections in the context of broader social and political changes. Abbott argues that Black Sections reflected the aspirations of a new generation, one that had marched with Darcus Howe and the Race Today Collective on the Black People's Day of Action in 1981 and had witnessed the subsequent insurrection in Brixton. Unlike their parents, who were more willing to tolerate inequality, this new generation demanded justice and power.[29] Abbott argues that the activists who came together to form Black Sections were, with a few exceptions, part of this new generation, which wanted to move from protest – looking to achieve their aims by exerting influence outside authoritative institutions – to power – by obtaining real authority within existing institutions. Finally, she argues that Black Sections reflected changes in the London Labour Party in particular. From the early 1980s, members of the new urban left associated with the CLPD, such as Ken Livingstone and Jeremy Corbyn, and others associated with *London Labour Briefing*, began supporting Black self-organization. Consequently, Black activists could be sure of support from London Labour's increasingly dominant left-wing faction.[30]

Conversations between Black councillors in Proffit and Bousquet's networks led to the foundation of Black Sections in the summer of 1983. The first meeting took place at 39 Chippenham Road, Westminster – Abbott's local constituency party office. The meeting led to the creation of the Black Sections steering committee.[31] Boateng describes Black Sections as 'a genuine bottom-up, grassroots movement of activists'.[32] Abbott puts it this way:

> It wasn't that somebody set up Black Sections and asked us to join. There were
> a group of us who were individual black activists in our parties, but who were

---

[28]　Ibid.

[29]　Interview with Diane Abbott, 18 March 2019. See also Terri Sewell, *Black Tribunes: Black Political Participation in Britain* (London: Lawrence & Wishart, 1990), ch. 5.

[30]　Ibid. See also Hilary Wainwright, *Labour: A Tale of Two Parties* (London: The Hogarth Press, 1987), 162–5.

[31]　Bunce and Linton, *Diane Abbott: The Authorised Biography*, 151.

[32]　Interview with Paul Boateng, 10 February 2020.

also informed by the politics of race and also post-colonial politics. We didn't start with the demand for Black Sections. We started by coming together and saying, 'How can we support each other, how can we get the left to pay attention to black struggles?'[33]

The arguments deployed for Black Sections evolved following the 1983 general election, but the core platform remained consistent. The primary demand was that people who were oppressed by white racism in Britain, or who had come from backgrounds of colonial oppression, should be allowed to organize themselves into formal sections within the Labour Party, and that these sections should have guaranteed representation at all levels of the party. This was modelled on the Women's Section and Labour's Youth Section. Abbott argues that they initially hit on the demand, on the basis that it was a way of presenting Black self-organization in a language that Labour activists could understand.[34] They also demanded that the party acknowledged it was not free from racism, that Black Sections should have representation at selection meetings and that there should be all-female and all-Black shortlists for parliamentary seats. Black Sections were also organized around a commitment to 'political blackness': an understanding of 'Black' that encompassed *everyone* adversely affected by white racism. Consequently, in some areas, Black Sections were predominantly African-Caribbean, in others largely Bengali, whilst some areas had a significant Cypriot membership.[35]

The Black Sections debate

Black Sections took their initial demands to the 1983 Labour Party conference.[36] The resolution for Black Sections, however, was not put to a vote. Rather, the conference agreed to establish a Working Party on Positive Discrimination, which would make recommendations on constitutional reform at the next conference. Nonetheless, the 1983 conference had important repercussions for Black Sections. The conference elected Neil Kinnock as the new party leader, with Roy Hattersley as his deputy. Kinnock was a passionate opponent of apartheid. Equally, whilst the left regarded Hattersley as the 'standard-bearer of

---

[33] Interview with Diane Abbott, 18 March 2019.

[34] Ibid.

[35] Jeffers, 'Black Sections in the Labour Party', 45.

[36] Muhammad Anwar, *Race and Politics: Ethnic Minorities and the British Political System* (London: Routledge, 2013), 119.

the old parliamentary right,[37] he represented the constituency of Birmingham Sparkbrook, where minority ethnic voters made up more than 35 per cent of the population, amongst whom historically as many as 90 per cent voted Labour.[38] Therefore, many of the leading members of Black Sections, from across the left/ right divide, assumed that Kinnock and Hattersley had good reasons for backing Black Sections.

In 1984, however, the party leadership came out firmly against the initiative. Kinnock set out his objections in an open letter published in *New Life*, a weekly newspaper read by many British Asians, at the end of June 1984. Essentially, he argued that 'racially segregationist' sections were a form of apartheid. Moreover, he argued that there could be no agreed basis for Black Sections, for whilst there were clear definitions of sex and age there was no way of defining 'black'. Consequently, whilst women's sections and youth sections could be based on clear definitions, Black Sections 'would create significant problems of racial definition which could lead only too easily to endless unproductive acrimony'.[39] Despite this, Kinnock argued that he supported many of the objectives of Black Sections.

Hattersley set out his opposition to Black Sections in a speech at the 1985 Labour conference. Like Kinnock, he professed himself to be against Black Sections on principle, arguing that it was an 'article of socialist faith' that 'all men and women are treated the same'. Like Kinnock, Hattersley linked this to the problem of definition. Rejecting political blackness, Hattersley, insisted that the correct term was 'the black and Asian British' or 'the ethnic minorities'. He argued:

> A group of men and women, of very different origins, with very different cultures, cannot be lumped together and generically and vacuously called 'the blacks' or the 'black and Asians', as if they all had the same problems, all had the same cultural background, all had the same aspirations, and all had the same interests. To lump the ethnic minorities together in that way is a deeply patronising view of those of our citizens.[40]

Party conferences were also opportunities for Black Sections to restate their case and counter Kinnock and Hattersley's arguments. Abbott, who spoke for Black Sections at the 1984 conference, argued that 'The actual experience when

[37] Richard Heffernan and Mike Marqusee, *Defeat from the Jaws of Victory* (London: Verso, 1992), 37.
[38] Sewell, *Black Tribunes*, 18.
[39] 'Black Sections – Neil Kinnock', *New Life*, 29 June 1984.
[40] Off-air recording of BBC footage of the Labour Party conference, 30 September 1985, British Film Institute Archive.

you set up Black Sections, is far from being ghettos, far from being apartheid, they draw black people into the party and they maximise black involvement.'[41] On the issue of apartheid, she claimed:

> We've been accused of apartheid. I'll tell you what's apartheid: all white parties in multi-racial constituencies, that's apartheid. An all-white House of Commons, that's apartheid. We are providing a remedy for this apartheid.[42]

Turning to definition, Lambeth councillor Sharon Atkin, who was born in Ealing to an Irish mother and West Indian father, argued:

> People here say they don't know the definition of black. Well, I'll address that problem. The National Front know the definition of black. The police know the definition of black. The [Department of Health and Social Security] know the definition of black ... So why is it such a problem for the leadership of our party?[43]

More generally, Black Sections claimed that, rather than advocating racial equality, Hattersley's approach to Black people in the Labour Party was essentially colonial in nature. Linda Bellos, who had been active in the feminist movement and having joined Black Sections rose to prominence as Leader of Lambeth Council in 1986, responded to Hattersley's insistence that Black and Asian people had different interests by accusing him of employing 'divide and rule' tactics, tactics that were recognizable from British India. Moreover, working with Howe and veteran left-wing activist Tariq Ali, Black Sections pointed to evidence of the manipulation of recruitment and membership in Hattersley's constituency in a documentary on Channel 4. Days before his 1985 conference speech, *The Bandung File* revealed evidence that Hattersley relied on the support of local 'godfathers' in the Asian community. These 'godfathers' packed the membership of Hattersley's local party, on some occasions casting votes on behalf of fictitious members, allowing Hattersley to control the local party organization. In return, *The Bandung File* claimed, Hattersley prioritized the immigration cases presented to him by these local 'godfathers' and ignored those that reached him through other routes.[44] The relationship, then, reproduced the patron–client dynamic that had been rife in British India. Abbott's alternative

---

[41] Off-air recording of BBC footage of the Labour Party conference, 3 October 1984, British Film Institute Archive.

[42] Ibid.

[43] Off-air recording of BBC footage of the Labour Party conference, 30 September 1985, British Film Institute Archive.

[44] 'Till death us do part', *Bandung File*, Channel 4, 26 September 1985. See also Les Back and John Solomos, *Race, Politics and Social Change* (London: Routledge, 1995), 87.

was Black Sections, which would allow Black people to take 'part in the decision making as equals. Black people should stop being clients and start wielding real political power.' Abbott's argument exposed one of the weaknesses in Kinnock's position. His thinking was based on a simplistic distinction between integration and segregation. Abbott pointed out that integration was more problematic than Kinnock realized. Abbott backed Black Sections as a method through which Black people could integrate from a position of strength and, in so doing, could integrate as equals, rather than clients.

The revelations from Hattersley's constituency were indicative of a broader point: the campaign against Black Sections was motivated by political calculations independent of high-minded principle. This first became clear following the selection of Trinidad-born Peter Hamid, a member of the Black Sections steering committee, to stand for Labour in the Enfield Southgate by-election at the end of 1984, when Michael Portillo retained the seat for the Tories. Whilst the Tory majority dropped more than ten thousand, significantly, the main beneficiaries were the SDP–Liberal Alliance, and Labour's vote was cut in half. Soon after Hamid's defeat, Nicholas Harman, writing in the *Sunday Times*, presented what he claimed was the view from Labour high command: 'Lots of Labour professionals, some of them sincerely anti-racist, are blaming Hamid's wretched performance on the fact that he is black.' The result, Harman predicted, 'will make local Labour parties even more unwilling than previously to adopt black candidates'.[45] Kinnock's papers bear this out. Kinnock's thinking was informed by Marian Fitzgerald's *Political Parties and 'the Black Vote'*, a report prepared for the Labour leader following the 1983 election. Fitzgerald argued that in criticizing the Tory approach to race, Labour had 'walked straight into the trap'. The Conservatives, she argued 'had not needed to run a racist campaign … they simply provoked Labour into making statements from which white racists might safely be left to draw their own inferences'. More generally, Fitzgerald argued that appeals to Black voters would lead to a net drop in Labour's vote because the number of white voters which would become alienated would outweigh the Black voters that Labour attracted.[46]

A private letter from Hattersley to Kinnock, from the summer of 1985, also links his opposition to Black Sections to his electoral concerns. He wrote:

---

[45] 'The black and the red', *The Sunday Times*, 16 December 1984.
[46] *Political Parties and 'The Black Vote'*, December 1983, The Papers of Neil Kinnock, Churchill Archive Centre, University of Cambridge.

I, however, counsel caution about finding some common ground with black sections [*sic*] supporters. We are in no danger of losing the ethnic minority vote. Indeed, as far as the Asian community is concerned, they are more likely to desert us because they fear extreme infiltration than because they resent the absence of positive discrimination within the party.[47]

Hattersley's concerns were not entirely devoid of principle. As Hattersley explained in his 1985 Conference speech, the interests of 'the ethnic minorities' were identical to those of the white working class. Consequently, the real interests of 'the black and Asian British' were the same as the electoral interests of the Labour Party. Moreover, there was no need for Black Sections, as Black people could rely on white Labour ministers to act in their best interests. Again, for Black Sections this approach conceived Black people as the passive recipients of the largesse of well-meaning whites. Atkin addressed this at the 1985 Labour conference stating 'Roy Hattersley relies on the black vote to return him to Parliament. And what do they call him there? "Hatterjee!" Well he's not my Guru!'[48]

During 1985 it became clear that the leadership was no longer engaging in debate. Rather, they were using their dominant position on the NEC to put pressure on Black Sections. Russell Proffit's selection as Labour candidate in Lewisham East was overturned by the NEC, due to Black Sections' involvement in the selection meeting. Proffit was reinstated by the Lewisham party following a year-long campaign by Black Sections.[49] Moreover, following their battle with the Trotskyist group Militant, the Labour leadership increasingly took the view that Black Sections were extremists, who wanted to use separate sections to infiltrate the party. As a result, the NEC passed a resolution banning 'separatist activity'. Immediately prior to the 1987 election, Atkin was deselected as the Labour candidate for Nottingham East on this basis.[50] The NEC ruled that even though Atkin had not been found guilty of the charge, the mere accusation warranted deselection. Abbott recalls that she and the other Black Sections candidates received warnings from party head office that they would be deselected if they spoke out on Atkin's behalf.[51]

---

[47] Letter from Roy Hattersley to Neil Kinnock, 7 May 1985, Records of Roy Hattersley, Hull University Archives, Hull History Centre.

[48] Off-air recording of BBC footage of the Labour Party conference, 30 September 1985, British Film Institute Archive.

[49] 'Commemorating 25 years of the Labour Party Black Sections', Hansib Publications, 2008, 10.

[50] Bunce and Linton, *Diane Abbott: The Authorised Biography*, 189–90.

[51] Interview with Diane Abbott, 18 March 2019.

Militant

The debate over Black Sections did not necessarily correspond to divisions between left and right in the party. Profitt, for example, was regarded as a moderate and Atkin as a left-winger. Equally, whilst members associated with *Briefing* and the CLPD supported Black Sections, there was resistance from other parts of the left. *Tribune*, for instance, was sympathetic to Black rights as anti-racism in theory but saw no reason why Black people should lead the fight for racial justice in practice.

Militant was a fierce opponent of Black Sections. Militant, which dominated Liverpool City Council in the early 1980s, saw the discrimination and unemployment facing Black people in Liverpool in the same way they saw all issues: as a class problem. Following the Toxteth riots, Derek Hatton, then deputy leader of Liverpool City Council, explained that, whilst accepting that discrimination existed, Militant's position was that the problems of the Black community are a class problem, and a socialist problem, and must therefore be solved within that wider framework.[52] Thus, he asserted that racism must be tackled at its root, by mobilizing the working class to push through socialist programmes that tackle poverty and mass unemployment. Consequently, Militant argued that campaigns for Black representation threatened to reduce class to 'just another category, along with race, sex, disability, age etc.'[53] The success of Black Sections, it argued, 'would jeopardise the building of unity amongst blacks and whites'.[54] Moreover, they argued that initiatives to advance Black rights would alienate many white working-class people from the struggle.[55]

From this perspective, Liverpool's Militant-dominated council refused to introduce policies to explicitly address racism. In 1984, Sam Bond, a London building surveyor, was appointed Liverpool City Council's Principal Race Relations Adviser. Bond was immediately boycotted by NALGO and the Black Caucus of Liverpool Race Relations Liaison Committee, who argued that he was neither from Liverpool nor qualified for the role. Moreover, the Black Caucus – a group of locally elected councillors and local Black representatives – added that Bond was only chosen because he shared Militant's view of race relations.[56] To protest Bond's appointment, members of the Black Caucus occupied Hatton's

---

[52] See 'British reformists in action: when Militant ran Liverpool', *Workers Hammer*, no. 210 (Spring 2010).

[53] 'Black Sections – constitutional substitute for socialist policies', *Militant*, Spring 1986.

[54] 'The inner cities erupt – what lies ahead for blacks in Britain', *Militant*, Spring 1986.

[55] Ibid.

[56] Michael Crick, *Militant* (London: Faber & Faber, 1984); P. Evans, 'Militants accused of Stalinist tactics', *The Times*, 1986.

office until he agreed to reconsider the appointment. Hatton agreed, but later withdrew his decision. On Militant's account, Hatton and colleagues were taken hostage, threatened with physical violence and had no option but to sign the agreement the Black Caucus gave them.[57] Critics subsequently accused Militant of perpetuating racist myths of Black people as violent and criminal.[58]

The reaction to Bond's appointment must be seen against the wider backdrop of the council's history of failure to fund and support initiatives that had been agreed by the Race Relations Liaison Committee. These included ethnicity monitoring, the establishment of a working party on racial harassment on council estates, and a Department of Environment-backed sheltered housing scheme for elderly Black people.[59] A damning Runnymede Trust report, endorsed by local community and religious leaders, accused the council of thwarting and undermining the Black community by cutting off grants to Black groups and by freezing appointments to race relations roles. The council also came under fire when it was noted that fewer than 1 per cent of their employees were Black compared to 7 per cent of Liverpool's population.[60] In Liverpool, 'where positive initiatives have been taken, this has largely been in spite of, and not thanks to, its local Labour Party'.[61]

In Liverpool, the relationship between the Labour Party and the Black community grew progressively worse. The council's Race Relations Liaison Committee stopped meeting and was later replaced by an Equal Opportunities Committee, a Labour march was cancelled when the Black Caucus were rumoured to be attending, and eventually, Militant set up its own Black front organization, the Merseyside Action Group.[62]

Similarly, in Wolverhampton, there was a 'tendency within the Labour Group which, although not Militant, [was] not dissimilar in terms of its effects to those of Liverpool's Labour Group'.[63] Gideon Ben-Tovim et al. argued that the group's class-first, colour-blind approach resulted in the 'virtual absence of black faces' in the council.[64] The Wolverhampton group also opposed positive action, failed

[57] Peter Taaffe and Tony Mulhearn, *Liverpool – A City That Dared to Fight* (London: Fortress Books, 1988).

[58] 'Militants accused of Stalinist tactics', *The Times*, 1986.

[59] Gideon Ben-Tovim, John Gabriel, Ian Law and Kathleen Stredder, *The Local Politics of Race* (London: Palgrave, 1986).

[60] 'Liverpool council to face race inquiry', *The Times*, 1986.

[61] Ben-Tovim et al., *The Local Politics of Race*, 77.

[62] Crick, *Militant*.

[63] Ben-Tovim et al., *The Local Politics of Race*, 77.

[64] Ibid., 89.

to consult Black organizations on decisions affecting the Black community and made little use of government funding for race related initiatives.

Founder of *Militant* Peter Taaffe argued that positive discrimination and ethnicity-based quotas served to redistribute jobs from white to Black workers. In fact, he argued that the entire race relations industry was the ruling class' attempt to neutralize Black radicalism and garner support within the Black community by buying off the Black petit-bourgeois. In this, Taaffe agreed with Roy Hattersley, who argued that Black Sections were a group of middle-class careerists who had no connection to the working class.[65] Interestingly, some Black radicals had similar suspicions. For example, Ambalavaner Sivanandan asserted that 'Black Sections are no more representative of black working people than the Labour Party is of white.'[66] Taaffe argued that accusing white people of racism risked creating fratricidal strife within the working class.[67] Instead of separatist action, Taaffe asserted, Black and white workers needed to unite in the struggle for socialist change.[68]

Moving towards a universal struggle

Whilst Hatton and Hattersley couched their objections to Black Sections in terms of class, critics have pointed to serious problems with this perspective. Abbott cut through Militant's rhetoric of class at the 1984 Labour conference, arguing that Militant rejected Black Sections simply because they could not control the movement.[69] Additionally, Stephen Small argues that reducing racism to matters of class does little to improve the position of Black people.

> If all 'racial discrimination' ended today black people would remain at the bottom because of their economically disadvantaged position ... But it is also clear that many aspects of 'racialised' inequality cannot be reduced to class discrimination, nor can they await resolution until class inequality has been eliminated. This is not simply a theoretical contention, it is an historical fact which is clear from slavery, abolition, reconstruction and black power.[70]

[65] Letter from Roy Hattersley to Neil Kinnock, 7 May 1985, Records of Roy Hattersley, Hull University Archives, Hull History Centre.
[66] Ambalavaner Sivanandan, *Communities of Resistance: Writings on Black Struggles for Socialism* (London: Verso, 1990), 203.
[67] Taaffe and Mulhearn, *Liverpool – A City That Dared to Fight*.
[68] Crick, *Militant*.
[69] Off-air recording of BBC footage of the Labour Party conference, 3 October 1984, British Film Institute Archive.
[70] Stephen Small, 'Racialised relations in Liverpool: a contemporary anomaly', *New Community* 17, no. 4 (1991): 523.

Paul Gilroy argues that class analysis must be overhauled if it is to be of relevance to modern struggles against oppression and marginalization. The British left, Gilroy says, fails to understand that power is no longer confined to the labour process. Such a view is race blind at best and at worst Eurocentric.[71] He argues that radical collective action comes from groups who find the premises of their collective existence threatened. These groups do not fit neatly within traditional definitions of class, and instead are based on collective identities, traditional roots and social ties.[72]

Like Gilroy, Sivanandan is critical of Eurocentric notions of the working class. He maintains that the industrial working class is crucial to the socialist struggle, but it now exists in the 'Third World' and with those from the 'Third World' who live in the West. Sivanandan adds:

> There is a class war going on within Marxism as to who – in the period of the deconstruction of industrial capitalism and the recomposition of the working class – are the real agents of revolutionary change: the orthodox working class, which is orthodox no more, or the 'ideological classes' who pass for the new social force or forces.[73]

These new social movements, as defined by identity (e.g. the women's, anti-racism or LGBTQ movements) or issues (such as environmentalism) have the potential to radicalize class struggles. 'Black struggle – for human dignity and true freedom – far from being divisive of, or in competition with, socialism, actually lies within and advances its best traditions.'[74]

Sivanandan points to the Black struggles of the 1960s and 1970s and the insurrections of 1981 and 1985 as examples of collective movements that originated from need and community, not choice and personal identity. They were by nature, multifaceted but unrelenting in their struggle against the ruling class. By moving 'from their particularities to the whole and back again to themselves' social movements like Black rights movements have the potential to produce a new universal struggle for 'human worth, dignity, genuine equality, the enlargement of the self'.[75] Darcus Howe advances a similar analysis, arguing that the white Labour movement had been bought off by years of social democracy.

---

[71] Paul Gilroy, 'You can't fool the youths … race and class formation in the 1980s', *Race & Class* 23, nos 2–3 (October 1981): 207–20; Paul Gilroy, *There Ain't No Black in the Union Jack: The Cultural Politics of Race and Nation* (London: Hutchinson, 1987).

[72] Ibid.

[73] Sivanandan, *Communities of Resistance*, 169.

[74] Ibid., 275.

[75] Ibid., 91.

For Howe, migrant groups who experienced capitalism at its most exploitative in the colonies and in the metropolis had the historic role of reawakening the white working class.[76]

Conclusion

Black Sections had a considerable political impact. Starting in London in 1983, it quickly became a national movement. The first annual national Black Sections conference, which took place in Birmingham in July 1984, attracted three hundred delegates, and by 1987, thirty-five constituency Labour parties had informal Black Sections, twenty of these were in London with the others being spread throughout Britain's big cities.[77] At a local level, Black Sections was responsible for increasing Black representation on councils. Indeed, the number of Black councillors in London rose from around 50 in 1982 to 150 in 1986, with significant increases in areas such as Birmingham, Bradford and Leicester.[78]

Keith Vaz, who became involved in Black Sections around the time of the 1984 European elections and went on to become Britain's longest serving Asian MP, argues 'we would never have had the first four black MPs but for Black Sections'.[79] Abbott concurs, arguing that the breakthrough in 1987 occurred in spite of the Labour leadership's antipathy. Indeed, the leadership's hostility to Black candidates continued beyond the election. In 1989, the Labour Party used new powers to deselect Martha Osamor ahead of a by-election in the south London Vauxhall constituency, and to impose a shortlist which contained no credible Black candidates. Nonetheless, Linda Bellos argues that Black Sections' breakthrough in 1987 was important, as it dispelled the myth that white people would not vote for Black candidates. In the longer term Bellos argues that other parties followed Labour's lead, so that in time 'even the Conservative Party managed to select credible Black candidates'.[80] Vaz agrees, noting that a 2019

---

[76] Robin Bunce and Paul Field, *Renegade, the life and times of Darcus Howe* (London: Bloomsbury, 2017), 226.

[77] Jeffers, 'Black Sections in the Labour Party', 43–6.

[78] Muhammad Anwar, 'Ethnic minorities' representation voting and electoral politics in Britain, and the role of leaders', in Werbner and Anwar, *Black and Ethnic Leaderships in Britain*, 38; and 'Diane Abbott, Race Relations Conference', in Bunce and Linton, *Diane Abbott: The Authorised Biography*, 124.

[79] Interview with Keith Vaz, 19 November 2020.

[80] Private correspondence with Linda Bellos, 18 November 2020.

Conservative Cabinet containing an Asian Chancellor and Asian Home Secretary was only possible because of the fight for representation over previous decades. Indeed, whilst the 1980s is usually remembered as the decade in which the right won the economic argument, for a time at least, it was also the decade in which, as Bellos contends, Black Sections, 'women, lesbian, and gay and general decent socialists' won the social argument.[81] Vaz attributes Black Sections' successes to the movement's emphasis on 'self-identification, and self-organization with a very clear mandate. The purity of the Black Sections movement was … activists deciding for themselves what they wanted to achieve in respect of representation.' This, he argues, together with effective organization and an intelligent campaign, led to the 1987 breakthrough. Subsequently, Labour leaders 'have tried to establish their own way of achieving representation'. These initiatives have failed, in part, he explains, due to the fact that they were not rooted in self-organization and, in part, due to the 'Balkanisation' of ethnic minority communities, often along ethnic and religious lines, which has made co-ordination far more difficult to achieve.[82] Looking to the future, Vaz argues that 'the best way for the leadership now to grapple with race issues is to start talking policy'.[83]

For Abbott, who at the time of writing remains the only one of the quartet elected in 1987 still to sit as an MP, Black Sections has a clear message for Labour at the beginning of the new decade:

> Labour should remember that respecting and facilitating black involvement in the party makes it stronger. We have seen how black voters were key to Joe Biden's victory [in November 2020]. It was black voters in cities like Philadelphia, Detroit and Atlanta who brought Pennsylvania, Michigan and Georgia home for Biden. And just as black voters were a great strength to Biden, they will be a huge strength to Labour. But the issues that Black Sections raised all those years ago are still extremely relevant today; not taking the black vote for granted and better black representation at every level in the party.[84]

In that sense, Abbott argues that Labour should finally deliver on the demands that Black Sections made more than three decades ago. Russell Profitt concurs, arguing that if Labour is to be a truly progressive political force it must facilitate the greater involvement and representation of Black people, rather than 'presenting itself as thinking it knows best, as too often is the case with Party representatives'.

---

[81] Ibid. For a similar argument, see Jonathan Davis and Rohan McWilliam, *Labour and the Left in the 1980s* (Manchester: MUP, 2018), 1–22.

[82] Interview with Keith Vaz, 19 November 2020.

[83] Ibid.

[84] Private correspondence with Diane Abbott, 16 November 2020.

The same is true of left-wing factions, which Profitt says should give up their desire to '"lead" on black and Asian involvement'. In practical terms, Profitt argues that as 'society is changing continuously, so structures need to be fluid enough to accept this'. This includes the development of 'alternative ways of increasing involvement and participation', which he argues are necessary 'should [Labour] wish to be more attractive to the targeted communities in future'.[85]

Whilst Black Sections undoubtedly had many progressive consequences, the debate within the Labour Party crystalized arguments that are still mobilized today against independent groups that campaign for racial justice. Indeed, the debates of the 1980s were an early example of an ongoing issue, which Professor Salman Sayyid describes as 'the paradox of anti-racism'[86]: Labour was a party in which everyone deplored racism, but a party in which racism persisted. Similar dynamics are still at work today. During 2020, white opponents of Black Lives Matter, on both sides of the Atlantic, claimed to deplore racism whilst disputing the right of Black people to define their own terms, to articulate their own interests and to pursue their own strategies for liberation, whilst at the same time characterizing Black radicals as extremists. For Black Sections, anti-racism was only meaningful in a context where Black people organized themselves, Black people articulated their own demands and Black people led the fight for racial justice. Debates about racism and anti-racism, the terms of integration and the problems of segregation are part of contemporary politics. In that sense, the debates surrounding Black Sections are as relevant today as ever.

[85] Private correspondence with Russell Profitt, 24 November 2020.
[86] Salman Sayyid, 'Post-racial paradoxes: rethinking European racism and anti-racism', *Patterns of Prejudice* 51, no. 1 (January 2017): 9–25.

11

'This party is a moral crusade, or it is nothing': Foreign aid and Labour's ethical identity

Charlotte Lydia Riley

… if anybody in this Conference is tempted to luxuriate in the irresponsible impotence of Opposition rather than sear his knuckles, and sometimes his conscience, in the hard graft of government responsibility, I hope he will remember that when Labour loses offices in Britain it affects not only us here, it affects millions around the world.

Denis Healey, speech at Labour Party Conference, 1 October 1970

For us as democratic socialists there can be no retreat from our duties as citizens of the world. And as people who believe that the great privilege of strength is the power that it gives to help people who are not strong, we understand where our obligations are. If the morality won't convince people, if ethics won't, let the practicalities convince them.

Neil Kinnock, speech at Labour Party Conference, 11 October 1985

It is perfectly obvious that Labour stands for sharing, kindness, gays, single mothers and Nelson Mandela as opposed to braying bossy men having affairs with everyone shag shag shag left right and centre and going to the Ritz in Paris then telling all the presenters off on the Today programme … it is important to vote for the principle of the thing, not on the itsy bitsy details about this per cent or that per cent.

Bridget Jones (Helen Fielding) in *Bridget Jones's Diary*,
The Independent, 29 January 1997

In October 1962, standing before conference attendees in Brighton, Harold Wilson famously defined the Labour Party as 'a moral crusade or … nothing'.

This morality at the heart of the party shaped its electoral ambitions: the party would not 'sail into power under any flags of convenience' such as those afforded by a 'timorous and defeatist' Lib-Lab pact. Rather, Labour would be elected to govern 'on one basis only – to seek a majority on a socialist mandate'.[1] Wilson's speech to conference the following year is more famous, as his invocation of the White Heat of technological revolution positioned Labour as the party of the future and is often cited as instrumental in its victory the following year. But in October 1964, at the first conference after their narrow electoral victory, Wilson did not repeat the 'white heat' refrain. Instead, he called back to another theme in the speech:

> In my speech at Scarborough I said: There is no standing aside, no comforting refuge in abstentions or vetoes, we are either against oppression, or we condone it. In these issues, there can be no neutrals, no escape. For in this shrinking world, whilst political isolationism invites danger, and economic isolationism invites bankruptcy, *moral* isolationism invites contempt.[2]

He went on to argue that the government needed to take a strong stand against racism, at home and abroad, because 'This Labour Party of ours is more than a political organisation: it is a crusade, or it would be better that it did not exist'.[3]

It is a little unfashionable to argue that Wilson's politics were a 'moral crusade', given his reputation as an 'unprincipled' prime minister, and the general sense that the lesson for Labour from Wilson's tenure as leader is of the importance of pragmatism and forward-thinking.[4] But this reading fails to account for how ideology figured in Wilson's political life. Not just socialism in the abstract, but the Labour Party specifically, was imbued with a sense of moral righteousness for Wilson; he wanted the party to win elections in order to gain power, but the rejection of 'flags of convenience' was not just a cold calculation of the limits of governing in coalition. Labour's destiny was to bring socialism to Britain: whilst the white heat of technology burned bright, so did the inherent morality of the party's mission. The connection between socialist politics and moral authority can be read through a religious lens: Wilson was raised Baptist, at university

---

[1] 'The Chairman's Address: "On the Threshold of Victory"', *The Times*, 2 October 1962.

[2] Emphasis added. This is not, in fact, a quotation from his speech in 1963; rather, it seems to be paraphrasing a general feeling Wilson believed he had conveyed. Harold Wilson, 'Leader's Speech, Brighton, 1964, http://www.britishpoliticalspeech.org/speech-archive.htm?speech=162 (accessed 13 September 2021).

[3] Ibid.

[4] Kevin Hickson and Andrew S. Crines, *Harold Wilson: The Unprincipled Prime Minister?* (London: Biteback, 2016); Glen O'Hara and Helen Parr, 'Introduction: The Rise and Fall of a Reputation', *Contemporary British History* 20 (2006): 295–302.

joined the evangelical Oxford Group over the Oxford Labour Party and, when he eventually joined Labour in Huddersfield, said he had done so as it stood for his 'highest moral and religious ideas'.[5] Indeed, Wilson paraphrased Acts 17.26 in his argument for an anti-racist politics at home and overseas, saying 'He hath made of one blood all nations to dwell upon the Earth.'

Morgan Phillips' assertion that the Labour Party owed as much to Methodism as Marx is often highlighted by the right of the party; it is a pithy line supposedly coined by Denis Healey for a speech by Phillips at the Socialist International Conference in Copenhagen in 1953.[6] Keir Hardie argued that socialism was 'at bottom, a question of ethics or morals'; Robert Blatchford, the socialist campaigner and journalist, argued that socialism was 'ethically right', and it was this ethical dimension that should drive the left beyond mere collectivism.[7] And it is clear that for many on the left, particularly at the beginning of the century, their socialism was rooted in a form of Christian socialism; this has been explored, for example, in the context of institutions such as the Labour Churches at the end of the nineteenth century, or in work drawing out the connections between pacifism and the left in Britain during the First World War and in the interwar period.[8]

But there is a distinct lack of scholarship that centres moral questions in the work of the Labour Party in the twentieth century. There has been little academic scholarship that seeks to more broadly explain the conflation between a sense of moral and ethical rightness and the Labour Party, which clearly exists amongst sections of the British public and can be seen in popular culture to the extent shown in the above quotation from *Bridget Jones's Diary*. Why is it possible to assert, as Bridget does, that Labour is the party of 'sharing, kindness, gays, single mothers and Nelson Mandela', to broad understanding – if not agreement – by readers both within and without the party?

The full question of the connections between morality and socialism, and ethics and the Labour Party, is too broad to be explored in this chapter. Instead, I focus here on one aspect of morality that perhaps explains the inclusion of Nelson Mandela at the end of Bridget's list: the question of foreign aid, in the

[5] Ben Pimlott, *Harold Wilson* (London: William Collins, 2016), 39, 47; 'Obituary: Lord Wilson of Rievaulx', *The Independent*, 24 May 1995.

[6] James Callaghan, *Time and Chance* (London: Harper Collins, 1987).

[7] Lawrence Black, 'Social Democracy as a Way of Life: Fellowship and the Socialist Union, 1951–9', *Twentieth Century British History* 10, no. 4 (1999): 507.

[8] Mark Bevir, 'The Labour Church Movement, 1891–1902', *Journal of British Studies* 38, no. 2 (1999): 217–45, https://doi.org/10.1086/386190; Stephen Yeo, 'A New Life: the Religion of Socialism in Britain, 1883–1896', *History Workshop Journal* 4, no. 1 (1 October 1977): 5–56; Paul Bridgen, *The Labour Party and the Politics of War and Peace, 1900–1924* (London: Royal Historical Society, 2009).

context of broader discussions around Labour and Britain's approach to the Global South. In this discussion, by focusing particularly on the 1960s and the 1990s, I trace a line from Barbara Castle to Robin Cook, to show a continuity of thinking about overseas aid within the Labour Party from the end of empire to the end of the twentieth century.

The ethical questions around foreign aid and assertions of moral goodness have been explored particularly in the fields of political economy and philosophy.[9] Tomohisa Hattori, for example, argues that multilateral aid agencies can be understood as exercising a form of beneficence that can be interpreted within a framework of Aristotelian virtue ethics. More broadly, as he sets out, liberal justifications for foreign aid can be read as making an ethical claim either via first, the argument that aid fulfils an 'imperfect obligation' to help the global population meet basic needs within their fundamental human rights; second, the idea that aid is essentially a utilitarian practice that demands that nations with technical expertise should share this globally for the greater good; or third, that aid is part of a broader humanitarian principle.[10] The idea that humanitarianism is itself inherently ethical or morally good has been challenged in turn by the work of historians of humanitarianism, who have outlined the complex connections between the humanitarian and the political, and between charity, altruism, national identity and the national interest.[11] Historians in this field have also worked to question the separation between imperialism and humanitarianism that has been posited by authors like Michael Barnett and which serves to elide the connections between modern humanitarian work by governments and non-governmental organizations (NGOs) and the imperial expansion and developmentalist colonialism of colonial metropoles in the nineteenth and twentieth centuries.[12]

It is in the context of this work that this chapter is framed: aid cannot be extricated from imperialism ideologically or practically, but political actors on the left still attempt to engage with questions around foreign aid within a broadly ethical framework. Indeed, this ethical framework is key to explaining

---

[9] See, for example, Deen K. Chatterjee (ed.), *The Ethics of Assistance: Morality and the Distant Needy* (Cambridge: CUP, 2004); Garrett Cullity, *The Moral Demands of Affluence* (Oxford: OUP, 2004); William Aitken and Hugh La Follette, *World Hunger and Morality* (London: Pearson, 1995).

[10] Tomohisa Hattori, 'The Moral Politics of Foreign Aid', *Review of International Studies* 29, no. 2 (2003): 230–1.

[11] See for example Bronwen Everill, Emily Baughan, Eleanor Davey, Kevin O'Sullivan, Tehila Sasson and Matthew Hilton, 'Humanitarianism and History: A conversation', *Past and Present* 241, no. 1 (2018): e1–e38, https://doi.org/10.1093/pastj/gty040.

[12] Michael Barnett, *Empire of Humanity: A History of Humanitarianism* (Ithaca, NY: CUP, 2011); Bronwen Everill, review of Humanitarianism and Humanitarian Intervention, review no. 1141, https://reviews.history.ac.uk/review/1141 (accessed 13 September 2021).

how Labour is able to embrace aid as a policy despite the complex political roots of British aid and development programmes. Thinking about how Labour has positioned overseas aid as a moral component of its policy programme can help us to explore how the party deals with (or fails to deal with) these complexities, but it can also help us to take seriously the idea that morality shapes voters' political engagement. If morality were not seen as an aim in Labour Party policy, aid would not be presented to voters so frequently as an innate moral good; what does this tell us about aid and about Labour? Exploring the ways in which the Labour Party has historically been concerned with crafting an ethical identity around these policies can push us to ask questions about how that ethical identity might be bought into by voters, and what might happen if their faith in that ethical platform is shaken.

As I have already argued, modern and contemporary aid and development policies can only be understood within a framework of imperial and decolonization politics. Building on the work of Anna Bocking-Welch and Joseph Hodge, I posit that British aid and development programmes were a way of maintaining international networks and connections at moments when it looked like they might break down.[13] Government aid and development programmes have their origins in colonial policies, just as international aid and development NGOs are rooted in charitable responses to empire, such as missionary activity in the eighteenth and nineteenth centuries. As the European metropoles shifted in the postwar period to a more 'developmentalist' approach to their colonial possessions, and with the increasing importance of actors such as the UN, the WHO and the FAO in transnational politics, NGOs also increasingly moved away from straightforwardly philanthropic or charitable projects to 'the more technical goal of "development"'.[14]

The issue of foreign aid and overseas development has been historically associated with the Labour Party specifically in the context of Labour's engagement with colonial rule and postcolonial foreign politics.[15] The first Colonial

---

[13] Anna Bocking Welch, *British Civic Society at the End of Empire: Decolonisation, Globalisation, and International Responsibility* (Manchester: MUP, 2018); Joseph Morgan Hodge, *Triumph of the Expert: Agrarian Doctrines of Development and the Legacies of British Colonialism* (Athens: Ohio University Press, 2007).

[14] Matthew Hilton, Nick Crowson, Jean-Francois Mouhot and James McKay, *A Historical Guide to NGOs in Britain: Charities, Civil Society and the Voluntary Sector since 1945* (London: Macmillan, 2012), 45–6.

[15] For more on this, see Charlotte Lydia Riley, '"The winds of change are blowing economically": the Labour Party and British overseas development, 1940s–1960s', in Andrew W. M. Smith and Chris Jeppesen, *Britain, France and the Decolonization of Africa: Future Imperfect?* (London: UCL, 2017).

Development and Welfare Act was passed in 1940 by Malcolm MacDonald, son of the former Labour leader and prime minister Ramsay MacDonald. The Act was renewed in 1945 under the newly elected Attlee government, and several more times after the war into the 1950s and early 1960s; in addition, the Colonial Development Corporation continued to promote capital projects (and still exists today, in amended form, as the CDC Group PLC). Arthur Creech Jones, the Colonial Secretary for much of the Attlee government, had been one of the founding members of the Fabian Colonial Bureau; he was influential in pushing the Colonial Office to embrace social welfare programmes as well as economic development strategies, such as focusing on primary education, the provision of maternity and child health services, and the formation of trade unions for African workers.[16]

From 1961 to 1964, under the Conservative government led by Harold Macmillan, the Department of Technical Co-Operation was responsible for technical assistance to foreign countries; the Commonwealth Relations Office granted capital aid to Commonwealth countries; the Foreign Office was in charge of all capital aid to foreign countries outside the Commonwealth. In 1964, these functions were combined into the Department of Overseas Development (ODM) by Harold Wilson's first Labour government. The ODM was the first time that British overseas aid was delivered to a generalized set of recipients 'overseas' rather than maintaining the distinction between colonies, ex-colonies and other foreign nations. But British aid policy in the 1960s clearly demonstrated a continuation of attitudes and approaches that were forged in colonial rule. In this way, the former metropole was able to maintain its relationship with its former colonies through overseas aid and development programmes, echoing the style of imperialism adopted during the postwar Labour government.

Although in many ways Barbara Castle, the first Minister of Overseas Development, set the tone for postcolonial British aid programmes, the ODM was not the final word in British overseas aid and development policy. In 1970, Edward Heath's new Conservative government rolled up responsibility for overseas aid into the Foreign and Commonwealth Office (FCO). In 1974, when Wilson was re-elected, Labour re-established the ODM (although later merged it again with the FCO) with Judith Hart, Frank Judd and Reginald Prentice serving as Ministers for Overseas Development. In 1979, the Conservative diminution of aid under foreign policy was continued by Margaret Thatcher, with aid administered from the Overseas Development Administration subsumed entirely

---

[16] Ibid.

within the FCO; in 1997, Tony Blair created the Department for International Development (DFID). DFID survived the coalition government of 2010 and the subsequent Conservative governments, despite figures such as Priti Patel, who later served as Secretary of State for International Development, calling for the department to be closed. However, in summer 2020 it was announced by Boris Johnson that DFID was to be closed, with aid once again becoming part of the FCO, now renamed the Foreign, Commonwealth and Development Office. Aid and development is clearly a partisan issue in British politics and the Labour Party clearly has historically had a distinctive approach to foreign aid. But how has this been constructed as a moral duty or an ethical concern?

When Denis Healey derided those who would luxuriate in the 'irresponsible impotence' of opposition rather than risk their knuckles and conscience in government, in the 1970 conference speech quoted above, he did so by appealing to their sense of global responsibility. When Healey said angrily that a Labour loss 'affects not only us here, it affects millions around the world', he was making the claim that the Labour Party had a particular approach to foreign policy; Labour being in power therefore made a difference even to those who were not part of the British polity. This counters the IR-inflected historiography that asserts that British foreign policy is not partisan and that the Foreign Office ultimately controls British action overseas through a rational, realist assessment of the nation's aims and objectives on the world stage, or that Labour – or British socialism more widely – has never had much interest in foreign policy compared to domestic politics.[17] This chapter instead builds on the work of Rhiannon Vickers, who argues that the Labour Party has historically had a distinctive foreign policy built on internationalist 'meta-principles' that included 'a belief in progress and an optimistic view of human nature'.[18] Although Vickers concludes that Labour has rarely been able to operate a socialist foreign policy – even at times when this would have been accepted by the party as a whole – because Britain's major allies have consistently been drawn from capitalist nation states, I argue that this has not stopped the party from framing some aspects of foreign policy as inherently 'socialist' or more specifically Labourite. In fact, Labour voters and members actually have a clear sense themselves of what a

---

[17] David Howell, for example, argues that both the Attlee government and Wilson governments were committed ultimately to realpolitik, in *British Social Democracy: A Study in Development and Decay* (London: Croom Helm, 1976), 144–9 and 267–74; James Hinton argues that British socialism made little contribution to foreign policy, in *Protests and Visions: Peace Politics in Twentieth Century Britain* (London: Hutchinson, 1989), 33.

[18] Rhiannon Vickers, *The Labour Party and the World, Vol. 1: The Evolution of Labour's Foreign Policy 1900–51* (Manchester: MUP, 2000), 5.

'Labour' foreign policy should look like and how it should differ from that of the Conservative Party.[19]

Overseas aid and development policies have had a particular salience within this imagination. One factor in this is the necessity to understand government aid and development programmes within a broader context of international charity and humanitarianism. For many people outside the sector, aid and development are difficult to extricate from charity and humanitarianism. A 2003 study by MacDonnell et al., for example, demonstrated that public support for aid is associated with the belief that most aid is in the form of humanitarian assistance, and a Mass Observation directive in 2008 found that most people who supported the idea of British government aid cited 'projects focused on individuals and/or communities and the provision of particular resources (for example schools or access to water)', projects far more associated with NGO activity than the work that had been funded by DFID as part of the Official Development Assistance (ODA) fund.[20] This blurring of categories is important because it demonstrates that for many of the British people, government aid and development policies are actually understood as acts of international altruism. This understanding is, however, partisan: Labour supporters are more likely to support aid spending to reduce global poverty, and less likely to support aid spending being used for policies that would act in Britain's economic self-interest, than supporters of the Conservative Party.[21]

When Healey made his speech, he had just returned from apartheid South Africa. As he told the conference, he had spent a week travelling around the country speaking to opponents of apartheid, 'to black people, to white people, to Trade Unionists, professors, churchmen and journalists', about their experience of and resistance to apartheid. He invoked these people to justify his assertion that Labour needed to win at home to do good overseas: 'there was one thing on which all those men and women told me they had been united: that when the news reached them at the end of June of the defeat of Harold Wilson's

---

[19] Although this split has been complicated by the fact that much public opinion foreign policy now also needs to be understood through the lens of Leave v Remain. See for example Sophia Gaston, *UK Public Opinion on Foreign Policy and Global Affairs: Annual Survey – 2020* (London: British Foreign Policy Group, 2020), https://bfpg.co.uk/wp-content/uploads/2020/06/BFPG-Annual-Survey-Public-Opinion-2020-HR.pdf (accessed 13 September 2021).

[20] IDS WORKING PAPER 353, Public Perceptions of International Development and Support for Aid in the UK: Results of a Qualitative Enquiry (The Mass Observation Project Winter 2008 Directive – Part 2).

[21] Sophia Gaston, *UK Public Opinion on Foreign Policy and Global Affairs: Annual Survey – 2020* (London: British Foreign Policy Group, 2020), 32.

Government they felt it as a bitter, personal tragedy and as a blow for freedom in South Africa as a whole'.[22]

This might sound only like a useful rhetorical device to galvanize the Labour Party to resist luxuriating in opposition, and perhaps it was. But it is supported by the global response to the election of the Wilson government in 1964, and the appointment of Barbara Castle as Minister for Overseas Development. Castle was active in the anti-apartheid movement – she received the Oliver Tambo medal in 2004 in recognition of her work – and had been instrumental, too, in exposing the Hola Camp atrocity in parliament in 1959.[23] In addition, her brother Tristan (always known as Jimmy) Betts was appointed Oxfam's first African field director in 1961. Castle's long-standing interest in issues of development and postcolonial politics were well-known internationally, and she received letters of congratulations from around the globe, including from actors involved with the anti-apartheid campaign. So, for example, Arthur Goldreich (the Israeli–South African artist and anti-apartheid stalwart) wrote: 'I'm quite certain that you and your party are to stay for years and years and that Britain and the rest of the world will benefit from it. I wish South Africa fell under the mantle of your ministry – we'd see a great deal more "development" than is obvious at the present time.'[24] Similarly, Barney Desai, from the South Africa Coloured People's Congress, believed that 'The victory of Labour; Mr Wilson's elevation to the Premiership and the inclusion of persons of your fibre in the Government of the UK, gives us great hope that justice and morality will replace expediency and self-interest, in British dealings with South Africa.'[25] And Suriya Wickremasinghe, of the Afro-Asian Solidarity Association of Ceylon, confided that 'We are confident that the new government of Britain will take a more positive line on South Africa than its predecessor, and that in general its foreign policy will be in sympathy with the aspirations of the people of Africa and Asia.'[26] The international community, then, received and amplified the idea of a specifically Labour Party approach to colonial policy, as well as the idea that this approach was rooted fundamentally in a distinctive moral framework.

---

[22]   Healey, 'Thursday afternoon – South Africa', Labour party conference proceedings 1970, 251.

[23]   Caroline Elkins, 'The Struggle for Mau Mau Rehabilitation in Late Colonial Kenya', *The International Journal of African Historical Studies* 33, no. 1 (2000): 47.

[24]   Arthur Goldreich, Tel Aviv, to Castle, 19 October 1964, MSS Castle 260: Letters of Congratulation upon re-election as MP and appointment as Minister for Overseas Development, October–December 1964, Bodleian Library, University of Oxford.

[25]   Barney Desai, South Africa Coloured People's Congress (living in London), to Castle, 20 October 1964, MSS Castle 260.

[26]   Suriya Wickremasinghe, Ass Sec to Afro-Asian Solidarity Association of Ceylon, to Castle, 20 October 1964, MSS Castle 260.

For many British politicians and members of the public, aid and development were mechanisms by which Britain could maintain a global role, even as decolonization reduced the size of the formal empire; as well as formally, through hard power, they also represented new forms of engagement for ordinary British people with a new post-imperial world. This continued desire for an international role by both the government and the people had multiple overlapping motivations: it could be a desire to continue empire by other means, to recapture British 'greatness', or to maintain connections in areas now looking to either the USA or USSR in the Cold War battle for hearts and minds. These types of arguments were mostly, but not only, to be found on the right of the political spectrum, including the right of the Labour Party. An opinion piece from January 1964 in the *Sunday Times* is a good example of this approach: overseas aid was 'a matter both of duty, as an ex-colonial Power, and of self-interest, as the central figure in the pattern of Commonwealth partnerships. Aid may not in the short run buy off Communism, subversion or other forms of extremism, but in the long run it is probably the best contribution towards the stability of the new countries.'[27]

Many on the British political left argued for aid and development programmes from a slightly different perspective – focusing more on duty to the colonies and colonial populations, and then a debt incurred to recently independent nations. Labour figures including Wilson, Castle and Hart, all believed that aid was a way in which Britain could and should work to reduce global poverty and inequality, especially as these inequalities were injustices that the imperial system had heightened and codified.

In Wilson's 1953 book *The War On World Poverty*, he set out what he saw as 'Britain's duty' in a world where 'the gunboat has given way to the tractor; the pro-consul to the imperial engineer'.[28] Wilson's conception of a modern world was one in which imperialism was 'over'; instead, he wanted to see Britain and America work together to build on postwar development initiatives such as British colonial development programmes and the American Point IV plan, and to do so within the context of an international authority on development through the United Nations, including cooperation with the Soviet Union if possible. But at the end of the book, he argued that if America could not be convinced that this were their mission, a new Labour government should 'go it alone'.[29] He rooted Labour's commitment to overseas aid in 'the fifty years' march

---

[27] 'The Legacy of Empire', *The Sunday Times*, 26 January 1964, 14.
[28] Harold Wilson, *The War on World Poverty* (London: Gollancz, 1953), 202.
[29] Ibid., 199–202.

out of industrialism and inequality towards social justice and the welfare state'.[30] The war on world poverty of the book's title was Britain's 'historic mission', partly because hunger is a threat to world peace, partly because it is a limit on global productivity.[31] But as Wilson made clear, above all, this should be couched as an ethical challenge: 'It is not a question of self interest or power politics. It is a moral imperative. We are rich and they are poor, and it is our duty to help them.'[32]

Hart, who first served as Minister of Overseas Development in 1969, before serving two stints as Minister for Overseas Development in the 1970s, also formulated a conception of overseas aid that made a moral case for Labour supporting these policies. In her book *Aid and Liberation: A Socialist Study of Aid Politics* she rejected the idea that aid should be framed through 'the suffocating and cosy political neutralism of well-meaning compassion'.[33] She framed her own experience of British aid policy through the work of the Haslemere Group, a non-party organization comprising a mixture of NGOs and charitable organizations, which had in 1968 drawn attention to the failures of the international aid regime – 'at best, a wholly inadequate payment for goods received, at worst another name for the continued exploitation of the poor countries by the rich' – and demanded that charities stop being 'polite, respectable and ineffective' and instead demand that Western governments 'respond realistically to the desperate human need of the poor world'.[34] Hart argued that, despite the limitations of the aid system, Britain must not simply opt out and thus 'evade the responsibility and guilt that any former imperial power must bear for the pattern of past events, which … produced the poverty gap'.[35] Instead, a socialist government must develop a working definition of aid that, for example, prioritized public sector mechanisms for development over privatized solutions, just as it would do at home.[36] Britain under a Labour government must 'accept a moral and political commitment to the development of the Third World', because of the 'universality of the fight against poverty and injustice'.[37]

Aid, therefore, was not simply an aspect of British foreign policy; it was a moral duty, and one for which the Labour Party should feel it had a distinct

[30] Ibid., 203.
[31] Ibid.
[32] Ibid., 25.
[33] Judith Hart, *Aid and Liberation: A Socialist Study of Aid Politics* (London: Gollancz, 1973), 235.
[34] Haslemere Declaration Group and Third World First, *The Haslemere Declaration*, April 1968.
[35] Hart, *Aid and Liberation*, 241.
[36] Ibid., 244.
[37] Ibid., 279–80.

responsibility. A *Sunday Times* leader from 1969 amplified this notion that aid was a distinctly Labour policy. Headlined 'Let the People Give', the piece argued that there were 'few votes in overseas aid' but that 'support for it has always been a distinctive feature of Labour's philosophy' and that the issue was 'close to the soul, so to speak, of the party'; Labour was, in fact, 'pulsating with idealism' on the issue.[38] The invocation of the party's 'soul', however self-consciously, shows how the idea of aid and charity had become part of a broader discussion around the moral economy of international relations by the late 1960s.[39]

The Labour Party's aid policy was interrupted by their election loss in 1970; the 1974–9 government continued the earlier policies and tone, but against an ever-more fractious political background that pushed discussions about overseas aid out of the spotlight. Labour itself was of course pushed into the shadows from 1979 to 1997; in this long period of opposition, the party's natural supporters directed their energies into a broader range of civil and civic activism, beyond parliamentary politics. For many of them, this was inflected by the increasing focus on issues surrounding what was then commonly referred to as the 'Third World', such as the Nestlé baby-milk scandal, the campaign around the contraceptive injection Depo-Provera and the events of Band Aid/ Live Aid in response to the Ethiopian famine. Tehila Sasson, for example, has demonstrated how War on Want was able to mobilize consumers within a moral economy that connected consumer ethics to questions of poverty and morality, leading to the rise of the 'fair trade' movement.[40] This popular mobilization of British 'care' about the people of the 'Third World' could be part of mass culture – for example, in the increasingly ubiquitous charity single.[41] But it was also a distinct presence in left-wing activist spaces, where it took on a particularly critical tone to explore the intersections between political and moral questions: for example, in the pages of the feminist zine *Spare Rib*.[42] As prefigured by the

---

[38] 'Let the people give', *The Sunday Times*, 16 November 1969, 12.

[39] This is still true today, with much discussion of capitalism and the potential for a moral economy drawing on ideas about aid and charity. See for example Tehila Sasson, 'The Gospel of Wealth', *Dissent*, 22 August 2018, https://www.dissentmagazine.org/online_articles/tim-rogan-moral-economists-critique-capitalism-book-review (accessed 13 September 2021).

[40] Tehila Sasson, 'Milking the Third World? Humanitarianism, Capitalism, and the Moral Economy of the Nestlé Boycott', *The American Historical Review* 121, no. 4 (October 2016): 1196–224, https://doi.org/10.1093/ahr/121.4.1196.

[41] Lucy Robinson, 'Putting the Charity Back into Charity Singles: Charity Singles in Britain 1984–1995', *Contemporary British History* 26, no. 3 (2012): 405–25, https://doi.org/10.1080/13619462.2012.703026.

[42] See for example 'Third World: Powdered Milk Kills', *Spare Rib* 34 (April 1975): 26; 'Powdered Milk Kills: Nestlé sues Third World Campaigners', *Spare Rib* 36 (June 1975): 20; 'Depo Provera: 3rd World Women not told this contraceptive is trial', *Spare Rib* 42 (January 1976): 22–3; '"Better a Woman gets cancer in 30 years than pregnant now" Depo Provera in use', *Spare Rib* 69 (April 1978): 28.

Haslemere Declaration, against the radical ideological backdrop of Thatcherism, British humanitarian and aid NGOs such as Oxfam, War on Want, the Campaign Against the Arms Trade and the World Development Movement became both increasingly explicitly 'political' and critical of the British government, and increasingly keen to mobilize British citizens in support of their campaigns, for example through letter-writing and the lobbying of constituency MPs.[43] This can also be set within a wider internationalist focus on the activist left, such as the protests against the American military base at Greenham Common and the establishment of the Greenham Common camp by feminist socialist activists. There increasingly arose, then, a type of holistic political identity that connected – for example – donating to Oxfam, listening to musicians associated with the Red Wedge collective, reading *Spare Rib*, going on CND marches and voting for Labour.[44] It is within this framework that Bridget Jones constructs her theory of Labour's political and moral identity.

The 1997 Labour manifesto declared that the party believed Britain had 'a clear moral responsibility' to combat global poverty and inequality.[45] The manifesto declared the intention to reinstate a department for international development, independent of the Foreign Office. The manifesto focused to a large extent on the potential for aid and development as enacted through trade agreements and the European Union. The Department for International Development was created in May 1997 and was headed until her resignation in May 2003 by Clare Short.

The creation of DFID should not be understood only as an invention of Tony Blair's new government. Rather, it should be seen within the context not only of the history of aid outlined here during the 1940s and the 1960s – when Labour developed a moral approach to aid whilst in government – but also in the 1980s and 1990s, when Neil Kinnock sought to refocus the party after successive defeats to the Conservatives. The centrality of aid and development to the offer made by Kinnock to the electorate speaks to the importance of aid and development within a new moral framework of Labour politics. Aid and development allowed Britain to position itself on the world stage as an ethical actor (at least until proven otherwise in other areas of foreign policy) and, as it

---

[43] Clare Saunders, 'British Humanitarian, Aid and Development NGOs, 1949–Present', in Hilton et al., *NGOS in Contemporary Britain*, 44–9.

[44] This has often been emphasized in relationship to the campaigns of the Greater London Council (GLC) but can be seen across all regions of Britain. See for example Daisy Payling, '"Socialist Republic of South Yorkshire": Grassroots Activism and Left-Wing Solidarity in 1980s Sheffield', *Twentieth Century British History* 25, no. 4 (December 2014): 602–27, https://doi.org/10.1093/tcbh/hwu001.

[45] Labour Party Manifesto, 'New Labour: Because Britain Deserves Better' (Labour Party, 1997).

was an area where Britain had historic (in fact, imperial) experience, it was a way for the country to maintain an authoritative and dominant role in international organizations and on the world stage. But this would not have been accepted within the Labour Party or – most importantly – by its supporters, if it had been this visibly cynical; aid-as-soft-power is, after all, the consistent manifesto promise of the Conservative Party. Labour's commitment to aid went beyond these strategic concerns; building on the politics of the 1960s, the Labour Party in the 1980s framed their commitment to foreign aid as an unmistakably moral concern.

At Labour conference in 1985, Kinnock spoke to his fellow 'democratic socialists' of the need to commit to, not retreat from, their 'duties as citizens of the world'. He spoke of the 'obligations' that a strong nation such as Britain had to help poorer nations and argued that part of Britain's 'place in the world' (a contested concept, after decolonization) was not only to give the poor the means to feed and clothe themselves but also to 'develop their economy, to find their freedom'. He framed this partly as a practical concern, in Britain's material interest – 'we live together or we decay separately'. But this practical concern was presented only as a last resort: 'if the morality won't convince people, if ethics won't'.[46] The Labour report *Modern Britain in a Modern World: For the Good of All* from that year reiterated that aid was a 'moral duty' for Britain under Labour, as part of the party's 'plans for a modern Britain in a modern world'; a Labour Party *Talking Points* pamphlet on 'Overseas Aid: Britain's Place in the World' from the following year described aid as a 'moral obligation'.[47]

This is the longer context of the creation of DFID, which should also be understood as being an important part of the 1997 Labour government's focus on pursuing an 'ethical' foreign policy. In May 1997, only twelve days after the election, Robin Cook – then the newly appointed Foreign Secretary – made a speech to outline the core principles which would underpin Labour's activities overseas. Cook argued that in the 'age of internationalism' and a 'world in which nation states are interdependent', foreign policy was 'not independent from domestic policy but a central part of any political programme'.[48] The speech is

---

[46] Neil Kinnock, Foreword: 'Labour Party Conference, October 1985', in *Modern Britain in a Modern World: For the Good of All* (Labour Party, 1985).

[47] *Modern Britain in a Modern World: For the Good of All* (Labour Party, 1985), 27; Labour Party 'Overseas Aid: Britain's Place in the World', *Talking Points* 65 (September 1986).

[48] Robin Cook, 'Mission Statement for the Foreign and Commonwealth Office', speech delivered at Locarno Suite, FCO, London, 12 May 1997.

best remembered for Cook's assertion that Labour needed to follow 'an ethical foreign policy'.[49] In fact, he never used this phrase to describe his plans for the Foreign Office. Instead, he argued that British foreign policy 'must have an ethical dimension'; this statement can perhaps best be understood in the context of the final words of the speech, which proclaimed that the new mission statement would 'make Britain once again a force for good in the world'.[50] The rhetoric harks back to an imagined past of British greatness and, combined with the focus on British power lying within its position in the international community, can be seen as a repudiation of British foreign policy in the 1980s under Mrs Thatcher. In fact, Cook clearly locates Labour's approach to foreign policy in opposition to the policies followed under the previous eighteen years of Conservative rule, which he identifies as the pursuit of 'not so splendid isolation'.[51] In this way, aid and development programmes are presented part of a British return, not to a glorious past of greatness – nothing so triumphant or so tinged with imperialism – but to its rightful *moral* position on the world stage.[52]

This emphasis of the 'ethics' of foreign policy was fundamental to much of the discussion of DFID within the Labour Party. In the House of Commons, Short claimed that 'ethics [would] be at the heart of [Labour's] international development policy', fitting into the narrative created by Robin Cook earlier that month.[53] This emphasis was repeated later by other Labour MPs, such as Julia Drown, MP for Swindon South, who proclaimed herself 'proud to be part of the Labour Party' because of its commitment to 'reverse the increase in the polarities of wealth and to give prominence to development issues'.[54] Oona King, MP for Bethnal Green and Bow, argued that Labour was offering 'fairness, not favours' internationally as well as domestically, and emphasized the role of government action in international development: 'we cannot privatise the problems facing the planet'.[55] Overseas aid and development, therefore, was framed as a moral issue that was fundamentally connected to the values of the Labour Party, and this continued throughout Short's tenure as minister.

---

[49] Chris Brown, 'On Morality, Self-Interest and Foreign Policy', *Government and Opposition* 37, no. 2 (2002): 173–89.

[50] Robin Cook, 'Mission Statement for the Foreign and Commonwealth Office'.

[51] Ibid.

[52] I am grateful for Nick Garland for prompting this idea.

[53] Claire Short, Development Policy (Ethical Issues), HC Deb 21 May 1997, vol. 294, c. 90.

[54] Julia Drown, International Development, HC Deb 01 July 1997, vol. 297, c. 187.

[55] Oona King, International Development, HC Deb 01 July 1997, vol. 297, c. 171.

Conclusion

Labour, then, has historically used narratives around overseas aid and development to construct an image of itself as a moral actor in the world. For the Attlee government, and especially for Arthur Creech Jones, colonial development policies were an 'ethical' way of being imperialists; for the Blair government, overseas development was an 'ethical' way of having a foreign policy in the developing world. Under Wilson and Kinnock, Labour Party thinking bridged the gap between imperialism and overseas development through the framework of morality, 'duty' and ethics.

To argue that Labour has developed a sense of aid as a moral obligation is not to argue that Labour policies towards the Global South should be above criticism. Historically, for the Labour Party, it is clear that aid and development has been a way of engaging with the developing world without having to engage with the history of violent exploitation that characterized Britain's historic relationship with these populations, and a way of denying that the party itself had any complicity in this history. In this manner, Short was able to claim in a letter to the Zimbabwean agricultural minister that the Blair government was 'a new government with diverse backgrounds without links to former colonial interests' – indeed, that as she was Irish she was 'colonised, not coloniser' – even whilst refusing to support reparative land acquisition programmes, which were rooted fundamentally in Britain's recent colonial past.[56]

In 2017 the Labour Party published a policy paper, written by Kate Osamor in her position as Shadow Secretary of State for International Development, entitled *A World for the many not the few: The Labour Party's vision for international development*. The document drew on some of the motifs of Labour's popular Corbynite manifesto, *For the many not the few*, to set out a socialist internationalist approach to aid. The document took a rights-based approach to poverty reduction and politicized problems such as 'poverty, hunger, inequality, injustice and climate change' both as interconnected and 'not natural'.[57] Surprisingly, perhaps, given the context of its creation, it lauds 1997 as a 'radical and revolutionary' moment for the creation of DFID, and repeats too the argument for an ethical foreign policy.[58] But it also argues that in 1997, DFID rejected aid as an act of 'short-term national interest' and instead established

---

[56] Claire Short to Kumbirai Kangai, Zimbabwean Minister of Agriculture and Land, 5 November 1997.
[57] Kate Osamor, *A world for the many not the few: The Labour Party's vision for international development* (Labour Party, 2018), 9.
[58] Ibid., 11.

'a higher moral purpose of poverty reduction', to which the document argues a Corbyn Labour government would return.[59] The invocation again of aid as a *moral* issue demonstrates the lasting impact of discussions in the 1960s and the 1990s on British politics today. It is interesting that a Corbyn Labour Party chose to amplify the achievements of the Blair government in establishing DFID, despite sustained and developed criticisms of international aid as a tool of neo-colonial control.[60] Perhaps this indicates that aid is a space where there is in fact a great degree of consensus within the Labour Party, that could in fact be used to reduce division in other areas.

As I have argued throughout this chapter, aid and development policies are an integral part of Labour ideology, as central to the party's identity as the welfare state at home. Questions of morality in overseas aid have been historically developed and discussed by Labour thinkers and there is a coherent and consistent canon of Labour thinking on this issue which should not be ignored or downplayed. Future Labour governments – in a world which is no less unequal than that surveyed by Harold Wilson in the middle of the last century – should be empowered by the fact that Labour's most successful leaders have been those who have advocated with clear voices for overseas aid spending, and should continue to make a case for aid, not only for short-term political gain but also as part of the moral framework of the Labour Party itself.

[59] Ibid., 5.
[60] See for example Mark Lagan, *Neo-Colonialism and the Poverty of 'Development' in Africa* (London: Palgrave Macmillan, 2018).

Part Four

12

'What did the 1983 manifesto ever do for us?'

Colm Murphy

If the average Labour member knows anything about their party's history, they will know that the 1983 general election was a catastrophe. A glance at the horror show of electoral statistics reminds us why. After four years of a polarizing Conservative administration (featuring a vicious recession, urban rioting, IRA hunger strikes and accelerated deindustrialization) Labour lost three million votes and achieved a popular vote share of only 27.6 per cent. The outcome was a landslide majority of 144 seats for Margaret Thatcher.[1] When elected leader soon afterwards, Neil Kinnock exhorted party members to 'remember how you felt' in the aftermath and promised 'never, ever again will we experience that'.[2]

Labour crumbled to this historic defeat for many reasons, including a post-Falklands popularity boost for Thatcher, the legacies of factional division and the dysfunctional organization of Michael Foot's beleaguered party.[3] A major contributor to Labour's struggles was its radical manifesto – memorably condemned by the waspish MP Gerald Kaufman as the 'longest suicide note in history'.[4] This 'suicide' folk memory of 1983 was crucial for the later development of the party. Kinnock and John Smith both consciously moved away from key 1983 commitments over the 1980s and 1990s.[5] The evangelists of 'New Labour'

---

[1] Colin Rallings and Michael Thrasher, *British Electoral Facts* (London: Biteback, 2009), 48, 50.

[2] Ian Aitken, 'Kinnock takes charge', *Guardian*, 3 October 1983, 1.

[3] Jon Lawrence, *Electing Our Masters: The Hustings in British Politics from Hogarth to Blair* (Oxford: OUP, 2009), 222–3.

[4] David Butler and Denis Kavanagh, *The British General Election 1983* (Basingstoke: Macmillan, 1984), 280.

[5] Eric Shaw, *The Labour Party Since 1979: Crisis and Transformation* (London: Routledge, 1994). For Labour's changing electoral sociological outlook, see Florence Sutcliffe-Braithwaite, '"Class" in the Development of British Labour Party Ideology, 1983–1997', *Archiv für Sozialgeschichte* 53 (2013): 327–63.

saw the manifesto as the crowning disgrace of an 'Old Labour' addicted to policies like nationalization, price controls and 'beer and sandwiches' corporatism.[6]

In this chapter, I will argue that this impression does a disservice to the intellectual ferment within the British left over the 1970s and early 1980s. A diverse array of sympathetic figures both inside and outside the Labour Party – including not just democratic socialists, but 'High Tory' Keynesians, trade unionists, radical liberals and communists – spent the best part of a decade developing an interlocking set of policies known as the 'Alternative Economic Strategy' (AES). To a significant extent, the 1983 manifesto was the culmination of these intellectual currents. The AES stands testament to one of the most creative moments of policymaking in Labour's history. At the very least, it deserves a more considered appraisal.

In making this argument, I am not going to pretend that the manifesto was an astute or electorally appropriate pitch to Britain in 1983. In political terms, it was disastrously misguided. Nor will I ignore the dubious assumptions behind some of its commitments. Many of the criticisms of 1983 bear out. However, blanket dismissal is an unwise approach for those reflecting on the party's past. It prevents us from listening beyond the sound and fury, for those quieter and subtler insights that can help us today.

This chapter returns the 1983 manifesto to its true context: the political and intellectual upheaval of Labour's left after Harold Wilson's first government. It provides, firstly, a more accurate picture of the origins of the 1983 manifesto than claims of 'Old Labour'.[7] For its authors, the AES was a cutting-edge socialist response to the upheavals of the 1970s. At the time, it was far from obvious that they were wrong, as attested by the interest of Treasury officials and liberal social democrats in different parts of the strategy. Secondly, this chapter draws attention to elements of the 1983 manifesto that jar against conventional accounts of its unmitigated folly. These include the debts it owed to the 1974 manifestoes – which, though not runaway triumphs, were electorally successful. In some ways, such as its policies for working women, the 1983 manifesto even anticipated New Labour's landslide-winning 1997 platform. Thirdly, it shows that key theorists behind the AES were far from diehard ideologues, as they changed their minds on major issues in the early 1980s. This not only helped Kinnock overhaul his party's programme

[6]   Peter Mandelson, *The Third Man: Life at the Heart of New Labour* (London: HarperPress, 2010), 65–9.

[7]   For criticism of the term, see Eric Shaw, 'Retrieving or re-imagining the past? The case of "Old Labour", 1979–94', in Jonathan Davis and Rohan McWilliam (eds), *Labour and the Left in the 1980s* (Manchester: MUP, 2017), 25–43.

and lay the groundwork for 1990s electoral successes, it also suggests a subtler lesson. During the 1970s, Labour's social democrats reacted mostly with hostility to arguments of AES theorists, even some of their more constructive ideas. This was counterproductive. It alienated social democrats from the dynamic ideas of their day, which in turn contributed to the radical tenor of Labour's platform. As counter-intuitive as it may seem, social democrats today can draw some positive as well as the more obvious negative insights from *A New Hope for Britain*.

The manifesto, and its flaws

It is customary at this point to list Labour's 1983 commitments, building a cumulative impression of blinkered radicalism. Labour pledged an 'emergency programme of action', which included a 'massive programme for expansion' in public and industrial investment, housebuilding, welfare and social service expenditure, and a 'crash programme of employment and training'. Alongside audaciously reflating the economy, Labour promised to reshape Britain's industries, political economy and power structures. To protect its reflation from spiralling prices and speculative financial attack, Labour would not just devalue the pound and reinstate price and exchange controls but also introduce import controls and other forms of economic protectionism. A 1983 Labour government would establish a new National Investment Bank, give the state powers to assume shareholding ownership of large private companies and direct other firms through plans agreed jointly by business, trade unions and the government. It would not only renationalize recently privatized public companies but also socialize the private economy by facilitating a major expansion of industrial democracy (through, for example, sponsoring worker-owned firms and legislating for workers on boards). In foreign and defence policy, Labour would withdraw from the European Economic Community 'well within the lifetime of a Labour government', cancel the Trident nuclear programme, refuse to deploy Cruise missiles on Greenham Common and remove American nuclear bases from Britain.[8]

There were no illusions amongst Labour supporters about the radicalism of their platform, and how it would be interpreted by finance, business and the British establishment. In his 1983 book (which, unluckily, was published

---

[8] Iain Dale (ed.), *Labour Party General Election Manifestos, 1900–1997* (London: Routledge, 2000), 239–89.

just after Labour's defeat), Putney's parliamentary candidate Peter Hain wrote dramatically about the scale of the task if Foot had entered Downing Street. During the 'first few hours' after it had become 'apparent that Labour has won the election' – which 'could conceivably be before the votes are actually counted' because of the exit poll – Labour would need to impose 'emergency controls on foreign currency and capital movements', devalue the currency and appoint a 'socialist Governor of the Bank of England'. By the end of the 'first weekend', NATO should be 'informed that Britain intends to go non-nuclear' and the European Economic Community (EEC) told that Labour would enact its policies regardless of its regulations. The House of Lords, meanwhile, 'should be warned' that if it tried to revise any legislation, Labour would immediately flood the second chamber with hundreds of peers to engineer a 'socialist majority'.[9]

This was not only bracing stuff, but fatally ambitious. Many of the subsequent criticisms of the manifesto, and of the Labour left in the early 1980s, are wholly justified. This is especially obvious in foreign and defence policy. In 1983, Labour's platform was (with the exception of Euroscepticism) without precedent and in the case of unilateralism violently out of step with public opinion. Unilaterally abandoning the nuclear deterrent, though a cherished aim of Michael Foot and the resurgent Campaign for Nuclear Disarmament, was electorally toxic.[10]

How did Labour end up saddled with commitments so out of step with public opinion? To answer that, we must look closely at the party's internal politics over the 1970s. Labour's emerging platform was, to a large extent, the product of the left's march through the party's institutions and the trade union movement. The left gained ground after the failure of Harold Wilson's National Plan and the *In Place of Strife* controversy disillusioned supporters.[11] Additionally, in some constituency parties, the left advanced due to the entry of a new generation of leftists (often inspired by post-1968 liberation movements).[12] Through their newfound voting power at the annual conference, Labour's left seized control of key NEC policy committees, using them to flesh out a new agenda.[13] These

---

[9] Peter Hain, *The Democratic Alternative: A Socialist Response To Britain's Crisis* (London: Penguin, 1983), 165–6.

[10] Butler and Kavanagh, *The British General Election 1983*, 282.

[11] James E. Cronin, *New Labour's Pasts: The Labour Party and its Discontents* (Edinburgh: Pearson, 2004), 135.

[12] The extent of this phenomenon can be exaggerated – and the rise of the left varied locally. See Daisy Payling, '"Socialist Republic of South Yorkshire": Grassroots Activism and Left-Wing Solidarity in 1980s Sheffield', *Twentieth Century British History* 25, no. 4 (2014): 602–27; Steven Fielding and Duncan Tanner, 'The "Rise Of The Left" Revisited: Labour Party Culture In Post-War Manchester and Salford', *Labour History Review* 71, no. 3 (2006): 211–33.

[13] Mark Wickham-Jones, *Economic Strategy and the Labour Party: Politics and Policy-Making, 1970–83* (Basingstoke: Macmillan, 1996), 8.

committees, however, had flawed priorities. As Labour's left-wing research director Geoff Bish admitted in a post-mortem of the 1983 defeat, they largely ignored public opinion research.[14] Hence, the inclusion of commitments like unilateralism in the first place.

There were other problems too. Because the NEC developed a new agenda in explicit opposition to a largely unenthusiastic parliamentary party and (Shadow) Cabinet, the left's advance came at the cost of an intensely divided party. Once Labour entered government, the party seemed to have parallel policymaking structures at Transport House and Whitehall. This made incoherent messaging and public spats inevitable – which in turn undermined Labour's public image. The most dramatic example of this was during the 1976 conference, when Denis Healey, the Chancellor of the Exchequer, was forced to defend his crisis-fighting policies whilst barracked and booed from all angles. Similarly, during the 1983 election, Healey (now the party's deputy leader) equivocated over the party's unilateralist stance, a policy he was well-known to oppose personally. Days of harmful headlines resulted.[15]

Even aside from the imperatives of electoralism and party unity, some of the manifesto's policy combinations were inappropriate for the early 1980s. Labour's lack of realism in 1983 was largely a product of its unhappy recent experience in power. Between 1974 and 1979, ferocious headwinds – including spiking inflation, slowing growth and civil-sectarian violence in the north of Ireland – had buffeted both Wilson and his successor Jim Callaghan as they tried to steer the ship of state. Moreover, razor-tight election results meant that they could rely only on tenuous parliamentary majorities and short-term coalitions. The 1974–9 government had tried to tackle inflation and industrial strife with corporatist negotiation and semi-voluntary incomes policies (the 'Social Contract'). But after a speculative run on the pound in 1976, which led the IMF to demand fiscal retrenchment as a condition of its financial support, it became harder for Labour to hold its side of the corporatist bargain, even though it continued to demand wage restraint. Sharp spending cuts, the 'Winter of Discontent' and an outraged activist base were the unhappy consequences.[16] With memories of these spectacular failures of pay restraint still raw, Labour's 1983 manifesto ruled

---

[14] Geoff Bish, 'Future Policy Development: A Preliminary Note by the Research Secretary', RD: 2806/July 1983, in Labour History and Archives Study Centre, People's History Museum (hereafter, PHM), Labour Party Archive, Home Policy Committee papers.

[15] Butler and Kavanagh, *The British General Election 1983*, 95.

[16] Kathleen Burk and Alec Cairncross, *'Goodbye Great Britain': The 1976 IMF Crisis* (New Haven, CT: Yale University Press, 1992), 55–6; Tara Martin López, *The Winter of Discontent: Myth, Memory, and History* (Liverpool: LUP, 2014).

out a government-imposed incomes policy. Yet, it simultaneously pledged the empowerment of trade union bargaining, a currency devaluation, and a massive fiscal expansion – all of which risked an inflationary spiral. Given their other commitments, Labour's refusal to even consider an incomes policy to keep prices down was, to be blunt, a triumph of wishful thinking.[17]

In combination, all these flaws reflected some well-known weaknesses of the Labour Party in the early 1980s: an addiction to unwieldy lists of policies secured through factional slate politics, a mistaking of grassroots activist enthusiasm with popular support and an unwillingness to confront unwelcome trade-offs.

State holding companies and multinationals

Nonetheless, the intellectual thinking behind the 1983 manifesto cannot be reduced to these flaws. Labour's platform was, in many ways, the product of extensive debates on the future of the national social-democratic mixed economy. The historian Guy Ortolano has recently stressed the 'dynamism' of social democracy during the difficult 1970s, and Labour's policymaking is no exception in this regard.[18]

It is often forgotten that the meat of Labour's 1983 pledges for planning and public ownership had been party policy for nearly a decade – in which time Labour had *won as well as lost elections*. In a decade that saw stuttering economic growth, high inflation and titanic industrial disputes – due in part to the destabilization of the world economy after the fall of Bretton Woods and the 1973 oil crisis – space opened for more daring political programmes. 'Monetarism', advanced in America by Milton Friedman and in Britain by influential commentators like Samuel Brittan, was one such programme, but a rejuvenated democratic socialism was another.[19] This was reflected in both of Labour's 1974 manifestos, which famously promised a 'fundamental and irreversible shift in the balance of power and wealth in favour of working people and their families'.[20] This promise, and the accompanying policies, were based on the iconic conference document, *Labour's Programme 1973*, a foundational text for what became known as the

---

[17] Jim Tomlinson, *Monetarism: Is there an Alternative? Non-Monetarist Strategies for the Economy* (Oxford: Basil Blackwell, 1986), 34–5, 62–6.

[18] Guy Ortolano, *Thatcher's Progress: From Social Democracy to Market Liberalism through an English New Town* (Cambridge: CUP, 2019), 21.

[19] Michael Oliver and Hugh Pemberton, 'Learning and Change in Twentieth-Century British Economic Policy', *Governance* 17, no. 3 (2004): 415–41, at 429–32.

[20] Dale, *Labour Party General Election Manifestos*, 192; Wickham-Jones, *Economic Strategy*, 54, 62–5.

'Alternative Economic Strategy'. Many of its landmark commitments, such as planning agreements and state holding companies, featured in both the 1974 and the 1983 manifestos. These policies were not inherently unelectable.

The AES was also at the cutting edge of socialist and social democratic policymaking in the 1970s. This is not always obvious, as it relied on other appeals too. The strategy did draw ideological energy from the classic socialist aim of increasing democratic control over the economy, and from the left's long-standing fascination with an efficient industrial economy.[21] Left tribunes like Tony Benn also drew on mythologized versions of Labour and radical history to sell these policies on the conference floor.[22] However, this should not obscure the fact that the *policy* thinking behind these pledges was far from nostalgic.[23] Their intellectual architects were responding directly to the upheavals of the 1970s – and to larger, structural changes in Western capitalism.

The key thinker was the former civil servant, left-wing economist and future Labour MP for Vauxhall, Stuart Holland. Co-opted onto the relevant NEC committees, Holland developed a distinctive interpretation of why governments were struggling to manage the economy. Whilst recognizing contingent contexts, like the 1967 run on the pound and the OPEC oil crisis, he blamed the growing concentration of industrial production into a few massive companies. Wilson's attempts at 'indicative' planning had underestimated the market-leading power of private firms in leading sectors. For Holland, the rise of oligopolies made a mockery of the alleged competitive benefits of capitalism.[24] Holland also used this argument to declare another era-defining economic trend: the rise of 'multinationals' in Western capitalism. For Holland, multinationals threatened the economic sovereignty of the nation-state. Firms could use 'transfer pricing' to avoid taxes in national jurisdictions. They could sidestep monetary policy by raising funds from retained profits or the Eurodollar market. They could move production or investment funds from one country to another, chasing lower costs or better quality. The multinationality of their production undermined the effectiveness of exchange-rate changes.[25] Given that both corporatism

---

[21] Tony Benn, *Arguments for Democracy*, ed. Chris Mullin (London: Penguin, 1982); Jim Tomlinson, 'The Labour Party and the Capitalist Firm, c.1950–1970', *The Historical Journal* 47, no. 3 (2004): 685–708.

[22] Richard Jobson, 'A New Hope for an Old Britain?: Nostalgia and the British Labour Party's Alternative Economic Strategy, 1970–1983', *Journal of Policy History* 27, no. 4 (2015): 670–94.

[23] Jobson, 'A New Hope for Old Britain?', 671–2.

[24] Stuart Holland, *The Socialist Challenge* (London: Quarter Books, 1975), 48–61.

[25] Ibid., 75–92. Stuart Holland, 'The New Economic Imperatives', RD:473/November 1972, in London School of Economics, The Papers of Peter Shore (hereafter, LSE SHORE/)10/3.

and postwar Keynesianism were premised on a 'national economy', all these possibilities were threatening to a Labour Party policymaker.[26]

Holland argued that, to properly respond to these trends, the British state needed to intervene more directly in capitalist production to ensure that it served wider society. It should reinvest the profits of multinationals in domestic industries, improve their productivity and competitiveness, and thus ensure the achievement of wider social goals such as full employment and greater regional equality. All this required extending public ownership and control. Yet, crucially, Holland did not seek inspiration from Herbert Morrison-style nationalization. He looked instead to experiments in 'state holding companies' in countries like Italy, France and Japan. He was particularly impressed by the *Istituto per la Ricostruzione Industriale* (originally a 1930s Fascist creation, but an institution that became central to Italy's postwar reconstruction), which took direct stakes in successful companies and used them to direct investment, employment, production locations and trade. For other companies, Holland argued for planning agreements, through which the state would coordinate production in ways that boosted national economic output and competitiveness.[27]

Although he would have chafed at this description then, Holland's programme was largely Wilsonism with added adrenaline and a dash more radicalism over property rights. It drew on successful recent precedents in Western Europe and East Asia to advance a new, more interventionist industrial strategy, which aimed to finish what Wilson started and 'modernize' Britain's economy. In the context of the 1970s, when the state had a far more extensive role in the economy generally, Holland was essentially arguing for the 'entrepreneurial state' as a way to improve economic competitiveness, and to constrain the more negative impacts of what later became known as 'globalization'.[28]

Holland's politics did become more sharply left wing as the 1970s progressed. During the decade, he became associated with Tony Benn, the Campaign for Labour Party Democracy, and other stalwarts of state socialism. As a result, his ongoing advocacy for a state shareholding presence in dynamic sectors of the economy quickly radicalized into a demand for controlling shares in twenty-five out of the top one hundred UK companies. Wilson, unsurprisingly, rejected

---

[26] David Edgerton, *The Rise and Fall of the British Nation: A Twentieth Century History* (London: Allen Lane, 2018).

[27] Holland, *Socialist Challenge*, 177–83, 223–5; Holland, 'The New Economic Imperatives'.

[28] Mariana Mazzucato, *The Entrepreneurial State: Debunking Public vs Private Sector Myths* (London: Anthem Press, 2013). In 2017, Holland spoke favourably about Mazzucato's ideas, whilst also noting their differences to his work, especially on state share ownership. Stuart Holland and Martin O'Neill, 'Hope amidst despair?', *Renewal* 25, nos. 3–4 (2017): 90–100, at 91–3.

this pledge categorically before the 1974 elections and refused to countenance it in office, but it remained a totem on the conference floor.[29] Intervention on that scale was not securely grounded. Apart from anything else, it relied on the assumption of extensive multinational profits, just waiting out there for the state to reinvest efficiently. The profits crises of the early 1970s and then the vicious recession of 1980–1, made that assumption doubtful.[30]

Still, this radicalization was not inevitable. Due to its origins in empirical studies of continental social democracy, the intellectual substance of Holland's platform was not the inherent preserve of Labour's left. In the 1960s, Holland had been a civil servant working directly with Wilson, and in the early 1970s his ideas about state holding companies were examined with interest by liberal social democrats like Roy Jenkins and Bill Rodgers – both members of the 'Gang of Four'.[31] Moreover, Holland's worries about multinationals were widely shared across the Western European social-democratic left in the 1970s.[32] Even young Scottish Labour activists like Gordon Brown were highlighting the importance of multinationals.[33]

Creativity and innovation

The other important feature about the AES was its evolution. It was a living, breathing entity. New policy agendas featured in a succession of landmark statements like Labour's Programme 1976, Labour's Programme 1982 and a joint TUC-Labour Party document on planning.[34] Labour's policy platform thus responded to a variety of emerging issues after 1973, including the growing presence of women in the workplace, feminist campaigns inside the party, low pay, industrial democracy and deindustrialization. Although the AES's responses were often inadequate, they sometimes had enduring consequences.

---

[29] Wickham-Jones, Economic Strategy, 63–4.
[30] Mark Wickham-Jones, 'The challenge of Stuart Holland: the Labour Party's economic strategy during the 1970s', in Lawrence Black et al. (eds), Reassessing 1970s Britain (Manchester: MUP, 2013), 123–49, at 137–42.
[31] Ibid., 126.
[32] Willy Brandt, Bruno Kreisky and Olof Palme, 'A European Correspondence', New Statesman, 17 September 1976, 366–9.
[33] Gordon Brown, 'Introduction: The Socialist Challenge', in Brown (ed.), The Red Paper On Scotland (Edinburgh: EUSPB, 1975), 7–22, at 11–14.
[34] TUC–Labour Party Liaison Committee, Economic Planning & Industrial Democracy: The Framework For Full Employment (London: Labour Party, 1982).

The best example of the latter point is Labour's evolving approach to gender equality. The AES was hardly a beacon of feminism. In 1981, a prominent journalist and socialist feminist, Anna Coote, famously critiqued the AES for being obsessed with (male-dominated) manufacturing industry, and accused the party of ignoring feminist ideas relating to the politics of care.[35] Yet, Labour's left did consciously try to respond to this critique – indeed, in the early 1980s, feminist campaigners in the party were usually associated with the party's left. The 1983 manifesto pledged a minimum wage (as did New Labour's 1997 manifesto), which it stressed would especially help working women. It also promised to strengthen equality legislation and expand the provision of childcare.[36] Most strikingly, Labour's 1983 manifesto pledged the creation of a ministry for 'equality between the sexes'. Although many more conflicts lay ahead, New Labour's 'Minister for Women' can trace its origins back to 1983. Labour's policies had a long way to go to address the demands of feminist activists of the 1970s and 1980s, but the stirrings of change are clearly discernible. This is even clearer at a municipal and local level. As others have argued, the early 1980s municipal left explored new campaigns about gender, sexuality and race, which anticipated consensus politics of later years.[37]

Another emerging theme was industrial democracy. To many political observers in the 1970s, the direction of travel appeared to be towards greater involvement of organized labour in the economy through the democratization of the firm. Because Thatcher chose to confront the trade unions after 1979, and largely succeeded, this is difficult to conceptualize in hindsight. Still, as historians like Emily Robinson and Florence Sutcliffe-Braithwaite have argued, the instability of the 1970s was partly the result of a 'decline in deference' and rise in 'popular individualism'. These trends did not necessarily lead to Thatcherite individualism; movements for industrial democracy, driven by restive shop stewards, were another potential outcome.[38] During the 1970s, many trade unionists attempted to establish worker-owned or worker-controlled production, often acting independently of national trade union leaders – most famously in the Upper Clyde shipyards and the Lucas Aerospace factories. Consequently, many commentators saw democratizing industry as a durable solution to the waves

[35] Anna Coote, 'The AES: a new starting point', *New Socialist* (November/December 1981), 4–7.

[36] Sarah Perrigo, 'Women and Change in the Labour Party 1979–1995', in Joni Lovenduski and Pippa Norris (eds), *Women in Politics* (Oxford: OUP, 1996), 116–29, at 121.

[37] Jonathan Davis and Rohan McWilliam, 'Introduction: new histories of Labour and the left in the 1980s', in Davis and McWilliam (eds), *Labour and the Left in the 1980s*, 1–22, at 14–15.

[38] Emily Robinson et al., 'Telling Stories about Post-War Britain: Popular Individualism and the "Crisis" of the 1970s', *Twentieth Century British History* 28, no. 2 (2017): 268–304.

of strikes in the late 1960s and early 1970s. This impression was not confined to Labour's left. The wish to expand joint bargaining to new areas of company governance was also articulated by social democrats like Giles Radice (the same politician that, in the early 1990s, wrote the *Southern Discomfort* pamphlets which influenced New Labour's electoral strategy).[39] Even previous sceptics like Anthony Crosland were won over to industrial democracy by the mid-1970s.[40] Hence, Harold Wilson's government pushed through the Bullock Commission, which recommended workers on boards in the teeth of CBI opposition.[41]

Labour's policymakers responded directly to this growing support for industrial democracy and adapted the AES accordingly.[42] The 1983 manifesto included pledges on funding worker co-operatives, expanding joint bargaining into new areas of company governance and the inclusion of trade unions in the development of state plans. Here, admittedly, there was a glaring tension between Labour's sincere wish to expand industrial democracy and its enthusiasm for centralist 'planning'. As Mark Wickham-Jones perceptively notes, the belief that these goals could coexist relied on a distinctly heroic assumption: that Westminster's planning priorities could be reconciled with empowered, restive and radicalized shop stewards.[43] It was also far from clear whether enough trade unionists were themselves especially keen to help manage a capitalist firm, steeped as they were in Britain's strong tradition of 'free collective bargaining'.[44] Nonetheless, the AES clearly responded to a dynamic political current of its day.

The same can be said about the inclusion of protectionism in Labour's 1983 manifesto. The advocacy of import controls, which the party first endorsed in 1976, may seem like a throwback to the 1930s, and some of its support arose simply from trade unionists looking to protect their jobs.[45] But it also gained support from the cutting-edge Keynesian (not socialist) theory of its day. The logic was twofold. First, like many in 1970s Britain, Labour Party members anguished about the signs of deindustrialization.[46] At the time, it was widely

---

[39] Giles Radice, *The Industrial Democrats: Trade Unions in an uncertain world* (London: George Allen & Unwin, 1978); Giles Radice, *Southern Discomfort* (London: Fabian Society, 1992).

[40] Anthony Crosland, *Socialism Now and other essays*, ed. Dick Leonard (London: Jonathan Cape, 1974), 49–52.

[41] Adrian Williamson, 'The Bullock Report on Industrial Democracy and the Post-War Consensus', *Contemporary British History* 30, no. 1 (2016): 119–49.

[42] TUC–Labour Party, *Economic Planning & Industrial Democracy*; Holland, *Socialist Challenge*, 270–4.

[43] Wickham-Jones, *Economic Strategy*, 186. See also Holland, *Socialist Challenge*, 289–90.

[44] Williamson, 'The Bullock Report', 128–9.

[45] Wickham-Jones, *Economic Strategy*, 74–6.

[46] Jim Tomlinson, 'De-industrialization Not Decline: A New Meta-narrative for Post-war British History', *Twentieth Century British History* 27, no. 1 (2016): 76–99.

believed that a strong manufacturing sector and a healthy trade balance were crucial for sustainable economic growth (a theory that has recently regained popularity). Import controls would give a Labour government time to intervene in British industries and reverse deindustrialization. Second, it would enable Labour's planned attack on unemployment. Protectionism would, it was argued, protect Labour's fiscal expansion by preventing it from sucking in imports, weakening sterling and fuelling inflation.

The prime intellectual source here was not Holland, who never supported import controls, but rather the prominent post-Keynesian academics at the Cambridge Economic Policy Group (CEPG) – especially Francis Cripps and Wynne Godley.[47] Cripps was one of Tony Benn's leading advisors, and Benn was one of the most prominent champions of import controls in the Cabinet.[48] The CEPG's brand of Keynesianism was heterodox, and I do not have the space to do it justice here. The crucial point is that its advocacy of protectionism was, whilst controversial, not a fringe position – it was taken extremely seriously by economists, commentators and civil servants during the 1970s.[49] Godley and Cripps were given extended column inches in quintessentially establishment newspapers like *The Times* to explain their theories.[50] Godley, an aristocratic former Treasury official, was not a socialist at all, but rather a self-proclaimed 'One Nation' Tory.[51] Whilst Labour did not fully buy their theories, the CEPG clearly influenced several Labour politicians from Tony Benn to Peter Shore and made their mark on Labour's 1983 manifesto. Their advocacy of import controls was contentious (and, it must be said, unclear if it would work). But it was not based on either nostalgia or swivel-eyed radicalism.

Incompatible with social democracy?

This creativity and ability to incorporate ideas from diverse sources was not as apparent on Labour's right. Partly, this was due to bad luck. Handed Ted

---

[47] Wynne Godley, 'Britain's Chronic Recession – Can Anything Be Done?', September 1978, LSE SHORE/11/1.

[48] Peter Jay, 'Making sense of Mr Benn', *The Times*, 24 April 1975, 21; Burk and Cairncross, *'Goodbye Great Britain'*, 48–9; Francis Cripps et al., *Manifesto: A Radical Strategy for Britain's Future* (London: Pan Books, 1981).

[49] John Maloney, 'The Treasury and the New Cambridge School in the 1970s', *Cambridge Journal of Economics* 36 (2012): 995–1017.

[50] Wynne Godley and Francis Cripps, 'Need for unconventional methods', *The Times*, 9 January 1973, 17.

[51] Alan Shipman, *Wynne Godley: A Biography* (Basingstoke: Palgrave Macmillan, 2019), 184.

Heath's poisoned chalice in 1974, the Labour right struggled to unify over a platform during the Wilson–Callaghan governments. Coherence is easier to find during good years, when social democrats can unify over state spending. Harder times tend to expose divisions. As Stephen Meredith has shown, the right's Croslandite consensus over Keynesian welfare spending and incomes policies collapsed under the pressure of inflation, industrial strife and European integration, a fracturing capped off with the 1981 schism.[52] By 1983, Labour's right was intellectually marginal. It had been worn out by factional warfare and had suffered the untimely deaths of its leading intellectual MPs, Crosland in 1977 and John Mackintosh in 1978, followed by an exodus of defectors in 1981. Whilst it had managed to stage a factional 'fightback' in the early 1980s, it had little time (and, as Labour's chance of winning an election receded after the Falklands war, little inclination) to develop an alternative platform.[53]

Nonetheless, misfortune cannot fully account for the intellectual struggles of Labour's social democrats. Put simply, they did not help themselves. Despite some interest in the state holding company and community politics in the early 1970s, over the decade the party's right cut itself off from some of the most dynamic intellectual currents of its day. One Labour activist, Tony Blair, said as much in 1982.[54] When confronted by the AES in 1973–4, leading social democratic writers like Crosland and Mackintosh were unsurprisingly scathing. Yet, their dismissal of the left's agenda as 'populist socialism' or 'monolithic industry nationalization' revealed a preference for attacking a strawman of reheated Bevanism, rather than the substance of the strategy.[55] Former Labour MP and SDP defector David Marquand developed an even less generous critique. His famous 1979 attack on working-class consciousness in the House of Commons tearoom may reflect an interesting motivation behind the creation of the SDP. But his argument that Labour's left was hostile to intellectuals demonstrates a real lack of understanding of the social makeup of the new left.[56] Even when Marquand did explore the thinking behind Bennism, hostility outweighed constructive engagement. Reviewing Holland's *The Socialist Challenge* in

---

[52] Stephen Meredith, *Labours old and new: The parliamentary right of the British Labour Party 1970–79 and the roots of New Labour* (Manchester: MUP, 2008), 18.

[53] Dianne Hayter, *Fightback! Labour's traditional right in the 1970s and 1980s* (Manchester: MUP, 2005).

[54] Tony Blair, *Tony Blair In His Own Words*, ed. Paul Richards (London: Politico's, 2004), 14–15.

[55] Crosland, *Socialism Now*, 28, 39; John P. Mackintosh, *John P. Mackintosh on Parliament and Social Democracy*, ed. David Marquand (London: Longman, 1982), 158–9.

[56] David Marquand, 'Inquest on a Movement: Labour's Defeat & Its Consequences', *Encounter* (July 1979): 8–18.

1975, Marquand admitted that Holland was probably 'right' to focus on the state holding company. He also made some insightful critiques of Holland's naivety on an incomes policy and overestimation of multinational power. But these insights were submerged beneath a needless torrent of aggressive and patronizing criticism: Holland's case was 'glib', 'cocksure', 'grating', 'sloppy', 'nonsense', 'dangerous' and a 'destructive fantasy'. Despite briefly conceding the potential of the state holding company, Marquand dismissed Holland's case as 'pour[ing] new wine into the old bottles of Clause Four'.[57]

This failure to engage fully may be more significant than it first appears. This chapter has already observed that, whilst Holland undeniably radicalized over the 1970s, his politics were in many ways technocratic and empirical. Central elements of his pitch could have been reconciled with a more consensual social democracy. This is especially the case for a state holding company, the inspiration for which mainly came from social democratic (and Christian democratic) governments abroad. If that is the case, though, then the question becomes: how did these policy ideas turn into the 1983 manifesto? Part of the blame must lie with the left for radicalizing the National Enterprise Board into a pledge to 'nationalize' twenty-five of the top one hundred UK companies. It does appear, though, that hostile incuriosity from Labour's right was also at fault. Over the 1970s, Holland himself became increasingly frustrated with Labour's social democrats for not taking his case seriously.[58] Consider this passage, written in 1978:

> [F]ormer ministers appear never to have read the new industrial policy proposals for the NEB [National Enterprise Board] or Planning Agreements elsewhere than in the columns of a hostile press ... Thus Roy Jenkins stated on television that he was in favour of a State Holding Company with selective shareholdings in enterprise, but not in favour of 'dogmatic nationalization' of the kind envisaged in the NEB proposals, apparently not realizing that the Party's proposals were for a State Holding Company with controlling shareholdings, very similar to that which he himself earlier proposed in a series of major speeches.[59]

There was clear red water between Holland and Jenkins on several issues. But it is plausible that, especially in the early 1970s, these undoubted differences could

---

[57] David Marquand, 'Clause Four rides again', *Times Literary Supplement*, 26 September 1975, 1095.

[58] Although this is probably due partly to hindsight, Holland later stressed the cross-factional appeal of his ideas. Stuart Holland, 'Alternative European and economic strategies', in Black et al., *Reassessing 1970s Britain*, 96–123, at 109.

[59] Stuart Holland, 'Planning Disagreements', in Holland (ed.), *Beyond Capitalist Planning* (Oxford: Basil Blackwell, 1978), 137–65, at 147.

have been submerged into an internally unifying platform – a frequent political necessity for a large, unwieldy edifice like the British Labour Party. This would, however, have required the leading intellectuals of Labour's social-democratic wings to take some of the workable ideas from the left more seriously. Holland's clear annoyance with Jenkins' misrepresentation is suggestive. It hints that, perhaps, Labour's social democrats missed a chance to engage constructively with new left-wing ideas, and thus shape Labour's policy agenda in a more favourable direction.

This possibility of a less confrontational interpretation of the thinking behind the AES is bolstered by the subsequent direction of its key policymakers, like Holland and Cripps, over the 1980s. Even before the 1983 election, many were beginning to *change their minds* on key aspects of the strategy. For example, despite the firm Euroscepticism of the Bennite left, both men looked increasingly to a coordinated pan-European reflation as a response to the global recession, and even to a European industrial strategy. In 1982, Cripps was one of the first Bennites to openly flirt with abandoning the then totemic pledge of withdrawal from the European Community.[60] This revisionism demonstrated their capacity for intellectual and political openness. The possibility for a different outcome is also suggested by the fruitful engagement of Neil Kinnock's reformist Labour Party after 1983. On the issue of Europe, for instance, Kinnock drew directly on Holland's arguments when, in 1984, he first signalled Labour's abandonment of its European withdrawal policy.[61] Similarly, Richard Carr has ably traced the evolution of the proposal for a National Investment Bank (NIB) over the 1980s, which shows how policies in the 1983 manifesto were adapted into a more electorally healthy platform. Whilst the AES's plan for the NIB to compel funds from pensions and nationalized banks was quickly ditched, the institution itself remained Labour policy well into the 1990s, and served as one of the vehicles for Kinnock's 'supply side socialism'. When social democrats like Roy Hattersley and Bryan Gould engaged with the questions underpinning the AES, constructive policies could be the result.[62]

Why is it worth dwelling today on these points of potential overlap between the thinking behind the 1983 manifesto and a more consensual social democratic platform? The journey of Holland into the arms of the party's 1970s left provides,

---

[60] Francis Cripps and Terry Ward, 'Road to recovery', *New Socialist* (July/August 1982): 22–6.

[61] Holland, 'Alternative European and economic strategies', 116, 122; Neil Kinnock 'New Deal for Europe', in James Curran (ed.), *The Future of the Left* (Cambridge: Polity Press, 1984), 231–45.

[62] Richard Carr, 'Responsible capitalism: Labour's industrial policy and the idea of a National Investment Bank during the long 1980s', in Davis and McWilliam, *Labour and the Left in the 1980s*, 90–109.

I suggest, a cautionary tale for social democrats today. As tempting as it may be, and as factionally useful as it can prove, the centre-left should avoid stereotyping the ideas of other traditions in the labour movement and broader left. I frankly acknowledge that this will not always be possible, but whenever it is, social democrats should actively seek creative dialogue, and even points of potential consensus, with other parts of the left.[63] Otherwise, they can find themselves – like David Marquand in 1979 – marginalized from the dynamic debates of their day. The last few years have been a period of undoubted creativity for the intellectual left, symbolized by the 'Green New Deal' and the 'Preston Model'.[64] The details, scale and strategic underpinnings of these ideas may be open to challenge,[65] but the injustices of inequality and the climate emergency, which they tried to address, still demand policy responses. Now that Keir Starmer's leadership has allowed social democrats to return from their own bout of internal exile, they may find it worthwhile to reflect on the mistakes of their forebears.

---

[63] As convincingly argued in Karl Pike and Andy Hindmoor, 'Do As I Did Not As I Say: Blair, New Labour and Party Traditions', *The Political Quarterly* 91, no. 1 (2020): 148–55.

[64] Martin O'Neill and Matthew Brown, 'The road to socialist is the A59: The Preston model', *Renewal* 24, no. 2 (2016): 69–78; Adrienne Buller, 'Where next for the Green New Deal?', *Renewal* 28, no. 1 (2020): 26–36.

[65] Colm Murphy, 'The unspoken dilemmas of Corbynomics', *Renewal* 27, no. 3 (2019): 5–13.

13

Neil Kinnock: A reassessment

Jonathan Davis and Rohan McWilliam

When assessing Neil Kinnock's record as leader of the Labour Party (1983–92), the three standard viewpoints elaborated by Martin J. Smith in 1994 remain strikingly relevant today. Firstly, Kinnock is still seen by some as the 'vacillating and verbose leader who was not intellectually able enough to challenge Margaret Thatcher'. He was, ultimately, an 'electoral failure'.[1] The view that Kinnock failed because he was a winner at neither the despatch box nor the ballot box was difficult to shift at the time and has remained so ever since. However, Kinnock was arguably the greatest political orator since Aneurin Bevan, equipped with a charismatic magnetism that many actors would kill for. And, yet (like his mentor Michael Foot before him), his was a form of oratory that seemed old fashioned even in the 1980s, reminding many of a past they wanted to get away from. Indeed, his tendency to continually reference Bevan (as well as the 1945 Labour government) made him appear backward looking, even anachronistic. Kinnock did not impress as a major thinker either, and in the early 1990s, was notoriously hounded in the pages of the *New Statesman* by the Oxford political scientist R. W. Johnson for his alleged failure to understand economics.[2]

The second opinion advanced by Smith came from the left. It argued that Kinnock 'misused his left-wing credentials to take control of the party' and then forced it to 'abandon its commitment to socialism'. Kinnock thus moved Labour closer towards the centre of British politics in order to make it a 'social democratic or even a Thatcherite party'.[3] If we replace 'Thatcherite' with 'Blairite', then this accusation has a contemporary feel to it.

---

[1] Martin J. Smith, 'Neil Kinnock and the modernisation of the Labour Party', *Contemporary Record* 8, no. 3 (Winter 1994): 555–66, 555.

[2] Martin Westlake (with Ian St John), *Kinnock: The Biography* (London: Little, Brown, 2001), 458–9.

[3] Smith, 'Neil Kinnock and the modernisation of the Labour Party', 555.

The third interpretation that Smith identified is, however, just as relevant and correct now as it was nearly thirty years ago, and it is this view that we intend to build on here. It argues that Kinnock's time as leader was 'extremely successful' as he transformed the party 'in a way that eluded all previous leaders'. The previous views are 'oversimplifications', meaning that a more nuanced analysis – addressing the 'demoralization of the party' after 1983 with its rancorous divisions, and the way it was 'ideologically divorced from the electorate' – is necessary to 'provide a fairer assessment of the Kinnock leadership'.[4]

Overall, this chapter will argue that the reforms introduced by Kinnock need to be seen in a more positive light than has often been the case, not only because they helped to make Labour electable again (albeit under a new leader in the 1990s) but also because Labour in the early 2020s needs to escape from its retrospective ideological navel gazing more quickly than it did in the 1980s if it wants to stand a chance of beating the Conservatives at the next election (currently due in 2024). In this chapter, we also explore the comparisons between Kinnock and Keir Starmer. Kinnock was never able to make the electoral breakthrough that he and Labour hoped for, but he did encourage voters to look again at Labour and took the party almost to the brink of victory in 1992. He could not convince enough people that he could – or should – be prime minister, of course, but he began to make Labour's ideology more relevant to a swathe of the British electorate, at a time when countries across the world were rejecting socialism as it had existed for nearly a century.

The importance of this should not be underestimated, and neither should Kinnock's successes. As Britain moved rightwards during the Thatcher years, Kinnock ensured that Labour remained together in the face of challenges from the left and right and continued to be the main alternative to the Conservatives. In so doing he emerged as the pivotal, if not only potential, figure to lead the party through the process of reconciliation with the new global order emerging as deindustrialization and the turn towards the free market gathered pace. His reward was mixed of course, as, though he kept the party united, he was not the person to lead Labour into government.

Kinnock's electoral failure might not recommend him as a model to be followed; few people today describe themselves as 'Kinnockite' (a term that was not even used that much in the 1980s). He should, however, be reappraised, and given greater credit, as a political figure who combined enduring issues of social

----

4   Ibid.

justice with an adjustment to the way in which the global and British industrial economies were changing in the 1980s.[5]

This chapter will reassess Kinnock's efforts to move the main elements of Labour's domestic agenda, paying particular attention to debates concerning the role of the state and the free market, Kinnock's efforts to challenge the left's suspicion of affluence and engaging with the affluent society. We do not seek here to explore Labour's problem with communicating its message, which have been memorably treated in the likes of Philip Gould's *The Unfinished Revolution*.[6] Whilst the party's progress during the Kinnock years is often interpreted through the lens of New Labour, this is not the only way to interpret what was a distinctive moment in progressive politics in the UK.

A need for change: adjusting to the 1980s

Neil Kinnock realized how far and how fast the world was changing in the 1980s, as consumerism and the consequences of deindustrialization took hold. Together with fellow reformers, he sought to adapt Labour's socialist views to make them seem more relevant for this new world. For some, this was nothing more than a rejection of the party's core beliefs that made Labour distinctively socialist. For others, it was a necessary recalibration of aspects of party policy that voters had rejected in the previous two elections.

This new 1980s world was guided by emerging neoliberalism, a concept that influenced the political thought of a specific group of right-wing thinkers across the globe in the 1970s. It was promoted by Milton Friedman and the so-called 'Chicago School' of economists, and found a home in Augusto Pinochet's Chile.[7] With the advent of Mrs Thatcher as leader of the British Conservative Party in 1975 and prime minister in 1979, Friedman's ideas – favouring small-state individualism, greater entrepreneurship and monetarism – entered into the mainstream of British economic and political debate, and found in Mrs Thatcher a champion who fervently believed that contemporary politics had been too geared 'towards the collectivist society' as people had 'forgotten about

[5] Jonathan Davis, *The Global 1980s: People, Power and Profit* (London: Routledge, 2019).
[6] Philip Gould, *The Unfinished Revolution: How New Labour Changed British Politics For Ever* (London: Abacus, 2011 [1998]), 36–155.
[7] For more on this, see Eduardo Silva, 'The Political Economy of Chile's Regime Transition: From Radical to "Pragmatic" Neo-liberal Policies', in Paul W. Drake and Iván Jascić (eds), *The Struggle for Democracy in Chile, 1982–1990* (Lincoln: University of Nebraska, 1991).

the personal society'. She saw it as her duty to 'change the approach' with the objective of politics being 'to change the heart and soul'.[8] As her views developed, neoliberalism in Britain became better understood as the catch-all term she gave her name to – Thatcherism'.[9]

The sociologist Stuart Hall called Thatcherism a 'struggle for hegemony within the dominant bloc' and argued that it was radical in its 'commitment to break the mould, not simply to rework the elements of the prevailing "philosophies"'.[10] It was an attempt to revolutionize people's thought processes and their instincts, to encourage them to embrace competition, free markets, consumer choice and lower retail prices. But this new focus on consumerism, though popular with many, also brought with it an assault on public services, strong community links, the notion of society and the idea of putting people before profit.

This phenomenon was not confined to just Chile and the United Kingdom. New ways of thinking about the market spread across the globe in the 1980s and socialist and communist parties were forced to change their thinking and their views of the modern world accordingly. François Mitterrand's French socialist government adopted neoliberal policies, Mikhail Gorbachev's *perestroika* introduced individualism into Soviet socialism, and Deng Xiaoping opened China up to Western businesses and capitalist economics. Globalization forced capitalism's critics to dramatically rethink things, as they embraced market economics in different ways.[11] Labour was firmly part of this global shift in thinking, and, just as others engaged more positively with market forces, it sought out ways to respond to a new narrative that hailed free markets and individualism as the future. More profoundly, it had to deal with the fact that Mrs Thatcher had managed to speak to people's aspirations, not least when it came to home ownership. Philip Gould's focus groups in the mid-1980s associated Labour with 'houses that all looked the same' (i.e. council housing) and a stale uniformity. Voters feared that Labour would restrict their freedom to buy their council house and move up the housing ladder.[12] What was disturbing about Thatcherism was the fact that it seemed to express the desire of a new kind of society that had emerged in the 1970s, which the left did not understand.

---

[8] Margaret Thatcher, 'Interview for *Sunday Times*', 3 May 1981, http://www.margaretthatcher.org/document/104475 (accessed 13 September 2021).

[9] For more on the development of Thatcherism, see Stuart Hall, 'The Great Moving Right Show', *Marxism Today*, January 1979 and Ben Jackson and Robert Saunders (eds), *Making Thatcher's Britain* (Cambridge: CUP, 2012).

[10] Hall, 'The Great Moving Right Show', 16.

[11] For more on this, see Davis, *The Global 1980s*, chs 5, 8 and 16.

[12] Gould, *The Unfinished Revolution*, 49, 83.

None of this meant Labour would reject the idea that the state could and should still look to protect the weak and vulnerable, or that it would no longer believe that there was still such a thing as society. But it did mean that Kinnock came to see the world differently from how he had interpreted it earlier in his political career, and this in turn meant that radical change was coming to Labour. Nothing was seen as sacred as the party grappled with a new economic and political vision in response to society's changed needs. Labour did not reject its progressive, socialist and internationalist legacies. As we showed in our edited collection, *Labour and the Left in the 1980s*, it remained part of the global fight for socialism, sided with feminists in a male-dominated society, fought racism at home and abroad and challenged homophobia in the shape of the government's Clause 28.[13]

The enabling state

From almost the beginning of her time in office, Mrs Thatcher made the case that there was no alternative to her policies. It fell to Kinnock to insist that there was another way, which, true to ongoing Labour policies, he located in the state. The radical right had challenged the use of state power, arguing that it served to produce unaccountable and inefficient bureaucracies that, combined with bloated union power, failed to serve the public interest. Former Labour supporters, such as the economist John Vaizey, had left the party and moved rightwards because they had come to distrust any overwhelming use of state power.[14] The orthodoxy in the 1980s became about reducing public expenditure and *dirigiste* state intervention in order to allow the market to do its work, whilst the record of the 1974–9 Labour government appeared to suggest that the goal of Keynesianism in one country was no longer sustainable.

Kinnock was no political *naïf* when it came to how the economy worked, despite never having served as a minister. His background provided a deep understanding of the coal industry (and the people dependent upon it) and his time as a backbencher in the 1970s had involved serving on the Commons Select Committees for Public Expenditure (1971–3) and the Nationalized Industries (1973–8). The latter role required an extended investigation of the

---

[13] These issues are all dealt with in Jonathan Davis and Rohan McWilliam (eds), *Labour and the Left in the 1980s* (Manchester: MUP, 2018).

[14] John Vaizey, *In Breach of Promise: Gaitskell, Macleod, Titmuss, Crosland, Boyle: Five Men who shaped a Generation* (London: Weidenfeld and Nicolson, 1983).

steel industry in 1977, which had experienced severe losses, and suggested to the young Kinnock, at a time when he regularly attacked capitalism, that manpower reductions were inevitable. As he put it, the problem was that there were 'too many steel producers and too few steel consumers'.[15] Right from the start, he was ready to confront difficult issues caused by the shift towards deindustrialization.

As leader, Kinnock was inevitably swept up in arguments about the 'British disease': the country's ongoing stagnation and failure to effectively modernize, in contrast with much of Europe and Japan in the postwar period. Where Harold Wilson was able to call confidently for a 'revolution in the white heat of technology', Kinnock had to contend with a darker and more defeatist climate. His initial approach can be found in the book he wrote in 1986, entitled *Making Our Way*. Whilst it is fair to say that as a thinker Kinnock was no Anthony Crosland, the book presents an attempt to deal with the problems of Britain as it struggled in the age of Thatcherism. It had its roots in a lecture he gave to the Industrial Society on 20 January 1986. The title was significant; its emphasis on the act of 'making' evoked a future in which investment in manufacturing was an alternative to deindustrialization. As Kinnock put it in the preface to the book, 'democratic socialism is the politics of production'.[16] He also argued that the turn to service industries (whilst important in themselves) was not sufficient to sustain the economy.[17] Kinnock was therefore at odds with the larger forces of globalization that were shifting manufacturing to other parts of the world. What Labour failed to do was to own the issue of 'modernity' which damaged its appeal to workers in the south of England. As David Marquand put it, Kinnock's Labour was the 'product of the age of steam, hobbling arthritically into the age of computer'. It succeeded in appealing 'to the casualties of change rather than to the pacemakers'.[18] At the same time, Kinnock's party had a strong message for those communities that would, a generation later, be labelled as 'left behind'.

Kinnock's vision called for a renewed relationship between government, unions and manufacturers, effectively maintaining the corporatist relationships of the earlier generation that Thatcherism rejected. The roots of these arrangements went back at least to the 1930s, but they flourished under prime ministers from Macmillan to Callaghan, who subscribed to the notion of

---

[15] See Westlake, *Kinnock*, 109–10, at 110.

[16] Neil Kinnock, *Making our Way: Investing in Britain's Future* (Oxford: Basil Blackwell, 1986), vi.

[17] Ibid., 73.

[18] David Marquand, 'Neil Kinnock: The Progressive as Moses', in Marquand, *The Progressive Dilemma: From Lloyd George to Blair* (London: Phoenix, 1999 [1991]), 212.

planning as a spur to economic progress. This period generated organizations such as the National Economic Development Council (NEDC) and the National Economic Development Office, which became known as 'neddies' for short.[19] These institutions supplied an answer to the problem of how to modernize the economy and generate growth although the belief in the transformative power of neddies, and planning in general, declined in the 1970s. Significantly, Kinnock praised the work of the NEDC, whose role was being sidelined by Mrs Thatcher (it was later abolished by John Major in 1992). He noted that in its origins it was intended as the British equivalent of the *Commmisariat Général du Plan* (1946–2006), which had shaped postwar economic planning in France. The British version, in his view, had never been given the tools to bring all the major economic players together to boost British industry; instead, it had merely become a consultative body. Kinnock therefore proposed a major expansion of its activities so that it covered all of manufacturing.[20]

For Kinnock, the alternative to Thatcherism was both an 'enabling' and a developmental state. In the latter, the state invests both in production but also in research and development to modernize and shape the economy. In this thinking, government could not solve all the problems of manufacturing, but it had to be part of the solution. Kinnock was also very clear about the countries he wished to emulate – Japan, West Germany, Sweden, France and Italy, rather than the American model of capitalism.[21] Whilst talking of democratic socialism, Kinnock in effect staked his claim to be a continental social democrat.

A Wilsonian emphasis on government-promoted research became a central thread of Kinnock's leadership. In 1986, he called for the establishment of a new ministry of science, which would co-ordinate its activities with the department of trade and industry.[22] In his 1990 conference speech at Blackpool, he said 'we have got to employ science', calling for the modernization of the transport system, the diffusion of new technologies throughout industry and a shift in spending from military to civil research, 'in order to get better economic value for public investment'. He also placed a lot of emphasis on the concept of a national training strategy, that was being promoted by his employment spokesman, Tony Blair.[23] He returned to the theme the following year, attacking

[19] Glen O'Hara, *From Dreams to Disillusionment: Economic and Social Planning in 1960s Britain* (Basingstoke: Palgrave, 2007).

[20] Kinnock, *Making our Way*, 107–10.

[21] Neil Kinnock, *Thorns and Roses: Speeches, 1983–1991* (London: Hutchinson, 1992), 84.

[22] Kinnock, *Making our Way*, 125.

[23] Kinnock, *Thorns and Roses*, 194, 199.

the Conservatives for cutting support for research and development and insisting that 'economic success will be built on converting scientific inventiveness into competitive industrial production'. He hailed British science for its innovations in fibre optics, catalytic converters, body scanners, holograms and microwave technology, before complaining that their subsequent development had taken place in other countries.[24] Foreshadowing the economy of the future, Bryan Gould's working party on the productive and competitive economy in 1988 even proposed the next Labour government invest in building a fibre optic network that would cover the whole of Britain.[25]

Underpinning Kinnock's economic strategy was the construction of a national investment bank – an idea that was brought back into Labour policy by Jeremy Corbyn's team after 2015. This was an attempt to contest Britain's historic over-reliance on the City of London, although Kinnock acknowledged that the 1980 Wilson committee found no evidence of any lack of finance for British industry. As Richard Carr has shown, the idea of such a bank went as far back as the 1930s and had been advanced in the early 1980s by both Tony Benn and Michael Foot.[26] Kinnock wanted a British equivalent of the French *Credit National* or the German *Kreditanstalt für Wiederaufbau*, which invested in long-term projects to their countries' benefit. The bank would not just offer funding, but also technical and managerial assistance.[27] Kinnock's account of what a national bank would do went through various permutations during his time as leader. Notably, its aims would become modest, focusing not on how to remould capitalism in a socialist direction but rather on offering a force that would enable industries to capture key markets.[28] Labour's identity as a modern continental social democratic party was complete.

The affluent society

Another dimension of Kinnock's journey with Labour was coming to terms with the rise in living standards in the country. Rising affluence and the development of a consumer society had long been a problem for the party. Ever since the

---

[24] Ibid., 215–16, at 215.

[25] Bryan Gould, *Goodbye to all That* (Basingstoke: Macmillan, 1995), 204.

[26] Richard Carr, 'Responsible capitalism: Labour's industrial policy and the idea of a National Investment Bank during the long 1980s', in Davis and McWilliam, *Labour and the Left in the 1980s*, 90–109.

[27] Kinnock, *Making our Way*, 110–13.

[28] Carr, 'Responsible Capitalism', 104.

1950s, Labour had not known how to react to it.[29] Even in his firebrand days, Kinnock had always acknowledged that, in order to assist the victimized, one had to get the votes of those who were satisfied with the status quo. Simply focusing on squalor risked having nothing to say about the reality of much of modern Britain.

Kinnock addressed this in his 1987 conference speech in Brighton, insisting that affluence and consumerism should not be seen as a curse. It had, after all, offered a Labourist spin on the fact that poorer people in the 1950s could suddenly afford cars, washing machines, televisions and their first ever foreign holidays. These things, he insisted, were provided by 'people doing lots of very hard work, working overtime, so that they could get these things'. Such advances should not, he argued, be seen as the enemy of left-wing thought, which was meant to be about helping ordinary people 'get on'. He caustically quoted his friend Oliver Jones in Tredegar who told the young Kinnock that if socialism 'needs misery to give it a majority, God forbid we have the misery'. In the most well-known section of this speech, he cited the words of Ron Todd, the leader of the Transport and General Workers' Union: 'What do you say to a docker who earns £400 a week, owns his house, a new car, a microwave and a video, as well as a small place near Marbella? You do not say … let me take you out of your misery brother.'[30] This kind of awareness of the importance of aspiration and the changing nature of the working class shaped Labour politics from 1987 through to at least 2015.

Similarly, Kinnock sought to address the popularity of the Thatcherite emphasis on individualism, freedom and choice. In 1988 he insisted that, 'the collective is the means not the end, and the end is the advancing, the nourishing, the encouragement, the succouring, the reward of the merit of the individual'. Labour, he proclaimed, was the consumer's party, but insisted that freedom to consume was dependent on decent education, health care and housing.[31] This emphasis also chimed with the approach developed in deputy leader Roy Hattersley's book *Choose Freedom*, which squared freedom with equality as Labour values, whilst accepting some of the efficiencies of a market economy.[32] These arguments were not new (they can also be found in Crosland's 1956

---

[29] Lawrence Black, *The Political Culture of the Left in Affluent Britain, 1951–64: Old Labour, New Britain?* (Basingstoke: Palgrave Macmillan, 2003).

[30] Kinnock, *Thorns and Roses*, 129–33.

[31] Ibid., 157.

[32] Roy Hattersley, *Choose Freedom: The Future for Democratic Socialism* (London: Penguin, 1987).

Future of Socialism) but they did reposition Labour and provide an opening for the party's policy review.

On cultural matters (such as sexuality and race) Kinnock was personally liberal but was aware that many Labour voters were not. Although it was heavily conflicted over issues of personal identity, Kinnock's Labour Party ultimately stood for forms of social liberalism that have proved more enduring than the Conservatives' emphasis at that time on family values (which David Cameron's party later had to disown). Labour opposed the notorious Section 28 of the 1988 Local Government Act which prevented local authorities from what it viewed as the 'promotion' of homosexuality. Whilst Labour was attacked in the press for its so-called 'loony left' (often a dog whistle allusion to its liberal view on race), the party managed to get the first Black MPs elected in 1987. If Kinnock's Labour failed to win the economic argument, it played a role in winning the social and cultural ones.[33]

Labour Party Policy Review

The year 1987 saw Labour lose its third election in a row, when the Conservatives were returned to power with a majority of 102. Labour's promises were still not as appealing as the Conservatives', but it did have some successes at the election. It maintained its second party status after a challenge from the SDP–Liberal Alliance; it increased its share of the vote to 30.8 per cent (up from its historic low of 27.6 per cent four years earlier) and cut the government's majority by forty-two seats.

Culturally and socially, Labour contributed much to the struggles for equality in Britain in the 1980s. Economically, however, it was still struggling to keep up – both with the Conservatives and with the major changes to the global economy that were underway. Kinnock recognized that the party's values and ideas needed to be reshaped to fit a globalizing world, which was starting to be governed by new rules.[34] It was this fact that led him to launch the Policy Review after the election defeat, where he and his supporters examined the party's core beliefs, looked to establish what democratic socialism meant in the late 1980s and began to consider how it would deal with the possible issues of the 1990s. Indeed, at a Policy Review Group meeting in November 1988, it was

---

[33] See Davis and McWilliam, *Labour and the Left in the 1980s*.
[34] For more on this, see Davis, *The Global 1980s*, chs 2, 5 and 13.

noted that the following decade would be one of 'economic challenges and new opportunities'. Here, they argued, Britain would face an intensely 'competitive environment in the 1990s' because changes to the EEC's internal market 'will sharpen competitive pressures throughout British industry, creating a far more challenging environment than that of the oil-cushioned eighties'.[35]

Although the Review focused on various areas of Labour policy, its main consideration was how the party would engage with the market economy and what this would mean for the party's ideological world view as defined by its socialist traditions. It was accepted by one of the various Policy Review groups that Labour's 'central task' was 'to re-establish the economic case for socialism'.[36] This meant 'developing an operational expression of the Labour Party's fundamental belief that the economy should be organized in a manner which best serves the material interests of the majority of the people'. And it would require 'both the pursuit of efficient, *sustainable* economic performance, and the distribution of the fruits of production in a manner which, whilst rewarding effort, sustains community and provides every person with the material platform on which to build self-reliance and self-respect'.[37]

With the aggressive push towards individualism from the Thatcherite right, Labour had to develop a new narrative, and this saw the party consider a form of aspirational socialism, which promoted individual and collective welfare. As Kinnock wrote a year before the election in his own version of *The Future of Socialism*, 'As socialists the advancement of collective freedoms is central precisely because it offers the best hope of advancing individual freedom.'[38] And as discussions during the Policy Review about Labour's vision and values continued, it was stated that the party's beliefs were based on 'the potential and equal worth of individuals as well as the importance of strong communities and democracy'.[39]

This was part of the wider reconsiderations that ran through the Review as the Labour hierarchy engaged in a major rethink of Labour's socioeconomic plans and its wider political thought. This was not an entirely new reform process in this era. As Colm Murphy shows in the previous chapter, the party was already considering 'the future of the national social-democratic mixed

---

[35] Neil Kinnock Papers, KNNK 2/2/14: Policy Review December 87–November 88, Policy Review Group meeting, 16 November 1988: 'Values, Vision and Strategy', Churchill Archives Centre, Churchill College, Cambridge.

[36] Kinnock Papers KNNK 2/2/14: 'People at Work Policy Review Group', December 1987, 1.

[37] Ibid., 2–3, original emphasis.

[38] Neil Kinnock, *The Future of Socialism*, Fabian Tract 509 (London: Fabian Society, 1986), 4.

[39] KNNK 2/2/14: Policy Review Group meeting, 16 November 1988: 'Values, Vision and Strategy', 1.

economy'.[40] In some ways, this was a continuation of that earlier process and over time, democratic socialism morphed into a more recognizably social democratic programme, as consumerism and market-based economics shaped Kinnock's ideas. Of course, this was not welcomed by the left of the party, which largely remained devoted to the Alternative Economic Strategy. Accepting that market forces would have to play a bigger role in its thinking was one thing; reconciling this with the traditional view of what socialism meant was another thing entirely. But the party's turn to the market for answers under Kinnock was very much part of the left's response to the neoliberal turn. The crisis in Labour was part of the wider crisis in the global left, as it responded to the changing needs and desires of a society shaped by consumerism, a changing workforce during deindustrialization and a growing individualism encouraged by the government. The Policy Review was therefore a necessary process Labour had to go through, because the issues that had once defined British politics were changing dramatically.

One of the most significant breaks with Labour's past was to accept that nationalization would no longer be a core part of the party's programme. Kinnock and his shadow chancellor John Smith moved away from favouring large-scale public ownership and state intervention in nationalized industries. Labour would not look to renationalize those that had been privatized by Mrs Thatcher. The aim now was to introduce greater flexibility into production by using a mixture of market- and non-market-based ownership.

The 'People at Work Policy Review Group' paper from December 1987 discussed this further, and the argument presented was an important insight into how the reformist wing of the party now felt about the role of markets. Essentially, we see here that there was a broad acceptance of market forces, but by no means blind and total support, as the problems were highlighted just as much as the benefits. It was noted that in the:

> ... pursuit of the objective of improving performance one of the most difficult tasks will be to define the desirable scale and composition of state intervention in the operation of markets. Markets can be an efficient means of guiding and production, and of enhancing the community of interest between producer and consumer. The market can be a powerful creative force, providing a competitive stimulus to innovation and to provision of variety and choice. But markets also impose very short-term pressures which result in the immediate waste or even destruction of resources and which seriously jeopardize long-run efficiency.

[40] See chapter 12, above.

The market is inefficient in the provision of goods and services the benefits of which are not all bought and paid for, whether these be the social benefits of a well-educated population or the reduction in traffic congestion (and death and injuries) resulting from a well-run, heavily-subsidized railway network. The asymmetry of power in the market place results in the exploitation both of workers and consumers, and in self-perpetuating inequity.[41]

One conclusion drawn was that Labour had to 'use markets boldly, opening up new avenues of competition where the very high levels of concentration and market control prevalent in Britain are limiting consumer choice and product innovation. Equally, we must design more efficient means of decisive intervention in the market place.'[42] This approach developed into a wider policy based on the idea that state intervention would be used to promote industrial investment, rather than overall control of industry via a renationalization programme. This was quite a shift away from Labour's traditional starting point. But whilst it certainly encouraged a boldness in its thoughts about its strategy, purpose and values, Kinnock's promise that 'society mattered' held good. Although he accepted the new national and international economic realities, Kinnock also promised that Labour would use the market differently, and that it would have different priorities such as funding the National Health Service. He also promised there would be no 'slide to the right' or 'concession to Thatcherism'.[43]

The Policy Review was not meant to be a rejection of Labour's socialism, in the same way as Mikhail Gorbachev's *perestroika* in the Soviet Union was not meant to be a rejection of Soviet socialism. Both Kinnock and Gorbachev continued to use the language of socialism as they reshaped it to fit the new realities. And, just as happened in the USSR, this process of rethinking Labour's ideological framework saw socialism come to mean something quite different from what it had meant in previous decades.[44] Now market forces were not to be railed against or rejected as they would play a much greater role in Labour's thinking. However, they were to be used for socialist purposes because the end goal for Labour was still the creation of a strong society that benefitted the majority, not just the rich and powerful. As the Policy Review Group made clear when discussing the party's socialist values

---

[41] KNNK 2/2/14: 'People at Work Policy Review Group', 4–5.

[42] Ibid.

[43] Kinnock, *Thorns and Roses*, 158.

[44] For more on Labour and the Soviet Union, see Jonathan Davis, 'Neil Kinnock's *perestroika*: Labour and the Soviet influence', in Davis and McWilliam, *Labour and the Left in the 1980s*, 113–31.

in November 1988: amongst 'the key values which must inform the work of this group are: equality, justice, security, participation, self-determination, democracy and collective values'.[45]

The need for the Policy Review was driven by Labour's poor electoral performances in the 1980s, but one of its primary purposes was to rethink what socialism meant in a globalizing world. The language of socialism was still prevalent in some of the Review's conclusions, but by the 1992 general election even this had gone, and socialism was not mentioned in Labour's manifesto.[46] In this, we can see that one logical – though by no means inevitable – outcome of the Review was the eventual emergence of 'New Labour'. Kinnock may not have meant this as the long-term direction of travel for the party, but it is clear that the Review paved the way for New Labour, and thus played a crucial role in the making of the modern Labour Party.

The different ideas put forward by party members, together with the arguments and debates that occurred during Neil Kinnock's tenure as Labour leader, are appearing again as Keir Starmer reshapes the party along the lines that he believes can see Labour win the next general election. Kinnock and Starmer are two different leaders working in very different circumstances of course, but there are some important similarities. For example, they both inherited a divided party after a disastrous election defeat, and they both endured a hostile political environment. However, Kinnock was a left-wing firebrand who moved the party closer to the centre whilst fighting against a formidable opponent in Mrs Thatcher, whilst Starmer does not share Kinnock's Bevanite background or his rhetorical fluency. Instead, he is praised for his forensic ability to pick holes in his opponents' arguments.

Starmer's problem is that Boris Johnson so far has proved to be an untouchable prime minister whose clever campaigning and populist style have allowed him to ride out many storms, particularly those concerned with the Covid-19 pandemic. He is seen by his supporters as a politician who kept his promise and delivered Brexit, and he is thus invested with a lot of political capital. And despite the appallingly high death toll, the successful vaccine roll-out has only strengthened this image of a politician who gets things done. Kinnock had to deal with Mrs Thatcher who was perceived as someone who

---

[45] KNNK 2/2/14: Policy Review Group meeting, 'Values, Vision and Strategy', 2.

[46] Labour Party General Election Manifesto, 'It's time to get Britain working again', 1992, http://www.labour-party.org.uk/manifestos/1992/1992-labour-manifesto.shtml#build (accessed 13 September 2021).

'saved the country' (from socialism and economic decline). Starmer is dealing with Johnson who is also seen as a saviour (from the EU and Covid-19). However, whilst Mrs Thatcher was not someone who could be underestimated, Labour has continued to underestimate Johnson and his ability to appeal to voters. No amount of portraying him as out of touch and corrupt has changed voters' minds, meaning that Labour will need a different approach to taking on Johnson in the post-Brexit, post-Covid world.

We must also note another important difference in the Kinnock–Starmer comparisons, and this is the parliamentary majority that Starmer is faced with. Mrs Thatcher's victory in 1987 saw her government maintain a large majority, and, although Labour ate into it in 1992, it still fell some way short of overturning it. Today, Labour again has a huge task regarding the parliamentary numbers, but some of the areas that turned away from the party in December 2019 are seen as having only lent their votes to the Tories, implying only temporary support for Johnson and the Conservatives. It is not a given that voters in these places will return to Labour, but their traditional Labour roots and the current polling for Starmer offer hopeful signs that lost 'Red Wall' seats can be won back, if the message is coherent and the policies are right. Starmer's Labour may therefore also benefit from a policy review.

The starting point of any kind of political reflection on Kinnock and Starmer would have to acknowledge the different electoral geographies facing both leaders. Where Kinnock could rely on the old Labour heartlands in the industrial communities for votes, Starmer will have to work hard to win back those who have turned away from Labour, most recently at the 2019 election. However, as Labour Together's *Election Review* acknowledges, the problem runs deeper than that, with many traditional supporters believing that the party 'no longer seems to represent people like me'.[47] The difficulty for Starmer will be winning these voters back whilst holding on to those who do see Labour as their party. And then there is Scotland. In the 1980s, the Scottish National Party (SNP) was not the force it is today, and Labour was the dominant party. However, since 2015, Labour has been all but wiped out electorally by the SNP, so it must either work out how to win Scotland back, or how to win without Scotland.

---

[47] Labour Together, *Election Review*, 2019, https://www.labourtogether.uk/ (accessed 13 September 2021), ch. 2.

Conclusion

What are we to make of Neil Kinnock's record as leader of the Labour Party? This was undoubtedly a period of political defeat but also, we argue, one of political vitality and creativity on the left.[48] The 1980s saw remarkable vitality in progressive ideas. This was the heyday of *Marxism Today*, which developed its 'New Times' analysis, but there were also remarkable writings produced by progressive figures such as David Marquand, Ben Pimlott, Beatrix Campbell, Andrew Gamble, Tom Nairn and John Lloyd.[49] These were different figures but pointed to the need for Labour to rethink its attitude to the constitution, the voting system, defence, markets and more. Above all, they raised questions about how to empower citizens. Whilst Kinnock was not directly responsible for this (and was often criticized by these people), there was a strong sense that the Labour leadership was asking its supporters to think in new ways.

Kinnock shaped the progressive culture of his times. *Our* times, however, need to go beyond lazy caricatures and references to the 'Welsh windbag', as he is often portrayed. Even Kinnock's harshest critics admit that he held the party together and arguably saved it: the 1983 election result, when it almost came third in the popular vote, suggested a future in which Labour might be eclipsed by the SDP–Liberal alliance. Kinnock's leadership was one reason that did not happen. He was, however, more than just an effective party manager. He proved a effective talent spotter, bringing on the kind of people who shaped the politics of the next decade and beyond, including the likes of Patricia Hewitt, Charles Clarke, Peter Mandelson, Gordon Brown and Tony Blair. And he took his party on a journey that prompted a major rethink of political ideas and priorities.

Kinnock identified a soft left position, which he in effect proclaimed as the essence of the Labour Party's identity. He pursued a strategy of isolating Tony Benn and the far left, which made differences between the soft left and right seem immaterial. This was crystallized in his attack on Militant at the 1985 Bournemouth conference, which at the time involved immense personal bravery. Yet this kind of serious soft left position nevertheless found some of

---

[48] This is an argument we expand upon in Davis and McWilliam, *Labour and the Left in the 1980s*.

[49] Beatrix Campbell, *Wigan Pier Revisited: Poverty and Politics in the Eighties* (London: Virago, 1984); Andrew Gamble, *Britain in Decline: Economic Policy, Political Strategy, Political Strategy and the British State* (London: Macmillan, 1985); David Marquand, *The Unprincipled Society: New Demands and Old Politics* (London: Cape, 1988); Tom Nairn, *The Enchanted Glass: Britain and its Monarchy* (London: Radius, 1988); John Lloyd, *A Rational Advance for the Labour Party* (London: Chatto and Windus, 1989); Ben Pimlott, Anthony Wright and Tony Flower (eds), *The Alternative: Politics for a Change* (London: W.H. Allen, 1990).

the issues of the 1980s difficult to respond to, especially the miners' strike of 1984–5, where Kinnock was caught between supporting the kind of people he was brought up with, and the revolutionary tactics of Arthur Scargill. The strike famously posed the question, 'whose side are you on?' Kinnock's answer was not clear.

Kinnock developed an approach to the British state that contrasted with Thatcherism and had the strategic attraction that it could command support across much of the Labour Party. The idea of the 'developmental state' was written off by the Thatcher-shaped orthodoxy of the 1980s as the product of a failed consensus in politics. However, as the economist Mariana Mazzucato has shown, government investment has always been crucial in the development of wealth creation, a truth eclipsed by the New Right fixation with market-based solutions.[50] Kinnock may well have been ahead of his time.

Neil Kinnock took the Labour Party on an intellectual journey that ultimately ended in defeat. He can thus be seen as occupying a similar space in history to Mikhail Gorbachev. Although very different in their reach and ability to effect change – the leader of the opposition in Britain was obviously less influential than the leader of the USSR – both significantly reformed their party's ideologies and made them relevant to the new world that was emerging; both were the only leaders who could do this at that time, and both were denied the chance to see through the consequences of their ideological rethinking. There is a political tragedy here as the ideas put forward by Kinnock and Gorbachev could, at the very least, have blunted the harsher edges of the globalized corporate capitalism that came to define the 1990s.

Kinnock's problem was arguably that he was too much a creature of the Labour Party. One could not imagine him in any other party. He embodied a particular kind of Labourism that meant that he could not appeal to so-called Middle England voters – the key figures in the marginal constituencies who became integral to the party's retail offer in the mid-1990s. Indeed, Kinnock's failure was that it was never clear which voters he wanted in order to build a winning coalition. His was a strategy that was ultimately geared up to increasing Labour's votes in seats it already had. Yet the criticism of New Labour that is now common (that it enjoyed 'wide but shallow' support) is not one that could be made of Kinnock's Labour, which retained a strong sense of its history and values. How Neil Kinnock might have fared as prime minister, we will never

---

[50] Mariana Mazzucato, *The Entrepreneurial State: Debunking Public vs Private Sector Myths* (London: Penguin, 2018 [2013]).

know. Yet we have argued here that he had insights into the potential role of the state and about social justice that Labour neglects at its cost. Kinnock in many ways made New Labour possible, but he offered a form of politics that was significantly different.

14

Past, present and future: Tony Blair and the political legacy of New Labour

Andrew Hindmoor and Karl Pike

Introduction

Imagine not having an opinion about Tony Blair. It's not easy, even if you try. A March 2021 poll by YouGov showed that, unsurprisingly, 99 per cent of Labour Party members had an opinion on the former prime minister; and that for 54 per cent of them it was a favourable one, for 45 per cent an unfavourable one. For Gordon Brown, the result was very different: 81 per cent had a favourable opinion, only 18 per cent an unfavourable one. Given how closely their political fortunes were entwined, this is a striking difference.[1]

The Labour Party has not won a general election since Blair left office in 2007. The Blair–Brown governments increased expenditure on health and education; reduced child and pensioner poverty; enacted big constitutional changes; and established civil partnerships. These are not inconsiderable achievements.

However, they have not come close to securing a positive legacy for Blair. Instead, and to his critics in the party, Blair is defined by Iraq, public service reform and tuition fees. It wasn't always the case, of course. Blair may never have been loved by many Labour activists, but there was a time when he could convince Labour members, often against the odds, of the rightness of his and New Labour's mission, of his desire to build on the work of his predecessors and to engage with the party's traditions.

Rightly or wrongly, it is difficult to imagine perceptions of Blair within Labour changing dramatically. He keeps popping up in the media pronouncing on the

---

YouGov survey of 1073 Labour Party Members, 17–24 March 2021, https://docs.cdn.yougov.com/icjepi77jw/Internal_Labour_Member_Release_210329_W.pdf (accessed 13 September 2021).

issues of the day. But rather than adopt the tried-and-tested, ex-leader role of cheering his successors from the side lines, Blair has chosen to comment upon the contemporary state of the Labour Party, the failings of its current leaders and the development and delivery of government policy. Blair is typically well-informed, well-briefed, keen and more than able to communicate his suggestions. His interventions during the Covid crisis saw him ask legitimate questions of the Conservative government's strategy, for instance on vaccinations. As the journalist Decca Aitkenhead observed in June 2020, following a lengthy interview with Blair, he has 'constructed a post-Downing Street existence in which he continues to operate for all the world as if he's still running the country'.[2]

So, in Tony Blair's case, the invitation to think afresh about the legacy of Labour's past leaders is a particularly interesting one. Who Blair is, and interpretations of what he stands for – particularly within a changing Labour Party – remain subject to the actions of Blair and his interactions with other political figures.

Our argument here has three parts. First, rather than simply talk about Blair and Blairism as if they were a single and coherent phenomenon, which arrived fully formed in the early 1990s, we need to recognize that Blair said, thought and did different things at different stages of his thirteen-year term as Labour leader. Just as Colin Hay and Stephen Farrall have argued that we can 'periodise' Thatcher and Thatcherism,[3] we think that it is possible to periodize Blair and Blairism, whilst suggesting that different features may be drawn from different parts of this history. Here, we distinguish between five phases of Blair and New Labour, from the early opposition figure and his 'Social-ism' to the post-Downing Street Blair of recent fame and fortune. What Blair says today, we must remember, is not necessarily what the Blair of 1994, 1997 or 2001 might have said. Of course, there is much that's familiar and has remained a core part of his political identity. But much has changed too, as anyone would reasonably expect.

Second, we should be wary of extrapolating from Blair, New Labour and the political, economic and social circumstances of the 1990s and 2000s, a set of more general and timeless 'lessons' about the Labour Party of today or the Labour Party of the future. Not only that there are different Blairs

---

[2] Decca Aitkenhead, 'Tony Blair on ambition, housework and still living like a prime minister', *The Sunday Times*, 28 June 2020, https://www.thetimes.co.uk/article/tony-blair-on-ambition-housework-and-still-living-like-a-prime-minister-50qnzmcc5 (accessed 13 September 2021).

[3] Colin Hay and Stephen Farrall, 'Establishing the Ontological Status of Thatcherism by Gauging its "Periodisability": Towards a "Cascade Theory" of Public Policy Radicalism', *British Journal of Politics and International Relations* 13, no. 4 (2011): 439–58.

at different stages, New Labour's achievements and failings need to be understood in the specific context of their time, and that this means we should be wary of easy 'then and now' comparisons. Hence, our emphasis in the second part of this chapter is on the state of the economy during the time Blair was leader and the complex and, we think, unique relationship with Gordon Brown.

Third, and following from these two points, we suggest that it is simply not plausible to cast Blair and New Labour as either, and unconditionally, betrayer or saviour of the Labour Party. Failures, successes, and all things in between, can be found in different forms at different times during Blair's time as Labour leader.

Blair in stages

We contend that whilst Blair retained his core political brand and identity across the span of his active political career, his outlook changed and his priorities inevitably shifted. In the place of 'one Blair', what follows are five periods of Blair: early Blair (early 1980s); Blair the convincer (1994–2000); restless Blair (2000–2003); uncompromising Blair (2004–7) and post-Downing Street Blair (2007 onwards).

Early Blair

Our first Blair is, without doubt, the most marginal one, but we include him here as a rejoinder to anyone who thinks they know everything there is to know about him or who doubts that his politics ever evolved. In 1982, in the aftermath of his defeat as the Labour candidate in the Beaconsfield by-election, Blair visited Australia, where he had lived as a child, and delivered a paper to the politics department at Murdoch University in Perth.[4] At the time, Labour was in all sorts of trouble and the Conservatives, experiencing a rise in support following the Falklands War[5] and economic recovery, were, suddenly, odds-on to win the next general election. Blair was looking ahead.

---

[4] This section draws on our published work presenting a fuller analysis of the lecture and Blair's period as opposition leader: Karl Pike and Andrew Hindmoor, 'Do As I Did Not As I Say: Blair, New Labour and Party Traditions', *The Political Quarterly* 91, no. 1 (2020): 148–55.

[5] Harold D. Clarke, William Mishler and Paul Whiteley, 'Recapturing the Falklands: Models of Conservative Popularity, 1979–83', *British Journal of Political Science* 20, no. 1 (1990): 63–81, 79.

He started his presentation by attacking the Conservatives' competence and, less obviously, the centrist Social Democratic Party, which 'appealed to middle-aged and middle-class erstwhile Labour members, who have grown too fat and affluent to feel comfortable with Labour and whose lingering social consciences prevent them from voting Tory'. He then went on to eviscerate the right of the Labour Party whose leaders had 'basked for too long in the praise of the leader writers of the *Financial Times*, *Times* and *The Guardian*'. They were, he argued, too timid and predictable and had become 'managers of a conservative country'. A future Labour government, he warned, would come into 'sharp conflict with the power of capital, particularly multinational capital' and needed to be ready for that moment. Labour's left, he suggested, was in thrall to outdated 'dogmas' (read Marxism) but a new generation of left-wing activists had nevertheless energized the party and promoted new and important policy issues such as the environment and social equality.[6]

This was, at the time, quite iconoclastic stuff but is now rarely commented upon (there are a few exceptions, such as John Rentoul's early biography of Blair).[7] Blair had not yet been selected as the prospective Labour candidate in Sedgefield and so was free to say what he wanted. But what he said then was very different to what we might expect now, and a reminder that Blair, the self-styled modernizer, proved to be a clean break not only with Labour's left but also with its traditional right wing. In the years following his election in 1983, Blair's political identity was constructed and framed as one projecting *rapid* modernization in the context of a more *gradually* changing Labour Party. He was soon on the frontbench, and recorded in his memoir that, in terms of 'modernizing' policy, he considered himself 'the most forward' at that time, whilst taking 'some care to remain with the pack and not to become so isolated that I could be picked off'.[8] For Blair, progress after Labour's 1987 election defeat was too slow. Under Neil Kinnock's leadership, and then with John Smith, Blair consistently pushed for more change. He has since reflected (in a way inextricably tied to his own ambitions) that 'by 1992 I was almost forty. I had been in Opposition for a decade. The thought of another five years of merely incremental steps towards change in the party that was so obviously needed, filled me with dismay'.[9]

[6] Tony Blair, Lecture at Murdoch University, Perth, 1982.
[7] John Rentoul, *Tony Blair* (London: Little Brown, 2001). An edited version of Blair's lecture at Murdoch University is also available in Paul Richards (ed.), *Tony Blair: In His Own Words* (London: Politico's, 2004).
[8] Tony Blair, *A Journey* (London: Hutchinson, 2010), 48–9.
[9] Ibid., 51.

Blair the convincer

After his election as Labour leader in 1994, comfortably beating John Prescott and Margaret Beckett, Blair carried his party before him. Tony Benn recorded in his diary that the newly elected leader had made a 'really quite radical' speech about which he had 'no complaint'.[10] Blair gained overwhelming approval to rewrite Clause IV, dropping the totemic – though much debated and under-utilized – commitment to public ownership. He carried a vote on Labour's draft manifesto. During this period, Blair spoke, time and again, about Labour's 'head and body problem'.[11] By this, he meant the history of Labour's leaders (the heads) saying one thing and the activist base (the body) saying something quite different and more radical. For a time Blair was so convincing, he seemed to have solved the problem.

This period was not, as it is sometimes portrayed, one of a consistently safety-first, un-ideological, Blair. Alongside the argument about what a revised Clause IV ought to say, Blair, time and again, in a way which was not true of his later years in office, discussed, spoke and wrote about his party's history, its ideological traditions and the legacies bequeathed to it via Fabianism, Marxism and Blair's favoured 'ethical socialism'. This was the period of Blair's 1994 Fabian Society pamphlet *Socialism* and his lecture on the place of the 1945 Attlee government in Labour's past, present and future.[12] Blair was not particularly interested in proselyting on behalf of the classic works of socialist theory. He rarely namechecked Crosland's *The Future of Socialism*, the lodestar of social democratic revisionism. Blair's reluctance to 'adopt a thinker' from the party's past, however, did not mean he was immune to it. His interest in liberalism, and the 'progressive dilemma' (the need for those fighting the Conservatives to find common ground, rather than fight one another and lose elections) was as sincere as his initial desire to form a closer political working relationship with the then leader of the Liberal Democrats, Paddy Ashdown.

In electoral terms this was the age of 'big tent' politics, and New Labour couldn't have done it any better. A triple figure majority after four successive general election defeats and, post-1997, a sustained double-digit opinion poll lead over a self-indulgent Conservative Party was a remarkable and sustained success. This is the period, too, where many of the achievements that comprise

---

[10] Tony Benn, *Free At Last! Diaries 1991–2001* (London: Hutchinson, 2003), 258.

[11] Philip Gould, *The Unfinished Revolution* (London: Abacus, 2011), 258.

[12] Tony Blair, *Socialism* (London: The Fabian Society, 1994); Tony Blair, *Let Us Face the Future: the 1945 anniversary lecture* (London: The Fabian Society, 1995).

New Labour's 'greatest hits' were released: the National Minimum Wage, devolution settlements in Scotland and Wales, the Good Friday Agreement, Sure Start centres, the Human Rights Act, increases in Child Benefit and Winter Fuel Payments. In 1997, New Labour had campaigned on a minimalist manifesto. In office, it was more ambitious in its reforms, including the unexpected.

Yet, Blair the convincer was nothing if not politically eclectic. Against the expectations of his supporters, he stuck by his promise to stick by the Conservatives' spending plans. Despite all the talk of forging a new 'radical centre' he was quite ruthless, post-1997, in marginalizing the Liberal Democrats and pouring cold water on talk about electoral reform. The 'tougher' stance on asylum policy began to emerge, with policies and initiatives sometimes appearing driven by media outcry. So New Labour was, in short, and during this period, a mixed bag of a government which was hard to simply pigeon-hole as either a neoliberal-driven betrayal of socialist values or a reinvention of Labour's long-standing social democratic tradition.

Restless Blair

In January 2000, Blair was interviewed by David Frost on *Breakfast with Frost* where he was pushed to defend Labour's record on the NHS in the midst of a winter flu pandemic. Pleading, at first, for a 'sense of balance' and time to put things right, Blair, suddenly, clicked into gear and started talking about 'substantial extra resources for the Health Service': saying that, within five years, 'we will be in a position where our Health Service spending comes up to the average of the European Union'.[13] Suddenly, New Labour had redefined itself as the party of targeted public spending largesse.

Health expenditure rose from 4.7 per cent of GDP in 2000 to 6.2 per cent in 2005. Other countries were also starting to spend more on their public health systems. But in the UK, the rate of increase was the largest and, within a few years, translated into higher numbers of doctors, nurses and hospitals and improved waiting times and mortality rates. Under New Labour, public expenditure on health, education and social security increased faster than it had under previous Labour governments, and there were sizeable reductions in child and pensioner

---

[13] BBC Breakfast with Frost Interview Transcript, 16 January 2000, http://news.bbc.co.uk/hi/english/static/audio_video/programmes/breakfast_with_frost/transcripts/blair16.jan.txt (accessed 13 September 2021).

poverty.[14] From 2000 onwards, New Labour sought to make a political virtue of spending more on public services and, in doing so, portrayed the Conservatives as the party of cuts. After the fiscal incrementalism of the late 1990s, this was quite a shift.

In addition to public spending and public sector reform, the period following the 2001 election was defined, in large part, by 9/11 and Blair's unwavering response to it. The Iraq war has, of course, become a touchstone issue in the Labour Party: coming to define how politicians are seen, either on the basis of their votes at that time or their subsequent views upon it. Every party leader elected since Labour left office has stated his opposition, at the time and since, to the conflict. Sir John Chilcot, who chaired the Iraq inquiry, said in his public statement in 2016 that 'military action at that time was not a last resort' and that 'the judgements about the severity of the threat posed by Iraq's weapons of mass destruction - WMD - were presented with a certainty that was not justified'.[15] Significantly, given how the military occupation went, the report found that whilst Blair had 'recognised the significance of the post-conflict phase', he did not:

> press President Bush for definite assurances about US plans, did not consider or
> seek advice on whether the absence of a satisfactory plan called for reassessment
> of the terms of the UK's engagement and did not make agreement on such a plan
> a condition of UK participation in military action.[16]

It may be true that President Bush would have invaded Iraq regardless of what Blair did, but this does not diminish Blair's responsibility for the decision to join the United States in that invasion, nor the mistakes that let Iraq spiral into chaos.[17]

Public spending and Iraq were the two issues that consumed Blair's second term and went some way, alongside fierce debates over public sector reform, towards defining New Labour's legacy. Political lessons can be drawn from them both. But perhaps what they reveal is the extent to which Blair, once derided as someone who would say or do anything to get elected, emerged, as time went on,

---

[14] Maurice Mullard and Raymond Swaray, 'New Labour Legacy: Comparing the Labour Governments of Blair and Brown to Labour Governments since 1945', *The Political Quarterly* 81, no. 4 (2010): 511–52, 512. Robert Joyce and Luke Sibieta, 'An assessment of Labour's record on income inequality and poverty', *Oxford Review of Economic Policy* 29, no. 1 (2013): 178–202, 194.

[15] Sir John Chilcot's public statement, 6 July 2016, https://webarchive.nationalarchives.gov. uk/20171123124608/http://www.iraqinquiry.org.uk/the-inquiry/sir-john-chilcots-public-statement/ (accessed 13 September 2021).

[16] The Report of the Iraq Inquiry: Executive Summary, 123, https://assets.publishing.service.gov.uk/ government/uploads/system/uploads/attachment_data/file/535407/The_Report_of_the_Iraq_ Inquiry_-_Executive_Summary.pdf (accessed 13 September 2021).

[17] Jon Davis and John Rentoul, *Heroes or Villains* (Oxford: OUP, 2019), 256.

as somebody convinced of the rightness of his beliefs and actions – in the case of the Iraq war, in our view too convinced.

Looking back, he was right to judge that the health service, and other vital public services, had been neglected badly. They needed significant, indeed historically unprecedented, increases in funding. That policy decision was also lethal for the Conservative Party, which from 2001 onwards was continually on the back foot when it came to public services. His instinct to partner resources with reform is perhaps also understandable. Few contemporary commentators argued that *all* the NHS needed was money. In talking about choice and responsiveness, Blair irritated the left of his party but struck a broader public chord. The 2001 election win, and what the manifesto meant for Labour's future, is important here. Blair said of a Parliamentary Labour Party meeting soon after the election that his MPs 'felt they had won on one basis; I felt I had won on another'.[18] Blair, at this time, clearly wanted a lot more in terms of reform than many of his colleagues really thought necessary. It was the seed for multiple problems with his party later down the line.

Uncompromising Blair

In 2004, Blair came close to resigning the premiership and leaving office for good. With the (significant) caveat that his medium-term policy objectives must be supported by his chancellor, he told Gordon Brown he would stand down prior to a 2005 election: a commitment he has since come to believe was wrong in principle.[19] Regardless, he confided to those close to him that he was tired of the job. In May 2004, Alastair Campbell recorded in his diary that 'the PM was on the point of resignation'.[20] Allies perceived Blair as 'drifting' politically.[21] Yet what emerged from Blair's period of gloomy reflection on his own political mortality was a conviction that only he could properly pursue New Labour reforms. So, he opted to stay and try to secure as much time as he could.

Blair then went into policy overdrive. Tired of seeing his own ideas sidelined by the Treasury and derided by his party, he decided to simply push ahead: making it clear that he no longer really cared what others thought about him or his ideas. It was the beginning of Blair's thoroughly uncompromising time

---

[18] Blair, *A Journey*, 340.

[19] Ibid., 497.

[20] Alastair Campbell, *Outside, Inside, Diaries, Vol. 5: 2003–2005* (London: Biteback, 2016), 235.

[21] Ibid., 258.

as Labour leader: something which would, ultimately, spell the end of his premiership and (finally, in Brown's view) the succession of his chancellor.

This was the age of Blair refusing, publicly at least, to take one rhetorical step backward when it came to Iraq. It was the age of Blair fighting long and hard for an extension to detention periods for suspected terrorists and of fighting large parts of his own party to introduce university top-up fees. And, above all, it was this Blair who, having once complained to an audience of venture capitalists (who else?) about the 'scars on my back' received as a result of his efforts to reform the public sector, decided that modernization of the NHS and education system must, come what may, now follow higher spending.

Blair himself dated his break with the 'older' version of New Labour to the period approaching the 2001 election which then took a few years to become visible.

> I date from that time … my clear break with the thinking that had dominated even New Labour policy up to then: that the public and private sectors operated in different spheres according to different principles. New Labour had indeed weaned the party off its hostility to the private sector, but now we moved on from the 1990s version of New Labour to something more consistent with a twenty-first century mindset.[22]

This is a classic piece of Blair rhetoric, and one many will have become accustomed to over the years. There is more than a hint here, that whilst those around him – read, we think, chiefly Brown – were okay with some of the *easier* New Labour ideas, only *he*, Tony Blair, was prepared to properly honour the New Labour creed, embrace the future and take the difficult but right decisions on markets and competition.

This way of thinking shaped the reform/anti-reform narrative which poisoned the final years of Blair and Brown's partnership. They stumbled through the 2005 election together, securing another just-about-comfortable majority but the cracks papered over for the campaign by trusted aides (including Campbell) soon reappeared.

Yet by this stage, Blair was unwilling – or unable – to compromise. He believed he was right and had taken the tough decisions. The journalist Steve Richards appositely observed that 'throughout his career as leader and prime minister, Blair sought solutions that would either be popular, or else the least unpopular that his extensive skills could contrive. The truth is that whilst Blair regarded his early popularity as vindication for his actions, he managed to take his later unpopularity as a form of vindication too'.[23]

---

[22] Blair, *A Journey*, 283–4.
[23] Steve Richards, *Whatever It Takes* (London: Fourth Estate, 2010), 431.

Post-Downing Street Blair

As we write this in early 2021, Blair continues to shape (not always positively) his own legacy. He does so through the positions he takes, the language he uses and the decisions he makes: not least the way he has, in the past, chosen to make money.[24]

Blair also invested a great deal of time between 2015 and 2020 in attacking Jeremy Corbyn. That Blair truly believed Corbyn's leadership would be destructive for Labour, and ultimately bad for the country, was always very clear. Yet, one often got the sense that his criticisms, whilst pointed, could sometimes strengthen rather than damage Corbyn in so far as the latter was the tangible embodiment of the party's unease with the former. Corbyn campaigned for the Labour leadership against Blair and against the Iraq War. When Blair criticized him, in 2015 and then regularly afterwards, Corbyn returned to what was in many ways a core message for his leadership: 'yes, I'm not that guy'

It is easy to see the post-Downing Street Blair, who flirted with Change UK, as being the 'real' 'see, I told you so' Blair. But the up-and-coming politician who derided Labour defectors to the SDP in the early 1980s was also Tony Blair. We need to read and reflect upon the whole of New Labour's history – how its leaders interpreted the world, progressive politics and dilemmas at different moments in time. For Blair, that means including his days door-knocking with Michael Foot as a fresh-faced candidate; making waves in opposition as the (then junior) partner of Blair and Brown; and his time as a leader who thought and wrote on socialist ideology. It means reflecting on the prime minister who left the Conservative Party reeling – on the defensive regarding public spending and embarking upon its own 'modernization' – a politician who, with determination and energy, played a leading role in securing peace in Northern Ireland, and who robustly defended Britain's role as a friend and partner to other European countries. And it means comprehending a leader – one who agonized so much over domestic reform – seemingly committed to a US president who, along with senior officials, oversaw the fiasco of the invasion of Iraq.

---

[24] What Blair would do after leaving office, and how much money he would make, was talked about from 2007 onwards. In 2016, Blair closed his advisory firm, with a report in the *Financial Times* stating the business had 'muddied his post-government career by making millions of pounds from an array of controversial clients ranging from oil companies to the authoritarian government of Kazakhstan'. 'Tony Blair shuts down advisory firm that made him millions', *The Financial Times*, 20 September 2016, https://www.ft.com/content/d1d6830e-7f4f-11e6-bc52-0c7211ef3198 (accessed 13 September 2021).

The constants

We have argued that Blair changed before, during and after his time in Downing Street and that any nuanced assessment of his legacy needs to take this into account. There is not one single Blair, and whatever 'Blairism' is, it means something different today than it did twenty years ago.

But we also need to recognize that Blair's time as Labour leader between 1994 and 2007 reflects, at times quite clearly, two other very clear political and economic contexts, which applied then but do not apply now: the 'great moderation' of the world (and British) economy in the 1990s and 2000s and the very personal, often dysfunctional, often devastatingly effective, relationship between Blair and Gordon Brown.

'It's the economy, stupid'

Tony Blair was born, in Edinburgh, in 1953, and educated privately at Fettes College in Edinburgh. After a gap year in which he had tried his hand as a music promoter, he left London in 1972 to study Jurisprudence at Oxford where, slowly, he gravitated towards politics. This was the year after the collapse of the Bretton Woods system and a year before the OPEC oil crisis: the two events which, with the benefit of hindsight, we now know marked the beginning of the end of the postwar boom. Blair graduated, went back to London and eventually joined the Labour Party in 1975. A year later, James Callaghan warned delegates to Labour's conference in Blackpool that the country was facing an impending economic crisis.[25]

Skip forward two decades and Blair became Labour's leader in 1994, shortly after the British economy had emerged from a two-year recession in which GDP had fallen by nearly 2 per cent, and at a moment when the world economy was embarking upon an era of 'great moderation' characterized by stable growth, falling unemployment, rising incomes, low inflation and low interest rates.[26] Between 1992 and 2007 UK economic growth averaged 2.8 per cent a year; median household income, adjusted for inflation but before housing costs, rose from £360 to £499 a week; inflation averaged 2.8 per cent and unemployment

---

[25] Andrew Hindmoor, *12 Days that made modern Britain* (Oxford: OUP, 2019), 7–31.
[26] Ben Bernanke, 'The Great Moderation', Remarks by Ben Bernanke, Eastern Economic Association, 20 February 2004, https://www.federalreserve.gov/boarddocs/speeches/2004/20040220/ (accessed 13 September 2021).

fell to just over 5 per cent. This was, looking back, if not a golden era, then an economically pleasant one.

Blair left office in June 2007 at – just about – a time of his choosing. Two months later, France's biggest bank, BNP Paribas, froze €1.6 billion in hedge fund accounts, which had been hit by the implosion of the US subprime market. In September 2007, the Northern Rock bank fell apart and the slow car crash of the global financial crisis began. Eventually, and in the UK, this resulted in £137 billion of public money being used in loans and capital to stabilize the banking system;[27] a recession in which GDP fell by 4 per cent in 2009; and an increase in public debt from 41 per cent of GDP in 2007, to 83 per cent by 2012.[28]

Judged in terms of the timing of his entry and exit, Blair could not have done things any better. He arrived at the party just as it was warming-up and left shortly before it went wrong. But it is vitally important that we bear this global economic context in mind when we remember New Labour, let alone seek to draw lessons from it.

For the most part, New Labour pursued a pretty modest economic policy agenda. The Bank of England was given its formal independence. Welfare and tax policy were realigned to ensure that work paid, or at least that it paid more than unemployment. New Labour's basic political and economic strategy was to let the economy grow, keep regulating the City of London with a 'light-touch' and use the resulting tax revenue to support higher welfare redistribution and increase public spending and investment. And, at the time, with the Bank of England, the International Monetary Fund (IMF) and the Organisation for Economic Co-operation and Development (OECD) all publishing generally glowing reports about the UK economy, this strategy made sense. There was no pressing case upon New Labour and the Treasury to intervene to fix the economy because the economy seemed to be doing fine on its own and to help matters further, Blair, perhaps against his own best political judgment, had been talked out of a potentially calamitous push to join the single currency.[29]

To say that the strategy made sense, does not mean that the strategy was flawless. We now know that New Labour was too ready to do too little. It may have recognized evidence of growing regional imbalances, falling productivity and a failing vocational education sector, but it did not do enough about them.

---

[27] 'Bank rescues of 2007–09: outcomes and cost', House of Commons Library Briefing Paper, Number 5748, 8 October 2018.

[28] On the more general impact of the financial crisis in the UK, see Andrew Hindmoor, *What's Left Now* (Oxford: OUP, 2018), 173–8.

[29] Ed Balls, *Speaking Out: Lessons in Life and Politics* (London: Hutchinson, 2016), 155–72.

Its redistribution agenda was insufficient to reverse the historic high that income inequality had reached under the Thatcher and Major governments. Indeed, there was 'a small increase in overall measures of income inequality during Labour's period in office' following the big increases of the 1980s.[30] It played around with, but never really committed to, an industrial strategy. Above all, New Labour came to depend far too heavily, in terms of both taxation and national prestige, on banking and finance.

We have already argued that it is a mistake to think about Blair and Blairism as if it were a single and coherent phenomenon. There were different Blairs at different times. But there were also, to complicate matters further, possible Blairs that we never saw. Imagine that the financial crash had come early: in 2003/4 rather than 2007/8. It is simply not true to say that New Labour renounced Keynesianism.[31] But, for the most part, New Labour did not have to do much Keynesian demand-management because sufficient demand was not the economic problem it faced. Yet if the economy had crashed whilst he was prime minister, would Blair have led from the front in advocating a Keynesian approach and stronger state intervention in the way Gordon Brown did? Or would he have sought to hold Brown back? It has been said that just as 'there are no atheists in fox holes, there are no free-market libertarians in a financial crisis'.[32] But we can't know what Blair would have done because economic history worked out differently and this puts limits around the legacy for which we can now judge him.

For the same reason, we need to be careful about extrapolating from Blair and New Labour's past to more contemporary economic conditions. Long before Covid-19 created a new crisis for Britain's economy, the long-term costs of austerity in terms of low public and private investment and low productivity were apparent. Jeremy Corbyn advocated a robustly interventionist economic strategy including higher borrowing for public investment, an active industrial strategy, corporate governance reform, public ownership, higher corporate taxes and the introduction of a financial transactions tax. Blair was shocked and outraged. But Blair was prime minister during the boom, not the bust. He simply did not have to deal with the same economic conditions as his successors and,

---

[30]   Joyce and Sibieta, 'An assessment of Labour's record on income inequality and poverty', 187.

[31]   See Ben Clift and Jim Tomlinson, 'Credible Keynesianism? New Labour Macroeconomic Policy and the Political Economy of Coarse Tuning', *British Journal of Political Science* 37, no. 1 (2007): 47–69.

[32]   Jeff Frankel, '"No Atheists in Foxholes."? No Libertarians in Financial Crises', *Views on the Economy and the World*, 17 July 2008, https://www.belfercenter.org/publication/no-atheists-foxholes-no-libertarians-financial-crises (accessed 13 September 2021).

to this extent, Theresa May's repudiation of free-market certainties when she entered office in 2016 is more telling than Blair's critique.[33]

In the end, this is about politics as well as economics. Blair has never wavered in his argument that elections are won from the centre-ground. But as Corbyn told the Labour Party conference in 2017, the location of the centre-ground changes:

> It is often said that elections can only be won from the centre ground. And in a way that's not wrong – so long as it's clear that the political centre of gravity isn't fixed or unmovable, nor is it where the establishment pundits like to think it is.[34]

Survey data shows that when it comes to the public's views about the appropriate balance between public expenditure and taxation, attitudes have changed and are closer to the left.[35] This does not mean that Corbynism would, sooner or later, have broken through and convinced voters – ultimately, Corbyn failed badly at the 2019 election. But, equally, we should be careful of thinking that what worked for New Labour then, would work now.

The Blair–Brown relationship

In opposition after 1994, New Labour had what was called a group of 'Big Guns',[36] which met to discuss strategy and comprised Blair, Brown, deputy leader John Prescott, Robin Cook, the shadow foreign secretary and Campbell. Beyond this, there were key advisors like Peter Mandelson and party heavyweights like David Blunkett. That the 'Big Guns', along with many of its extensions, was dominated by men is not remarked upon enough. New Labour was incredibly male. Harriet Harman has a revealing story about what became the infamous 'Blair's Babes' photocall to welcome the historic intake of Labour women MPs in 1997. 'I wanted to have a photo taken of all the new Labour women MPs', Harman recollected. 'We told Number 10 but, to our dismay, found that they had automatically assumed Tony would be in it … Tony's presence would turn it into a photograph of a powerful man surrounded by a large group of women.'[37]

[33] BBC News, 'Theresa May vows to be "one nation" prime minister', 13 July 2016, https://www.bbc.co.uk/news/uk-politics-36788782 (accessed 13 September 2021).
[34] Jeremy Corbyn, 'Speech to the 2017 Labour Party Conference', 27 September 2017.
[35] Hindmoor, *What's Left Now*, 48.
[36] Alastair Campbell, *Prelude to Power, Vol. 1, 1994–1997* (London: Hutchinson), 84.
[37] Harriet Harman, *A Woman's Work* (London: Allen Lane, 2017), 193.

The 'Big Four' set-up changed after 1997. First, more and more political authority ran through Numbers 10 and 11 Downing Street. The 'Big Four' became two. Second, the personal and political relationship between the big two fell apart. Much of the debate about the Blair–Brown relationship has majored on deals: about who said what to whom and when. We won't restate much of that here, other than to say that despite the plethora of biographies and diaries we still don't know what we should believe.

Instead, we offer two observations – one mostly about Brown and the other about Blair. Brown argued in his memoir that both men had different interpretations of what modernization meant: something that became particularly acute after the 2001 election. He suggested:

> The truth is I was always up for modernisation. However, I was never up for a narrow interpretation of it that made the test of being a moderniser how much privatisation and liberalisation I bought into and whether I was now agnostic on inequality.[38]

This pretty pointed challenge towards Blair has as much validity as the Blair camp's counter-argument, that whilst Brown had a politically effective attack line on Blair's agenda, he didn't have an agenda of his own and this became painfully clear when Brown became prime minister. It is the truth of both of these points that holds lessons for their successors. There *were* different interpretations of modernization and these different interpretations were long-standing. They cannot solely be reduced to Brown's ambition to replace Blair. That there were differences is hardly surprising. People interpret the world differently, they change and they prioritize different things. The problem was that efforts to reconcile different interpretations ceased in the second half of New Labour's period in office. Brown failed to develop his alternative and both sides failed to try and find any common ground or to debate their differences (outside of newspaper briefings). Blair, for his part, gave up trying to find a guiding ideology. The enduring lesson for Labour, we believe, is that ideational debate – whether through restatement or the reconciliation of different ideational strands – is integral to Labour's coherence, and to its capacity to govern. Labour is a political party that cares too much about too many ideological issues for a leader to suggest they don't matter. The Blair–Brown relationship at its best *did* take this seriously. Indeed, 1994's famous 'Granita pact', which is so often presented in terms of leadership ambitions, also amounted to a principled ideological

---

[38] Gordon Brown, *My Life, Our Times* (London: The Bodley Head, 2017), 184–5.

compromise, where Brown was given the authority to drive economic policy inside and out of the Treasury.

The second point we offer is about Blair's leadership and his decision to maintain the Blair–Brown duopoly. In a sense, the question of whether Blair should have removed Brown from the Treasury is secondary to what it says about Blair's leadership that he didn't. Nobody can read the diaries and memoirs of New Labour and not feel exhausted by the feuding: the kind of rows and falling outs that filter down to day-to-day procedural fights amongst not just two people, but groups of people. Clearly, that style of working was far from ideal. Yet in keeping Brown as chancellor, Blair knew he wasn't just trying to keep on board someone he believed Labour and the government needed. He was maintaining the biggest internal check-and-balance on his own power that was possible within the government. For sure, there was an un-ignorable political risk in removing Brown anyway, particularly as Blair's power within the Labour Party waned. But the contradiction between Blair wanting to solidify a policy legacy whilst retaining the powerful figure he believed was frustrating it, cannot be ignored. And there's a good reason for not doing so. Being challenged is a good thing for a political leader and was, at times, good for New Labour.

That Brown has a very different relationship with his party to Blair today is an important point to reflect upon. Blair and Brown co-authored New Labour and were (often) co-decision makers for the decade they spent running Number 10 and the Treasury. Throughout their partnership, both wrestled with the dilemmas of 'modernization' and the compromises that appear inevitable at the top of British politics. Yet, despite leading Labour to defeat in 2010, Brown has a more comfortable position within his party and with its past. The distance Blair has placed between himself and Labour since he left office – something, no doubt, he would say subsequent leaders have also contributed to – is important for understanding how Blair is understood today, and for what lessons can be learnt from the Blair leadership. Quite simply, the distance between Blair and his party makes the former's interventions on social democratic politics less effective – and the job of those unwilling to trash all of Blair's legacy harder.

Conclusion

In this chapter, we have attempted to 'periodize' Blair's time as Labour leader: a form of analysis that both contextualizes his contribution and reveals his interpretations of long-standing Labour traditions. Blair was not an alien in the world of the Labour Party. Early Blair distinguished himself, and was clearly a modernizer, but he was also working from within a very recognizable ideological tradition. As leader, Blair sought to change his party as the final step to achieving power and being able to change the country. He achieved both, in part because of his capacity to convince. But he did not foist change upon Labour. He made a case, alongside formidable political allies – principally Brown – and won. It was from around 2001 that Blair began to increase the distance between himself, his party and some of the traditions which constitute Labour's people and its practices. When Labour was delivering huge increases in public spending, and big, impactful policies to increase life chances, Blair was mulling whether this was really 'reform'. That widening gap soured the Blair–Brown relationship further, and saw a prime minister and leader increasingly talking a different talk, and walking a different walk, to his party.

15

Renewal beyond New Labour: From the LCC to Corbynomics

George Morris, Emily Robinson and Florence Sutcliffe-Braithwaite[*]

'Labour – the natural party of opposition?' So opened the first issue of *Renewal: A Journal of Labour Politics*. In 1993, just as in the late 1950s, following a series of General Election losses, the left was divided into factions, each of which explained – and proposed to reverse – these defeats with competing diagnoses of social change.[1] Were economic trends, cultural shifts and changing social expectations to be accommodated, challenged or waited out? John Smith was taking a cautious approach to reforming Labour (pejoratively dubbed by some the 'one more heave' approach),[2] whilst others had begun to write off the party as doomed by sociological reality.[3] *Renewal*'s line was similar to that of the emerging New Labour project: Labour needed to modernize itself and to the task of modernizing Britain. The journal set out to give Labour a space to think through the array of challenges it faced, and to do so in a critical and pluralist spirit, arguing that '*Renewal* must become a significant means for making the changes that are needed in Labour.'[4]

---

[*] The authors would like to thank Sue Goss, Ben Lucas, Paul Thompson, Neal Lawson, Martin McIvor and Ben Jackson for giving up their time to answer questions about *Renewal*'s history; the analysis contained in this chapter and any errors are, of course, the authors' own.

[1] On the 1950s, see Lawrence Black, *The Political Culture of the Left in Affluent Britain* (Basingstoke: Palgrave, 2003).

[2] See Bryan Gould, *Goodbye to All That* (London: Macmillan, 1995), 224–5; Peter Mandelson, *The Third Man: Life at the Heart of New Labour* (London: HarperPress, 2010), 149ff.; Tony Blair, *A Journey* (London: Hutchinson, 2010), 51; Jack Straw, *Last Man Standing: Memoirs of a Political Survivor* (London: Macmillan, 2012), 190–1.

[3] For debate about whether Labour's only option was coalition, see Anthony Heath, Roger Jowell and John Curtice, *Labour's Last Chance? The 1992 Election and Beyond* (London: Dartmouth Publishing Co., 1994). For historical analyses of New Labour, see Steven Fielding, *The Labour Party: Continuity and Change in the Making of 'New' Labour* (Basingstoke: Palgrave Macmillan, 2003); Stephen Driver and Luke Martell, *New Labour*, 2nd edn (Cambridge: Polity, 2006).

[4] Paul Thompson, 'Labour – the natural party of opposition?', *Renewal* 1, no. 1 (1993).

The story of the rise of New Labour has been narrated by its own adherents as the tale of a heroic group of 'modernizers' updating the party and its policies for the late twentieth century.[5] To others, New Labour had capitulated to Thatcherism or at least its 'neoliberal' component.[6] This is a story with two sides: modernizers and traditionalists, moderates and socialists. But this framing simplifies Labour's past, flattening a diverse tradition into the category of 'Old Labour',[7] and also imposes a false uniformity and teleology on the story of modernization.[8] Blair's project was never the only version of modernization, and nor was it inevitable that it would win. Once we see modernization as a diverse *set of projects* it becomes possible to see strong continuities in the pages of *Renewal*, even as it went from being associated with Blair, to becoming a venue for the development of Corbynomics. It also suggests a way of interpreting Keir Starmer's attempts to situate himself in a tradition of Labour leaders – Attlee, Wilson and Blair – who all 'saw it as their task to modernise Britain' in a way that does not have to mean uncritically returning to Blairite policies.[9]

As the current editors of *Renewal*, we inevitably offer a partisan take on its history, and particularly on its recent years. But the journal is now almost thirty years old – slightly older than the youngest of its editors – and we think we are in a privileged position to examine its continuities and changes. It is significant that we, like many of the journal's previous editors, are all, in different ways, historians of modern Britain. The consistent thread in *Renewal*'s approach to politics has been the effort to situate Labour within the contexts of the particular times in which it finds itself. This is how it has been able to be a critical friend to both Blair and Corbyn, and how it has counselled the party to avoid the ahistorical defeatism of the question with which we opened this chapter.

---

[5]   See Philip Gould, *The Unfinished Revolution: How the Modernisers Saved the Labour Party* (London: Abacus, 1998).

[6]   See Leo Panitch and Colin Leys, *The End of Parliamentary Socialism: From New Left to New Labour* (London: Verso, 1997).

[7]   See Tim Bale, 'The logic of no alternative? Political scientists, historians and the politics of Labour's past', *British Journal of Politics and International Relations* 1, no. 2 (1999): 192–204.

[8]   Colm Murphy, 'Futures of socialism: "modernisation" and "modernity" on the British left, 1973–1997', PhD thesis, Queen Mary, University of London, 2020.

[9]   Keir Starmer, speech to Labour Party Conference, Doncaster, 22 September 2020, https://inews. co.uk/news/politics/keir-starmer-speech-full-text-labour-leader-conference-2020-address-today-doncaster-655612 (accessed 13 September 2021).

Beginnings

The new journal, edited by Paul Thompson, emerged from the politics of the Labour Co-ordinating Committee (LCC), of which Thompson was chair.[10] Set up in 1978, and initially aiming to challenge the party leadership from the left – for example, backing Tony Benn against Denis Healey for the deputy leadership in 1981 – the LCC moved away from the hard left, and became increasingly involved in the battle against Militant as the 1980s progressed. From the late 1970s, there was an upsurge of anxiety on the left about Labour's electoral prospects in an age of deindustrialization and huge social change. This was sparked most notably by Eric Hobsbawm's Marx Memorial lecture of 1978, 'The forward march of Labour halted?', published in the influential Eurocommunist journal *Marxism Today* and widely debated across the left.[11] In this ferment of debate, LCC members discussed in detail, as early as 1982, the evidence of a decline in class-based voting, a growing rejection of the big, bureaucratic state and the need to learn from and work with new social movements.[12] Following the bruising election defeat of 1983, such anxieties were turbocharged. The LCC published a statement, 'After the landslide', which argued that Labour's policies – such as the Alternative Economic Strategy – had been right, but needed to be communicated differently. It called for deep reflection on what had gone wrong, and a process of 'modernising' the party.[13] It was in this context that the politics of *Renewal*, the 'soft left' and 'modernization', were formed. The drive to modernize the party and the country went hand in hand: constitutional and electoral reform, greater pluralism and the devolution of power were all needed within Labour as well as outside. The 'high watermark' of the influence and organizational clout of the LCC came with the achievement of one-member-one-vote under John Smith.[14] This was, as Ben Lucas, another former LCC chair, recently reflected, important in building the perception that there was a left beyond the old trade union left and the Militant left – a pluralist left concerned with freedom.[15]

---

[10] On the history of the LCC, see Paul Thompson and Ben Lucas, *The Forward March of Modernisation: a History of the LCC, 1978–1998* (London: LCC, 1994).

[11] Eric Hobsbawm, 'The forward march of Labour halted?', *Marxism Today*, September 1978, 279–86.

[12] Charles Clarke and David Griffiths, *Labour and Mass Politics: Rethinking our Strategy* (London: LCC, 1982).

[13] Nigel Stanley, 'After the landslide – The Labour Co-ordinating Committee (LCC) on the 1983 election', 15 December 2019, https://medium.com/0040;nigelstanley/after-the-landslide-the-labour-co-ordinating-committee-lcc-on-the-1983-election-fff03b2a5018 (accessed 21 September 2020).

[14] Ben Lucas interview with FSB, 10 November 2020.

[15] Sue Goss interview with FSB, 9 November 2020.

In the run up to the 1992 general election, however, it seemed as though the LCC was 'stagnating politically' and that 'without more deep-rooted intellectual underpinnings, the soft left could not lead the struggle for actual renewal in and beyond the party'.[16] Election defeat only confirmed that, as Paul Thompson recalled, 'Labour had failed to develop [a] serious modernising project'.[17] Whilst the soft left felt that the factional battle had been won, with their ideas forming the core of a new consensus, they also knew that the LCC's position within party structures meant it was not well placed to develop and communicate complex ideas.[18] This was the work that *Renewal* was created to do. Whereas the LCC channelled grassroots pressure,[19] *Renewal* aimed 'to reach outwards to the broader intellectual policy community and to wider independent, left voices': Ernesto Laclau, Bob Jessop, Michael Rustin, Geoff Hodgson, Sally Tomlinson, Anne Phillips and Lynne Segal were all on its editorial board.[20] Its goal was, like the LCC before it, 'to get a Labour government',[21] but the journal aimed to advance this cause by developing *ideas and electoral strategy* for a modernizing Labour Party.

Neal Lawson took on the practical side of running the journal in its early years, slowly developing an editorial role and becoming co-editor with Thompson; soon after its foundation the journal entered into an agreement that radical publishers Lawrence & Wishart would take over the administration and production, with the journal remaining politically independent. From Lawrence & Wishart, Sally Davison joined the editorial group, and though the politics of publisher and journal differed, with Lawrence & Wishart tending towards the 'Gramscian side of the Communist Party' represented in the 1980s by *Marxism Today*, a shared commitment to pluralism and a shared political sensibility formed the basis for collaboration.[22] From the beginning, then, *Renewal*'s desire to 'modernize' Labour aligned it with the New Labour 'project'. But its 'critical and pluralist spirit also meant that it would not be a mere cheerleader. In time, this would lead to a parting of ways.

---

[16] Paul Thompson email correspondence, 27 October 2020.

[17] Ibid.

[18] Sue Goss interview.

[19] See Jake Watts, 'Narratives of organisational reform in the British Labour Party, 1979–2014', PhD thesis, University of Sussex, 2017, 91.

[20] Paul Thompson email correspondence.

[21] Neal Lawson interview with FSB, 27 October 2020.

[22] Sally Davison email correspondence, 16 November 2020. It is also worth noting that such collaboration was not unusual: Demos was founded by Martin Jacques and Geoff Mulgan, both of whom came from *Marxism Today*, with the latter going on to become Blair's Director of Policy. Nina Temple, the General Secretary of the Communist Party of Great Britain who oversaw its dissolution, became a champion of constitutional and electoral reform through Democratic Left (later the New Politics Network) and the Make Votes Count coalition, and later worked for the Social Market Foundation; she was also a member of *Renewal*'s editorial board.

'The shock troops of Blairism'? 1994–7

Patrick Wintour, *Guardian* journalist, LCC member and *Renewal* contributor, later described those associated with *Renewal* as 'the shock troops of Blairism in 1994–5'.[23] This perhaps says more about the misperception of the New Labour project in these years than it does about *Renewal* itself. The political causes that animated the journal in its early years were constitutional reform, democratic renewal, political equality, and stakeholder capitalism.[24] Its other key concern before 1997 was to deepen the party's strategic engagement with changes in the electorate and new approaches to political campaigning, channelling ideas, for example, from Bill Clinton's Democratic Party.[25] All of these elements fed into Blair's modernization project, as David Halpern and Stewart Wood suggested in their comparison of the 1979 Tory manifesto with Blair's *The Road to the Manifesto* in 1997, in which they described New Labour as offering a potentially transformative moment akin to the Thatcher revolution.[26]

The journal encouraged the idea that it was an organ of Blairism by changing its strapline soon after its foundation from *A Journal of Labour Politics* to *A Journal of New Labour Politics* (a decision which was controversial amongst the editorial team and which proved to be temporary), and offering Blair several opportunities to develop his ideas in its pages, in 1993 and again as leader in 1995.[27] In 1995, in a statement of his agenda as leader, Blair identified two key questions facing Labour at the end of the twentieth century – how to manage globalization, and how to establish a new set of social rules and a strong civic society.[28] The soundbites were there already; the piece featured the phrase 'tough on crime and tough on the causes of crime' twice. New Labour, wrote Blair, wanted to transcend the solutions of the old left and the new right, which were both unfit to tackle the problems now facing Britain and the world. This newness, though, also entailed 'reclaiming' values that had traditionally been Labour's – family, freedom and responsibility – and criticizing some elements of the Thatcherite

---

[23] Patrick Wintour, 'Devolving public services "must be Labour aim"', *Guardian*, 15 January 2003, https://www.theguardian.com/society/2003/jan/15/publicservices.politics (accessed 13 September 2021).

[24] Though the journal did publish some critical pieces on 'stakeholder capitalism': Peter Metcalfe, 'Stakeholding versus corporatism', *Renewal* 4, no. 4 (1996).

[25] Patricia Hewitt and Philip Gould, 'Labour and Clinton's New Democrats', *Renewal* 1, no. 1 (1993): 45–51.

[26] David Halpern and Stewart Wood, 'Comparable revolutions? Thatcherism 79 and Labour 97', *Renewal* 4, no. 4 (1996).

[27] Tony Blair, 'Why modernisation matters', *Renewal* 1, no. 4 (1993): 4–12.

[28] Tony Blair, 'Power for a purpose', *Renewal* 3, no. 4 (1995).

consensus: in place of individualism, he argued for 'building a meritocracy'. He framed this as commonsensical, with the common sense residing both in the 'working class' and 'so-called Middle England'. In mapping out a new path for Labour, Blair praised *Renewal* for having 'recognised the need for modernisation from the beginning' and described it as 'a valuable forum for debate'.[29]

The historian Peter Mandler, writing in the US leftist magazine *Dissent* on the eve of New Labour's landslide, described *Renewal* as 'amateurish, under-resourced, marginal – a general staff without an army'.[30] *Renewal* was certainly small and it was, indeed, run on a shoestring, but its editors never intended to lead an army. The journal was part of a growing ecosystem of think tanks: IPPR, the New Economics Foundation and the Social Market Foundation had all launched in the late 1980s; Demos followed in 1993, Progress in 1996 and Policy Network in 2000. There were also shorter-lived organizations with zeitgeisty names: Catalyst (active from 1998 to the early 2000s) and Nexus (active in the late 1990s). The latter was set up by Neal Lawson, Stewart Wood and David Halpern, with links to Number 10, and promoted itself as 'the first online think-tank'.[31] This was an attempt to extend the conversation beyond the party, but took the form of an academic/policy network, not a mass movement. The aim was to influence a Labour leadership that was notably uninterested in movement politics.[32] Whilst this may have run against the democratizing instincts of the *Renewal* team, with their LCC heritage, in the early years they were content to leverage their connections with the leader's office and other prominent MPs.[33] Later on, Lawson's frustration would be channelled into the pluralist membership organization Compass, but this was still the 'honeymoon period', when alternative power bases seemed unnecessary.[34] *Renewal*'s link to the LCC faction meant, too, that the journal was reported on, and its editors published, in the mainstream left press, particularly the *Guardian* and *New Statesman*, giving its ideas broader publicity.[35]

---

[29] Ibid.

[30] Peter Mandler, 'A popular front of the mind? "Centre-left" journalism in Britain today', *Dissent* (Spring 1997): 103–6.

[31] Neal Lawson interview.

[32] See Watts, 'Narratives of organisational reform'.

[33] Paul Thompson email correspondence; Neal Lawson interview.

[34] Paul Thompson email correspondence.

[35] Patrick Wintour, 'Former Labour allies round on Blair', *Guardian*, 9 August 2004, https://www.theguardian.com/politics/2004/aug/09/uk.labour (accessed 13 September 2021).

Nevertheless, even before Labour entered government, *Renewal* was offering critiques of the 'project'. Martin Kettle, reviewing Peter Mandelson and Roger Liddle's book *The Blair Revolution*, noted that 'the most articulate parts of the party' had been unwilling to discuss the book – 'more like a Communist Party attitude than a Labour one'. He found the book itself to be symptomatic of this: exceedingly cautious and characterized by 'New Labour Newspeak'.[36] Many of the central planks of *Renewal's* modernization programme – like stakeholder capitalism – were only adopted by the leadership briefly or in diluted form. Some of the core team would later regret not having pushed harder in this phase to embed their approach in the New Labour project, and not having developed a more radical programme of economic reform.[37] Whilst parts of the constitutional reform programme developed by the soft left network including Charter 88, the LCC and *Renewal* were enacted in 1997–9, Sue Goss, who was involved in all three, described it as the 'tragedy of New Labour' that even in 1997 it was unable to imagine it would have the power to achieve big things.[38] The wider project, in Ben Lucas' analysis, was 'cheapened and narrowed' by being hitched to the 'flimsy' posturing of 'Cool Britannia'; the serious project of restructuring the state was reduced to a rather nebulous gesturing towards 'modernization'.[39]

'Blair's conscience'? 1997–2007

As Labour approached power, *Renewal* was keen to hold New Labour to its transformative promise, and to ensure that the 'project' was not mere sloganeering; it could not mean simply the abandonment of old principles, but demanded the formation of new ones. As Mandler put it, '*Renewal* sees its role as Blair's conscience'.[40] Giving the Nexus inaugural lecture, Robin Cook lamented the intellectually stifling pressures of a 24-hour media cycle and a hostile press keen to jump on any dissent or radicalism from political practitioners.[41] Without space to think, New Labour politicians would need to rely on the work of organizations like *Renewal* and Nexus in 'keeping open our

---

[36] Martin Kettle, 'Peter Mandelson and Roger Liddle: *The Blair Revolution*', *Renewal* 4, no. 2 (1996).
[37] Ben Lucas interview. See also Stuart White and Martin O'Neill, 'That was the New Labour That Wasn't', *Fabian Review* 125, no. 1 (2013): 14–17.
[38] Sue Goss interview.
[39] Ben Lucas interview. See also Alan Finlayson, 'Tony Blair and the Jargon of Modernisation', *Soundings* 10 (1998): 11–27.
[40] Mandler, 'A popular front of the mind?'.
[41] Robin Cook, 'A radical agenda for the new millennium', *Renewal* 5, no. 1 (1997).

lines of communication to people blessed with the freedom of thinking beyond the next bulletin'. Academics, think tankers and intellectuals could take on the 'exciting task of providing the cutting edge of the advance party of radical thought', allowing politicians to cross the minefield 'after some of the mines in the way have been exploded', Cook suggested.[42]

The emphasis of *Renewal* in Labour's early years in power was on fleshing out the idea of the Third Way, which had thus far been defined primarily by what it was not. Stuart White argued that there were multiple versions of the Third Way available, with some offering a genuinely modern social democracy and others simply being forms of left-wing Toryism; within the Labour tradition, he suggested, it might be more useful to think in terms of a 'new revisionism'.[43] White traced the core principles of the normative framework of the Third Way as 'opportunity', 'responsibility' and 'community'. Within this framework there were potential fault-lines – between leftists and centrists, or liberals and communitarians – over how core principles should be interpreted and implemented; should 'opportunity', for example, be seen in meritocratic or egalitarian terms? White argued that those adopting the language of the Third Way must be more precise about what they meant, or the concept was useless. In a 2002 *Renewal* article, setting out an agenda for a second term, David Miliband wrote that the Third Way was still 'defined negatively rather than positively'. 'Incumbency', he argued, 'no less than insurgency demands fresh thinking.'[44] Yet the very vagueness of the Third Way project was part of its appeal to those in power, and *Renewal*'s efforts to give it greater definition could only go so far.

Attempts to define the Third Way and to influence the New Labour project ran alongside a growing sense of disappointment. In late 1998 *Marxism Today* famously reconvened for a special issue, featuring a cover image of Blair with the word 'Wrong',[45] but as early as March that year, Neal Lawson and Simon Buckby, a journalist who had been Labour's director of advertising in the 1997 election campaign, had written a cover story for the *New Statesman*, which contrasted modernizers whose goal remained a more equal society ('the new social democrats'), with those who had, Lawson and Buckby wrote, 'failed to escape from the influence of neo-liberalism'.[46] They suggested that New Labour was too

---

[42] Cook also criticized the name 'Nexus' as a symptom of the modernizers' obsession with the new, and wondered why the group had not drawn on the treasury of socialist history and named itself after a figure like William Morris.

[43] Stuart White, 'Interpreting the "third way": not one road, but many', *Renewal* 6, no. 2 (1998).

[44] David Miliband, 'Maintaining our radicalism in a second term', *Renewal* 10, no. 2 (2002).

[45] *Marxism Today*, special issue, 1998.

[46] Simon Buckby and Neal Lawson, 'Third way? No way, Tony', *New Statesman* 11, no. 495 (13 March 1998): 16–18.

focused on day-to-day firefighting and on maintaining electoral credibility, and that it was failing to build public support for more radical moves to make Britain a more egalitarian and democratic place. The intervention was described in the *New Statesman* as New Labour's 'first split'.[47]

These tensions made their way into the pages of *Renewal*. In a debate with Philip Gould, Paul Thompson argued that 'New Labour has succeeded in burying the past but largely failed to fashion a future'. Gould countered that the left's tendency to be disappointed by Labour in office contained within it a 'mindset of betrayal' – an obsession with ideological purity that had led to the need for modernization in the first place. For Thompson this response epitomized the problem: 'What you and many in New Labour ranks seem to find harder to deal with is that criticism may exist from within a modernising perspective.' New Labour in office had become too centralized, domineering and controlling; more focused on catching up with perceived public opinion than committed to changing it. The lack of any guiding ideas or principles meant that the leadership had become convinced that modernization was whatever New Labour ministers did, and all who opposed them, including the different modernizing tendency represented by *Renewal*, were 'enemies of progress'. Modernization was, as a result, now 'largely emptied of any meaning'.[48]

The ambivalence of the relationship could be seen when *Renewal* turned ten in 2003. Blair not only agreed to host a seminar in Downing Street to celebrate, but his office admitted that they were running out of policy ideas. Capitalizing on this opportunity to 'make the case for a second wave modernising strategy', *Renewal* used the event to set out what its founders later described as 'a reasonably coherent and confident agenda' based on the journal's work on equality, liberty and fraternity, political economy and citizenship.[49] The leaders of Demos and IPPR also spoke in support of this broad agenda. Yet they all, Paul Thompson recalled, 'met a wall of defensiveness and hostility'.[50] Their thinking was out of step with the government's. New Labour had already concluded, thought Thompson and Lawson, that 'more markets and even less of the public realm' were the key to renewing the project.[51] The following month, Gordon Brown hosted a birthday party for the journal in the Commons. All the talk,

---

[47] See also Neal Lawson interview.
[48] Paul Thompson and Philip Gould, 'Is New Labour still new? A debate, *Renewal* 11, no. 1 (2003).
[49] Neal Lawson and Paul Thompson, 'Reflections on an extended conversation with New Labour', *Renewal* 15, no. 1 (2007).
[50] Paul Thompson email correspondence.
[51] Lawson and Thompson, 'Reflections on an extended conversation with New Labour'.

Robin Cook noted in his diary, was about Blair's enthusiasm for the US-led war in Iraq, and for the derailing of Cook's proposed reforms to the House of Lords. Brown gave a well-received speech, and Cook noted that many of those present had 'scuppered [Brown's] ambitions for the leadership in 1994 by throwing their support behind Tony'. Now most of them would have preferred a Brown premiership.[52] *Renewal* was increasingly attributing the social-democratic features of the New Labour project to Brown.[53]

Renewal continued to push New Labour to be bolder. Before the election of 2005, the journal challenged a third term Labour government to broaden its social democratic horizons. Martin McIvor noted the legacy of the new left in New Labour's exploration of the democratization of public services, a legacy which Blairite approaches to Labour's past had deliberately forgotten.[54] John Denham argued that the government needed to expand social justice into the market, by recreating 'progressive institutions' within it, rather than regarding them as parallel fields. He also noted that the involvement of the private sector in public services had brought 'private sector conditions of employment and a narrow, contractual view of their relationship with the public service'.[55] Sue Goss, similarly, argued that a 'resilient, self-confident social democracy has a public realm in which market values and market relationships don't apply'.[56] A roundtable on feminism, including Patricia Hewitt, Ruth Lister and Polly Toynbee, proposed a feminist agenda for Labour. They called, amongst other things, for reform of employment law, the universal availability of Sure Start, a statutory duty to analyse the gendered effects of government policies, and a feminist economic/industrial strategy.[57] After the election, Danny Dorling issued a challenge to the idea that class was becoming less significant in politics, arguing that class structure had changed, but that inequalities in health, wealth and geography were growing, and remained profoundly important as drivers of electoral behaviour: Labour needed to understand and respond to this rather than deferring to narratives of class 'dealignment' in voting.[58]

[52] Robin Cook, *The Point of Departure* (London: Simon & Schuster, 2003): 302–3.
[53] Lawson and Thompson, 'Reflections'.
[54] Martin McIvor, 'Communities in control?', *Renewal* 12, no. 1 (2004).
[55] John Denham, 'The case for a "New Labour" third term', *Renewal* 12, no. 4 (2004).
[56] Sue Goss, 'The reform of public service reform', *Renewal* 13, nos 2–3 (2005).
[57] Scarlett Maguire, 'Roundtable: what do we make of the "F" word now?', *Renewal* 12, no. 3 (2004).
[58] Danny Dorling, 'Class Alignment', *Renewal* 14, no. 1 (2006): 8–19.

'Renew and radicalize, 2007–16

In 2007, Blair gave way to Brown. At the same time, Lawson and Thompson stood down as editors of the journal and were succeeded by Martin McIvor. In their parting editorial, Lawson and Thompson looked back with disappointment at what they now felt had not been a dialogue but a monologue. Instead of the new politics they had hoped for, they had got 'post-politics and an implicit agreement with the end of history thesis in which the USA and the markets were perceived to have won'.[59] The alternative roads that were available to New Labour – the roads mapped out by the journal – had not been taken. 'If the past years have taught us anything, it is this – expecting Labour to renew and radicalize itself solely from within its own resources is a waste of time.' But they were also surprised that *Renewal*, first conceived following the fourth successive election defeat in 1992, had survived for so long. In 'a modest symbolic change' the journal now changed its strap line to 'a journal of social democracy', indicative of a desire to widen the conversation to encompass more of civil society, and not simply those within the Labour Party. The outgoing editors pointed to Compass, the campaigning think tank founded by Lawson in 2003, as a space in which this form of politics could be organized, and the journal retained links to and affinities with Compass under McIvor.[60] Lawson later recalled having learned the lesson 'that journals and think-tanks were important, but not enough. You also need a way to shape the party'.[61] Accordingly, Compass placed more emphasis on building a membership.

In an essay in 2003, Patrick Wintour asked 'Did *Renewal* make a difference?'[62] The journal had been helpful to Blair in the early days of his leadership of the party, thought Wintour. It had avoided becoming a faction or a think tank, an academic journal or a 'propaganda sheet', and was 'one of the few spaces in which social democrats can have a grown-up discussion without someone shouting betrayal'. It had remained at the cutting edge, and also maintained 'an honourable and consistent critique': it had been seriously interested in devolution, and was early to criticize excessively centralized public services, the culture of evaluation, targets and inspection in Labour's first term, and Blair's 'redistribution by stealth' policy. Yet it had never managed to win widespread support for proportional

---

[59] Lawson and Thompson, 'Reflections'.
[60] Martin McIvor email correspondence.
[61] Neal Lawson interview.
[62] Patrick Wintour, 'Did *Renewal* make a difference?', *Renewal* 11, no. 1 (2003).

representation or a progressive alliance, and at times its academic tendencies had meant sacrificing the clarity of expression needed to win a debate.

The palpable disappointment of the outgoing editors in 2007 suggests another limit to *Renewal*'s usefulness: a journal of ideas committed to connecting ideology and practice only worked if those in power joined the dialogue. New Labour's limited engagement with the journal – in theory one of the few left institutions sympathetic to the 'project' – was indicative of its attitude more widely. As Thompson's debate with Gould suggested, anybody not entirely supportive of every aspect of government policy was viewed with suspicion. A journal committed to intellectual inquiry and political pluralism could only get so far against this bunker mentality.

McIvor's editorship began with the hope that Brown could renew the social democratic tendencies of the government.[63] The 'architect' of much of what was deemed good about New Labour was now 'at the helm'. Brown seemed to recognize the need to relaunch with a new narrative, and a desire to find a new approach to the state.[64] McIvor's intention was to 'draw out and even radicalize' aspects of Brownism – such as building a progressive national identity, and creating an active state – and also to 'challenge potential weaknesses' – such as Brown's tendencies to technocracy and centralization.[65]

Yet soon Brown's government seemed to be losing its way.[66] When the global financial crisis hit in 2008, social democrats missed their moment to challenge the 'neo-liberal paradigm' because, McIvor argued, they had 'no alternative political economy to offer in response'.[67] New Labour had effectively depoliticized the economy, preferring to transfer wealth from higher tax yields into better public services, rather than addressing the problems inherent in the capitalist model itself. As Hopi Sen commented in 2011, looking back on the period from the perspective of a long-time supporter of Brown, the crash exposed the short-sightedness of Brownism.[68] It also effectively ended Labour's period in office. The leadership election that followed saw candidates enthusiastically declaring an end to the New Labour era; much of the critique that *Renewal* had developed

---

[63] Martin McIvor, 'The problem of social democracy', *Renewal* 15, nos 2–3 (2007): 6–10.

[64] Martin McIvor, 'The problem of Britain', *Renewal* 16, no. 1 (2008): 5–6.

[65] Martin McIvor email correspondence.

[66] Martin McIvor, 'Crisis and opportunities', *Renewal* 16, nos 3–4 (2008): 6–7.

[67] Daniel Leighton and Martin McIvor, 'Political economy after the end of history', *Renewal* 17, no. 3 (2009): 5–9.

[68] Hopi Sen, 'We need to talk about Gordon', *Renewal* 19, nos 3–4 (2011); the piece was widely discussed: see 'Hopi Sen: Labour has no future if it refuses to confront the ghosts of its past', *The Independent*, 24 September 2011.

over the past decade now seemed to be the consensus. But McIvor worried that 'there is something too easy about all of this'.[69] There was far too little discussion of the reality of power, and the structural forces acting on Labour in government. 'New Labour', he wrote, 'was shaped by powerful ideological, institutional, and economic forces far greater than a few renegade individuals.' The loss of power – to some extent inevitably – prompted the journal to focus on the external social, cultural, and economic factors which provided the context not only for Labour's electoral fortunes, but also for its experiences in power.

Labour's recent past continued to haunt the party. In 2011, McIvor and his successor as editor, Ben Jackson, wrote that Milibandism was hampered by New Labour's legacy on cuts and public services, which had shaped the political context that made the Coalition's damaging programme of austerity possible.[70] But the Miliband years proved in some ways a congenial time for *Renewal*. If Blair and Brown had tended towards control freakery rather than intellectual pluralism, Miliband was self-consciously interested in ideas. His leadership of the party, McIvor wrote, 'felt like a fruition of many of the lines of thought that the journal had tried to encourage and contribute to'.[71] *Renewal* attempted to probe and develop the emerging political economy of Miliband's Labour, particularly the idea that became known as 'predistribution', and the set of ideas that concerned 'Blue Labour': community, nation, place, and identity. As Jackson recalled, there 'seemed to be a decent chance Labour might win in 2015', so in these years it seemed that *Renewal* could play an important role in forming and testing 'a new governmental project for the left'.[72]

In the wake of the financial crisis, and with centre-left parties in trouble across Europe, it was clear to many that a thorough critique of 'neo-liberalism' was needed, and a new political economy required. This was one of the key tasks to which *Renewal* turned. Bringing academic ideas into Labour strategy and policymaking circles was a key part of the journal's activity, drawing in research such as Anne Wren's work on the political economy of the service transition.[73] There was sustained engagement with the Milibandite idea of 'predistribution', which expressed the aspiration – indeed the need – in a period of sluggish growth and constricted public finances, to think about how the

---

[69] Martin McIvor, 'The lessons of power', *Renewal* 18, nos 3–4 (2010): 6–8.

[70] Ben Jackson and Martin McIvor, 'The long game', *Renewal* 19, no. 2 (2011): 5–7.

[71] Martin McIvor email correspondence.

[72] Ben Jackson email correspondence.

[73] Anne Wren, 'The political economy of the service transition', *Renewal* 21, no. 1 (2013): 67–76.

economy might be re-engineered to produce more equitable distributions of income and wealth. Natan Doron saw Martin O'Neill and Thad Williamson's book on the Rawlsian idea of 'property owning democracy' as one model that might give rise to a different 'pre-distribution';[74] whilst Joe Guinan, drawing on the work of the Democracy Collaborative think-do tank in the United States, looked to the possibility of democratizing capital, though community wealth building, worker cooperatives, and the like.[75] An important set of ideas were being drawn together here: as Doron put it, they offered the glimmerings of a 'genuine paradigm shift in political economy'.[76]

Some of the journal's long-standing concerns, however, lessened in significance in the Miliband years. After the Liberal Democrats entered the coalition government with David Cameron's Tories in 2010, the prospects of a 'progressive alliance' of any sort dimmed, and *Renewal,* accordingly, turned away from debates about the construction of such an alliance, and refocused on debates internal to the Labour Party. In contrast, Compass broke its formal ties with Labour at this point, in an attempt to revivify this agenda.

The experiences of 2015 suggested that voters were not convinced by the sort of soft leftism Miliband had offered: the party was defeated in the general election, and the subsequent landslide election of Jeremy Corbyn as party leader shifted control of the party to the hard left.[77] But Jackson's last editorial, at the end of 2015, was optimistic that there was common ground between the centre, the soft left and the Corbynites on three key issues, all of which broke with New Labour.[78] First, there was a newfound consensus on the need to reduce economic inequality, and a recognition that 'predistribution' – a progressive re-engineering of the workings of the economy – was needed as well as redistribution. Second, there was a widespread belief in the need to tackle inequalities of power, as well as income and wealth. And third, there was a renewed emphasis on mutualism and civic mobilization. The journal would continue to develop these themes in the coming years, though the factional divides in Labour, far from lessening, would only grow deeper.

---

[74] Natan Doron, 'Property-owning democracy and pre-distribution', *Renewal* 20, nos 2–3 (2012): 150–3.

[75] Joe Guinan, 'Social democracy in the age of austerity and resistance: the radical potential of democratising capital', *Renewal* 20, no. 4 (2012): 9–19.

[76] Natan Doron, 'Property-owning democracy and pre-distribution', *Renewal* 20, nos 2–3 (2012): 150–3, at 150.

[77] See Eunice Goes, *The Labour Party under Ed Miliband: Trying but Failing to Renew Social Democracy* (Manchester: MUP, 2016).

[78] Ben Jackson, 'Labour's ideology: towards common ground', *Renewal* 23, no. 4 (2015): 5–10.

'Critical friends and worthy opponents', 2016–20

The first editorial by Florence Sutcliffe-Braithwaite and James Stafford in 2016 reflected back on Paul Thompson's first editorial in 1993.[79] At both moments, the electoral prospects for social democrats looked bleak. But it had been easier, wrote the new editors, to 'detect and adapt to the mood of the times' in 1993 than it was in 2016. Meanwhile, the settlement reached by New Labour in power had unravelled, with many of the gains made over its thirteen years in power being undone in a term of the Coalition. And Labour itself had been transformed by the election of Jeremy Corbyn. As Alan Finlayson argued in a subsequent issue, Blair had not been the start of something new so much as the end of something old – the politics of retail offers had come to an end, and the new politics of Corbynism seemed to offer something more relevant to the times.[80] The editors were instinctively sceptical of Corbynism, as might be expected from a journal of the soft left that had been enthusiastically committed to modernization, but they aimed to offer a space to both 'critical friends and worthy opponents' of the new Labour leader, as the journal had under Blair, Brown and Miliband.

The journal set out to engage with and develop the new political economy that was emerging from John McDonnell's office, which began to be called 'Corbynomics'. It published, for example, an interview with Matthew Brown of Preston Council on the community wealth building strategy the council was enacting;[81] an analysis by commissioning editor Christine Berry of how the government's stake in RBS could be used to create a new framework of local and regional banks lending to small and medium-sized businesses; and a debate on Universal Basic Income.[82] The journal also developed a serious interest in re-examining the new left and the hard left of the 'long 1970s', carrying an interview with Stuart Holland, an analysis of the Institute for Workers' Control, and pieces on community activism and new left critiques of social democracy.[83] This was not just an attempt to reckon with the origins of Corbynism, but something much

[79] James Stafford and Florence Sutcliffe-Braithwaite, 'Reorienting the left', *Renewal* 24, no. 1 (2016): 5–13.

[80] Alan Finlayson, 'The present crisis and the questions we must ask,' *Renewal* 24, no. 3 (2016): 5–14.

[81] Martin O'Neill interviewing Matthew Brown, 'The Road to Socialism is the A59: The Preston Model', *Renewal* 24, no. 2 (2016): 69–78.

[82] Mat Lawrence and Neal Lawson, 'Basic income: a debate', *Renewal* 24, no. 4 (2016): 69–79.

[83] Martin O'Neill interviewing Stuart Holland, 'Hope Amidst Despair?', *Renewal* 25, nos 3–4 (2017): 90–100; Joe Guinan, 'Bring back the Institute for Workers' Control', *Renewal* 23, no. 4 (2015): 11–36; Alex Campsie, 'Populism and Grassroots Politics: "New Left" Critiques of Social Democracy, 1968–1994', *Renewal* 25, no. 1 (2017): 62–75; David Ellis, 'On Taking (Back) Control: Lessons from Community Action in 1970s Britain', *Renewal* 25, no. 1 (2017): 53–61.

more radical: an attempt to find 'roads not taken' in the intellectually fertile and vibrant period after 1968, focusing on grassroots mobilization, decentralization of power and economic democracy – the issues that had animated the LCC.

The surprise result of the 2017 general election seemed to offer hope that a truly transformative Labour government might be around the corner. 'The prospects are exhilarating', wrote the editors. 'But the volume of work needed to prepare the party for government remains formidable.'[84] As in the 1990s, the journal tasked itself with doing that work. It sought to further develop, critique and test the emerging ideas of 'Corbynomics', and to strategically position these ideas as the basis for a possible policy consensus to unite different factions of the party. It now regarded Corbyn in a way not dissimilar to its view of Blair twenty years earlier.

The most influential output of the journal in this period, an essay by commissioning editors Joe Guinan and Martin O'Neill, was an analysis of the emerging political economy.[85] This clearly drew on themes that Guinan, O'Neill, and others had developed within and outside the pages of the journal in the Miliband years (indeed, as Colm Murphy wrote in 2019, calls for a paradigm shift in political economy had important 'roots in Ed Miliband's "predistribution" agenda', though they were 'turbocharged' under Corbyn's leadership).[86] Guinan and O'Neill characterized the party's economic thinking as having undergone an 'institutional turn' – instead of focusing solely on state ownership or redistribution, Labour now believed that the task was to transform and build institutions of the economy in a more democratic and sustainable direction. As in any such intervention, the essay's analysis of the new political economy, and its tracing of the different intellectual influences old and new, was not simply descriptive, but added to the coherence it argued was there. The essay was unusually widely received for a contribution to *Renewal*: it was discussed in the *Economist*, and the *Guardian* referenced *Renewal* for the first time in a decade.[87] The journal hosted an ongoing conversation about this thesis, with critiques and calls for the

---

[84] James Stafford and Florence Sutcliffe-Braithwaite, 'Ready for government?', *Renewal* 25, nos 3–4 (2017): 6–15.

[85] Joe Guinan and Martin O'Neill, 'The institutional turn: Labour's new political economy', *Renewal* 26, no. 2 (2018): 5–16.

[86] Colm Murphy, 'The unspoken dilemmas of Corbynomics', *Renewal* 27, no. 3 (2019): 5–13.

[87] 'Corbynomics would change Britain – but not in the way most people think', *The Economist*, 17 May 2018, https://www.economist.com/britain/2018/05/17/corbynomics-would-change-britain-but-not-in-the-way-most-people-think (accessed 13 September 2021); Ben Tarnoff, 'Next left: Corbyn, Sanders and the return of socialism', *Guardian*, 17 December 2018, https://www.theguardian.com/books/2018/dec/17/the-next-left-socialism-in-the-uk-and-the-us (accessed 13 September 2021).

expansion of its central ideas into, for example, the international arena.[88] It also attempted to bring the constellation of ideas around the 'institutional turn' into conversation with other ideas about how to re-engineer the British economy, notably those proposed by the IPPR's Commission on Economic Justice, and those associated with the 'Everyday Economy' or 'Foundational Economy' approach, which promotes economic well-being in the parts of the economy that all citizens rely on in everyday life. Political economy was not *Renewal's* only concern in these years – there was also work on Europe and climate change (often linked to economics),[89] on Labour's changing electoral base and on the new form of political mobilization represented by Momentum.[90] But it was in the sustained attempt to test, deepen and develop a new political economy that *Renewal's* strategy in these years most clearly bore fruit.

The journal was nervous on the eve of the 2019 election; an editorial written in advance celebrated the party's transformation into a party of 'thoroughgoing economic radicalism' whilst acknowledging Labour's dismal poll numbers.[91] Crushing defeat forced the journal into what an editorial described as 'the end of illusions'.[92] Labour's radical economic agenda had not been translated into a compelling electoral or communications strategy; the average voter was more likely to see Corbyn as representing a return to state ownership than to associate him with an 'institutional turn'. Ideology and strategy remained disconnected. The editors wrote with regret that *Renewal* had 'stopped asking hard questions about the party's effectiveness as a vehicle for that policy radicalism, either as an electoral or as a governing proposition'. It was 1993 again, again.

[88] Anthony Painter, 'Can Labour break free?', *Renewal* 26, no. 3 (2018): 5–8; Murphy, 'The unspoken dilemmas of Corbynomics' David Adler, 'The international institutional turn: the missing ingredient in Labour's new political economy', *Renewal* 27, no. 4 (2019): 11–22; Matthew L. Bishop and Anthony Payne, 'The left and the case for "progressive reglobalisation"', *Renewal* 27, no. 3 (2019): 79–95.

[89] On Europe, see Andy Tarrant and Andrea Biondi, 'Labour's programme and EU law', *Renewal* 25, nos 3–4 (2017): 66–89; this formed one subject of a joint seminar on Europe with IPPR. On climate change, see Lisa Nandy, 'What is the significance of the Paris Agreement?', *Renewal* 24, no. 1 (2016): 47–52; Jon Burke and Mika Minio-Paluello, 'Street-level climate politics', *Renewal* 26, no. 3 (2018): 9–20; Polly Billington, 'Climate Change is a Class Issue', *Renewal* 25, no. 2 (2017): 48–52; Franziska Paul, '"No jobs on a dead planet" Energy democracy, public ownership, and union opposition to mega-energy projects', *Renewal* 26, no. 3 (2018): 21–9.

[90] Adam Klug, Emma Rees and James Schneider, 'Momentum: a new kind of politics', *Renewal*, 24, no. 2 (2016): 36–44; Jessica Garland, 'A new politics? The challenges of multi-speed party membership', *Renewal* 24, no. 3 (2016): 40–7; Jon Lawrence, 'Movement politics, the electoral machine, and the "masses": lessons from the early Labour Party', *Renewal* 24, no. 3 (2016): 34–9.

[91] James Stafford and Florence Sutcliffe-Braithwaite, 'If the tide goes out', *Renewal* 27, no. 4 (2019): 5–10.

[92] George Morris, Emily Robinson, James Stafford and Florence Sutcliffe-Braithwaite, 'The end of illusions', *Renewal* 28, no. 1 (2020): 5–10.

Conclusion

In the almost thirty years of its existence, *Renewal* has undergone a transformation that at face value seems strange. In the 1990s it pitched itself as the vanguard of the 'modernizing' project and New Labour, and by the end of the 2010s it provided a space for the elaboration of Corbynomics. But as we have argued, characterizations of *Renewal* in the 1990s as the agent of Blairism obscure as much as they reveal: the journal was committed to soft left 'modernization', but this involved a different – more radical and more expansive – set of concerns than the narrow interpretation offered by Blair. In fact, the continuities in the journal's approach are more striking than the ruptures: underlying the apparent transformation from champion of modernization to critical friend to Corbynism have been a core set of political principles – and an approach to history – which mean that the transformation is not so strange at all.

Renewal was Blairite in that it believed that New Labour offered some of the solutions facing the country, and the party, in the 1990s. But it never believed that electoral success without a guiding vision was desirable, and it sought to expand the horizons of Labour's vision. It did not believe, as some successors to Blairism have persisted in believing, that New Labour was the solution for all time. The renewal of social democracy has always depended on the analysis of the signs of the times. Under Corbyn, the journal sought to suggest new questions and find new answers to problems that simply were not present in the 1990s.

This is not to say that the projects of Blairism and Corbynism were analogous. Blairism was fixated on strategy at the expense of ideas, whereas Corbynism eventually revealed itself to be all ideas and no strategy. Blairism stifled debate within the party and neutered its democratic structures, whereas Corbynism brought with it an explosion of radical thinking and a reanimation – mainly for the worse – of factional politics.

Both projects struggled with the problem of connecting ideas and strategy, something that *Renewal* was founded to solve, but with which it has continued to grapple. Political practitioners, as the story of *Renewal* suggests, have limited interest in small journals of ideas. There are structural reasons for this. *Renewal's* readership remains limited mainly to intellectuals, policy professionals and academics. Yet *Renewal* also shows that a journal wishing to be at the intellectual vanguard can have its uses. The transformation of the left media ecosystem over the past thirty years has brought new media to the fore – think of the role of

Novara in Corbynism, for example. And long-form semi-academic analysis still has a role in providing, as Cook suggested, 'the cutting edge of the advance party of radical thought'. The internet – social media, blogs and new publications and media outlets with a big online presence – has democratized the circulation of ideas, in ways that might be assumed to 'crowd out' a long-form, quarterly publication, but it has also offered new opportunities to publicize the journal. *Renewal*'s somewhat elite organizational form has sometimes seemed at odds, however, with the movement-style politics that has returned since the 1990s – whether Compass or, more recently, Momentum.

Whilst it has been obvious since the days of the LCC that national and party renewal must go hand in hand, the temptation for the Labour leadership to centralize and control the party (and indeed the country) will always be strong. A journal hoping to influence that leadership is not necessarily best placed to persuade it otherwise. But *Renewal* has provided a space for dialogue between factions of the party and a forum for debating, in a spirit of critical friendship, the policies and strategies of successive leaders. Because *Renewal* was not and is not a faction within the party, it has been able to deal with the two extremes of contemporary Labour history, whilst remaining committed to a core set of values. These are its belief in the need for radical action to create a more egalitarian and democratic country, in the need to analyse the social, economic and political context in order to develop a political strategy appropriate to the times; and in the need for pluralist debate. But these dealings have never been straightforward. If it has successfully held open a space for soft left politicians and policy debates,[93] *Renewal*'s relationship to Labour since 1993 has also mirrored that of many party members: initial excitement about each attempt to transform the party, followed by disillusionment. It has yet to truly reckon with the factors that have stood in the way of these successive, if very different, attempts.

---

[93] Sue Goss interview; Paul Thompson email correspondence.

Part Five

16

The Labour Party and aspiration

Jeremy Nuttall

Don't understand aspiration? You've got a bloody cheek to say that. We know more about aspiration than any millionaire's kid who was in the Bullingdon Club. They don't know what aspiration is. They were born there. We had to fight our way up … We understand aspiration. Nobody understands aspiration better than people who come from modest backgrounds and want to build for themselves, and particularly their children, a better future. That is at the centre, the core of Labour's values.[1]

The speaker was an animated Neil Kinnock, former leader of the Labour Party, on Nicky Campbell's BBC Radio Five Live phone-in show on 30 September 2009. He was responding to Campbell's claim that 'the Labour Party never used to understand this word; they do far more now – "aspiration"'.[2] The suggestion hit a raw nerve. Not unfairly, Kinnock pointed out that he was the son of a miner, the first in his family to secure a place at university and a former leader of the opposition. But the subject of aspiration has long been an uneasy, uncertain one for Labour, and, it may be added, its historians.

The immediate context of Kinnock's retort was the reaction to then Labour prime minister Gordon Brown's speech to the party conference the day before. Kinnock was defending the Brown government's economic policy and criticizing the Conservatives' prioritization of an inheritance tax cut for the better-off. But Campbell reminded him that it was this very policy, announced by Shadow Chancellor (and aforementioned 'millionaire's kid') George Osborne in October 2007, that was credited with boosting the Conservatives' poll ratings sufficiently

---

[1] Nicky Campbell's phone-in, BBC Radio 5 Live, 30 September 2009, https://www.youtube.com/watch?v=PGhPvVb3dak&lc=UggLcUoyG13a03gCoAEC (accessed 11 November 2020).

[2] Ibid.

to deter Brown from calling an early general election. Osborne, Campbell posited, had understood people's appetite for aspirational policies in a way that Labour was struggling to do, just as it had in the past.[3]

The past, of course, could not but be interpreted by Kinnock as including his own period as leader, which comprised a significant proportion of those post-1979, but pre-New Labour years, during which the party lost four consecutive general elections, its failure to adapt sufficiently to a rising aspirational social mobility frequently seen as a major underlying cause of its defeats. There was, however, also a more current target for the charge: Brown himself, seen by critics as having lost the wide national, aspirational appeal of his three-time election-winning predecessor, Tony Blair. The following year, Brown would indeed be defeated at the ballot box, bringing to an end Labour's longest (and at the time of writing, last) spell in office.

Yet, despite the consequential nature of the role of aspiration in Labour's past and present, exemplified by the mix it provoked in Kinnock of passionate advocacy with the uneasy awareness of something long unresolved, it is not a theme that has greatly aroused the interest of political scientists and historians. The related subject of affluence has certainly generated work by sociologists. Particular debate has centred around John Goldthorpe and David Lockwood's *The Affluent Worker* studies from 1968 and 1969, based on research in Luton, which disputed that the new or better-off working class had now become either more middle class, or inclined to break its allegiance with the Labour Party.[4] But this debate has surprisingly little influenced the writing of *political* history, with the exception of *The Political Culture of the Left in Affluent Britain*, Lawrence Black's excellent study of the left's struggle to come to terms with affluence in the 1950s and 1960s.[5] Certainly, when compared to the voluminous political history literature on the concept of equality, that of aspiration – and the related ideas of social mobility, opportunity and affluence – have been subject to considerably less attention.[6] The words appear to conjure up associations with liberalism or conservatism, the very consideration of them perceived as akin to diluting a focus on socialist egalitarianism, through distraction by these seemingly less ideologically ambitious, 'meritocratic' ideals.

---

[3] Ibid.

[4] John H. Goldthorpe and David Lockwood, *The Affluent Worker* (Cambridge: CUP, 1968, 1969); Stuart Middleton, '"Affluence" and The Left in Britain, *c.* 1958–1974', *The English Historical Review* 129 (2014): 138, 130–1.

[5] Lawrence Black, *The Political Culture of the Left in Affluent Britain, 1951–64* (Basingstoke: Palgrave Macmillan, 2003). For more scepticism about the arrival of affluence, see Middleton, '"Affluence"'.

[6] For example, Ben Jackson, *Equality and the British Left* (Manchester: MUP, 2007); N. Ellison, *Egalitarian Thought and Labour Politics: Retreating Visions* (London: Routledge, 1994); Geoffrey Foote, *The Labour Party's Political Thought*, 3rd edn (Basingstoke: Macmillan, 1997).

Methodologically, too, because the claim to represent aspiration has been, by its nature, contested across the different parties, writing about it would require the construction of cross-party, or comparative narratives by historians accustomed to charting the fortunes of Labour in isolation.

The subject is well worth pursuing. It is argued here that prior to New Labour, and subsequent to it, the party has suffered in important respects from not taking the issue of aspiration seriously enough, and some of the reasons for this neglect are suggested below. Two further lines of argument must supplement and qualify this. The first is that if New Labour sought, with significant success, to appropriate the mantle of aspiration from the Conservatives, this has not been without its own unresolved intellectual problems, such that New Labour alone does not provide a wholly transferrable blueprint for social democratic aspirationalism in the 2020s. Secondly, whilst it is right in part to identify aspiration as a recurring historical and contemporary *problem* for Labour, one might be just as struck by the party's ability, at certain crucial junctures, to embrace it more constructively, without undermining its own, more recognizably social democratic ideals. Indeed, it has been Labour's periodic ability to forge an agenda *combining* an appeal to equity and fairness with a zeitgeist-capturing vision of aspirational dynamism that has – as in 1945, 1964 and 1997 – characterized its moments of greatest success, both electoral and governmental, and it has the potential to do so again.

The Labour Party has been out of power for much of its existence, more so than the Conservatives, and more than, for instance, either the American Democrats, or the Victorian-era Liberal Party. For prolonged periods, in the 1920s and 1930s, again in the 1950s, for much of the 1980s and 1990s, and from 2010 onwards, the party experienced sustained periods in opposition. The reasons for this are complex and various, but historians have pointed to one important and enduring factor being Labour's difficulty in sustaining an aspirational cross-class appeal, amidst an evolving social context of rising standards of living, within which class loyalties became increasingly fluid over the course of the century. Laura Beers has probed the tensions within the party over the first half-century of its existence after 1900, between its desire on the one hand to appeal as a broadly based national, moderate, cross-class and even (though less completely) cross-gender party – an approach certainly favoured by one of its most influential early leaders, Ramsay MacDonald – and on the other its function as a sectional interest group of the organized, male manual working class.[7]

[7] Laura Beers, *Your Britain. Media and the Making of the Labour Party* (Cambridge, MA: HUP, 2010).

By the 1950s, as Black has shown, both Hugh Gaitskell and Aneurin Bevan, though leaders of fiercely rival factions within the party, had a tendency to dismiss the emerging new domestic consumer goods as 'gadgets', symbolizing a broader socialist disengagement from the rapidly emerging societal 'affluence'.[8] Affluence was seen by many in the party as principally a threat, whether because of its creation via the capitalist system, or the supposedly morally corrosive effect of its glossy superficiality. Black perceives this as a missed opportunity, suggesting that socialists could have appropriated affluence by defining it in more positive, and, moreover, in potentially more socially co-operative and progressive terms. Instead, 'the left contrived to alienate itself from affluence by describing it so unfavourably'.[9] In contrast, as Ball and Holliday have explored, the otherwise seemingly elite-orientated Conservatives in fact proved surprisingly adept at adjusting to the heightened twentieth-century expectations of social mobility, and thus 'made the advent of democracy an opportunity rather than a peril'.[10]

Labour's opponents have certainly repeatedly levelled the charge that, in its preoccupation with equalizing economic and educational systems and resources, it lacks an understanding of the desire of individuals, in an actually existing society of unequal abilities, efforts and character attributes, to excel, make their own way or 'get on'. Labour had a habit of 'attributing all existing evils to Capitalism', claimed the Liberal Party in 1929, neglecting that progress relied on individual 'spirit'.[11] For the leading Liberal economist John Maynard Keynes, Labour had to 'put on an appearance of being against anyone who is … more skilful, more industrious, more thrifty than the average'.[12] 'Labour is against spreading … freedoms and choice to all our people', Margaret Thatcher later claimed. 'Labour's policies are a vote of no confidence in the ability of British people to manage their own affairs'.[13]

Moreover, the more perceptive within Labour itself were alive to this danger. Reflecting on the new affluence of the 1960s and 1970s, Labour's Chancellor in the 1974–9 government, Denis Healey observed that 'class feeling was receding. Living standards had risen substantially, and most of the British people now felt

[8] Black, *Affluent Britain*, 27–8.
[9] Ibid., 191.
[10] Stuart Ball and Ian Holliday, 'Mass Conservatism: An Introduction', in Ball and Holliday (eds), *Mass Conservatism. The Conservatives and The Public Since The 1880s* (London: Routledge, 2002), 2, 12.
[11] British Library of Political and Economic Science, London, Liberal Party Papers, 15/1, 154, Liberal Candidates' Handbook, 1929; 15/3, 6, Speakers' Notes, 1931.
[12] King's College, Cambridge, Keynes Papers, PS/4, Keynes, Liberal Summer School, 3 August 1929.
[13] Margaret Thatcher Foundation website, speech, House of Commons, 22 November 1990, https://www.margaretthatcher.org/document/108256 (accessed 18 September 2020).

that they had something to conserve; so self-interest was no longer sufficient by itself to promote greater equality.'[14] Nor was it exclusively the 'modernizing' right or revisionists who noticed such trends. Just as New Left thinkers in the 1960s, through their 'cultural turn', took affluence seriously as a new force shaping popular political and cultural outlooks, so one of the leading thinkers on the 'soft left' in the 1980s, Bryan Gould sought to revisit the relationship between *Socialism and Freedom* in 1985.[15] There was a danger, Gould warned, that the Conservatives, through their promotion of council house sales, entrepreneurship and share ownership were now seen as 'the liberator of working-class ambitions'. He suggested that 'Labour could not hope to be re-elected if we allowed ourselves to be seen as a party which stopped people from doing things, which prevented them from realising their aspirations.'[16]

Yet, if the party in the 1980s and early 1990s, under Kinnock's often skilful leadership, clawed its way back to a position of competence and respectability, the final product was in some ways more similar to a variant of 1950s Croslandite revisionism (symbolized by the party's egalitarian deputy leader Roy Hattersley) than an engagement with the different, heightened aspirational culture of the late twentieth century. Kinnock's own treatment of the subject of aspiration exhibited the double-sidedness with which this chapter began: an awareness that some kind of intellectual update *needed* to happen, but an uneasy vagueness about whether it really could or should. Hence, the brevity and haziness of his conclusion, in a 1986 volume of speeches, that 'our beliefs exist to promote upward mobility of whole countries and, by definition, the individuals within those countries'.[17]

If Labour had (and has) a problem with aspiration, it begs the question why. Class was one important factor. There was consistently a sense that aspiration and affluence were somehow 'Other', whether materially beyond reach, from the point of view of the party's labourist working-class culture, or ideologically unpalatable, in the eyes of its middle-class intellectuals. Hence, the caricatures of uniformly malign capitalists, evident, for instance in leading Fabian Sidney Webb's 1923 denunciation of the 'sinister dominance ... of the private interests of the owners of great masses of wealth'.[18] The organized working-class trade union movement reached the peak of its power in the 1970s, just at the moment – unfortunately for Labour – when that expanding newly middle-class

[14] Denis Healey, *The Time of My Life* (London: Michael Joseph, 1990), 346.
[15] Bryan Gould, *Socialism and Freedom* (London: Macmillan, 1985).
[16] Bryan Gould, *Goodbye To All That* (London: Macmillan, 1995), 152.
[17] Neil Kinnock, *Making Our Way* (Oxford: Wiley-Blackwell, 1986), 194.
[18] Sidney Webb, *The Labour Party on The Threshold*, Fabian Tract 207 (1923), 9.

culture of surplus income, Spanish package holidays, televisions and freezers began to have substantial political heft. This was a growing culture of affluent individualism which long predated Mrs Thatcher's premiership and operated in part independently of it. In this sense, as Ewen Green observed, 'Thatcher was a creature of her time and not the creator of it'.[19]

Moreover, as recent research by Emily Robinson and others has shown, this affluent 'individualism' had liberating, liberal and indeed egalitarian implications as much as more exclusively self-orientated material ones.[20] An imaginative social democratic party might well have sought to harness these implications towards progressive ends, by articulating a vision of how a generous welfare state had been, and could continue to be, an enabler of aspirational social mobility. Yet, the six aims listed in the party's famously left-wing February 1974 manifesto, *Let Us Work Together*, included the promise of a 'fundamental and irreversible shift in the balance of power and wealth in favour of working people and their families', and to 'eliminate poverty', without making any mention of the socially mobile, or those who sat on the cusp between working- and middle-class status.[21]

Connected to class was a long-standing mistrust amongst many in Labour and the wider progressive intelligentsia of that so archetypal development of twentieth-century society, the spread of suburbia. Within this hostility, one witnesses a curious cocktail of social status envy, elitist snobbery and intellectual disdain. It extended to the outlooks of early-century New Liberal intellectuals. 'Politically it [suburbia] is a greater burden on the nation than the slum', wrote Leonard Hobhouse in 1904, lamenting the electoral success of villa Conservatism under Lord Salisbury, those 'feverish [suburban] hordes', agreed fellow Liberal Charles Masterman.[22] As John Carey has shown, this echoed a wider British (including left-wing) intellectual disdain for the emerging democratic, commercial, middle-brow culture, the likes of T. S. Eliot, D. H. Lawrence and George Orwell perceiving the people, in Carey's words, as essentially 'dead' of mind: 'the vulgar, trivial working millions, wallowing in newsprint'.[23]

---

[19] Ewen Henry Harvey Green, *Thatcher* (London: Bloomsbury Academic 2006), 196.

[20] Emily Robinson, Camilla Schofield, Florence Sutcliffe-Braithwaite and Natalie Tomlinson, 'Telling Stories About Post-War Britain: Popular Individualism and the "Crisis" of the 1970s', *Twentieth Century British History* 28 (2017): 268–304.

[21] *Let Us Work Together*, Labour Party General Election Manifesto, February 1974.

[22] Leonard Trelawney Hobhouse, *Democracy and Reaction* (New York: Barnes & Noble Books, 1973), 68; C. F. G. Masterman, *The Condition of England* (London: Faber & Faber, 2008; first published in 1909), 58.

[23] John Carey, *The Intellectuals and the Masses: Pride and Prejudice amongst the Literary Intelligentsia, 1880–1939* (London: Faber & Faber, 1992), 9–11. On this see also D. L. LeMahieu, *A Culture For Democracy: Mass Communication and the Cultivated Mind in Britain Between The Wars* (Oxford: Clarendon Press, 1988), 2–3.

Similar sentiments were later apparent in the left-wing film director Mike Leigh's iconic social commentary play, *Abigail's Party*, first televised in 1977, which movingly, humorously, alarmingly, yet also somewhat mockingly, portrayed the insecurities, snobbery and pretentiousness of the newly emerging middle-class world of home-owners, computer-operators and estate agents. Almost entirely absent from this otherwise powerful drama was any sense of countervailing suburban virtues, of people who had striven to rise. As Mark Clapson has illustrated, 'the suburban aspiration' has frequently operated as a long-term mobilizer of social mobility across class and ethnic divides.[24] Those who exhibited and pursued it had, in many ways, been Harold Wilson's people a decade before, indeed in some respects he was one of them himself. But many of them were about to relocate politically, just as they had socially and geographically.

To them, aspiration was a mindset as much as a material outcome. That aspiration spoke of the importance of character as much as social structures still further heightened its uncomfortableness to Labour, which was inclined to reduce problems to socioeconomic causation. 'At the back' of other contests over power, wrote even the relatively mainstream party leader Clement Attlee in 1937, has been 'the desire to use that power for economic ends'.[25] This is not to downplay the value of the social democratic insight that an emphasis on individual initiative and character was too often deployed by the political right as an excuse for preserving social disadvantage, and as a distraction from such disadvantage. As Orwell observed in 1939, too often the demand that ordinary people show 'a "change of heart" is in fact the alibi of people who do not wish to endanger the *status quo*'.[26] But there were arguably equal dangers for the left in going to the opposite extreme, in dismissing reference to individual endeavour and aspiration altogether, as nothing more than a cover for the legitimization of rampant free markets. In this mode, one contribution to a pamphlet published by the new left-wing think tank *Class* in 2015 went so far as to title itself 'Against Aspiration', on the grounds that 'aspiration is a rhetorical device that seeks to whitewash a neoliberal economic and political project and the staggering inequalities it produces'.[27] Increasingly, historians are developing more pluralist accounts of the causation and remedy of social inequalities, in which aspiration,

---

[24] Mark Clapson, 'The Suburban Aspiration in England Since 1919', *Contemporary British History* 14 (2000): 151–74.

[25] Clement Richard Attlee, *The Labour Party in Perspective – and Twelve Years Later* (London: Victor Gollancz, 1949), 33.

[26] George Orwell, essay, 'Charles Dickens', 1939, in Sonia Orwell and Ian Angus (eds), *The Collected Essays, Journalism and Letters of George Orwell*, vol. 1 (London: Secker & Warburg, 1968), 427, 445.

[27] Imogen Tyler and Bruce Bennett, 'Against Aspiration', in *What is Aspiration?: How Progressives Should Respond* (London: CLASS, August 2015), 6.

and the shortage of it reflect a complex mix of economic, educational and psychological factors, and in which the efforts of individuals and governments *both* matter to the achievement of progress.[28]

Much of the above fostered on the left a strain of pessimism about contemporary societal trends, a further psychological explanation for its reluctance to speak of aspiration and affluence. This reading of contemporary social history in at times one-dimensionally negative terms intellectually underappreciated the subtle mix of social advances alongside continuing injustices often at play in modern British society. Moreover, it also risked failing to reap the electoral dividends to a progressive party of appearing optimistic, constructive and forward-looking, as both Harold Wilson and Tony Blair, in their different ways, amply demonstrated. The perennial temptation of Labour figures was to look critically on even the most seemingly glorious of the party's own periods in office, as in the ever sceptical intellectual Bevanite Richard Crossman's comment, writing of the 1945–51 Attlee government, on 'how great were its failures', and 'how much further it might have taken us towards a true Socialist welfare state'.[29] Even Wilson himself later described his own 1964–70 government as marked by 'disappointment after disappointment'.[30] Robin Cook reflected thoughtfully and self-warningly in his 2004 memoirs on how 'leftist analysis by tradition tends to the gloomy ... end of the spectrum'.[31] As Andrew Hindmoor has recently explored, this pessimism is especially marked in relation to Labour's self-appraisals of the most recent decades in its, and the country's history, which could be 'remorselessly bleak and miserabilist', portraying a picture of 'dizzying levels of inequality, social decay, rampant individualism'.[32] Such a starkly negative portrait is, Hindmoor argues, both historically 'wrong and self-harming'.[33]

If Labour's wariness of the concept of aspiration stems from the above combination of class-based thinking, anti-suburbanism, economic reductionism and psychological pessimism, these were accompanied at certain points by an intellectual one-dimensionality, an inclination to see the polarities in ideological

---

[28] See Jeremy Nuttall, 'The Persistence of Character in Twentieth-Century British Politics', *Journal of Contemporary History* (2020), https://journals.sagepub.com/doi/10.1177/0022009420922584 (accessed 20 September 2021); J. Nuttall, *Psychological Socialism. The Labour Party and Qualities of Mind and Character, 1931–The Present* (Manchester: MUP, 2006).

[29] Richard Howard Stafford Crossman, *The New Statesman*, 28 November 1959.

[30] Harold Wilson, *The Labour Government 1964–70* (London: Weidenfeld & Nicolson and Michael Joseph, 1971), 18.

[31] Robin Cook, *The Point of Departure* (London: Simon & Schuster UK, 2004), 375.

[32] Andrew Hindmoor, *What's Left Now? The History and Future of Social Democracy* (Oxford: OUP, 2018), 2.

[33] Ibid.

objectives, to posit a desire for affluence and a concern about poverty as zero-sum alternatives, to pit a belief in meritocracy against a commitment to egalitarianism. Here, the sociologist and Labour activist Michael Young's highly influential *The Rise of The Meritocracy* (1958) is representative. In exposing with great persuasiveness the problems of a wholly meritocratic, competitive social system, it risked the appearance of condemning aspirational and acquisitive impulses altogether.[34]

In its exposing and challenging, from 1994, of many of these increasingly redundant obstacles to Labour adopting a more engaged and nuanced approach to the subject of aspiration, 'New Labour' – which was in fact a rather broad and diverse coalition within the party in those early years – deserves significant credit. Now, the suburban middle class were once again reclaimed as 'our people', as Blair told the party's 1995 conference.[35] Ideologically, the party's new third way, for all that it left intellectually unresolved, did, judged in the context of its time, have the considerable merit of moving beyond some of the starkest binary false intellectual choices that had characterized politics in the 1970s and 1980s. Aspiration could now at least be spoken of as something with the potential to be in *harmony* with social conscience and well-funded public services. Or, as Blair put it, 'you can be successful and care'.[36]

This ideological updating, which is too often and easily sneered at in its entirety, produced tangible benefits. The construction of an agenda for change that was purposeful, yet credible attracted a coalition of working- and middle-class support that was both broad and deep enough to sustain the party in power for thirteen years, by far its longest period in government. This allowed the party to implement a range of long-awaited social improvements, including a re-funding of the public realm, the alleviation of poverty, social liberalization and some measure of political decentralization. It has also significantly altered the electoral expectation levels of both major parties, albeit that Labour's losing habit has been resumed since 2010. It is too rarely observed that the Conservatives have in fact won only one really substantial electoral majority since 1987 (that in 2019), its grip on the archetypal aspirational or floating voter, now much less automatic and secure than it had been in either the 1950s or 1980s.

Yet, the party has struggled since 2010 to formulate a historically balanced and internally consensual appraisal of this, its own most recent period in

---

[34] Michael Young, *The Rise of The Meritocracy 1870–2033* (London: Penguin, 1958), 121, 135.

[35] Tony Blair, Labour Party Conference speech, 3 October 1995.

[36] Tony Blair, *A Journey* (London: Hutchinson, 2010), 8.

government. Too often, these years have been dismissed as little more than an extension of Thatcherism, seen as all the more insidious for their dressing in Labour clothes. Within this, a measured assessment of the continuities and discontinuities with 1980s policy is lost. As Ben Jackson has recently argued, 'labelling recent British political discourse as unvarnished "neo-liberalism" ... simplifies a more complicated picture'.[37] This lack of a sense of proportion in engaging with the past reflected itself, as it so often does, in an uncertainty within the party about what should come after New Labour. The problematic nature of this loss of self-confidence was highlighted by deputy leader Tom Watson in his 2016 party conference speech, which was widely seen as a rallying call to 'moderates' across the party. He warned delegates that 'trashing our own record is not the way to enhance our brand'.[38] But by this stage many in the party now echoed Corbyn's shadow chancellor John McDonnell's description in 2015 of 'this drivel' of 'all the old Blairite mantras that Labour has failed to be a party of aspiration, to occupy the middle ground and appeal to middle England'.[39]

However, if the above suggests that the newly ascendant Corbynite left of the party did not engage with the issue of aspiration sufficiently seriously, it should no less be noted that what remained of the Blairite right of the party were simultaneously struggling to be either willing or able to update their own conception of aspirational politics from its heyday in the 1990s and early 2000s. Indeed, it is arguable that whilst much attention is rightly paid to the party's loss of both intellectual dynamism and electoral appeal in the thirteen years after Blair departed from Downing Street in 2007, both of these declines had already begun to set in under the later Blair himself. In two particular respects, the powerful intellectual synthesis between aspiration and social conscience which Blair had earlier himself so nurtured was both unravelling and failing to evolve.

Firstly, although Blair, together with Gordon Brown had revitalized the public services with new resources, he became increasingly loathe to speak positively of an ethic of public service. He preferred now instead to advocate 'getting business ideas into public service practice'.[40] If this sat uneasily with his party (and Blair, ultimately fatally, too often forgot that whilst Labour leaders needed to think more of the country, they could not afford to wholly alienate their own party base), it also seemed strangely at odds with the very notion of a 'balance'

[37] Ben Jackson, 'Currents of Neo-Liberalism: British Political Ideologies and the New Right, c.1955–1979', *English Historical Review* 131 (2016): 826.

[38] Tom Watson, *Speech to Labour Party Conference*, 27 September 2016.

[39] John McDonnell, *Guardian*, 12 May 2015.

[40] Blair, *Journey*, 115, 119, 284, 686.

between state and market which lay behind his own third way. Here, by the end, it appeared, was not balance, but an over-correction of Labour's earlier statist excesses in favour of an uncritical laudation of competitive business zeal. In a sense, Blair had slipped into the very reductionist one-dimensionality he had so critiqued in 'Old Labour'.

Secondly, if this represented a loss of that intellectual equilibrium in support for the structures of both market *and* state, that mix of individual initiative and collective support which was needed to sustain an agenda of both equity and aspiration, it also constituted a loss in the definition of aspiration as a progressive *psychology*. If the earlier assumption had been that aspiration (although its meaning was never very systematically explored) was an essentially benign, even gentle motivational force, in which individuals could do well for themselves and their families, whilst also giving support to a more decent, liberal and equitable society, it now seemed to be defined in more competitive, macho and even aggressive terms. Blair's support for all that was 'modern', dynamic, innovative and thrusting led him, by his own intriguing admission, to a position where 'I sometimes underestimated the ruthlessness and amorality that can go with moneymaking'.[41] It was an outlook that also chimed with his increasing advocacy of what he would later term a 'muscular centrism', as evidenced by both British involvement in the Iraq War, and the way in which his later prime ministerial pronouncements became so dominated with the wider 'war on terror'.[42]

Both the ideological and the psychological implications of this for understandings of what a politics of aspiration meant are especially worthy of note, because they replicated a similar pattern in the approach, in the 1980s, of the non-Conservative political figure then most expressive of an aspirational agenda, David Owen. Initially, he, along with Roy Jenkins, through the creation in 1981 of the breakaway Social Democratic Party, had done much to promote a reinvigorated, cross-class progressive appeal designed to advance the relief of poverty and the furtherance of affluence alike. Jenkins, a figure once neglected by historians, perhaps due to his multiple political homes, but now the subject of several new studies, explained in 1981 that his new party wanted 'the support of all those whose aim in life is to get on, not hold on to what they've got', yet 'who believe that in getting on, they are … benefiting the community as a whole'.[43] Yet,

---

[41] Ibid., 115.

[42] Quoted in BBC News report, 22 March 2016.

[43] Bodleian Library, Oxford, Jenkins Papers, 318, speech, London, 24 June 1981. On Jenkins, see Jeremy Nuttall, 'Roy Jenkins and The Politics of Radical Moderation', *History* 104 (October 2019): 677–709; John Campbell, *Roy Jenkins. A Well-Rounded Life* (London: Jonathan Cape, 2014).

foreshadowing the evolution of the later Blair, when Owen assumed the party leadership himself in 1983, the ideological balance increasingly seemed to tilt rightwards in both policy and style, with markets, competition and combative party management foregrounded over the support for collective provision and care, to which the party still remained formally committed. Owen's emphasis was on 'financial rewards which stimulate people to innovate, experiment'.[44] Just as Blair increasingly privileged the mentality of muscularity, Owen wanted a political psychology that was 'distinct, tough, vital'.[45] Thus, as Dean Blackburn has explored, whilst initially generating fresh social democratic ideas for responding to the challenge of Thatcherism with a new synthesis of social justice with aspiration, by the end 'Owen glossed over ... how to pair up enthusiasm for the free market with concern for fellowship'.[46]

The importance of figures like Jenkins, Owen and Blair, and their often-innovative ideas in relation to aspiration reminds us that Labour, and wider progressive history has as much been shaped by varying conceptions of the ideological 'centre' as by the left. This centre now merits more explicit and systematic attention by political historians, so as better to understand both its strengths and its limitations.[47] As the above has sought to illustrate, the centre in the 1980s, 1990s and 2000s was not without its intellectual shortcomings, and the contemporary centre (across parties) has been slow to acknowledge and address these. It is not clear that centrist, third way thinking, in the years since New Labour, has yet managed, any more than Corbynism, to forge a fully coherent new progressive vision fit for the 2020s. This charge holds true of centrism within Labour circles, as well as of the Liberal Democrats and post-Cameronite One Nation Conservatives, both of the latter of which presently appear in a notably weakened state.

Blair himself continues to be in many ways the most intellectually fertile spokesperson for this centrist tradition, offering powerful advocacy against Brexit, and more widely. Speaking at a major event at King's College London in February 2020 to discuss Labour's past and present, he emphasized the importance of fresh thinking with 'big questions being posed'. It was still possible, he believed, to be idealistic, whilst connecting with people's real

---

[44] David Owen, *Face The Future* (Oxford: OUP, 1981), xix.

[45] David Owen, *Time To Declare* (London: Michael Joseph, 1992), 585, 593.

[46] Dean Blackburn, 'Facing The Future? David Owen and Social Democracy in the 1980s and Beyond', *Parliamentary Affairs* 64 (2011): 644.

[47] On the centre, see Jeremy Nuttall, 'The Centre in British Politics Since 1906', *Historical Research* 93 (May 2020): 353–78.

desires and lives: 'you can be clear and radical and still in the centre'.[48] Moreover, progressivism was now something broader than just Labour. Blair thought it an open question whether the present non-Conservative party structures would survive. Thus, progressive politics should be 'positioning itself absolutely in the future, building a broad alliance of people'.[49] He attached particular importance to developing new policies to chime with the 'technology revolution', which was now 'the biggest thing' in politics. 'It's the biggest opportunity, it's the biggest challenge, it's the biggest route to creating a different type of society and a better one' and symbolized the need for progressive politicians to proceed in a 'forward and modern-orientated way'.[50]

Here, Blair seemed to replicate both the virtues and the vices of the New Labour past, and of the contemporary British centre as a whole. It remained constructive, optimistic and intellectually creative in its desire to blend values with real world realities. Yet, it was simultaneously hazy on ultimate ideals, too content, perhaps, to see 'modernity' itself as a sufficient answer, too comprehensively seduced by modernity's glossy accessories (the market, technology) to offer a vision of how to mould it to progressive ends. Blair continued to denounce the spectre of 'old-style collectivism' in a way which now seemed a little lazily dated. What was the new style collective spirit that he *favoured* as distinct from opposed?[51]

The challenge now, therefore, may be for the party to explore new understandings of aspirational politics which move on from both the under-appreciation of aspiration apparent before New Labour, and the over-esteem of a too narrowly individualistic, macho definition of it into which New Labour later degenerated. If that points to a new aspirational politics for new times, what are the prospects and precedents for the Labour Party, and perhaps the wider progressive movement in Britain, being able to adapt to construct such a vision, and what are some of the policies which might ignite it?

History suggests there may be grounds for optimism. For whilst it certainly shows Labour frequently struggling to acknowledge and engage with affluence, modernity and aspiration, and thus to grasp the chance to shape their evolution for its own purposes, a historical observer might be just as struck by the consistency with which the party, and indeed wider progressive politics *has* risen to this challenge at those most pivotal moments, when the country has been

---

[48] '120 Years of The Labour Party: in Conversation with Tony Blair', King's College London, 20 February 2020.
[49] Ibid.
[50] Ibid.
[51] Ibid.

most ready for, and open to, social change. In 1906, in the case of the Liberal Party, then in 1945, 1964 and 1997, through Labour, election victories for the leading progressive party (in three out of the four cases large ones) have been followed by governments implementing substantial reforms. These staging posts are enough to significantly qualify, although not entirely to nullify, the much-employed characterization of the twentieth century as a 'Conservative century'. This is even more the case given that, as the proponent of the term Anthony Seldon himself points out, much of the Conservatives' undoubted *electoral* success depended on substantial *intellectual* borrowing from the new socioeconomic settlements that 1906, 1945, 1964 and 1997 embedded.[52]

Moreover, these reforming governments all managed to build both a rhetorical message and a policy agenda that made them seem more architects of a national vision of fairness and opportunity than sectionalist, class-based pursuers of their own interest, or ideological dogmatists. All, in their way, and by the standards of their day, *blended* meritocratic with egalitarian-collectivist impulses and, at least for a time, harnessed the possibilities of uniting a diverse electoral coalition behind the coming together of these objectives, rather than obsessing with the albeit real elements of long-term intellectual tension between them. In the early-century New Liberalism which intellectually underpinned the Liberal administrations, the oft-cited tension between a 'moral' agenda of encouraging individual initiative and character, and a 'mechanical' one, emphasizing the need for new institutions to provide collective welfare, was being superseded by a happy marriage of the two, which avoided the excesses of either individualism or statism. As its leading advocate Hobhouse put it in his seminal *Liberalism* (1911), it is 'the function of the State [is] to secure the conditions upon which mind and character may develop themselves'. Progress was 'not a matter of mechanical contrivance, but of the liberation of living spiritual energy', in which 'the generality of men and women are not only passive recipients but practical contributors'.[53]

The 1945–51 Labour government grafted socialism onto this New Liberal outlook, symbolized by its implementation of the Liberal William Beveridge's landmark 1942 report on social insurance and the maintenance of its belief in a balance between individual responsibility and social provision. Individual contributions were an important part of the enhanced national insurance

---

[52] Anthony Seldon, 'Conservative Century', in Anthony Seldon and Stuart Ball (eds), *Conservative Century* (Oxford: OUP, 1994), 17.

[53] Leonard Trelawney Hobhouse, *Liberalism* (Oxford: OUP, 1964; first published in 1911), 65–6, 72–3, 83.

schemes, but this was balanced by a free-to-all non-contributory National Health Service, funded out of general taxation. There was now a commitment to full employment. But the educational system retained a firmly meritocratic ethos, with the retention of grammar schools, seen by some leading Labour figures of this generation as a valuable ladder of opportunity for the most talented working-class children. Recognizing its 'twin purposes' of addressing social inequality *and* generating a strong economy, the party in this era insisted on its commitment to the aspirational: 'we shall encourage those who earn their money by hard work and ability'.[54]

Such an ethos was developed further by the intellectual Labour revisionists of the 1950s, notably Anthony Crosland, in his *The Future of Socialism* (1956), and Roy Jenkins, who, seeing the party lose electoral ground to the Conservative prime minister Harold Macmillan's 'never had it so good' appeal to affluent consumerism and expanding home ownership in the 1950s, recommended that it respond positively to these heightened aspirations. Following Labour's third consecutive general election defeat in 1959, Jenkins warned colleagues that they needed to address 'a misplaced feeling that the Labour Party is a narrow class Party, representing only the working class, and it is therefore natural for those who are beginning to do well in life to move away from it'.[55]

Jenkins would later serve as Chancellor in the second half of Wilson's 1964–70 Labour government, and the broad thrust of the revisionist approach on this issue was adopted by Wilson, albeit that he dressed his political realism in Bevanite clothes. An astute soother of party (and national) divides, Wilson skilfully bridged the duality pulling at him, egalitarian socialism and economic planning on the one hand, the wider 1960s mood for meritocratic scientific, technological and cultural modernization on the other, presenting them as mutually reinforcing. Stressing, in his speech to the party conference in Blackpool in September 1965, that his 'new Britain will be a Britain of opportunity', Wilson explained that this would both combat inequalities *and* enable the 'keen and thrusting' to advance.[56] Central to this double mission was education, its considerably enhanced funding and the rapid expansion of higher education, epitomizing that social democratic aspirationalism (replicated under Blair) in which the extension of opportunity through collective provision was expected to

---

[54] Labour Party manifesto, 1955, in Frederick Walter Scott Craig (ed.), *British General Election Manifestos 1900–1974* (London: Macmillan, 1975), 206.

[55] Jenkins Papers, 337, Fabian Society Lecture, 4 November 1959.

[56] Harold Wilson's speech at the Labour Party Conference, Blackpool, 28 September 1965, in Harold Wilson, *Purpose in Power* (London: Weidenfeld & Nicolson, 1964), 134, 150.

be matched by the individual responsibility of pupils and students to seize those opportunities.

History therefore shows complexity and contradictions in Labour's approach to aspiration, neglectful and wary of it, yet also at critical junctures capable of defining it in imaginative and progressively purposeful ways. Labour's character has been enduringly dual: sectionalist, bound by the constraints of at times outdated assumptions and class loyalties, yet repeatedly managing to emerge from this, usually after a period of defeat, internal combat, then renewed self-awareness, with an in many ways remarkably creative and generous-spirited cross-class, national vision and appeal. Ultimately, as David Cannadine has written of both the major British political parties across the twentieth century, Labour was 'transcending the division of society, even as in other ways they embodied it'.[57]

But if history demonstrates that the underlying political and intellectual capacity is there in Labour, will the next few years prove host to another of those critical phases where it develops an updated agenda, at once egalitarian and aspirational, and to inspire the breadth of support to return it to power? There appear three main contemporary challenges for such an outcome to occur. Firstly, Labour itself needs to regain unity and composure. Sir Keir Starmer, elected leader in April 2020, has restored its reputation for competence. He has also spoken of the importance of 'opportunity' and a forgotten societal middle.[58]

Secondly, there is the intellectual challenge of translating this into an aspirational policy agenda for the 2020s. This would likely foreground education, a less prominent subject in recent elections, but the prioritization of which has tended to be a signifier of progressive revival, as in 1964 and 1997. Education symbolizes more than the pursuit of a national re-skilling to reinvigorate the economy. At its deepest, it offers the promise of national uplift, on both an intellectual and a moral plane, individual and national aspiration combined. The definition of education should, however, broaden, encompassing esteem also for diverse forms of vocational education, apprenticeships and lifelong learning. Long-neglected policy areas, notably housing, should be newly prioritized. There is no contradiction between a reinvigorated agenda of home ownership, with active intervention to enable younger people to join the property ladder, *and* a much-enhanced social housing safety net. Both power and responsibility

[57] David Cannadine, *Class in Britain* (London: Penguin, 2000), 150.
[58] Channel 4, Labour leadership debate, 17 February 2020.

for economic and political decision-making must be imaginatively redistributed away from London.

Such a newly vitalized progressive policy agenda, more sensitive to recent critiques of globalization, the breakaway 'super-rich' and the 'left-behinds', is also essential, thirdly, to counter the problem that, as Eatwell and Goodwin have charted, 'across much of the West … populism is now a serious force'.[59] Nationalism and anti-immigrant feeling have intensified. Labour, with its increasingly London metropolitan associations, ponders how simultaneously to recover support from the diversely disaffected trio of Scotland, middle England and the deindustrialized North.

If recent years have shown the danger in complacently underestimating populism, there are, however, equal dangers in displaying excessive reverence for it, or overestimating its hegemony and durability, a danger which feeds on the left's aforementioned tendency to a periodic fashionable political pessimism. Joe Biden's victory in the November 2020 American presidential election, and its heralding of the end of the Trump administration, is an event which many would have been considered inconceivable only a year ago. Trump's support in the 'rust belt' states proved far from unreachable for the Democrats, just as the Conservatives' new 'blue wall' in northern England is not uniform, nor necessarily permanently politically reattached. If modern British history shows anything, it is that an aspirational agenda, generously and progressively defined, and articulated by convincing leadership, has an appeal which bridges many of the apparently immutable divides, between young and old, city and small town, and even nations.

That, indeed, is the final historical insight that the politics of aspiration offers. It is that the people, the organic character of society as a whole ultimately shape the course of political history, not simply the machinations of parties and their leaders. As Steven Fielding's insightful research has shown, at issue in politics, in the end, is as much the very national spirit as the specifics of more material policy agendas, and that popular spirit (or its absence) operates as either a real-world constraint, or an essential positive supporting force for what progressive governments can achieve.[60] If the history of British election results indicates that the people have often felt Labour fell short of representing their aspirations, Labour has frequently reciprocated, through a certain sense of disappointment

[59] Roger Eatwell and Matthew Goodwin, *National Populism* (London: Pelican, 2018), vii.

[60] Steven Fielding, Peter Thompson and Nick Tiratsoo, *'England Arise!': The Labour Party and Popular Politics in 1940s Britain* (Manchester: MUP, 1995).

in the perceived lack of idealism of the citizenry. Yet, as Jon Lawrence's recent work on the mix of popular sentiments of community and individualism in the country since the Second World War suggests, we should not underestimate the sophistication of the ways in which, both in the 1940s and since, people have sought 'a healthy balance between self and society'.[61] As the next stage of that evolution of the national character plays out in the coming years, a thoughtful aspirational politics could be well placed to harness it.

---

[61] Jon Lawrence, *Me, Me, Me? The Search for Community in Post-War England* (Oxford: OUP, 2019), 234.

17

Conclusion: Shaping Labour's future

Nick Thomas-Symonds

'The promise that brought us all into politics – to change the country for the better – is pointless if all we can do is object to endless Tory governments.'[1] With these words, spoken in Doncaster in September 2020, Sir Keir Starmer delivered the first leader's speech to a Labour Party conference in Yorkshire since Harold Wilson in Scarborough in October 1967. There was, as Starmer noted, something about his predecessor's speech that he wanted to emulate: Wilson's address was that of a prime minister who had been in office for three years. The debate about the Labour Party's history has to be an argument about how it forms governments that can transform people's lives. As Aneurin Bevan put it: 'The language of priorities is the religion of Socialism ... The argument is about power ... because only by the possession of power can you get the priorities correct.'[2]

As a biographer of Bevan, and Clement Attlee, with a book on Harold Wilson to come, I have spent many hours immersed in the achievements, trials and challenges of transformative Labour governments. What all Labour reformers have in common is a determination to take the experiences and injustices they have witnessed in communities and to offer solutions in a programme for government that could deliver meaningful change. Barbara Castle's 1970 Equal Pay Act, for example, was a response to the sewing machinists who made car seat covers at Ford's Dagenham plant who had stopped work after a pay regrading favouring male workers.

This collection, as its editor Nathan Yeowell set out in his introduction, aims to 'provide fresh perspective on the long-term effects and significance of Labour's

---

[1] Full text of Keir Starmer's speech at Labour Connected, 22 September 2020, https://labour.org.uk/press/full-text-of-keir-starmers-speech-at-labour-connected/ (accessed 13 September 2021).

[2] Report of the 48th Annual Conference (London: Labour Party, 1949), 172.

role as one of the two main parties of state'. History is always a contested space, but there are sobering facts about Labour history that do not lend themselves to any debate at all. They are a stark reality. Since the party became the official opposition at Westminster in 1922, there have been twenty-five general elections. The party has only triumphed in ten of them. Even fewer, eight, have been won with an overall majority, and only five of those have been higher than single figures. In 2022, Labour will mark a century as the Conservatives' principal competitor for power in British politics, yet it will only have been in government on its own, or in coalition, for thirty-five of those years.

This book divides Labour Party history into three periods. The first began on a Tuesday at the turn of the century: on 27 February 1900, 129 delegates met at the Memorial Hall on Farringdon Street in London and formed the Labour Representation Committee. It ended in the cataclysmic defeat of 1931, when, with leader Ramsay MacDonald, the party's first prime minister, having left to lead the national government, Labour was reduced to fifty-two seats in the House of Commons. Labour's second and third prime ministers, Clement Attlee and Harold Wilson, dominated the second period, leading the party for a total of thirty-three years between them, implementing profound economic and social change. It was the party's fourth prime minister, James Callaghan, whose election defeat in 1979 marked the end of Labour's dominance in the 1960s and 1970s. Callaghan sensed it was a watershed moment, telling his close aide Bernard Donoughue 'I suspect there is now … a sea change – and it is for Mrs Thatcher.'[3] The next forty years produced two more Labour prime ministers in Tony Blair and Gordon Brown, before the shattering defeat of 2019 reduced the party to its lowest number of MPs since 1935.

Thus, we stand at the start of a fourth period in Labour's story. The first, and fundamental, lesson we must draw from past defeats is that Labour can recover. That is not to say that a future Labour general election victory is inevitable, but it is a cause for optimism. Labour's values have not changed: the belief in a more equal society would be recognizable to any of the party's leaders from Hardie to Starmer. The challenge for every generation of Labour politicians is how to apply them to the circumstances of the country they find themselves in, to offer practical policies that can improve people's lives. Bevan, even after he left office, was still grappling with this when he wrote his seminal book, *In Place of Fear*.[4]

[3] Bernard Donoughue, *Prime Minister: The Conduct of Policy Under Harold Wilson and James Callaghan* (London: Jonathan Cape, 1987), 191.
[4] Aneurin Bevan, *In Place of Fear* (London: Quartet Books, 1990).

Attlee's landslide victory of 1945 was won not by looking back at the war years, but on moving forward to better times, as summed up in the title of the general election manifesto: *Let Us Face the Future*.[5] After another period of collective sacrifice during the coronavirus crisis, Labour must once again set out how it will shape the Britain of the next decade. At its centre must be a promise that things cannot go back to how they once were. We remember the thousands who lost their lives during the pandemic, and its heart-wrenching effects on families. We know its effects will be felt for years to come, from the life-chances of children in England for whom inadequate catch-up funding is being provided to failing businesses, lost jobs and a mental health crisis. Frontline workers, from police to firefighters and emergency medical services, to shop workers, delivery drivers, local government employees and child minders, kept our communities running in 2020–1. They put themselves at risk to help others. Their remarkable efforts showed that what people are paid does not reflect the value of their contribution to society, exposed the scale of the risk created by increasingly insecure work and the damage that inequality continues to cause across society.

Yet soon after the sound of the regular claps for carers faded away, it became clear that the Conservative government had learned nothing from the experience. Boris Johnson promised to 'build back better'.[6] Yet he seemed to have forgotten key workers. The reward for those who were there when the government needed them was a miniscule pay increase or a wage freeze. That the Tories failed to govern in the interests of working people would not surprise Hardie, but Bevan would point out that is the consequence of Labour not being in power.

All three postwar, election-winning Labour leaders captured the zeitgeist of their age. Attlee's promise of comprehensive welfare provision, mass housing and industries which worked in the public interest, rather than for private profit, matched the mood of the troops returning from overseas, and the war-weary public at home who questioned why, if Britain could plan effective provision for everyone in wartime, it could not also do the same in peacetime. Wilson's promise of building a new Britain 'forged in the white heat' of the scientific revolution, harnessing technological advancement for the benefit of the whole of society, ran with the mood of change in the 1960s.[7] Tony Blair's 1997 general

---

5   Iain Dale (ed.), *Labour Party General Election Manifestos 1900–1997* (London: Routledge, 2000), 51.
6   *Build Back Better: our plan for growth*, Policy Paper, 3 March 2021, https://www.gov.uk/government/publications/build-back-better-our-plan-for-growth/build-back-better-our-plan-for-growth-html (accessed 13 September 2021).
7   Report of the 62nd Annual Conference (London: Labour Party, 1963), 139–40.

election campaign song, D:Ream's *Things Can Only Get Better*, spoke to a country with decimated public services and a sleaze-ridden Tory government.

However, it is to Wilson, who won four general elections, that we should turn for a final piece of advice. As he put it: 'This Party is a moral crusade or it is nothing.'[8] A deadly virus has shone a penetrating light on the inequalities that exist in British society. There is an ethical and political imperative to offer a different future. The promise of changing the country for the better that has drawn people into the Labour Party since its formation, continues to inspire. Let us capture the spirit of post-pandemic Britain and ensure we do not face endless Tory governments in this next phase of Labour history.

[8] Report of the 61st Annual Conference (London: Labour Party, 1962), 89.

Further Reading

This is my attempt to present a consolidated Labour Party reading list of published material, bringing together works of history, politics, economics, sociology and biography. It covers all three 'ages' of the Labour Party, as well as themes and personalities not covered properly elsewhere in the collection.

Books

Abrams, Mark and Rose, Richard, *Must Labour Lose?* London: Penguin, 1959.

Ackers, Peter and Reid, Alastair J. (eds.), *Alternatives to State Socialism: Other Worlds of Labour in the Twentieth Century*, Basingstoke: Palgrave Macmillan, 2016.

Addison, Paul, *The Road to 1945*, London: Quartet, 1975.

Addison, Paul, *No Turning Back: The Peacetime Revolutions of Post-War Britain*, Oxford: Oxford University Press, 2010.

Adonis, Andrew, *Ernest Bevin: Labour's Churchill*, London: Biteback, 2020.

Ainsley, Claire, *The New Working Class*, Bristol: Policy Press, 2018.

Anderson, Paul and Mann, Nyta, *Safety First: The Making of New Labour*, London: Granta, 1997.

Andersson, Jenny, *The Library and the Workshop: Social Democracy and Capitalism in the Knowledge Economy*, Stanford: Stanford University Press, 2010.

Anwar, Muhammad, *Race and Politics: Ethnic Minorities and the British Political System*, London: Routledge, 2013.

Attlee, Clement Richard, *The Labour Party in Perspective – And Twelve Years Later*, London: Victor Gollancz, 1949.

Balls, Ed, *Speaking Out: Lessons in Life and Politics*, London: Hutchinson, 2016.

Beckett, Andy, *When the Lights Went Out*, London: Faber & Faber, 2009.

Beckett, Andy, *Promised You a Miracle*, London: Allen Lane, 2015.

Beckett, Francis, *Clem Attlee: Labour's Great Reformer*, London: Haus Publishing, 2015.

Beckett, Francis and Hencke, David, *Marching to the Fault Line*, London: Constable, 2009.

Beckett, Francis and Seddon, Mark, *Jeremy Corbyn and the Strange Rebirth of Labour England*, London: Biteback, 2018.

Beers, Laura, *Your Britain: Media and the Making of the Labour Party*, Cambridge, MA: Harvard University Press, 2010.

Beers, Laura, *Red Ellen: The Life of Ellen Wilkinson, Socialist, Feminist, Internationalist*, Cambridge, MA: Harvard University Press, 2010.

Benn, Tony, *Arguments for Socialism*, London: Penguin, 1980.

Benn, Tony, *Arguments for Democracy*, London: Penguin, 1982.

Benn, Tony, *Against the Tide: Diaries, 1973–76*, London: Hutchinson, 1989.

Benn, Tony, *Conflicts of Interest: Diaries, 1977–80*, London: Hutchinson, 1990.

Benn, Tony, *The End of an Era, 1980–90*, London: Hutchinson, 1992.

Bevan, Aneurin, *In Place of Fear*, London: Heinemann, 1952.

Bevir, Mark, *New Labour: A Critique*, London: Routledge, 2005.

Bevir, Mark, *The Making of British Socialism*, Princeton, NJ: Princeton University Press, 2011.

Bew, John, *Citizen Clem*, London: riverrun, 2016.

Black, Lawrence, *The Political Culture of the Left in Affluent Britain, 1951–1964*, Basingstoke: Palgrave Macmillan, 2002.

Black, Lawrence, Pemberton, Hugh and Thane, Pat (eds), *Reassessing 1970s Britain*, Manchester: Manchester University Press, 2013.

Blair, Tony, *Let us Face the Future: The 1945 Anniversary Lecture*, London: The Fabian Society, 1995.

Blair, Tony, *My Vision of a Young Country*, London: Fourth Estate, 1996.

Blair, Tony, *A Journey*, London: Hutchinson, 2010.

Blunkett, David, *On A Clear Day*, London: Michael O'Mara Books, 2002.

Blunkett, David and Jackson, Keith, *Democracy in Crisis: The Town Halls Respond*, London: Hogarth, 1987.

Bolton, Matt and Pitts, Frederick Harry, *Corbynism: A Critical Approach*, Bingley: Emerald Publishing, 2018.

Brivati, Brian, *Hugh Gaitskell*, London: Richard Cohen Books, 1996.

Brivati, Brian and Heffernan, Richard (eds.), *The Labour Party: A Centenary History*, Basingstoke: Palgrave Macmillan, 2000.

Brooke, Stephen J., *Labour's War: The Labour Party and the Second World War*, Oxford: Oxford University Press, 1992.

Brooke, Stephen J., *Sexual Politics: Sexuality, Family Planning and the British Left from the 1880s to the Present Day*, Oxford: Oxford University Press, 2011.

Brown, Gordon, *My Life, Our Times*, London: Bodley Head, 2017.

Brown, Gordon and Wright, Tony (eds.), *Values, Visions and Voices: An Anthology of Socialism*, Edinburgh: Mainstream, 1995.

Bullock, Alan, *Ernest Bevin*, London: Politico's, 2001.

Bunce, Robin and Linton, Samara, *Diane Abbott: The Authorised Biography*, London: Biteback, 2020.

Burk, Kathleen and Cairncross, Alec, *Goodbye, Great Britain: The 1976 IMF Crisis*, New Haven (CT): Yale University Press, 1992.

Butler, Lise, *Michael Young, Social Science, and the British Left, 1945–1979*, Oxford: Oxford University Press, 2020.

Callaghan, James, *Time and Chance*, London: HarperCollins, 1987.

Callaghan, John, Fielding, Steven and Ludlam, Steve (eds), *Interpreting the Labour Party*, Manchester: Manchester University Press, 2003.

Campbell, Alastair, *The Blair Years: Extracts from the Alastair Campbell Diaries*, London: Hutchinson, 2007.

Campbell, Beatrix, *Wigan Pier Revisited*, London: Virago, 1985.

Campbell, John, *Nye Bevan and the Mirage of British Socialism*, London: Weidenfeld & Nicolson, 1987.

Campbell, John, *Roy Jenkins: A Well-Rounded Life*, London: Jonathan Cape, 2014.

Cannadine, David, *Class in Britain*, New Haven, CT: Yale University Press, 1998.

Carr, Richard, *March of the Moderates: Bill Clinton, Tony Blair, and the Rebirth of Progressive Politics*, London: I.B. Tauris, 2019.

Castle, Barbara, *The Castle Diaries, 1974–76*, London: Weidenfeld & Nicolson, 1980.

Castle, Barbara, *The Castle Diaries, 1964–70*, London: Weidenfeld & Nicolson, 1984.

Castle, Barbara, *Fighting All the Way*, London: Macmillan, 1993.

Clarke, Charles and James, Toby, S. (ed.), *British Labour Leaders*, London: Biteback, 2015.

Clarke, Chris, *Warring Fictions*, London: Rowman & Littlefield, 2019.

Clarke, Peter, *Liberals and Social Democrats*, Cambridge: Cambridge University Press, 1978.

Coates, David, *Prolonged Labour: The Slow Birth of New Labour Britain*, Basingstoke: Palgrave Macmillan, 2005.

Cole, G. D. H., *Guild Socialism Re-Stated*, London: The Fabian Society, 1920.

Crewe, Ivor and King, Anthony, *SDP: The Birth, Life and Death of the Social Democratic Party*, Oxford: Oxford University Press, 1995.

Crick, Michael, *Militant*, London: Faber & Faber, 1984.

Crick, Michael, *Scargill and the Miners*, London: Penguin, 1985.

Crines, Andrew and Hickson, Kevin, *Harold Wilson: The Unprincipled Prime Minister?* London: Biteback, 2016.

Cronin, James E. *New Labour's Pasts: The Labour Party and its Discontents*, Abingdon: Routledge, 2004

Crosland, Anthony, *The Future of Socialism*, London: Jonathan Cape, 1956.

Crosland, Anthony, *Socialism Now*, London: Jonathan Cape, 1974.

Crosland, Susan, *Tony Crosland*, London: Jonathan Cape, 1982.

Crossman, Richard, *Labour in the Affluent Society*, London: The Fabian Society, 1960.

Crossman, Richard, *The Diaries of a Cabinet Minister, Volume 1: Minister of Housing 1964–66*, London: Hamish Hamilton & Jonathan Cape, 1975.

Crossman, Richard, *The Diaries of a Cabinet Minister, Volume 2: Lord President of the Council and Leader of the House of Commons, 1966–68*, London: Hamish Hamilton & Jonathan Cape, 1976.

Crossman, Richard, *The Diaries of a Cabinet Minister, Volume 3: Secretary of State for Social Services, 1968–70*, London: Hamish Hamilton & Jonathan Cape, 1977.

Cruddas, Jon, *The Dignity of Labour*, Cambridge: Polity Books, 2021.

Curran, James (ed.), *The Future of the Left*, Cambridge: Polity Press, 1984.

Darling, Alistair, *Back from the Brink: A Thousand Days at Number 11*, London: Biteback, 2011.

Davis, Jonathan and McWilliam, Rohan (eds), *Labour and the Left in the 1980s*, Manchester: Manchester University Press, 2017.

Davis, Jon and Rentoul, John, *Heroes or Villains?* Oxford: Oxford University Press, 2019.

Dell, Edmund, *A Strange and Eventful History: Democratic Socialism in Britain*, London: HarperCollins, 2000.

Desai, Radhika, *Intellectuals and Socialism: 'Social Democrats' and the Labour Party*, London: Lawrence & Wishart, 1994.

Diamond, Patrick, *The Crosland Legacy*, Bristol: Policy Press, 2016.

Diamond, Patrick, *The British Labour Party in Opposition and Power*, Abingdon: Routledge, 2021.

Donoughue, Bernard, *Downing Street Diary, Volume 1: With Harold Wilson in No. 10*, London: Jonathan Cape, 2005.

Donoughue, Bernard, *Downing Street Diary, Volume 2: With James Callaghan in No. 10*, London: Jonathan Cape, 2008.

Donoughue, Bernard, and Jones, George, *Herbert Morrison: Portrait of a Politician*, London: Weidenfeld & Nicolson, 1973.

Dorey, Peter, *Comrades in Conflict: Labour, The Trade Unions and 1969's In Place of Strife*, Manchester: Manchester University Press, 1989.

Drucker, H. M., *Doctrine and Ethos in the Labour Party*, London: HarperCollins, 1979.

Durbin, Elizabeth, *New Jerusalems: The Labour Party and the Economics of Democratic Socialism*, London: Routledge & Keegan Paul, 1985.

Durbin, Evan, *The Politics of Democratic Socialism*, London: Labour Book Service, 1940.

Edgerton, David, *Warfare State: Britain, 1920–1970*, Cambridge: Cambridge University Press, 2005.

Edgerton, David, *The Rise and Fall of the British Nation*, London: Allen Lane, 2018.

Ellison, Nicholas, *Egalitarian Thought and Labour Politics: Retreating Visions*, London: Routledge, 1994.

Fielding, Steven, *The Labour Party: Continuity and Change in the Making of 'New Labour'*, London: Palgrave, 2002.

Fielding, Steven, *The Labour Governments 1964–70, Volume 3: Labour and Cultural Change*, Manchester: Manchester University Press, 2003.

Fielding, Steven, Tiratsoo, Nick and Thompson, Peter, *'England Arise!' The Labour Party and Popular Politics in 1940s Britain*, Manchester: Manchester University Press, 1995.

Foot, Michael, *Another Heart and Other Pulses*, London: William Collins, 1984.

Foot, Michael, *Loyalists and Loners*, London: William Collins, 1986.

Foot, Michael, *Aneurin Bevan* (abridged version, edited by Brivati, Brian), London: Victor Gollancz, 1997.

Foote, Geoffrey, *The Labour Party's Political Thought, A History*, Basingstoke: Macmillan, 1997.

Gamble, Andrew, *Open Labour*, London: Rowman & Littlefield, 2018.

Giddens, Anthony, *The Third Way: The Renewal of Social Democracy*, Cambridge: Polity Press, 1998.

Glasman, Maurice, Rutherford, Jonathan, Stears, Marc and White, Stuart (eds.), *The Labour Tradition and the Politics of Paradox*, London: Soundings, 2011.

Goes, Eunice, *The Labour Party Under Ed Miliband: Trying But Failing to Renew Social Democracy*, Manchester: Manchester University Press, 2016.

Gould, Bryan, *Goodbye to All That*, London: Macmillan, 1995.

Gould, Philip, *The Unfinished Revolution: How the Modernisers Saved the Labour Party*, London: Little, Brown, 1998.

Graves, Pamela, *Labour Women: Women in British Working-Class Politics, 1918–1939*, Cambridge: Cambridge University Press, 1994.

Green, Ewen Henry Harvey, *Thatcher*, London: Bloomsbury Academic, 2006.

Gyford, John, *The Politics of Local Socialism*, London: Allen & Unwin, 1985.

Gyford, John and Haseler, Stephen, *Social Democracy: Beyond Revisionism*, London: The Fabian Society, 1971.

Haines, Joe, *The Politics of Power*, London: Jonathan Cape, 1977.

Haines, Joe, *Glimmers of Twilight: Harold Wilson in Decline: Murder, Intrigue and Passion at the Court of Harold Wilson*, London: Politico's, 2003.

Hale, Sarah, *Blair's Community: Communitarian Thought and New Labour*, Manchester: Manchester University Press, 2006.

Hall, Stuart and Jacques, Martin (eds), *New Times: The Changing Face of Politics in the 1990s*, London: Lawrence & Wishart, 1989.

Harman, Harriet, *A Woman's Work*, London: Allen Lane, 2017.

Harris, Jose, *William Beveridge: A Biography*, Oxford: Clarendon Press, 1977.

Harris, Robert, *The Making of Neil Kinnock*, London: Faber & Faber, 1994.

Hassan, Gerry and Shaw, Eric, *The People's Flag and the Union Jack*, London: Biteback, 2019.

Hatfield, Michael, *The House the Left Built: Inside Labour Policy-Making, 1970–1975*, London: Victor Gollancz, 1975.

Hattersley, Roy, *Choose Freedom*, London: Michael Joseph, 1987.

Hattersley, Roy, *Who Goes Home? Scenes from a Political Life*, London: Little, Brown, 1995.

Hayter, Dianne, *Fightback! Labour's Traditional Right in the 1970s and 1980s*, Manchester: Manchester University Press, 2005.

Healey, Denis, *The Time of My Life*, London: Michael Joseph, 1989.

Hickson, Kevin and Miles, Jasper, *James Callaghan: An Underrated Prime Minister?* London: Biteback, 2020.

Hindmoor, Andrew, *What's Left Now? The History and Future of Social Democracy*, Oxford: Oxford University Press, 2018.

Hobsbawm, Eric, *The Forward March of Labour Halted?* London: NLB, 1981.

Hobsbawm, Eric, *Politics for a Rational Left: Political Writings 1977–88*, London: Verso, 1989.

Holland, Stuart, *The Socialist Challenge*, London: Quartet Books, 1975.

Hollis, Patricia, *Jennie Lee: A Life*, Oxford: Oxford University Press, 1997.

Howell, David, *British Social Democracy, A Study in Development and Decay*, London: Croom Helm, 1980.

Howell, David, *MacDonald's Party: Labour Identities and Crisis, 1922–1931*, Oxford: Oxford University Press, 2002.

Hutton, Will, *The State We're In*, London: Vintage, 1996.

Jackson, Ben, *Equality and the British Left*, Manchester: Manchester University Press, 2007.

Jackson, Ben and Saunders, Robert, *Making Thatcher's Britain*, Cambridge: Cambridge University Press, 2012.

Jefferys, Kevin, *The Churchill Coalition and Wartime Politics, 1940–45*, Manchester: Manchester University Press, 1991.

Jefferys, Kevin, *Anthony Crosland: A New Biography*, London: John Blake, 1999.

Jenkins, Peter, *Mrs Thatcher's Revolution: The Ending of the Socialist Era*, London: Pan Books, 1989.

Jenkins, Roy, *A Life at the Centre*, London: Macmillan, 1991.

Jobson, Richard, *Nostalgia and the Post-War Labour Party: Prisoners of the Past*, Manchester: Manchester University Press, 2018.

Jones, Peter, *America and the British Labour Party: The 'Special Relationship' at Work*, London: I.B. Tauris, 1997.

Kampfner, John, *Blair's Wars,* London: The Free Press, 2003.

Kavanagh, Dennis (ed.), *The Politics of the Labour Party*, London: Routledge, 1982.

Kellner, Peter (ed.), *Thorns and Roses: The Speeches of Neil Kinnock, 1983–91*, London: Radius, 1992.

Kenny, Michael, *The First New Left*, London: Lawrence & Wishart, 1995.

Kogan, David, *Protest and Power: The Battle for the Labour Party*, London: Bloomsbury, 2018.

Kogan, David and Kogan, Maurice, *The Battle for the Labour Party*, London: Fontana, 1982.

Lawrence, Jon, *Speaking for the People: Party, Language and Popular Politics in England, 1867–1914*, Cambridge: Cambridge University Press, 1998.

Lawrence, Jon, *Electing our Masters*, Oxford: Oxford University Press, 2009.

Lawrence, Jon, *Me, Me, Me: The Search for Community in Post-War England*, Oxford: Oxford University Press, 2019.

MacDonald, James Ramsay, *Socialism and Society*, London: ILP, 1908.

MacDonald, James Ramsay, *Political Writings*, London: Allen Lane, 1972.

Mandelson, Peter, *The Third Man, Life at the Heart of New Labour*, London: HarperPress, 2010.

Mandelson, Peter and Liddle, Roger, *The Blair Revolution: Can New Labour Deliver?* London: Faber and Faber, 1996.

Marquand, David, *Ramsay MacDonald*, London: Jonathan Cape, 1977.

Marquand, David, *The Unprincipled Society*, London: Jonathan Cape, 1988.

Marquand, David, *The Progressive Dilemma: From Lloyd George to Kinnock*, London: Heinemann, 1991.

Marquand, David, *Britain Since 2018: The Strange Career of British Democracy*, London: Weidenfeld & Nicolson, 2008.

Marquand, David and Seldon, Anthony, *The Ideas That Shaped Post-War Britain*, London: Fontana Press, 1996.

McKibbin, Ross, *The Evolution of the Labour Party, 1910–1924*, Oxford: Clarendon Press, 1984.

McKibbin, Ross, *The Ideologies of Class: Social Relations in Britain, 1880–1950*, Oxford: Oxford University Press, 1990.

McKibbin, Ross, *Classes and Cultures: England, 1918–1951*, Oxford: Oxford University Press, 1998.

McKibbin, Ross, *Parties and People*, Oxford: Oxford University Press, 2010.

McSmith, Andy, *Faces of Labour: The Inside Story*, London: Verso, 1995.

Meredith, Stephen, *Labours Old and New: The Parliamentary Right of the British Labour Party 1970–79 and the Roots of New Labour*, Manchester: Manchester University Press, 2005.

Miliband, David (ed.), *Reinventing the Left*, Cambridge: Cambridge University Press, 1994.

Miliband, Ralph, *Parliamentary Socialism*, London: Allen & Unwin, 1961.

Minkin, Lewis, *The Labour Party Conference*, London: Viking, 1978.

Minkin, Lewis, *The Contentious Alliance, Trade Unions and the Labour Party*, Edinburgh: Edinburgh University Press, 1991.

Minkin, Lewis, *The Blair Supremacy: A Study in the Politics of Labour Party Management*, Manchester: Manchester University Press, 2013.

Moore, Charles, *Margaret Thatcher, The Authorized Biography, Volume 1: Not for Turning*, London: Allen Lane, 2013.

Moore, Charles, *Margaret Thatcher, The Authorized Biography, Volume 2: Everything She Wants*, London: Allen Lane, 2015.

Moore, Charles, *Margaret Thatcher, The Authorized Biography, Volume 3: Herself Alone*, London: Allen Lane, 2019.

Morgan, Kenneth O., *Portrait of a Progressive: The Political Career of Christopher, Viscount Addison*, Oxford: Oxford University Press, 1980.

Morgan, Kenneth O., *Labour in Power, 1945–51*, Oxford: Oxford University Press, 1984.

Morgan, Kenneth O., *Callaghan: A Life*, Oxford: Oxford University Press, 1997.

Morgan, Kenneth O., *Michael Foot: A Life*, London: HarperCollins, 2007.

Mudge, Stephanie, *Leftism Reinvented*, Cambridge, MA: Harvard University Press, 2018.

Nuttall, Jeremy, *Psychological Socialism: The Labour Party and Qualities of Mind and Character, 1931 to the Present*, Manchester: Manchester University Press, 2006.

O'Hara, Glen, *From Dreams to Disillusionment? Economic and Social Planning in 1960s Britain*, Basingstoke: Palgrave Macmillan, 2007.

O'Hara, Glen and Parr, Helen (eds.), *The Wilson Governments 1964–1970 Reconsidered*, Abingdon: Routledge, 2006.

Ortolano, Guy, *Thatcher's Progress: From Social Democracy to Market Liberalism Through an English New Town*, Cambridge: Cambridge University Press, 2019.

Overy, Richard, *The Morbid Age: Britain and the Crisis of Civilisation, 1919–1939*, London: Penguin, 2009.

Owen, David, *Face the Future*, Oxford: Oxford University Press, 1981.

Owen, David, *Time to Declare*, London: Michael Joseph, 1991.

Paterson, Peter, *George Brown*, London: Chatto & Windus, 1993.

Pimlott, Ben, *Labour and the Left in the 1930s*, Cambridge: Cambridge University Press, 1978.

Pimlott, Ben (ed.), *Fabian Essays in Socialist Thought*, London: Heinemann, 1984.

Pimlott, Ben, *Hugh Dalton*, London: Jonathan Cape, 1985.

Pimlott, Ben, *Harold Wilson*, London: William Collins, 1992.

Plant, Raymond, Beech, Matt and Hickson, Kevin (eds), *The Struggle for Labour's Soul: Understanding Labour's Political Thought Since 1945*, London: Routledge, 2004.

Pogrund, Gabriel and Maguire, Patrick, *Left Out: The Inside Story of Labour Under Corbyn*, London: Bodley Head, 2020.

Ponting, Clive, *Breach of Promise: Labour in Power, 1964–70*, London: Hamish Hamilton, 1989.

Pugh, Martin, *Speak for Britain! A New History of the Labour Party*, London: Bodley Head, 2010.

Radice, Giles, *Southern Discomfort*, London: The Fabian Society, 1993.

Radice, Giles, *Friends and Rivals: Crosland, Jenkins and Healey*, London: Little, Brown, 2002.

Rawnsley, Andrew, *Servants of the People: The Inside Story of New Labour*, London: Penguin, 2001.

Rawnsley, Andrew, *The End of the Party: The Rise and Fall of New Labour*, London: Penguin, 2010.

Reeves, Rachel, *Alice in Westminster: The Political Life of Alice Bacon*, London: I.B. Tauris, 2016.

Reeves, Rachel, *Women of Westminster*, London: Bloomsbury, 2018.

Rentoul, John, *Tony Blair*, London: Little, Brown, 2001.

Richards, Paul (ed.), *Tony Blair: In His Own Words*, London: Politico's, 2004.

Richards, Steve, *The Prime Ministers: Reflections on Leadership from Wilson to May*, London: Atlantic Books, 2019.

Robinson, Emily, *History, Heritage and Tradition in Contemporary British Politics*, Manchester: Manchester University Press, 2012.

Robinson, Emily, *The Language of Progressive Politics in Modern Britain*, Basingstoke: Palgrave Macmillan, 2017.

Robinson, Lucy, *Gay Men and the Left: How the Political Got Personal*, Manchester: Manchester University Press, 2007.

Rodgers, Bill, *Fourth Among Equals*, London: Politico's, 2000.

Russell, Meg, *Building New Labour*, Basingstoke: Palgrave Macmillan, 2005.

Sandbrook, Dominic, *White Heat: A History of Britain in the Swinging Sixties*, London: Little, Brown, 2006.

Sandbrook, Dominic, *State of Emergency, The Way We Were: Britain, 1970–1974*, London: Allen Lane, 2010.

Sandbrook, Dominic, *Seasons in the Sun: The Battle for Britain, 1974–1979*, London: Allen Lane, 2012.

Sandbu, Martin, *The Economics of Belonging*, Princeton, NJ: Princeton University Press, 2020.

Sassoon, Donald, *One Hundred Years of Socialism*, London: I.B. Tauris, 1996.

Saunders, Robert, *Yes to Europe! The 1975 Referendum and Seventies Britain*, Cambridge: Cambridge University Press, 2018.

Schattle, Hans and Nutall, Jeremy (eds.), *Making Social Democrats*, Manchester: Manchester University Press, 2018.

Seldon, Anthony, *Blair*, London: The Free Press, 2004.

Seldon, Anthony, *Blair Unbound*, London: Simon & Schuster, 2007.

Seldon, Anthony and Hickson, Kevin (eds.), *New Labour, Old Labour: The Wilson and Callaghan Governments, 1974–79*, London: Routledge, 2004.

Seldon, Anthony and Lodge, Guy, *Brown at 10*, London: Biteback, 2010.

Sewell, Terri, *Black Tribunes: Black Political Participation in Britain*, London: Lawrence & Wishart, 1990.

Seyd, Patrick, *The Rise and Fall of the Labour Left*, Basingstoke: Macmillan, 1987.

Seyd, Patrick and Whiteley, Paul, *New Labour's Grassroots*, London: Palgrave Macmillan, 2002.

Shaw, Eric, *Discipline and Discord: The Politics of Managerial Control in the Labour Party 1951–1987*, Manchester: Manchester University Press, 1988.

Shaw, Eric, *The Labour Party since 1979: Crisis and Transformation*, London: Routledge, 1994.

Shaw, Eric, *Losing Labour's Soul? New Labour and the Blair Governments*, London: Routledge, 2007.

Skidelsky, Robert, *Politicians and the Slump: The Labour Government 1929–31*, London: Penguin, 1970.

Skidelsky, Robert, *John Maynard Keynes: Economist, Philosopher, Statesman*, London: Penguin, 2003.

Sloane, Nan, *The Women in the Room: Labour's Forgotten History*, London: I.B. Tauris, 2020.

Sloman, Peter, *Transfer State: The Idea of a Guaranteed Income and the Politics of Redistribution*, Oxford: Oxford University Press, 2019.

Stedman-Jones, Gareth, *Languages of Class: Studies in English Working-Class History, 1932–1982*, Cambridge: Cambridge University Press, 1984.

Sutcliffe-Braithwaite, Florence, *Class, Politics and the Decline of Deference*, Oxford: Oxford University Press, 2018.

Tanner, Duncan, Thane, Pat and Tiratsoo, Nick (eds.), *Labour's First Century*, Cambridge: Cambridge University Press, 2000.

Tawney, R. H., *Equality*, London: Allen & Unwin, 1928.

Thomas-Symonds, Nick, *Attlee: A Life in Politics*, London: I.B. Tauris, 2010.

Thomas-Symonds, Nick, *Nye: The Political Life of Aneurin Bevan*, London: I.B. Tauris, 2014.

Thompson, Noel, *Left in the Wilderness: The Political Economy of British Democratic Socialism Since 1979*, Chesham: Acumen, 2002.

Thompson, Noel, *Political Economy and the Labour Party: The Economics of Democratic Socialism, 1884–2005*, London: Routledge, 2005.

Thorpe, Andrew, *A History of the British Labour Party*, Basingstoke: Palgrave Macmillan, 1997.

Timmins, Nicholas, *The Five Giants: A Biography of the Welfare State*, London: William Collins, 2017.

Tiratsoo, Nick (ed.), *The Attlee Years*, New York: University of Columbia Press, 1991.

Todman, Daniel, *Britain's War, Volume 1: Into Battle*, London: Allen Lane, 2016.

Todman, Daniel, *Britain's War, Volume 2: A New Word, 1942–1947*, London: Allen Lane, 2020.

Tomlinson, Jim, *The Labour Governments 1964–70, Volume 3: Economic Policy*, Manchester: Manchester University Press, 2004.

Tomlinson, Jim, *Managing the Economy, Managing the People: Narratives of Economic Life in Britain from Beveridge to Brexit*, Oxford: Oxford University Press, 2017.

Toye, Richard, *The Labour Party and the Planned Economy, 1931–1951*, Woodbridge: The Royal Historical Society, The Boydell Press, 2003.

Turner, Jacqueline, *The Labour Church: Religion and Politics in Britain 1890–1914*, London: I.B. Tauris, 2018.

Vickers, Rhiannon, *The Labour Party and the World, Volume 2: The Evolution of Labour's Foreign Policy since 1951*, Manchester: Manchester University Press, 2004.

Vickers, Rhiannon, *The Labour Party and the World, Volume 1: Labour's Foreign Policy Since 1951*, Manchester: Manchester University Press, 2011.

Wainwright, Hilary, *A Tale of Two Parties*, London: Hogarth, 1984.

Waters, Chris, *British Socialists and the Politics of Popular Culture 1884–1914*, Stanford: Stanford University Press, 1990.

Waters, Rob, *Thinking Black: Britain 1964–1985*, Berkeley: University of California Press, 2021.

Westlake, Martin, *Kinnock: The Biography*, London: Little, Brown, 2001.

Whitehead, Philip, *The Writing on the Wall: Britain in the Seventies*, London: Michael Joseph, 1985.

Wickham-Jones, Mark, *Economic Strategy and the Labour Party*, Basingstoke: Macmillan, 1996.

Williams, Francis, *The Fifty Years' March: The Rise of the Labour Party*, London: Odhams Press, 1950.

Williams, Shirley, *Politics is for People*, London: Allen Lane and Penguin, 1981.

Williams, Shirley, *Climbing the Bookshelves: The Autobiography*, London: Virago, 2009.

Wilson, Harold, *Purpose in Politics*, London: Weidenfeld & Nicolson, 1964.

Wilson, Harold, *The Labour Government, 1964–70: A Personal Record*, London: Weidenfeld & Nicolson and Michael Joseph, 1971.

Wilson, Harold, *Final Term: The Labour Government 1974–1976*, London: Weidenfeld & Nicolson and Michael Joseph, 1979.

Worley, Matthew (eds), *The Foundations of the British Labour Party: Identities, Cultures and Perspectives, 1900–1939*, Abingdon: Routledge, 2009.

Wright, Tony, G. D. H. *Cole and Socialist Democracy*, Oxford: Clarendon Press, 1979.

Wright, Tony, R. H. *Tawney*, Manchester: Manchester University Press, 1987.

Wright, Tony, *Socialisms: Old and New*, London: Routledge, 1996.

Young, John W. *The Labour Governments 1964–70, Volume 2: International Policy*, Manchester: Manchester University Press, 2003.

Young, Michael, *The Rise of the Meritocracy*, London: Penguin, 1958.

Journals

British Journal of Political Science, Contemporary British History, Encounter, English Historical Review, Journal of Political Ideologies, Labour History Review, Marxism Today, New Left Review, New Political Economy, Political Quarterly, Twentieth Century British History.

Online resources

The British Cartoon Archive (https://www.cartoons.ac.uk/)

Hansard 1803–2005 (https://api.parliament.uk/historic-hansard/index.html)

The Labour History Archive and Study Centre (https://phm.org.uk/collections/labour-history-archive-study-centre/)

The Margaret Thatcher Foundation archive (https://www.margaretthatcher.org/archive)

The Oxford Dictionary of National Biography (https://www.oxforddnb.com/)

Index